2 - 20 -14

W9-APM-777

Blue Ribbon Preserves

PUBLIC LIBRARY OF
SELMA & DALLAS CTY
1103 SELMA AVENUE
SELMA, AL 36701

Most HPBooks are available at special quantity discounts for bulk purchases for sales promotions, premiums, fund-raising, or educational use. Special books, or book excerpts, can also be created to fit specific needs.

For details, write: Special Markets, The Berkley Publishing Group, 375 Hudson Street, New York, New York 10014.

BLUE RIBBON PRESERVES

Secrets to Award-Winning
Jams, Jellies, Marmalades & More

LINDA J. AMENDT

HPBooks

HPBooks
Published by The Berkley Publishing Group
A division of Penguin Putnam Inc.
375 Hudson Street
New York, New York 10014

Copyright © 2001 by Linda J. Amendt
Text design by Tiffany Kukec
Cover design by Wendy Bass
Cover photo by Superstock

All rights reserved. This book, or parts thereof,
may not be reproduced in any form without permission.

First edition: July 2001
Published simultaneously in Canada.

The Penguin Putnam Inc. World Wide Web site address is
www.penguinputnam.com

Library of Congress Cataloging-in-Publication Data

Amendt, Linda J.
    Blue ribbon preserves : secrets to award-winning jams, jellies, marmalades and more /
Linda J. Amendt.
        p.   cm.
    Includes index.
    ISBN 978-1-55788-361-2
    1. Canning and preserving.   I. Title.

TX601 .A467   2001
641.4'2—dc21   2001016660

Printed in the United States of America

20   19   18

In loving memory of my mother and best friend,
Mary Louise Robbins Amendt.

Contents

Acknowledgments

I would like to express my deepest appreciation to all the people who helped make this cookbook a reality.

Special gratitude to my father, Lee Amendt, without whose support, belief in my abilities and encouragement to follow my dreams, this book would not have been possible.

To all the people who encouraged me to compete at the fairs and to share my recipes and expertise by writing this book: Jeanie and Earl Lee, my brothers Bruce and Brion and their families, Peg and John DePiazza, Sara D'Aquila and Richard Svoger, Carolyn and Mark Weiser, Sheila and Terry Inman, Sandra Manning, Rosa Lollar, Wanda Peterson, Troy Lopez, Marci Ruggeri, Matt Bootz and Leah Aretz: Thank you for believing in me.

To Carol Chybowski, who spent all those long and exciting days sitting with me through State Fair judgings and who never doubted that this book would be published.

To all of my tasters: Betty Welch, Clella Snider, MaryAlice Jessup, Heather Marks, Al Jessup and the gang from Seafare Inn: Clare and Scott Milhous, Gary and Shelley Milhous, Sara Houg, Carol Innes, Diane Watkins, Steve Tolli-son, Pam Chaffin, Charyl Baziak and Dan Gill, who willingly lined up to sample new recipes and share their opinions.

To Silvia Bishop and all the ladies in the Creative Living Department at the Los Angeles County Fair: Lorene Galligan, Lois, Dorothy, Donna, Beverly and everyone else for all your dedication and hard work to present a terrific display and outstanding fair every year.

To Willie Garrett and the California Living staff at the California State Fair for organizing a great fair and presenting an open judging that was both educational and entertaining.

To Amber Malinak, Culinary Superintendent, 1999 Montana State Fair; Marlene Brumfield, Culinary Superintendent, 2000 Montana State Fair and Susan Dickman, General Entry Coordinator, Colorado State Fair for their graciousness and helpful assistance with my entries and awards.

To the MontanaFair, State Fair of Texas, Kentucky State Fair, Tennessee State Fair and the Western Washington Fair for warmly welcoming a competitor from out of state.

To Lisa Rhoades and Dianne Wiley for their generosity and enthusiasm in delivering my entries to the Western Washington Fair.

To Lee Amendt, Betty Welch, Sara D'Aquila and Clella Snider for willingly undertaking the task of proofreading my manuscript.

To Sherry, Rochelle and Sylvia for all their hard work and efforts that enabled me to complete this project on schedule.

Foreword

My first encounter with Linda Amendt was completely anonymous. She was but one of many entrants in the preserved foods competition at the 1998 California State Fair. I was one of the six judges who had the taste delight of sampling a superb jar of Santa Rosa Plum Jam. After that competition, I had the pleasure of meeting Linda in person. Our discussion of some of the finer points of how to send winning entries to the fair left me with a lasting impression of the degree of professionalism that this competitor brought to the fair.

In the years following this first flavorful meeting, I would again have the opportunity to enjoy Linda's considerable talent. Carefully blending the freshest fruits and highest quality ingredients with a skill that can only come from years of patient practice and creative experimentation she continued to create culinary masterpieces. My most recent occasion to appreciate Linda Amendt's efforts came at the 2000 California State Fair where she again earned first place in the Sure-Jell Jam Competition with her outstanding Salsa Jam.

It is an honor and a privilege to recommend this collection of Linda's prizewinning recipes to canning aficionados old and new. Whether you are a veteran preserver or just taking your first walk through the garden of taste sensation known as preserved food, I am sure you will find Linda Amendt's carefully documented recipes and tips to making outstanding preserved food products a valuable addition to your reference library.

Linda Amendt's clear and concise explanation of the essentials to a successful preserving experience are covered in the Canning Basics chapter. She reviews safety and sanitation issues vital to the end product of preserved food, and includes a detailed glossary which clearly explains terms regularly used in canning recipes.

One of my favorite chapters is The World of Fair Competitions. Linda discusses in wonderful depth how to get the most enjoyment out of your fair competition experience, while avoiding some of the pitfalls that come from a lack of attention to the entry details outlined by the different regional fairs. As her history of fairs illustrates, we have come a long way since the inception of the first agricultural fair in 1811.

For those of you who have thought about entering competition, you will have the winning secrets of one of the most decorated competitors in the last decade of fair seasons. The fair competition circuit is losing one of its finest contestants but the consumers of Linda Amendt's new offering will soon discover what we judges already know, her products are always a treat. Linda has come full circle in her knowledge and we are truly excited that she has chosen to share that expertise with all of us.

Iris Dimond,
Family and Consumer Science Educator.
Judge, California State Fair Preserved Foods Competition; 1998, 1999, 2000.

Blue Ribbon Preserves

Introduction

Many of the cooking traditions once handed down from grandmother to mother and from mother to daughter have been forgotten. Now, one of these time-honored traditions, preserving fresh foods at home, is being rediscovered by new generations. A whole new crop of home canners is sprouting up across the country.

Once a necessity to pioneer survival, making homemade preserved foods is now a great way to provide yourself and your family with the best-quality food all year long. With basic canning and kitchen equipment and some time, you can make a wide array of delectable soft spreads and fruit to serve with breakfast or create tantalizing specialty sauces and vegetables to make gourmet dinners a snap. Home-canned exotic vinegars, flavorful syrups and juices, crunchy pickles, homemade ice-cream toppings and pie fillings are all within your reach. The possibilities are endless and are limited only by your imagination.

Men and women of all ages are discovering the benefits and delights of making their own jams and jellies, finding the sweet rewards of canning soft spreads, fruit and vegetables at home in their own kitchens. With increased concerns over pesticide residues and preservatives in commercially produced foods, health-conscious individuals are realizing the advantages of preparing their own preserved foods. The growing number of home gardens, farmers' markets and specialty produce markets in cities across the country provide home canners with an abundance of fresh, organically grown produce perfect for making preserved foods.

A store-bought spread cannot compare with the delightful, fresh-picked taste of a good homemade jam. The tantalizing, fruity aroma and intense flavor of strawberry preserves make any breakfast a special occasion. Apricots, canned at the peak of ripeness, spark memories of warm, sunny, summer days. Savoring the sweet, tangy goodness of a citrus marmalade is like opening a jar of bottled sunshine.

Creating homemade preserved foods of exceptional quality is not difficult, but it does require some patience, attention to detail and the use of only the best ingredients available. Anyone willing to put forward a little time and effort can reap the benefits and make their own homemade preserves with remarkably fresh flavor and silky-smooth texture.

Soft spreads are one of the most rewarding preserved foods you can make. They make great gifts, and there is a type of spread to suit everyone's tastes. Jams, jellies, marmalades, preserves and conserves share two things in common: They are each made with fruit that is preserved with sugar, and they are all jellied or set to a greater or lesser degree. Beyond that, they vary widely in their texture and method of preparation. Each of the spreads and their own specific preparation techniques will be discussed in detail.

In *Blue Ribbon Preserves,* you will find my expert advice on how to use modern canning techniques and equipment to create preserved foods that contain the maximum amount of flavor and have exceptional color. I will guide you through every step of the home-canning process, from the careful selection of ingredients and canning equipment, through the actual step-by-step process of canning, to my special techniques for creating the very best of each type of preserved food. You will gain the knowledge needed to confidently prepare your own wonderfully flavorful home-canned preserves. Everyone, whether you are an experienced canner or someone who has never tried home canning before, will find easy-to-follow recipes to produce outstanding quality preserves that will quickly become family favorites.

Local, county, regional and state fair competitions are growing and are filled with first-time entrants competing alongside the veteran canners. The rules and requirements of competition, while not complicated, can seem confusing, and they must be followed precisely in order to win. In *Blue Ribbon Preserves,* the exciting world of fair competitions and judging criteria are carefully examined, so those interested in trying their hand at competing will have a thorough understanding of how to successfully exhibit their preserved foods, impress the judges and win blue ribbons. Detailed information about how to contact the fairs and request their exhibitor handbooks and how to enter your exhibits is provided along with my expert, insider advice and secrets on what it really takes to win those blue ribbons. I encourage home canners of all ages and experience levels to discover for themselves the excitement and rewards of entering and competing in fair competitions. Winning that first blue ribbon is a joy you will never forget. And winning that blue ribbon, and many more after it, is not as hard as you may think.

Whether you plan to enter your homemade creations into competition at state, county or regional fairs or simply want to prepare flavor-packed preserved foods to share with your family and friends, *Blue Ribbon Preserves* is the ultimate resource to achieving both exceptional quality and expert results. I invite you to turn the pages and enjoy the wonderful world of homemade preserved foods for yourself. An exciting array of taste sensations awaits you.

Ingredients

Good, reliable recipes are essential for successful home canning, but they are only the beginning. The right jars, the careful selection, handling and preparation of the fruits and vegetables, accurate measuring of the ingredients, using the proper techniques and precise timing all play an important part in creating quality preserved foods.

QUALITY COUNTS

The importance of selecting ingredients for use in home canning cannot be stressed too strongly. The old adage, that you only get back out what you put in, is absolutely true when it comes to home canned foods. Quality ingredients are the most important factor in creating preserved foods that you will be proud to serve to your family and friends. You can follow every canning procedure to the letter, use every technique known to produce the best-preserved food you possibly can, but if you use inferior ingredients, the final product will be a disappointment. The outstanding flavor found in superior preserved foods comes directly from using the very best fruits and vegetables available and by not skimping on the quality of any ingredient.

FRESH FRUITS AND VEGETABLES

Fruits and vegetables are the primary ingredients and the main source of flavor in preserved foods and soft spreads. That is why in order to attain the best flavor in your homemade preserved foods, you must use the best-quality produce you can find. Select fruits and vegetables that are fully ripe, not overripe or underripe. Poorly ripened produce will affect the flavor, texture, color, appearance and keeping ability of your preserved foods. Underripe or overripe produce may also float or sink in the jars, fail to hold their shape and turn mushy during cooking or storage.

The fruits and vegetables you select should be fresh, firm, fully ripe and free of any signs of spoilage or bruises. Damaged fruit may have a tainted flavor and is more likely to contain bacteria or molds that could contaminate your preserved foods. No matter what other people may have told you, home canning is not the time to use imperfect produce, seconds or fruit that has fallen from the tree. If you use inferior ingredients when canning, you will end up with inferior preserved foods. Remember, what you have when you open the jars will only be as good as what you put into the jars in the first place.

Sort your fruits or vegetables according to their size and ripeness. For a uniform preserved food product, combine produce of similar size and ripeness together in the same batch. If the fruit is not fully ripe, wait another day or two before canning, but keep a close eye on it as the quality of fruit can deteriorate quite rapidly.

Before you make your preserved foods or soft spreads, taste the fruit you have chosen to use. Nothing is worse in home canning than to go through all the careful work to make a delightful soft spread and then find that the flavor of the finished jam or jelly is anything but delightful. There is no way to recover if the fruit you used had little or no flavor, or had an off taste. Only top-quality fruit can create a premium soft spread.

Home Garden Produce

The best fruits and vegetables to use for home canning are the ones you grow yourself in your own garden. You can harvest them at the peak of ripeness and have the finished preserved food in the jar within a matter of hours. Preserving the produce as close to harvest as possible will help the fruit and vegetables maintain their fresh flavor and firm texture.

The second best source of produce is from the home garden of a friend, neighbor or family member who is willing to share their abundant crop with you. In return, supply them with a few jars of the preserved food you create from their bounty. Not only will they be pleased with your thoughtfulness, they will happily supply you with more fruits and vegetables from their next harvest.

While fruits and berries that have reached maturity and full ripeness produce the most flavorful preserved foods and soft spreads, vegetables, with the exception of vine-ripened tomatoes, should be harvested before they reach full maturity. Mature vegetables may become tough and are likely to contain many seeds. They will often lose their shape and flavor and turn soft or mushy during preserving and processing. Tender, young vegetables make the best preserved foods.

When harvesting or storing fruits and vegetables before canning, do not pile them on top of each other as the weight and pressure of the fruit or vegetables on top may bruise or crush the ones below. Spread the fruit out in a single layer on soft towels until ready to use. If the fruit needs additional ripening time, turn the fruit every day so that the side on the bottom does not become bruised, making the fruit unfit for canning.

U-Pick Farms and Orchards

Excellent sources for top-quality produce are u-pick farms and orchards, where you actually go into the field or orchard and harvest the fruits and vegetables yourself. They present a wonderful opportunity to hand select perfect, fresh produce. Many growers and orchard owners open their gates each year to eager pickers. Apples, pears, peaches, apricots, cherries, grapes and berries are just some of the crops you can harvest yourself. Most u-pick growers belong to organizations that produce only organic crops, preferring to share a small portion with the birds, rather than treat their fruits and vegetables with potentially harmful pesticides.

I would not miss my annual trip to Bright's Cherry Ranch in Leona Valley, about ninety miles north of my Southern California home. Tree-ripened sweet cherries are beyond compare and this special adventure has become a family tradition. I look forward to cherry season every year with great anticipation and expectation.

Several years back, my parents and I spent a day in the country harvesting fruit from u-pick growers. First we went to an apricot orchard, where we picked over fifty pounds of the sunny fruit. Then we traveled a short ways to a boysenberry farm, where we were greeted out front by the friendly owner. She asked us if we were pickers or drinkers. "Drinkers," we asked? It turned out there was a small winery on the property and they were open for tastings. The owner explained that the drinkers usually did not start arriving until the afternoon so she figured we were probably pickers. Since it was just after eleven in the morning, we opened the trunk of the car to retrieve our picking baskets and boxes. "You're professional pickers!" the owner exclaimed when she saw our bounty of ripe apricots. Upon returning from the berry patch with our treasure, it was now after noon. So we asked our genial host if we could switch from being pickers and become drinkers. She led us into her cozy kitchen and uncorked the bottles of wine, which turned out to be really quite good.

Many u-pick farms and orchards request that you bring your own boxes or containers in which to carry your harvest home. Be sure you take flat boxes so that the delicate produce will not need to be stacked more than two or three layers deep in the box. Otherwise, when you get home, you may find that you have a deep container full of cherry juice or grape juice rather than the precious little gems you so carefully hand-picked from the branches or vines. I cringe when I see people dump ten pounds of perfect, tree-ripened cherries into a paper or plastic grocery sack and then haul it off to the trunk of their car for the long, hot drive home. When they reach their destination, half of the fruit will be crushed and the other half will be soft and covered with sticky juice.

Farmers' Markets

Farmers' markets are a great source for excellent-quality produce that is perfect for home canning. These markets often contain a mix of commercial growers and some home gardeners who have an abundant crop to share. Much of the produce may have been harvested that same morning, or late the previous afternoon, then brought fresh to the market. Most farmers' markets require that the produce be grown locally and that the growers use no pesticides. Check with the markets in your area.

When in season, green beans, corn, cucumbers, tomatoes, peppers, a variety of fresh fruits, berries and root vegetables can be found in abundance at farmers' markets. Many unusual and exotic fruits and vegetables can be found there as well. I enjoy going to a number of local farmers' markets just to see what is new and different. Be sure to go early, as near to opening time as possible, when the produce is freshest and the selection is plentiful.

Produce Markets

Many communities have produce markets where one or more growers sell their fresh fruits and vegetables. These markets can be a great resource for home canners. But just because the fruit is sold in a produce market, it does not mean that it was picked that same day. Much of the vegetables and fruit available in a produce market may have been grown locally, but were too ripe to survive shipping to the grocery store and supermarket distribution centers. This is a plus for the home canner because the produce was riper when it was harvested and will probably have a good flavor.

But sometimes the produce is too ripe, bruised or otherwise damaged. Shoppers need to inspect the produce carefully before buying. Some of it was probably harvested within the past 24 hours and may be in excellent condition, while other bins may contain produce that was picked over a week ago, or perhaps even longer. Watch out for special sales and deep discounts in price; these items may be old or damaged, leading to wasted produce and poor canning results. If the price looks too good to be true, it is probably a bad buy.

Roadside Stands

Growers will frequently set up produce stands along the edge of a road that runs past their fields and sell some of their crop directly to the public. These stands are an excellent source for fresh fruits and vegetables that are perfect for home canning. Strawberries, raspberries and other types of berries, peaches, apples, citrus fruits, corn, green beans, tomatoes, squash and all manner of other fruits and vegetables can be purchased from roadside stands. Buy produce early in the day, before it wilts from the heat, and also so you will have time to preserve it that same day.

Supermarket Produce

Much of the produce found in grocery stores does not make very satisfactory preserved foods. Because commercially grown fruit must survive the rough handling of long-distance shipping, it is usually picked green and ripens along the way or is chemically ripened in the warehouse before delivery to the stores. As a result, this shipped produce will have substantially less flavor than homegrown or locally grown fruit, which is allowed to ripen longer before being harvested. Store-bought fruit is frequently several weeks old and has been bruised or otherwise damaged along the way.

Vegetables are sturdier and usually travel better than fruit. As a result, the growers can harvest many vegetables closer to maturity, allowing them to develop more of their full flavor. However, delicate crops, such as green beans and peas, may lose some of their natural moisture, becoming wilted and limp during shipping. Corn begins to turn to starch as soon as it is picked and needs to be canned as close to harvest time as possible to retain its fresh flavor and texture. Because grocery store corn will have been harvested several days or weeks earlier, it will yield a poor quality, starchy canned product. Tomatoes destined for grocery stores are usually harvested fairly green and have a bland, underdeveloped flavor, even when fully ripe. You will be much better off using homegrown tomatoes or ones purchased from a farmers' market.

While grocery stores may not be considered the best place to buy fruits and vegetables for home canning, you can still find some excellent selections in the produce department. Get to know the produce manager of your local store. He or she can clue you in on the arrival of locally grown crops and produce that is ripe and in very good condition. Citrus fruits, apples, bananas, pineapples, and berries other than strawberries, are usually ripe and can readily be used for successful home canning. For brief periods during the peak of their specific seasons, ripe, locally grown apricots, peaches, pears, nectarines and plums can appear in grocery stores. Carrots, peppers, broccoli, cauliflower and rhubarb are usually all good choices. Cucumbers, which need to be pickled within 24 hours of harvest, should never be purchased from a grocery store because the crop may have been harvested weeks before delivery to the store.

Examine grocery store produce carefully before buying. Look for signs of bruising and rough handling. If fruit is underripe, bruises may not show up until the fruit begins to reach full ripeness. Select fruit that is already ripe and unblemished. Choose vegetables that are fresh, firm and crisp. Leave behind any produce that is underdeveloped, misshapen or too mature because it will make inferior preserved foods. Use the fruits and vegetables purchased from the store as soon as possible. Because they may have been sprayed with pesticides to prevent insect damage, just before using, wash fruits and scrub vegetables thoroughly. Be very gentle so that you do not damage the produce.

FROZEN FRUITS AND VEGETABLES

Some frozen fruits, especially berries, work very well for home canning. They may be used for making juices, syrups, vinegars and some soft spreads without sacrificing the flavor and quality of the preserved food. Blackberries, boysenberries, blueberries and raspberries are all good frozen fruit choices. Frozen strawberries, unless they were homegrown, do not have much flavor and do not retain their texture very well when thawed. Most other fruits that have been frozen were harvested slightly underripe so they could be prepared and frozen without losing their shape. As a result, their flavor is not well developed and they tend to make bland preserved foods.

If purchasing frozen fruit, buy fruit that has not had any sugar added to it. Fruit that has been frozen with sugar contains an unknown quantity of sweetener. Part of the sugar will have been absorbed into the fruit, while part will be dissolved in the juice released by the fruit as it defrosts. This extra sugar in the fruit or juice can cause havoc with the balance of ingredients in preserved food recipes and may cause soft spreads not to jell properly.

Frozen vegetables do not fare well when defrosted and reprocessed in home canned foods. Always use fresh vegetables for home-canning recipes.

BASIC INGREDIENTS FOR CANNING

Pectin

Pectin is a water-soluble substance that is found in the tissues of all fruits. Pectin is a natural thickening and jelling agent. It is what makes jams, jellies and other soft spreads jell. Underripe fruit contains more pectin than ripe fruit, but the flavor of underripe fruit is not well developed and makes poor tasting soft spreads.

The amount of pectin contained in fresh fruit varies widely by the type and variety of the fruit. Some fruits are naturally very high in pectin and may require little or no additional pectin to set. Other fruits have a low pectin content and must be combined with commercial pectin in order to jell. Recipes for soft spreads, and the amount of pectin added in proportion to the quantity of fruit and sugar in the recipe, are based on the quantity of natural pectin found in the type of fruit used to make the spread.

How Pectin Works

In the early 1900s, pectin was identified as the natural jelling substance in fruit. When combined with fruit, sugar and acid in the correct proportions and then heated, pectin causes the fruit mixture to jell or set.

When pectin molecules come in contact with fruit acid, chainlike structures in the pectin become charged and these chains fold in on themselves. The folded chains trap water from the fruit or juice, forming a gel. Excessive heat, or high heat for an extended amount of time during cooking, will cause the pectin to break down and prevent the product from jelling. The broken pectin chains will not be able to trap or hold the water. If the length of boiling time is not controlled when preparing soft spreads, you may damage the pectin and end up with a liquid jam or jelly.

Sugar increases the strength of pectin, allowing the pectin to trap more water and improve its ability to jell. It is important to use the right ratio of fruit, pectin, sugar and acid. The addition of too much sugar will allow the pectin molecules to gain too much strength. This excessive strength will make the jam or jelly set too firm and the spread will be tough. Too little sugar and the pectin will not have enough strength to support and maintain the gel.

Preparing soft spreads without the addition of extra pectin frequently yields unreliable results. To achieve better results without adding pectin requires the complex task of determining the actual pectin content of each batch of cooked fruit, then adding the sugar and acid in the correct proportions to form a gel. The extended cooking of the fruit before measuring the pectin, then of the mixture after the sugar and acid are added, will yield a finished spread with a definite cooked fruit flavor and a dark color. Jams, conserves and butters made without added pectin must be cooked for a long period of time and they actually thicken from the evaporation of juice rather than from the process of jelling. Unless watched very closely, the resulting preserve can become a thick, rubbery mass rather than a smooth, spreadable soft preserve.

Commercial Pectin

Commercial pectin comes in two forms, liquid and powdered. Liquid and powdered pectins are not interchangeable. Each requires a different balance of fruit, sugar and acid to attain the proper set. Powdered pectin is added to the fruit before cooking, while liquid pectin is added to the heated fruit and sugar mixture near the end of the cooking process.

Both forms of pectic are 100 percent natural and are derived from either tart apples or the white pith found under the colored peel of citrus fruits. Apples and citrus are both high in natural pectin, however the white pith from citrus is very bitter. Because pectins made from citrus fruits can retain this bitterness, affecting the flavor of the finished soft spread, most commercial pectins are made by extracting the natural pectin from apples. These commercial pectins are primarily imported in bulk form from Europe and then packaged here in the United States.

Canning without and with Added Pectin

When jams and jellies are made without the addition of a commercial pectin, at least one-quarter of the fruit used to make the spread must be underripe in order for the soft spread to set. This high proportion of underripe fruit can seriously change the flavor, texture and quality of the spread. Jams and jellies made without added pectin must also be cooked for a significantly longer period of time than soft spreads with added pectin. This extended cooking time reduces the fresh fruit flavor of the spread. Using a commercial pectin greatly reduces the amount of cooking time required, resulting in a soft spread with a truer, fresh and natural fruit flavor.

By using a commercial pectin to jell soft spreads, fully ripe fruit can be used, greatly enhancing the flavor and texture of the spreads.

Ripe fruit creates soft spreads with a full flavor and a smooth texture. With the shorter cooking time used in preparing spreads with added pectin, there is also less risk of scorching the fruit. By using commercial pectins when making soft spreads, you can achieve the outstanding flavor that can only be obtained with the use of fully ripe fruit.

Liquid versus Powdered Pectin

Although I have won a few awards with entries made from powdered pectin, I prefer the softer, more tender set achieved from using liquid pectin. The results are more consistent with liquid pectin. Jams and jellies rarely set up too soft or too firm when liquid pectin is used. Less juice or liquid is boiled away preventing overset spreads. Using liquid pectin instead of powdered pectin reduces the chance of cooking the spread too long after adding the pectin, thereby causing the spread to become too thick from the evaporation of too much juice, or to be too thin by overcooking the pectin and causing it to break down. Soft spreads made with powdered pectin tend to be firmer and stiffer in texture.

When using liquid pectin, the fruit and sugar are combined at the beginning of the cooking process rather than at the end as with powdered pectin. The sugar dissolves faster and more completely, reducing the possibility of crystals forming in soft spreads or of jellies becoming weepy. The sugar has more time to penetrate into the fruit, which nearly eliminates the chance that the fruit and juice will separate or that the fruit may float in the jars as the spread cools. When making preserves with liquid pectin, the whole fruit or fruit pieces and sugar can be combined then set aside to allow the fruit to absorb the sugar and release juice. This method, which does not work well with powdered pectins, replaces the air in the fruit cells with sugar, greatly decreasing the chances of the fruit floating to the top in the jars as the preserves cool.

There are other benefits to using liquid pectin as well. The flavors of all of the ingredients blend together better when they are combined earlier in the cooking process. Because the sugar is added to the fruit first, it dissolves and combines with the fruit creating a more liquid mixture. A thick fruit and powdered pectin mixture is also more likely to stick to the bottom of the pan and scorch.

When using a powdered pectin, the fruit or juice and the pectin are combined first and brought to a full rolling boil before the sugar is added. Over a high heat, the boiling fruit sputters and spatters unpredictably as trapped air bubbles struggle to escape from the fruit mixture. There is a very real risk of getting burned by this splattering fruit. When the sugar is combined with the fruit first, the increased volume of the fruit and dissolved sugar helps prevent the violent explosions from the trapped air bubbles. This reduces the chances of being splattered and burned by the boiling fruit pulp.

Be cautious about using soft spread recipes from cookbooks that just simply list the pectin ingredient as "one package powdered pectin." Each brand of powdered pectin requires a different proportion of fruit, sugar and acid in order for the spread to jell. Even packages of dry pectin with the same weight, but made by different manufacturers, do not possess the same jelling abilities. If you do not know the brand used to develop the recipe, your results may be very disappointing.

Because liquid pectin can deteriorate when exposed to warm temperatures for an extended period of time, store unopened packages in a cool location or in the refrigerator. Store opened pouches, tightly sealed, in the refrigerator. For best results, bring the pectin to room temperature before using. Check the expiration date marked on the package of pectin and use the contents before that date otherwise the soft spread may fail to set. Outdated pectin can break down and lose its ability to jell.

Many home canners misunderstand the purpose of the one-minute boiling time that is given in the instructions for the recipes that are found in the pectin boxes and also in canning cookbooks. They fear that if they boil the soft spread for even a few seconds longer than a minute, the pectin will either be destroyed and the spread will fail to set or that the pectin will seize up and they will be left with a tough, gooey mass they can barely spoon out of the pan. Don't panic, neither extreme is true. While cooking times should be watched closely and the mixture should not be undercooked, a few seconds extra cooking will not ruin the soft spread. This means that you can take a moment to turn off the timer before removing the pan from the heat, not that you should leave the pan on a hot burner while you get the jars ready.

Because liquid and powdered pectins are added to the fruit at different times, the cooking process is slightly different for each type of pectin. With liquid pectin, the final one minute of cooking at a full rolling boil after the pectin is added is to make sure that the pectin is equally distributed throughout the soft spread. The constant stirring during this boiling incorporates the pectin with the fruit and prevents the soft spread from scorching over the high heat.

For powdered pectin, the final one-minute full rolling boil after the addition of the sugar is to make sure that the sugar is completely dissolved. Any undissolved sugar may cause hard crystals to form in jams and other spreads and weeping to occur in jellies. While not harmful, these side effects of undissolved sugar lower the overall quality of the soft spread. The constant stirring during the last boil helps dissolve the sugar and prevent the spread from scorching.

The commercial pectins available today are all natural and produce consistent, reliable results without changing the natural flavor of the fruit. They are readily available in grocery stores and cooking supply stores across the country. Commercial pectins contain a higher acid level than homemade pectins, making them more effective than homemade pectins and producing more consistent results when making soft spreads.

Homemade Pectin

Some cooks prefer to use a homemade pectin when canning their jams, jellies and other soft spreads because they consider this pectin made from underripe apples to be "all natural." What they do not understand is that commercial pectins are also made from apples, are "all natural," and do not contain any preservatives or additives. In my experience, I have found that homemade pectins produce inferior results and I do not recommend the use of homemade pectin for making any soft spreads.

There are many disadvantages to using homemade pectin, which is usually made from unripe or underripe tart varieties of apples. Making the pectin is a lengthy, complicated and time-consuming process. Because the pectin content can vary from apple to apple, it is difficult to achieve a consistent jelling strength with each batch of homemade pectin. Jams, jellies and other soft spreads made from homemade pectin tend to be very soft and may not hold their shape or mound up in a spoon. Some will fail to set at all. Unripe apples also contain a high level of starch. Jellies made from homemade pectin will frequently turn cloudy within a few weeks of storage as a result of this high starch content. This is a very common occurrence with jellies and other soft spreads made from a homemade pectin.

When using homemade pectin in making jams, marmalades, preserves and conserves, there is a greater risk that the fruit will separate from the jelly and rise to the top of the jar, rather than be evenly suspended throughout the jar. This is caused by the soft set of spreads made with homemade pectin and the higher ratio of juice to fruit that results from using a homemade pectin base for jelling soft spreads.

Homemade pectin is frequently referred to as pectin stock because several cups of pectin are used as the base stock for making each batch of jam or jelly. Use of this apple pectin stock means that all jams, jellies and other soft spreads are made with an apple juice base to which other fruits and flavors are then added. The apple pectin weakens the true flavor of the fruit being used and significantly changes the taste of the finished soft spread. Homemade pectin is highly perishable and must be used within a few days or frozen, which can affect its ability to gel.

Sweeteners

Sugars

GRANULATED WHITE SUGAR: Granulated sugar is used in preserved foods to sweeten the food and to accentuate the natural flavor of the other ingredients. In addition to adding sweetness and enhancing the flavor in preserved foods, sugar also works as a natural preservative. In the canning of soft spreads, sugar plays other roles as well. It helps to extract the juices from the fruit, then helps to thicken those juices. Sugar works with the pectin to enable the spreads to set.

Depending on your personal preference, you may use either granulated white cane sugar or beet sugar when canning preserved foods. I recommend using cane sugar for making jams, jellies and other soft spreads because it tends to dissolve faster, reducing the chance of crystals forming in the finished spread. No matter which sugar you choose, be sure it is of the highest quality.

Do not use raw sugar or crystallized sugar for making preserved foods as both of these take sig-

nificantly longer to dissolve than granulated sugar. Because these sugars dissolve slowly, there is a much greater risk that they will not completely dissolve during the canning process. This increases the probability that hard sugar crystals will re-form in the soft spread or other preserved food. The larger grain of raw sugar and crystallized sugar makes it very difficult to obtain accurately measured quantities. One cup of raw or crystallized sugar is not equal to one cup of granulated sugar. As a result, the quantity of sugar in proportion to the fruit, acid and pectin in a soft spread recipe will be out of balance and the spread will fail to set properly.

SUPERFINE SUGAR: Superfine sugar, as its name suggests, is a finely ground form of granulated sugar. Sometimes called preserving sugar or caster sugar, it dissolves very quickly in fruit juice and other liquids. Superfine sugar is called for in curd recipes and some specialty preserve recipes, where the foods to be preserved are not heated to high temperatures and it is crucial that the sugar dissolves quickly. Measurements are the same for superfine sugar and granulated sugar. If you are unable to find superfine sugar in your local supermarket, regular granulated sugar may be briefly ground in a blender or food processor to create superfine sugar.

BROWN SUGAR: Brown sugar is not used much in home canning because its strong molasses flavor can quickly overpower the flavor of the fresh fruit, vegetables and other ingredients used in making preserved foods. It is primarily reserved for a few rich specialty dessert sauces and preserves that are enhanced by the brown sugar's rich and complex flavor.

CORN SYRUP: In some recipes, corn syrup is used in combination with sugar. The addition of the corn syrup helps to achieve and improve the desired texture of the preserved food. Using too much corn syrup will cause a soft spread to have a softer set as a result of the extra liquid in the sweetener. Corn syrup also contains vanilla extract, which can alter the taste of some fruits while enhancing the flavor of others. Using corn syrup alone or in large quantities can make a soft spread or other canned food cloyingly sweet and mask the other flavors in the preserved food.

HONEY: It is risky to substitute honey for the sugar called for in a preserved food recipe, especially with soft spreads. Honey contains additional liquid that can upset the balance of the recipe, causing the spread to fail to set properly. Many honeys have a strong flavor that can mask or overpower the natural flavor of the fruit and other ingredients. They may alter the taste of the preserved food or give it an unpleasant taste. Honey can seriously change the flavor of a soft spread and will cause more foam to develop on top of the fruit mixture as it cooks, requiring additional skimming before the spread can be ladled into the jars.

While I do not personally recommend it, honey may be substituted for about one-third of the granulated sugar called for in a soft spread recipe. But be aware that soft spreads made with honey tend to have a very soft set and will pick up the flavor of the honey. If you do decide to use honey in making your soft spreads, choose a very mild variety, such as clover or orange. Because of the texture and flavor changes that occur when using honey, soft spreads made with honey usually do not score very well with state and county fair judges. Unless there is a specific entry class for spreads made with honey, it is not a good idea to enter your soft spreads sweetened with honey into a fair competition.

ARTIFICIAL SWEETENERS: Artificial sweeteners are not recommended for use in the home canning of preserved foods. The high temperatures reached during canning and processing can cause the artificial sweeteners to turn very bitter, thus ruining the flavor of your preserved food. Fruit and juices may be canned without sugar and sweetened just before serving. Jams, jellies and other soft spreads require sugar to interact with the pectin and make the spreads set. Sugar substitutes will prevent the pectin from jelling and soft spreads made with artificial sweeteners will have a very poor texture. There are cookbooks available that give recipes and instructions for making soft spreads using fruit juice instead of sugar.

Acids

Acid brings out the full flavor of fruit. It also preserves the texture of pickles and helps soft spreads to jell properly. The correct acid level is also necessary to permit pickles and some fruits to be safely processed in a water bath canner. Depending on the type of food to be preserved, the recipe may call for the addition of either vinegar or lemon juice to increase the acid level.

The quantity of lemon juice, vinegar or any other acid ingredient called for in a recipe should never be reduced. The specified quantity of acid is needed to achieve the proper consistency of the food, to bring out the flavor of the ingredients, or to increase the acid level to inhibit bacteria growth so that the preserved food may be safely processed in a water bath canner.

VINEGAR: Vinegar is primarily used in the preparation of pickled foods. Because the vegetables used in preparing pickles have low acid levels, they are packed in a high-acid vinegar to allow them to be processed in a hot water bath. By this method, the pickles can be processed at a lower temperature and maintain their crisp texture, color and good flavor. Only commercially prepared vinegars should be used in home canning and they should have a minimum acidity level of 5 percent to ensure safe preservation. Homemade vinegars have an unknown acidity level and should never be used to preserve any form of home-canned food. Vinegars come in a variety of flavors and can be combined with other ingredients to make maximum use of these flavors. Commercial vinegars make an excellent base for the addition of fruits and other ingredients to create a variety of homemade flavored vinegars in a wide range of exotic tastes.

LEMON JUICE: In making preserved foods, lemon juice serves four main purposes. Lemon juice is frequently added to soft spreads to create the right acid balance to enable the pectin to work properly and achieve a spread with a good gel. Lemon juice protects the color of lighter fruits and prevents them from turning dark during storage, and brightens the color of red fruits, such as strawberries and cherries, to keep them from fading. Fresh lemon juice enhances and brings out the flavor of the fruit. Bottled lemon juice increases the acid level of low-acid fruits making it safe to process them in a water bath canner. If a recipe calls for the addition of lemon juice, it should not be left out.

Lemon juice is required to raise the acid level of certain canned fruits, particularly tomatoes, bananas and figs which tend to have low or variable acid levels. These recipes will specifically call for the use of a commercially bottled lemon juice, which is a reconstituted product and has a consistent acid level. Fresh-squeezed lemon juice should never be substituted for bottled lemon juice, because just like the fruits the juice is supposed to protect, fresh lemons can vary in their actual acid content. This uncertainty makes can-

ning lower acid fruits with fresh lemon juice a risky proposition. Commercially bottled lemon juice is produced to provide a consistent acid, while the acid level of fresh lemons can vary significantly. While this variation will not affect the setting ability of a soft spread, fresh lemon juice can allow the growth of bacteria in tomatoes and other low-acid fruits.

Bottled lemon juice may be substituted for fresh lemon juice, but it tends to give soft spreads an unpleasant, almost bitter flavor. For the best-flavored preserved foods, I recommend using only fresh lemon juice in recipes, such as most soft spreads, where the acid level of the fruit is already high enough to permit safe canning.

Fresh lemon juice should always be strained through a couple layers of fine-meshed cheesecloth to remove tiny seeds that can affect the texture of the preserved food. When making jellies, the lemon juice should be strained through a paper coffee filter to remove the pulp and fine particulate matter that can cause the jelly to become cloudy.

CITRIC ACID: Citric acid, which is available in powdered and crystallized forms at most health food stores and many drugstores, may be used in place of the bottled lemon juice required in some preserved food recipes to raise the acid levels for safe canning. It has a strong sour taste and the amount of sugar in a canned fruit recipe will need to be increased to compensate for this. Citric acid should not be added to soft spreads because increasing the sugar may upset the balance of the recipe, causing the spread not to set.

Other Ingredients
Butter
Many soft spread recipes call for adding a small quantity of unsalted butter to help reduce the amount of air that becomes trapped in the juice

when the fruit is heated or boiled. This trapped air rises to the top of the mixture in the form of foam, which must be skimmed from the surface before the spread can be ladled into the jars. Certain fruits like apricots and plums produce more foam than others. The butter helps to release the air bubbles and minimize the amount of foam produced as the fruit cooks.

Only a high-quality unsalted butter should be used in the preparation of preserved foods. Salted butter, reduced-fat butter, margarine, shortening, lard or any other butter substitute can impart an unpleasant flavor to the soft spread, or other preserved food, and should not be used.

In some soft spreads, such as Wild Blueberry Preserves (page 147), a larger amount of unsalted butter is called for and is added at the end of the cooking process rather than at the beginning. In this case, the butter is not used to reduce the foam but rather to give a richness to the spread that is similar to adding butter to a fruit pie filling. If you prefer, in most cases the butter may be omitted from a recipe without having a significant impact on the flavor or texture of the preserved food.

Because jellies are prized for their crystal clarity, butter should never be added when making a jelly. The fat in the butter will make the jelly turn cloudy. The fruit for jellies is cooked first to release the juice and the foam from the fruit is skimmed off before straining the juice to make it clear. If filtered properly, the juice will not produce any significant foam when it is reheated and made into a clear jelly.

Salt

In home canning, salt acts as both a flavoring and a preservative. When making pickles, large quantities of salt are used to draw excess moisture from the vegetables before beginning the pickling process. Pickles may also be packed in salt brine to preserve them in the jars.

Pickling salt, also called canning salt, and kosher salt both work well in home canning. They have larger crystals than table salt, have a good, clean flavor and dissolve easily. Do not use table salt for making preserved foods because it contains fillers to prevent it from caking that can interfere with the brining and canning of foods. Table salts containing iodine can also cause preserved foods, especially pickles, to turn dark. Sea salt may also contain minerals that can darken canned foods. Salt substitutes do not work well in home canning and should be avoided. They can turn bitter when heated and may give preserved foods an unpleasant flavor.

Water

Water plays an important role in the canning and preserving of pickles. Combined with salt to make a brine, it is used to draw moisture from cucumbers and other vegetables to keep them crisp and flavorful. Because hard water contains minerals that may cause pickles and other preserved foods to turn dark, tap water should not be used for home canning. Bottled drinking water and spring water also contain minerals that can darken the vegetables and are not recommended for making pickles. Soft water, which has had most of the hard water minerals filtered out, may be used for canning with acceptable results. If you use soft water and still have problems with your pickles darkening in the jars during storage, try using distilled water in both the brine and the syrup the next time you can pickles. I always use distilled water, which does not contain any minerals, for all of my pickling brines and syrups.

Antioxidants

To prevent light-colored fruits, such as pears, peaches and apples, from darkening while being prepared for canning or during storage in the jars, treat them in an antioxidant solution before canning. The commercial antioxidants, or fruit preservatives as they are commonly known, are a combination of citric acid and ascorbic acid and can be found in most grocery stores alongside the canning supplies. The crystals dissolve quickly in water to make a clear solution. As the fruit is peeled, it is dropped into the antioxidant solution to soak. The fruit should be removed from the solution after 20 minutes and rinsed under cool running water, otherwise the fruit can absorb too much of the acid and the finished preserved food may lack flavor and have a tart taste.

Ascorbic acid crystals, also known as vitamin C crystals, may be substituted for the commercial antioxidants with good results. Follow the same directions given in the recipes for making the antioxidant solutions. Ascorbic acid crystals may be purchased in bulk form at health food stores and are available at some drug stores. If you should happen to also have citric acid powder or crystals on your shelf, you may combine them with the ascorbic acid crystals in a ratio of three parts ascorbic acid to one part citric acid and use this mixture to make an antioxidant solution.

Clearjel Powder

Clearjel comes in two types: Instant, which is the one I use, and regular. Clearjel is a very fine modified cornstarch made from a special variety of corn. Compared to regular cornstarch, flour and tapioca, it has a superior thickening power and produces a smoother texture. Instant Clearjel immediately begins to thicken the sauce or pie filling when it is combined with liquid. It is not necessary to heat the liquid and starch mixture for it to thicken. Clearjel also does not have the chalky taste of regular cornstarch or flour, which must be cooked to remove this unpleasant flavor from the food.

Flour and cornstarch are not recommended for use as thickening agents in home canned foods because they can cause sauces, syrups and pie fillings to become thin and lumpy when heated to high temperatures for a period of time. Sauces and pie fillings may also separate during water bath processing or storage.

To prevent the possibility of small lumps from forming in sauces or pie fillings, thoroughly combine the Instant Clearjel with the superfine sugar called for in the recipe before adding the thickener to the liquid. The superfine sugar will separate the starch particles and help keep them from clumping together when combined with the moist ingredients.

Fruit Juices

Fruit juices are frequently used to enhance the flavor of preserved foods. For example, apples that are cooked in apple juice or apple cider will produce an intensely flavored applesauce or pie filling, while apples cooked in water will yield a product with only average flavor. Many of the marmalade recipes in this book call for using part water and part citrus juice for cooking the fruit and zest, rather than the traditional method of using just water alone. This gives the marmalade an extra burst of fresh fruit flavor that makes the spread memorable.

Fresh, frozen or canned fruit juices may also be used for canning fruit instead of using a sugar syrup. Be sure to select a mild juice that will complement the natural flavor of the fruit without overpowering it. White grape juice is a good choice for use with most all varieties of fruit.

Citrus Zest

Zest is the colored, thin, outer portion of the peel of citrus fruits. All of the flavorful citrus oils are found in the zest. It should be carefully removed from the fruit without taking any of the bitter white pith along with it. Zest is sliced into thin strips for use in marmalades and curds, and may be grated or finely chopped for use in other types of preserved foods.

Herbs and Spices

Whenever possible, use fresh herbs for making sauces and pickles as they produce a stronger and more pleasant flavor than dried herbs. Purchase new dried spices at the beginning of each canning season. Spices that have been open for several months will lose their flavor and intensity. To prevent the canning liquid or syrups used in pickling from becoming cloudy, always use whole spices instead of ground spices.

Nuts

Some recipes, such as conserves and ice-cream toppings, call for nuts as one of their main ingredients. While nuts may be used raw, they have a more intense, nutty flavor when they are toasted before being added to the other ingredients. Nuts should be added near the end of the cooking time to help maintain their crunchy texture and keep them from becoming mushy. Feel free to change the type of nut called for in the recipe to one that you prefer. In most cases, changing the variety of nut will not have a significant impact on the flavor or texture of the preserved food.

Dried Fruit

If a recipe calls for the use of dried fruit, it will usually contain instructions for plumping the fruit in fruit juice or a liqueur before adding it to the other ingredients. Water may also be used for plumping dried fruit. If dried fruit is added to the other ingredients without being plumped, it may draw too much moisture from the liquid ingredients, resulting in a very firm soft spread or a preserved food with a dry texture.

Extracts and Liqueurs

Extracts and flavorings may be added to preserved fruits and soft spreads to create special flavor combinations. To retain their intense flavor, extracts should be added close to the end of the cooking process. For the best flavor, use only pure extracts whenever possible. Avoid using an imitation flavoring whenever a pure extract of the same flavor is available. Pure extracts do cost more than imitation flavorings and the reason for the higher price is their superior flavor. This difference can definitely be tasted in the finished preserve. While a pure extract can enhance the preserved food with a true delicate flavor, an imitation flavoring can be harsh, leaving an unpleasant alcohol aftertaste.

Liqueurs are added to some preserved foods for special flavor. They are also used as the base for cordials. If you prefer, you can omit the liqueur from any soft spread or other preserved food, except for the cordials of course, without any major changes in texture. The liqueur may also be replaced with a fresh or canned fruit juice selected to complement the flavors of the other ingredients in the recipe.

ABOUT THE RECIPES

Proper preparation and careful measurement of the ingredients are important to the successful and safe preservation of home-canned foods. Always use exact measurements when preparing home-canned foods. Do not approximate the quantities of the ingredients; inexact measurements will affect the quality, texture and flavor of the preserved food, especially in soft spreads.

Fruits and vegetables should be peeled, pitted, sliced, chopped, crushed or cut into the size of pieces specified in the recipe. Processing times are based on the size and density of the food and the volume of the jar. Changes in either the size or density of the preserved food, or in the size of the jar used to can the food, can impair the ability of the heat to fully penetrate the product during processing and may result in an underprocessed preserved food.

The jar yields and the weight measurements for the fruits and vegetables listed in the recipes are all approximate. Each batch of preserved food and soft spread will vary slightly in the number of jars it actually fills and the amount of whole fruit that will be necessary to prepare the quantity of measured fruit needed in the recipe. This variation results from the size and shape of the fruit and vegetables used, their maturity and ripeness, as well as the juice or liquid content in their cells. These factors can change from harvest to harvest and from year to year. Whenever you prepare a batch of preserved foods, you may end up with a little bit more or a little bit less preserved food than the yield indicated in the recipe.

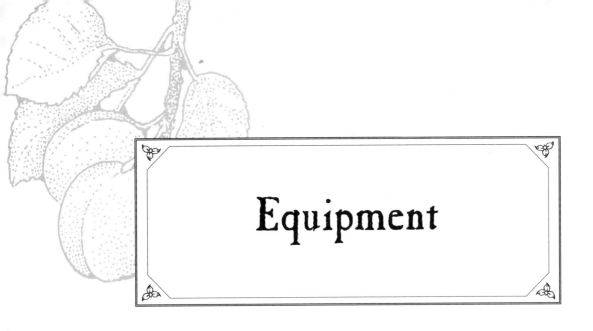

Equipment

Most of the equipment and utensils you will need for home canning are probably already in your kitchen. With the addition of a few other specialized pieces of equipment, such as a water bath canner or a pressure canner, and some canning utensils, you will be set to explore the exciting and flavorful world of preserving your own foods at home.

SELECTING EQUIPMENT

Always select good-quality, sturdy equipment and pans for use in home canning. Because of the acid content found in fruit and some of the other ingredients used in home canning, always use cooking equipment made from stainless steel or glass when making preserved foods. While aluminum pans allow for the fastest heating of food,

the natural acids in fruit and the vinegars used for pickling can chemically react with the metal and may pit the pan. Stainless steel is strongly recommended for all pans and most of the utensils used in making homemade preserved foods.

Never use pans, utensils or other equipment made from galvanized metals for home canning. The zinc coating on the galvanized metal can be dissolved by the fruit acids or vinegar. This dissolved coating is poisonous, and any preserved foods prepared in a galvanized pan should be considered dangerous and should not be consumed.

It is important to use the size of pan specified in the recipe because it determines how quickly the food will heat and how much liquid will evaporate during the cooking process. This is especially important when making soft spreads. If the pan is too small, not enough liquid will evaporate from the fruit mixture and the spread will be soft and runny. If the pan is too large, too much liquid could evaporate, resulting in a soft spread that may be very firm and rubbery in texture.

Basic Equipment for Canning

The wide variety of modern utensils and kitchen equipment available today has made home canning much easier and more reliable than

SUGGESTED EQUIPMENT

The following is a list of canning equipment, as well as some basic kitchen equipment and utensils, that you will want to have on hand when you home can preserved foods.

POTS AND PANS
8-quart stainless steel pan or stockpot
4-quart stainless steel pan or stockpot
2½- to 3-quart saucepan
1- to 2-quart saucepan for heating lids
Double boiler
Flat-bottomed bowl or pan for crushing fruit
Pressure canner
Water bath canner

SPECIAL EQUIPMENT
Apple corer
Bubble freer or plastic knife
Canning jars with two-piece lids
Cheesecloth
Cherry pitter
Collapsible wire basket for blanching fruit
Food mill
Jar lifter
Jelly bag (optional)
Lid wand
Melon baller
Pear corer
Pitting spoon or thin-bowled tableware spoon
Rubber or latex gloves for peeling chile peppers, pomegranates or beets
Sieve
Skimmer or slotted spoon for skimming foam
Strainer or colander

Tomato corer (sometimes called a huller), also great for strawberries
Wide-mouth funnel

STANDARD KITCHEN EQUIPMENT
Assorted-sized glass or stainless steel mixing bowls
Cooling racks or wooden board
Cutting board
Dish towels
Dry and liquid measuring cups
Instant read thermometer
Ladle
Long-handled spoon
Measuring spoons
Minute timer
Paper towels
Pot holders
Soft vegetable brush
Vegetable or potato masher

KNIVES
Chef's knife or utility knife
Crinkle-edge cutter for fancy pickles
Fruit knife or peeling knife
Paring knife
Vegetable peeler
Zester

in past years. There are all kinds of nifty gadgets and special tools that can be found in grocery store aisles and cooking stores to help you create truly spectacular preserved foods.

Jars

John Mason, in 1858, is credited with inventing the first tempered glass canning jar with screw threads that could be sealed airtight with a metal cap. When Mason's patent expired, the Ball brothers began producing glass canning jars using Mason's design. In the early 1900s, the rights to a two-piece German-made metal lid, lined with a rubberized gasket, were acquired by John Kerr. The modern age of home canning began when the Mason jar was combined with the Kerr vacuum-sealing lid and screw ring. Over the years, the methods used for sealing the jars have improved, but the basic jar and lid combination has remained the same.

Home-canning jars are made of clear tempered glass. Although some may appear slightly blue in color, they are still considered clear for canning and fair judging purposes. The jars come in a variety of shapes and patterns, ranging in size from 4 ounces to 1 quart. While 1½-quart and 2-quart canning jars can still be found, they are not recommended for use because they are so large that they would require a very long processing time for heat to penetrate to the food in the center of the jar. As a result, the food in the outer part of the jar would be overprocessed, destroying its color, texture and flavor.

Canning jars can be purchased with either regular or wide-mouth openings, making it easier to can a variety of foods. You may choose whichever size opening you prefer. The jars are packaged 12 to a box and include lids and screw rings. Jars made specifically for freezer canning should not be used for regular home canning, as they may break during processing and will not hold a tight seal.

Lids

Canning lids have a special sealing compound around the outer rims. Placing the lids in a pan of hot water for 10 minutes softens the compound and ensures a proper seal between the lid and the jar rim. (see more about lids, page 29). The purpose of the screw ring is to hold the lid in place during the processing and until the jars have cooled. When the jars are completely cooled, the screw rings are no longer needed and may be removed.

While jars and screw rings may be reused year after year as long as they are in good condition, lids can only be used once. New lids may be purchased separately and also come in boxes containing new screw rings.

Covering the top of soft spreads with melted paraffin is no longer an accepted method for sealing jars. It does not seal out air and allows bacteria and mold to grow in the jars.

Preserving Pan

The pan you select to use when preserving foods should be sturdy and made of stainless steel. It should be large enough to hold the food you will be preserving and also allow room for the food to expand during cooking. The fruit and sugar mixtures of soft spreads can double in volume as they boil, so take this into account when choosing a preserving pan. Recommendations for pan sizes are given in each recipe. The two standard pan sizes I use most often are a 4-quart and an 8-quart stockpot. I find that these two pans will handle about 90 percent of my home-canning needs.

Water Bath Canner

A water bath canner is used to heat process jars of high-acid foods to prevent contamination and seal the jars for storage. The canner consists of a large, deep pan with a metal rack in the bottom to hold the jars off the bottom and a snug-fitting lid. The pan should be about 4 inches taller than the height of the tallest jar you will be processing to allow the jars to be covered by 1 to 2 inches of water. Both the pan and the rack should be made of stainless steel to prevent rusting.

In 1810, Frenchman Nicolas Appert invented the process of packing food into glass jars, sealing them with a tight-fitting cork and then placing them in boiling water to create a vacuum inside the jars. Today, instead of the corks, we use jars with a two-piece lid and screw-ring closure to safely process high-acid foods in a hot water bath canner. This method creates a vacuum inside the jars and tightly seals the lids.

Pressure Canner

A pressure canner is a specialized piece of equipment used to heat process jars of low-acid foods with pressurized steam to kill bacteria spores and seal the jars for safe storage. The canner consists of a large, heavy-duty stainless steel pan with a rack to hold the jars, a tight-fitting lid that can be clamped down to seal the pan and a gauge to measure the pressure during processing. A pressure cooker is not the same as a pressure canner and cannot be substituted for a pressure canner.

The first pressure canner designed and sold for home use was created by American inventor A. J. Shriver in 1874. Modifications of this early canner design and the use of new materials have led to the modern pressure canners now used for the safe preservation of low-acid foods at home.

Measuring Equipment

While you might think that one type of measuring cup is the same as another, the two basic types of measuring cups, dry and liquid, are not interchangeable. Dry ingredients are measured by volume, while liquid ingredients are measured in ounces. Using the wrong measuring equipment will have a definite effect upon the quality and consistency of your preserved foods. For accurate measuring, invest in a sturdy set of both dry and liquid measuring cups.

Use plastic or metal graduated-size measuring cups specifically designed for dry ingredients to measure the dry ingredients. Heat-proof glass liquid measuring cups should be used for measuring all liquids, fruits and vegetables. Liquid measuring cups made of plastic are not recommended, as the plastic can absorb and retain strong flavors, even after washing, tainting the flavor of the next ingredients to be measured in the cup.

Measuring spoons should be graduated in size from ⅛ teaspoon to 1 tablespoon. While many cooks are used to adding a little of this or a little of that and estimating quantities that are less than a tablespoon, this is not a good practice for home canning. Making preserved foods is as much a science as it is a creative effort. Ingredients must be balanced in the correct proportions; otherwise, the preserved foods can fail to set or have a poor flavor blend—or even worse, be unsafe to eat. Accuracy in the measuring of all ingredients is key to creating successful preserved foods.

Jar Lifter

A jar lifter is a pair of heavy-duty tongs that are specifically designed to lower and raise filled home-canning jars into and out of a water bath canner or pressure canner. The jar lifter protects your hands from being burned by accidental contact with the hot water. Firmly grasp the jar with the lifter positioned around the neck of the jar, below the screw ring. Do not attempt to lift the jar by gripping it around the screw ring, as the jar can easily slip out of the grasp of the lifter, drop back into the pan and splash you with hot water or fall onto the counter or floor and break.

Lid Wand

A lid wand is an inexpensive, handy little tool that no home canner should be without. It is basically a long, plastic rod with a magnet on one end and is used to remove the lids from the pan of hot water in which they have been soaking to soften the sealing compound. Removing the lids from the hot water is a breeze with a lid wand.

Wide-Mouth Funnel

An indispensable piece of equipment, a wide-mouth funnel makes filling jars easier and less messy. It fits perfectly into canning jars with a regular-size opening and also works great in wide-mouth jars. The funnel may be made of either metal or heatproof plastic and can be found where canning supplies are sold, in cooking supply stores or ordered by mail.

Food Mill

A food mill is a piece of equipment designed to remove the seeds, skins and tough fibers from raw or cooked fruits and vegetables. It is especially useful when making butters, smooth sauces, applesauce or seedless jams. Food is placed into the mill, and the handle is turned to force the food through a metal disc perforated with small holes. Discs with different-size holes may be used, depending on the type of food to be milled, the size of the seeds to be removed and the desired consistency of the finished product. The seeds and skins are forced to one side, while the pulp passes through the disc. Using a food mill is faster and easier than trying to remove the seeds and skins from fruit by forcing it through a fine sieve.

The Foley food mill was the first food mill to be made readily available to the average consumer, and as a result, is the most commonly known brand. When purchasing a food mill, make sure that it is made of stainless steel. It will be sturdier, work better and last longer than the cheaper ones that are tin-plated or made from plastic. The tin-plated food mills tend to rust after only a few uses, and the plastic ones break easily.

Sieve

Fine-meshed sieves are useful for separating the juice from the fruit pulp when making jellies, syrups and vinegars. A sieve may be used in place of a food mill to separate the seeds and skins from the fruit pulp when making sauces and butters or to puree applesauce. Curds and many juices are also strained through a sieve. The mesh should be very fine to prevent small seeds and bits of fruit from passing through the sieve.

Metal sieves, other than those made from stainless steel, tend to rust quickly and can impart a metallic flavor to the food. Sturdy plastic sieves with a stainless steel mesh are an excellent choice because they clean up easily and will last a long time. Use a stiff brush to remove small food particles that may become trapped in the mesh, then rinse the sieve under running water until all signs of food and soap are completely gone.

Cheesecloth

Cheesecloth is used to strain fine pulp and seeds from juice or other liquids when making a variety of preserved foods. When preparing jellies, a sieve may be lined with several layers of cheesecloth to separate the juice from the fruit. Choose bleached or unbleached cheesecloth with a very fine weave. Do not use a loosely woven cheesecloth, as it will not trap all of the fine pulp from the juice or other liquid. My favorite cheesecloth is made by Norpro (see Mail-Order Sources, page 337). The cloth is strong, made of high-quality 100 percent bleached cotton and has a fine weave that is far superior to the many other brands I have tried.

Vegetable Masher

A vegetable or potato masher is the best tool to use to evenly crush fruits for making jams, conserves, other soft spreads and some sauces. It is more effective and consistent than trying to use the back of a large spoon to crush the fruit, as instructed in some cookbooks.

Food processors and blenders should not be used to prepare fruit for soft spreads because they chop the fruit unevenly and can quickly puree the fruit. Either occurrence will dramatically change the texture, quality and flavor of the spread. Preparing the fruit in a food processor or blender will also trap a significant amount of air in the fruit, which will turn to unwanted foam when the fruit is heated and cooked. This excess foam must be skimmed from the surface of the soft spread after cooking and can significantly alter the texture and yield of the spread.

Zester

A zester is a small tool with a row of evenly spaced small holes that is used to remove the colored peel from citrus fruits in very fine strips. It strips away only the outer, flavorful colored layer of the peel and leaves behind all of the bitter white pith. A zester is invaluable for making premium marmalades and smooth, flavorful curds.

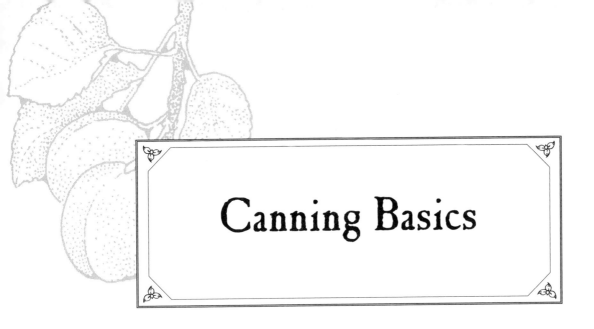

Canning Basics

Once you have mastered the basics of home canning, a whole new world of creating homemade preserves will open up to you. This adventure can be exciting as you explore new tastes, textures and flavor combinations. Learn how to preserve foods well and you will soon have family, friends and neighbors clamoring for more of your sweet and savory treats.

Top-quality produce makes the best-preserved foods. Fruits or vegetables that are bruised or show any signs of spoilage should not be used for canning. They may contain harmful bacteria that could contaminate your preserved foods.

CANNING SAFETY

Before we begin talking about canning techniques, a few words need to be said on the subject of home-canning safety. This section is not designed to scare you away from home canning, but to give you the reasons why it is important and necessary to use safe canning techniques and to correctly process jars of preserved foods. While today's modern methods of home canning yield preserved foods that are both delicious and safe to eat, care must be taken to follow the proper preserving procedures. Taking shortcuts can open the door to the possibility of bacterial contamination, which can result in dangerous preserved foods. Good hygiene and clean equipment are essential in the handling and preparation of any type of food.

Be wary about using canning recipes found in old cookbooks. They are often filled with old-fashioned techniques that could lead to disappointing results and ruined preserves. Even many of the recent books on home canning contain outdated and unsafe methods, continuing to perpetuate the problems of canning safety. If in doubt concerning the safety of a method or recipe, check with your local Cooperative Extension Service office.

Preventing Spoilage

Organisms that can cause food to spoil, such as bacteria, yeast and mold, are found in soil, water and even the air we breathe. Enzymes that are naturally present in raw fruits and vegetables can affect their color, texture and flavor. During processing, fruits and vegetables are heated to a high enough temperature for a long enough period of time to destroy these spoilage organisms. The heating process also stops the action of the enzymes that can quickly cause the deterioration of the food.

Clostridium botulinum bacteria is the organism of most concern in home canning. This is the bacteria that causes botulism. While *Clostridium botulinum* cells are easily killed by the temperatures reached during water bath processing, spores from the bacteria may continue to grow. High-acid foods, those foods having a pH level of 4.6 or lower, contain a sufficient acidity level to prevent spore growth in preserved foods.

Vegetables and other low-acid foods, such as meat and seafood, which have a pH level higher than 4.6, do not contain a sufficient acidity level to inhibit the growth of the bacteria spores. Because *Clostridium botulinum* cells thrive in the absence of air in moist, low-acid environments, low-acid foods must be processed in a pressure canner, where steam under pressure can heat the preserved foods to temperatures of 240F to 250F (116C to 121C), killing the bacteria spores and making the foods safe for storage and consumption.

Tomatoes have a borderline acidity level and require the addition of lemon juice or vinegar to make them safe for processing in a water bath canner. Jars of tomatoes that do not contain lemon juice or vinegar must be processed in a pressure canner to ensure the safety of their contents.

Always process high-acid preserved foods in a water bath canner after filling the jars. Although often seen as time-consuming and unnecessary by some home canners, this extra step will ensure that your preserved foods will be safe to eat for many months and will make great gifts for friends and family. If you make only a small amount of soft spreads for your own personal use, they may be stored in the refrigerator without processing and used within 2 months. However, because you have no real control over how the recipient will store a jar of preserved food, do not give away as gifts any jars that have not been water bath processed.

The Open-Kettle Method is no longer considered a safe way to can acid foods for long-term storage. In this method, jars were first sterilized in boiling water and then filled with boiling-hot preserves. After being covered with the lids and the screw rings tightened, the jars were turned upside down for 5 minutes to create a vacuum inside the jar. Unfortunately, this does not effectively seal out all potential contaminants.

Water Bath and Pressure Canning

There are two methods for processing preserved foods: water bath canning and steam pressure canning. Fruits and high-acid foods can be safely processed in a water bath canner, while vegetables and low-acid foods MUST be processed under pressurized steam.

Water bath processing is a safe and easy way to preserve high-acid foods, such as soft spreads, fruits, juices and pickles. Lemon juice or vinegar is added to some canning recipes to increase the acid level of the food to permit safe canning. To protect the quality of the preserved food, the lemon juice or vinegar called for in a recipe should not be reduced or omitted.

Vegetables and other low-acid foods must be processed in a pressure canner to prevent bacterial growth and ensure food safety. The types of food that require processing in a pressure canner include tomatoes that do not have lemon juice added to them, all vegetables that are not pickled with vinegar, meat, seafood, poultry and any other low-acid foods.

Pressure canners should not be confused with pressure cookers. They are not the same piece of equipment, do not work in the same way and are not interchangeable. Pressure cookers cannot be used to safely process and seal canning jars because they do not heat the contents of the jars to the correct temperature and can cause the jars to explode. When using a pressure canner, carefully follow the manufacturer's operating instructions that come with the canner. The failure to process low-acid foods in a pressure canner could have deadly consequences.

Other Safety Tips

- Never invert jars of preserved foods to seal the lids, even after water bath processing. Turning jars upside down in this old-fashioned way permits microscopic amounts of food or liquid to squeeze between the jar rim and the lid, allowing air and bacteria to enter the jar and causing the seal to fail.

- Sealing jars with paraffin is no longer an acceptable canning method. Paraffin does not seal the jars airtight and allows dangerous spoilage agents to enter the jars and grow in the preserved food. Never use paraffin to seal a jar.

- CAUTION: Do not use the oven, dishwasher, a nonpressurized steamer or a microwave oven to process filled jars of preserved foods. These unconventional methods fail to heat the contents of the jars to a high enough temperature to prohibit the growth of harmful bacteria, and they may cause the canning jars to break.

- When preparing pickles, use a commercial vinegar with a minimum 5 percent acidity level. Do not use homemade vinegars for pickling, as the acidity level is unknown and may be too low to ensure safe pickling.

- Fruits or vegetables that are bruised or show any signs of spoilage should not be used for canning. They may contain harmful bacteria that could contaminate your preserved foods.

Storing Canned Goods

Store jars of preserved foods in a cool, dry, dark place with temperatures that do not exceed 75F (24C) or drop below 40F (4C). Jar lids and screw rings can rust or corrode in moist environments, while light will cause preserved foods to darken in color. Excessive heat can trigger bacteria growth, and jars exposed to freezing temperatures may break. Proper storage of the jars will ensure that your homemade preserved foods will retain their natural color, texture and fresh flavor for the longest period of time.

Home-canned preserved foods that have been properly sealed and stored should maintain their quality for at least a year. After that time, although still safe to eat, the color and flavor of the food will gradually deteriorate.

Danger Signals

Never serve or taste the food from any jar until you have carefully inspected both the jar and its contents. Be sure that the jar is still well sealed and that the contents have a pleasant smell and appropriate color. If a jar of preserved food does not look right or smell right, do not eat the food.

When inspecting and opening jars of preserved foods, watch out for these dangerous signs of contamination:

- Broken seals or bulging lids
- Cloudy liquid in fruit, vegetables or pickles
- Fermentation (gas bubbles rising in liquid)
- Liquid or food leaking out from under the lid
- Contents spurting from under the seal when the jar is opened
- Mold visible on top of the food or on the underside of the lid
- Slimy or mushy food
- Unpleasant or unusual odor
- Unusual or badly discolored product

While spoilage is a rare occurrence in properly prepared, sealed and stored jars of home-canned preserved foods, it can happen. If you discover a contaminated jar, dispose of the contents so that no people or animals will come in contact with it. Throw away the lid and screw ring. Wash the jar in hot, soapy water, then place it on a rack or paper towel in the bottom of a deep pan of warm water. Make sure that the jar is completely submerged and covered by at least 1 inch of water. Bring the water to a full rolling boil and boil the jar for a minimum of 15 minutes. (A full rolling boil is a boil that cannot be stirred down.) Remove the jar from the pan and place it on a rack, wooden board or dish towel to cool.

Safety Guidelines

The following guidelines should be kept in mind when canning foods at home. Use common sense whenever preparing preserved foods.

- To prevent accidents and avoid contamination, be diligent about keeping your work area clean and clear. Food, utensils and equipment should always be handled with care to avoid potential problems and injuries.

- Whenever working with hot preserves, keep a bowl of ice water handy. Soft spreads can splatter, and the boiling, sugary mixture can quickly burn skin. If you do get hot preserves on your fingers or hands, never put them in your mouth to cool the temperature, as you will only succeed in burning the inside of your mouth as well. Stick your hand in the bowl of ice water instead.

- Canning jars should be kept hot until ready to use. Never ladle boiling hot preserved foods into room temperature jars, as the sudden temperature change may cause the jars to break.

- Use a specially designed and insulated jar lifter to load jars into and out of the hot water bath or pressure canner. Wet potholders transfer heat quickly, which can result in serious burns. Be sure to grasp the glass jar firmly, with the jar lifter positioned below the screw ring. Do not attempt to lift jars by the screw ring, as the jar lifter can easily slip and the falling jar may break or splash scalding water out of the canner.

- While either filling jars with hot food or cooling the hot jars after removing them from the canner, set the jars on a wire rack, wooden board or a dish towel. Hot jars set on a cold counter can break from the sudden change in temperature. When a canning jar breaks, it shatters, sending tiny pieces of glass everywhere.

- Avoid using abrasive materials or cleaners when washing canning jars, as they can scratch the glass, creating stress areas that may cause a jar to crack or break when filled with hot preserves.

- Keep small children and pets out of the kitchen when canning. With all the pans of hot preserves and boiling water, accidents can easily happen.

Canning Primer

Home canning has some specific methods and techniques that are used to make the canning process easier and yield better results.

Canning Terminology

Like any other form of cooking, home canning has its own specialized vocabulary. An understanding of these terms makes the process of canning preserved foods easier.

FOAM: The air that combines with the fruit juice and becomes trapped, then rises to the top during boiling.

FULL ROLLING BOIL: A rapid boil that breaks the surface and cannot be stirred down.

HEADSPACE: The amount of air space left in the jar between the top of the preserved food and the lid.

HOT PACK: Fruit, vegetables or pickles are heated in a syrup or other liquid for a few minutes, then packed into jars and covered with the hot syrup or liquid. This is the preferred method of preparation for most fruits and vegetables because air trapped inside the produce is released during heating. As a result, when the food is processed, there is no extra air to be released, the headspace remains the same and the product does not float in the jar.

PROCESS: To heat filled canning jars in very hot water or under pressurized steam for a specified amount of time to kill any potentially harmful bacteria and to deactivate enzymes.

RAW PACK: Unheated food, such as berries and other delicate fruits, is snugly packed into jars and covered with a hot syrup that has been boiled and cooled slightly.

SKIM: To use a slotted spoon to remove the foam from the top of a pan of preserved foods.

Preparing Jars

Wash the jars in a dishwasher. If your dishwasher has a sani-cycle, use it. Keep the jars hot until ready to use. Or, you may wash the jars by hand in hot, soapy water and rinse them thoroughly with hot water. Place the hand-washed jars in a large saucepan and cover them with hot water. Cover the pan and keep the jars hot until ready to use. Drain the jars just before filling.

Do not remove the jars from the dishwasher or hot water too soon. The jars should be hot when they are filled with hot food to prevent them from breaking as a result of the sudden temperature change. Another reason to keep the jars hot is because mildew can thrive in cold, wet jars.

Filling Jars

Fill the jars quickly, using a wide-mouth canning funnel and a ladle to make the job easier and less messy. When packing fruit, vegetables and pickles, fill one jar at a time, clean the rim and apply the lid before filling the next jar. When making soft spreads like jam or jelly, fill all the jars at once, otherwise the spread left in the pan will cool too much and begin to set up. The partially set spread will not pour smoothly from the ladle and will increase the possibility of air bubbles becoming trapped in the jars.

Always use a ladle to transfer any type of soft spread or preserve from the pan to the jars. Never pour a soft spread over the edge of the pan and into the jars. Any undissolved sugar granules picked up from the sides of the pan can result in the spread developing a grainy or gritty texture. Undissolved sugar may also cause the formation of crystals in jams, jellies, marmalades or other soft spreads.

Air Bubbles

Ladle jams and other soft spreads into the jars quickly, keeping the ladle close to the top of the funnel. Pouring the jam too slowly, or from too great a height, can cause air bubbles to become trapped in the spread. Besides affecting the overall appearance and quality of the soft spread, air bubbles can impair the vacuum seal of the jar and create spaces where bacteria could grow.

A nonmetallic knife, spatula or a great plastic gadget called a bubble freer should be used to remove any trapped air bubbles from the jars of preserved foods. A metal knife banged against the side or bottom of a hot jar may cause the jar to crack.

Trapped bubbles are a particularly common problem with fruits, vegetables and pickles, because the food is packed into the jars first and then covered with a hot syrup, water or pickling liquid. Carefully slide the plastic knife down between the preserved food and the inside of the jar. Gently press against the preserves to make a path for the air bubbles to escape. Repeat this procedure four or five more times around the jar or until all of the bubbles have been released. If necessary, add more liquid to the jar, raising the headspace back up to the correct level.

Headspace

When filling the jars, always leave the exact amount of headspace called for in the recipe. The headspace allows for the expansion of the preserved food and the air in the jar during the water bath or pressure canner processing. During processing, the contents of the jar expand and air is forced out under the lid. As the air remaining inside the jar cools, it creates a vacuum, pulling the lid tight against the rim of the jar.

If there is too much headspace, not enough air will escape from the jar to form a good vacuum and the lid may not seal properly. If there is too little headspace, some of the food may be forced out under the lid with the air, impairing the seal. Both of these situations can cause problems during storage. Improper headspaces lead to preserved foods that will deteriorate faster than normal, darken in color and lose flavor and texture. Jars with poor headspaces also run an increased risk of spoilage and contamination.

Before placing the hot lids on the filled jars, thoroughly wipe the jar rims, inside the top edge of the jar and the outside screw threads with a clean, damp cloth to dissolve and remove any spilled preserves. Either a lint-free cloth towel or paper towel works well for this job. Do not use a sponge to wipe the jar rims because it can harbor tiny food particles and potentially harmful bacteria that could contaminate the preserved food.

Lids

The jar lids used in home canning have a special sealing compound around the outside edge of the lid. Before being applied to the jars, the lids must be heated in hot water to soften the sealing compound.

To heat the lids, fill a small saucepan about half full of water. Bring the water to a simmer, then remove the pan from the heat. Drop the lids, one at a time, into the hot water with the sealing compound facing up. Cover the pan and allow the lids to heat for at least 10 minutes. Keep the lids and water hot over low heat until needed. Do not allow the lids to boil or the sealing compound may be damaged.

To remove the lids from the pan of hot water,

use a handy little tool called a lid wand. It is a long, plastic rod that has a magnet attached to one end. The magnet grabs on to the lid and lifts it out of the hot water while your hands stay safe and dry. This inexpensive gadget is better than trying to get the uncooperative lids out of the pan using a pair of kitchen tongs.

Take hold of the outer edge of the lid with your fingers, being careful not to touch the sealing compound, and remove it from the lid wand. Set the lid on top of the jar, with the sealing compound against the glass, and adjust it to center the lid over the jar rim.

When the lids are placed on the jars and screwed down with the rings, the sealing compound molds to the jar rim. During processing in a hot water bath or pressure canner, air is forced out under the lid as the contents inside the jars expand. As the jars and their contents start to cool, the remaining air inside the jar contracts, forming a vacuum, and pulls the lid down firmly against the jar forming a tight seal. As the jars cool, the sealing compound will set up firmer and the vacuum inside the jars will keep the lids in place.

Screw Rings

The purpose of the screw rings is to tightly hold the lids in place on the jars during processing. It is not necessary to keep them on the jars during storage. The rings may be removed from the jars 24 hours after processing, when the jars have completely cooled and sealed.

Hand-wash the screw rings in hot soapy water, rinse well and dry thoroughly. The rings should not be put in the dishwasher. Unless specifically instructed by the manufacturer, do not boil the screw rings or allow them to stand in water. Boiling the screw rings, or keeping them in hot water until ready to use, can promote the formation of rust on the rings.

Screw rings showing any signs of rust should not be used and should be discarded. The rust may prevent the screw ring from being screwed down firmly on the jar. Without a firm pressure on the lid during processing, some of the preserved food or liquid inside the jar may escape with the air. Food or liquid trapped between the jar and the lid may not allow a vacuum to form in the jar, preventing a tight seal.

Sealing Jars

Screw the rings on firmly by hand but do not twist too tight. The ring must be snug enough to keep the preserved food from seeping out from under the lid during processing, while still allowing air to escape and form a vacuum in the jar. If the screw rings are tightened down too much, the jars may not vent properly and the lids may buckle or the jars may break from the pressure inside the jars. Screwing the rings on with excessive force will also cause the sealing compound to squeeze out from between the lid and the jar, resulting in a poor seal. On jars where the lids and screw rings were applied too tightly, the seals may fail a day or two after processing.

Never retighten any loose screw rings after processing. This can force the still soft sealing compound to squeeze out from between the lid and the jar, allowing air back into the jar and causing the seal to fail.

Testing Jar Seals

After processing, allow the jars to cool, undisturbed, for 12 to 24 hours. As the jars cool, a vacuum forms inside the jars and the lids pull down tight against the jar rims. The lids usually make a pinging or popping sound when this happens. While this is a good sign, it does not guarantee that the jars are sealed.

When the jars are completely cool, check to see that the lids have formed a tight seal. Press down in the center of the lid with your finger. If the lid is concave and does not move, a good vacuum has formed and the jar is sealed. If the lid presses down and stays down, the jar should be adequately sealed, but mark the jar and use it first just to be on the safe side.

Should the lid flex up and down when pressed or make a popping sound, the jar has failed to seal and should be reprocessed with a new hot lid or stored in the refrigerator and used within a few weeks.

Reprocessing Unsealed Jars

A jar of preserved food that has failed to seal may be reprocessed within 24 hours. To reprocess a jar, empty the contents of the jar into a pan. Inspect the jar for nicks, cracks or deformities. If there is any sign of damage or irregularity, replace the jar with a new one.

Reheat the preserves to the original packing temperature indicated in the recipe (190F [88C], full rolling boil, etc.). Follow the recipe directions for skimming foam, cooling or any other special procedures. Pack the preserves into a clean, hot jar, wipe the jar rim and apply a new heated lid and a clean screw ring. If the jar was originally raw packed, the contents may be placed directly into a clean, hot jar and covered with hot liquid and sealed with a new heated lid and a clean screw ring. Reprocess the preserves using the same time, temperature or pressure specified in the recipe. Check the seal within 24 hours.

Fruit, vegetables and pickles that required reprocessing will be softer in texture than those that sealed properly the first time. Soft spreads that have been reprocessed will often have a firmer set due to the extra liquid that evaporates during the process of reheating the spread back up to the packing temperature. Because of this texture change, jars of reprocessed preserves should not be entered into fair competitions, as they will receive reduced scores from the judges.

Storing Preserved Foods

Store your jars of preserved foods in a cool, dry, dark location away from any heat sources or exterior walls. Properly stored preserved foods will keep well for up to a year. After that time the quality begins to deteriorate, the color darkens and the flavor fades. Plan on using or giving away your preserves within a year. This will also give you room to store your bounty from next year's canning.

If you choose to store your filled jars in the original boxes they came in, which I recommend, cut a piece of cardboard to fit in the bottom of the box, under the divider, to fill in the space between the bottom flaps. Without this extra piece of cardboard, the six center jars will stand on the uneven bottom of the box. This will result in the contents of the jar shifting and the headspace of your soft spreads will set on a sloping angle.

While this slanted headspace will not affect the quality or safety of the product inside the jars and is acceptable for home use, it will impair the perfect appearance of the soft spreads and can result in a substantial deduction in score from the judges of a fair competition. If you plan to exhibit your preserved foods at a fair, be sure to level the inside bottom of the boxes before storing the jars.

WATER BATH CANNING

Processing jars of high-acid preserved foods in a water bath canner protects the contents from bacteria growth and enzymes that could otherwise cause the food to rapidly deteriorate and even become dangerous. The two-piece lids and rings developed for modern home canning allow air to escape from the jar during the water bath, thereby creating a tight vacuum seal between the lid and the jar rim as the product cools.

Sterilizing the jars in boiling water before filling is no longer considered an acceptable substitute for water bath processing. Even in the few moments when the empty canning jars are removed from the hot water and turned upside down to drain before filling, bacteria and spores from the air can sneak in and attach themselves to the inside of the jars. All jars of high-acid preserved foods must be water bath processed to ensure safety.

Choosing a Water Bath Canner

There are a number of water bath canners available in specialty cooking and kitchen stores. The height of the water bath canner you will need depends on the size of the jars you will be processing. If you are making soft spreads or canning other types of preserves in pint or smaller jars, a standard-size water bath canner is fine. Contrary to what the labels say though, most canners are not deep enough to hold and correctly process quart jars.

To adequately process quart jars, a water bath canner must be at least—the very least—10 inches high. This height is necessary to accommodate the rack on the bottom, the 7-inch height of a quart jar, a minimum of 1 inch of water above the jar and another 1 inch of air space above the water level. I recommend using a water bath canner that is a minimum of 12 inches tall.

The other problem with the water bath canners found in stores is the flimsy rack that comes with them. The design of the rack is supposed to allow the cook to fill it with jars and then lower and raise them into and out of the water bath. But six or seven filled canning jars, especially quart jars, are quite heavy and difficult to lift and balance in a swaying rack. Once the rack is in the canner, the jars tend to lean against each other or even fall over. It is not a very good system.

The rack is necessary to insulate the jars from the high heat of the bottom of the pan and the burner below. It also allows the water to circulate around the entire jar, resulting in better heat penetration of the jar and its contents.

One option is to make your own water bath canner. Any large pot with a good-fitting lid that is deep enough will do. I use a tall, 20-quart stainless steel stockpot with a heavy-duty round cake cooling rack set in the bottom. It works great for all sizes of jars, keeping them upright and level during processing.

If you decide to assemble your own water bath canner, select a good-quality pan, then find a sturdy round metal rack that will fit snugly in the bottom. Finding the right size rack is the biggest challenge. A rack that is too big simply won't fit, while one that is too small may leave a large gap around the edge, causing the jars to tip over against the side of the pan. Keep looking until you find the right rack. If you locate a rack that is the right size but is not strong enough in the center to hold the filled jars, support it with a few used screw rings set in the bottom of the pan under the rack.

In case you just can't find a rack to fit your pan, several screw rings can be wired together to create a makeshift rack. Or a large dish towel folded over twice may be placed in the bottom of the canner to insulate the jars from the heat of the pan. These are not ideal solutions, but they will work in a pinch.

To efficiently heat water and maintain the proper temperature, a water bath canner should be no more than 4 inches larger in diameter than the element on your stove or cooktop. Keep this in mind when you shop for a canner. If you must use a small burner for the canner, allow extra time for the water to heat before processing the jars and check the water temperature frequently during processing.

Water Bath Processing

Enzymes, *Salmonella* bacteria and *Staphylococcus aureus* bacteria are destroyed at temperatures above 140F (60C). Molds, yeasts and *Clostridium botulinum* bacteria are destroyed at temperatures between 140F (60C) and 180F (82C). University studies have shown that temperatures between simmering and a full rolling boil will eliminate harmful bacteria and organisms and tightly seal the jars of high-acid preserved foods.

When processed at a full rolling boil, the cell structures of fruit and pickles can collapse, resulting in a canned product with a very soft texture. Processing at high temperatures can diminish the flavor of juices, and can also affect their texture. Fruit and juices can be safely processed at temperatures between 190F (88C) and 212F (100C). Pickles can be processed and pasteurized at 180F (82C). These lower processing temperatures keep the food from being overprocessed. As a result, fruit does not lose its shape and become mushy; pickles stay crisp and juices maintain their flavor, texture and color.

The United States Department of Agriculture (USDA) recommends water bath processing soft spreads for 5 minutes at 212F (100C). If you choose to process soft spreads in a boiling water bath at a full rolling boil of 212F (100C) or higher, the jars should not be processed for longer than 5 minutes. The quality, texture and flavor of soft spreads can be substantially diminished when processed at high temperatures for a longer amount of time. Preserves made from delicate fruits can be damaged and spreads, especially jellies, are susceptible to weeping when overprocessed. However, whenever you process soft spreads, or any other high-acid foods, in a water bath for less than 10 minutes, the empty jars must be sterilized in boiling water first, before filling, to reduce the chance of bacterial contamination.

Soft spreads may also be processed for 10 to 15 minutes in a 200F (93C) water bath. The longer processing time raises the temperature of the jar contents to a level sufficient to kill potential contaminants without damaging the quality of the preserves. This method eliminates the need to sterilize the jars before filling. The process works very well, kills any harmful bacteria and makes home canning both faster and easier. I prefer to process my jams, jellies and other soft spreads using this method.

Sterilizing Jars

To sterilize the jars, use a jar lifter to slowly lower empty, clean, washed canning jars into a large pan of hot but not boiling water. The pan should have a metal rack on the bottom, and the jars should be placed on the rack, spaced at least 1 inch apart and away from the sides of the pan. Add enough additional hot water so that the jars are submerged under at least 1 to 2 inches of water. Cover the pan and over medium-high to high heat, bring the water to a boil and boil the jars for a full 10 minutes. If you are at an altitude above 1,000 feet, add an additional 1 minute of boiling time for each 1,000 feet in elevation.

When the time is complete, turn off the heat and leave the jars in the hot water until ready to use. Just before filling the jars, use a jar lifter to remove the jars from the hot water and turn them upside down on a clean towel to drain. Fill the jars immediately to reduce the possibility of contamination from airborne bacteria and mold spores that can quickly attach to the inside of sterilized jars. While sterilizing the jars of short-duration processed soft spreads can significantly reduce the risk of spoilage, contamination can still occur if the jars are not handled carefully and sealed quickly. Contaminants can be transferred to the jars from the air, from your hands and nonsterile utensils, or by using a sponge or soiled cloth to wipe the jar rims before sealing the lids.

Safe Water Bath Processing of High-Acid Foods

1. Place the metal rack in the bottom of the canner. Set the canner on the stove or cooktop and fill it with water up to 4 inches from the top of the pan. If desired, add ¼ cup of vinegar to the water in the canner to help prevent mineral deposits from forming on the jars. Cover the pan and turn the heat to medium-high or high. In a teakettle or saucepan, begin heating 1 quart more water.

2. Prepare the food to be preserved according to the recipe instructions. Fill and seal the jars as instructed in the recipe.

3. Use a canning or candy thermometer to check the temperature of the water in the water bath. If the temperature is above 190F (88C), add a small amount of cold water to lower the temperature. Filled canning jars may break or shatter when lowered into water that is too hot, especially if the product in the jars was raw packed.

4. Using a jar lifter, lower each jar into the canner until it rests flat on the rack. Do not allow jars to touch the side of the pan and leave at least 1 inch of space between the jars for water circulation.

5. Check to see that the jars are covered by at least 1 to 2 inches of water. If necessary, add more hot water from the teakettle or saucepan. Leave a minimum of 1 inch of space between the top of the water and the top of the pan. If the pan is too full, use a small saucepan to ladle out the excess water, but do not allow water level to go below 1 inch above the jars.

6. Cover the pan and bring the water in the canner up to the processing temperature indicated in the recipe.

7. When the water in the canner reaches the required processing temperature, start timing the water bath. Reduce the heat under the pan and maintain at least the minimum water temperature, or slightly above, for the entire processing time.

8. Check the water periodically to make sure that the minimum processing temperature is maintained. If the temperature drops too low, turn up the heat until the water returns to the proper temperature, then begin the full timing again.

9. Process the preserved food for the full amount of time indicated in the recipe. The full time is necessary for the entire contents of the jar to reach the temperature needed to kill any harmful organisms. Do not reduce the processing time or all of the potential bacteria, yeasts and molds may not be destroyed.

10. When the processing time is complete, promptly remove the jars from the hot water bath using the jar lifter. Place the jars at least 1 inch apart on a cooling rack, wooden board a folded dish towel. Do not retighten any loose screw rings because you may damage or break the seal between the lid and the jar, allowing air and bacteria to enter the jar. Do not invert the hot jars after the water bath processing. Inverting the jars can cause the seals to fail, the vacuum to be released and bacteria to enter the jars.

11. Allow the jars to cool, undisturbed, for 12 to 24 hours, then check to make sure that all of the jars are tightly sealed.

TEMPERATURE AND TIME PROCESSING GUIDE

The following chart indicates the standard water temperatures and times that are needed for the safe processing of hot pack high-acid foods in

PRESERVED FOOD	TEMPERATURE	TIME
Jams, Jellies, Marmalades, Preserves, Conserves, Butters, Curds and Syrups	200F to 212F (93C to 100C)	4-ounce jars for 10 minutes Half-pint jars for 10 minutes Pint jars for 15 minutes
Fruit (whole or pieces) Fruit Sauces	190F to 200F (88C to 93C)	Times vary depending on the type of fruit, size of pieces and method of preparation (See recipe for exact time.)
Juices	200F (93C)	Pint jars for 15 minutes Quart jars for 15 minutes
Sauces and Relishes	212F (100C)	Pint jars for 15 minutes Quart jars for 20 minutes
Pickles (whole or pieces)	180F to 185F (82C to 85C)	Pint jars for 30 minutes Quart jars for 30 minutes

It is very important that you do not reduce the amount of processing time listed in the recipe. The jars must remain in the water bath for the full amount of time to kill any harmful bacteria that may be present, and to deactivate the enzymes that can cause preserved foods to spoil.

a water bath. The times may vary, depending on the method of preparation; so always check the recipe for the exact time. Unless otherwise directed in the recipe, the processing time should begin after the jars have all been loaded into the water bath and the water has reached the specified minimum processing temperature.

HIGH-ALTITUDE ADJUSTMENTS

If you live at an altitude above 1,000 feet, you will need to make some adjustments for the altitude by adding additional time to the standard water bath processing times given above. Increase the processing time as indicated in the chart below.

ELEVATION	ADD
1,001 to 3,000 feet	5 minutes to the processing time
3,001 to 6,000 feet	10 minutes to the processing time
6,001 to 8,000 feet	15 minutes to the processing time
8,001 to 10,000 feet	20 minutes to the processing time

PRESSURE CANNING

While most fruits and pickles contain an acid level that is high enough to protect them from the growth of harmful bacteria spores, making them safe for water bath processing, vegetables have a very low acid level and must be processed in a pressure canner. When canning vegetables and other low-acid foods, a pressure canner is the only safe and proven method for processing these types of preserved foods.

Pressure canners should not be confused with pressure cookers or pressure steamers. They are not interchangeable. Home-canned foods cannot be safely processed in either a pressure cooker or a pressure steamer. Only a modern pressure canner specifically designed for use in home canning should be used to process low-acid preserved foods.

Unfortunately, many cookbooks continue to mistakenly refer to pressure canners as pressure cookers, which perpetuates this misunderstanding and could result in serious bacterial contamination. Never use a pressure cooker to process any preserved food. The contents of the jars will not become hot enough to deactivate the enzymes or kill any present bacteria that could contaminate or seriously alter the quality and flavor of low-acid foods and vegetables.

Because of the extremely high temperatures reached under pressure, the natural color, texture and flavor of high-acid foods is often destroyed if they are processed in a pressure canner. To preserve their quality, high-acid preserved foods, such as fruit and tomatoes, should only be processed in a water bath canner.

Choosing a Pressure Canner

There are two basic types of pressure canners available for use in home canning: weighted-gauge canners and dial-gauge canners. Both work equally well and the canner you decide to purchase and use is a matter of personal choice and preference. Carefully read and follow the manufacturer's operating instructions that come with the canner.

A pressure canner consists of a large, heavy-weight pan with a tight-fitting lid that securely locks in place and is equipped with a dial-gauge or weighted-gauge for measuring the pressure. They come in a variety of sizes, with the 16-quart being the most popular and practical for the majority of home-canning jobs. The size of pressure canner you select will depend on the amount of canning you plan to do now and in the future.

Pressure Canner Processing

Before the beginning of each canning season, the gauge on a dial-gauge pressure canner should be checked for accuracy. A new gauge that has never been used before should also be checked. Most Cooperative Extension Service offices have the equipment needed to accurately test the gauge. If the gauge is off by 1 or 2 pounds, you can adjust the processing pressure accordingly. But if the gauge is off by more than 2 pounds, it really should be replaced to ensure correct processing.

Because of the increased risk of contamination in low-acid foods, processing times and pressures indicated in the recipes should be strictly followed. A decrease in either the time or pressure can result in dangerous food. Watch the pressure gauge carefully and use a timer to accurately keep track of the processing time.

Follow these steps for safe pressure canner processing. (Always read and follow the manufacturer's instructions that come with your pressure canner.)

1. Place the metal rack in the bottom of the canner. Set the canner on the stove or cooktop and

add 2 to 3 inches of water. An additional inch or 2 of water will be needed in pressure canners with weighted gauges that steam continuously during processing. Over low heat, begin heating the water to a simmer (180F [82C]).

2. Prepare the food to be preserved according to the recipe. Fill and seal the jars as instructed in the recipe.

3. Using a jar lifter, lower each jar into the canner until it rests flat on the rack. Do not allow the jars to touch the side of the pan, and leave at least 1 inch of space between jars for good heat circulation.

4. Place the lid on the canner and lock it in place according to the manufacturer's instructions. If you are using a dial-gauge canner, leave the petcock open. The petcock is the small hollow tube on the lid of a dial-gauge canner. It allows steam to escape while the canner is heating and is covered by a counterweight during processing. If you are using a weighted-gauge canner, leave the weighted gauge off of the vent. Increase the heat to medium-high. When steam begins to escape from the petcock or vent, set a timer for 10 minutes.

5. After the canner has vented for 10 minutes, close the petcock or place the weighted gauge on the vent. The canner will reach the correct pressure in about 5 minutes.

6. When the gauge indicates the canner has reached the correct pressure, set a timer for the amount of time specified in the recipe. Adjust the heat to maintain the correct pressure, or slightly above, throughout the entire processing time.

If the pressure drops below the required level for less than 5 minutes, return the canner to the correct pressure and add an additional 10 minutes to the remaining processing time. If the pressure drops below the required level for more than 5 minutes, return the canner to the correct pressure and reset the timer for the full amount of time indicated in the recipe.

7. When the processing time is complete, turn off the heat and, if possible, carefully move the canner off the hot burner. *Do not* open the petcock or remove the weighted gauge. Let the canner cool and depressurize until the gauge reads 0. This is an important part of the processing and is factored into the processing time requirement. Do not attempt to cool the canner by placing it under running water.

8. When the canner has finished depressurizing and the gauge reads 0, open the petcock or remove the weighted gauge from the vent. Wait for 2 minutes to allow the steam to vent, then unlock the lid and remove it, being careful to tilt up the far side of the lid first (away from you) to prevent the chance of being burned from any residual steam escaping from the canner.

9. Allow the jars to cool in the canner for 5 minutes to adjust them to the reduced temperature and reduce the risk of the jars breaking from the sudden temperature change as they are removed from the canner.

10. Using a jar lifter, remove the jars from the canner and place them on a wooden board covered with a clean cloth towel. Leave at least 1 inch of space between the jars for air circulation. Do not tighten any loose screw rings because you may damage or break the seal between the jar and the lid, permitting air and bacteria to enter the jar.

11. Allow the jars to cool, undisturbed, for 12 to 24 hours, then check to make sure that all of the jars are tightly sealed.

HIGH-ALTITUDE ADJUSTMENTS

If you live at an altitude above 1,000 feet, you will need to make some adjustments to the processing pressure given in the recipes. Increase the processing pressure as indicated in the chart below.

GETTING READY TO CAN

Select and Read Recipe

Select the recipe that you want to make. Read through the entire recipe carefully before you begin. Some recipes require several steps or may take more than one day to prepare. Be sure that you will have enough time to complete the project.

Do not double any of the recipes for soft spreads. If you want more jars of a particular variety of soft spread, make it in two or more batches. With the increased volume of fruit and sugar in a double batch, there is not enough surface area in the pan for the correct amount of liquid to evaporate from the mixture. The result will be several jars of tasty pancake syrup or ice-cream topping instead of a perfectly textured spread for toast or biscuits.

Never reduce the amount of sugar in a soft spread recipe. The exact measurement of sugar specified in the recipe is balanced against the quantity of fruit, acid and pectin and is needed to attain the right set. Sugar also acts as a preservative and inhibits the growth of bacteria and other spoilage agents.

When preparing soft spreads, the purpose of the final 1-minute boil is to thoroughly incorporate the pectin into the fruit mixture. Boiling the spread for longer than 1 minute after adding the pectin may allow too much liquid to evaporate, resulting in a soft spread that is too thick or firm. Omitting the final boil or boiling the mixture for less than 1 minute may result in a soft spread that either fails to set or only partially sets.

When preparing pickles and relishes, the quantity of vinegar in the recipes should not be reduced. The correct proportion of acid for the amount of vegetables is required to prohibit the growth of bacteria spores. If you desire a milder pickle, increase the amount of sugar in the pickling liquid.

Do not apply hand lotion to your hands at any time before or during the preparation of preserved foods. A greasy hand lotion can be transferred to the fruit or vegetables during handling, affecting the ability of the produce to absorb sugar or vinegar and changing the texture of the finished preserve. If the hand lotion contains a perfume or other scent, it can be picked up by the

ALTITUDE	DIAL-GAUGE PRESSURE CANNER	WEIGHTED-GAUGE PRESSURE CANNER
1 to 1,000 feet	11 pounds	10 pounds
1,001 to 2,000 feet	11 pounds	15 pounds
2,001 to 4,000 feet	12 pounds	15 pounds
4,001 to 6,000 feet	13 pounds	15 pounds
6,001 to 8,000 feet	14 pounds	15 pounds
8,001 to 10,000 feet	15 pounds	15 pounds

fruit and other ingredients, causing the preserved food to develop an unpleasant or off flavor. Before you begin canning, wash your hands thoroughly. Avoid using a hand soap with heavy moisturizers or perfumes, as they can also be transferred to the food and taint the flavor of the preserved food. Save the moisturizers and hand lotions for use after the canning is done.

Organize Ingredients

Check your cupboards and pantry to be sure you have all of the ingredients you will need to make your preserved foods. For best results, buy or harvest fully ripe, fresh produce not more than 24 hours in advance of canning. Slightly under-ripe fruit may be allowed to ripen for a few days, as long as it is watched carefully. Highly perishable produce, such as strawberries or pickling cucumbers, should be used on the same day they are harvested. Citrus fruits may be kept for about a week, if properly stored in the refrigerator.

Use only the finest, freshest ingredients and produce you can find to create your preserved foods. The quality of your finished preserves will directly relate to the quality of the ingredients you put into them.

Organize Equipment

Gather all of the equipment, tools and utensils you will need to complete the recipe. Have the jars, lids, pans, water bath canner, pressure canner, spoons, ladles, jar lifter, lid wand, canning funnel, measuring spoons and dry and liquid measuring cups within easy reach.

Use only standard Mason-type canning jars with two-piece lids and rings that are specifically designed for home canning. Never use mayonnaise or baby food jars or any other commercial jar, because they are not tempered to withstand the temperatures reached during water bath or pressure canner processing and can easily break.

Visually inspect all jars and lids for flaws, cracks, chips, nicks, scratches and sharp edges. Discard any damaged or imperfect jars or lids.

CANNING STEP-BY-STEP

Follow these simple canning steps to make blue ribbon quality preserved foods in your own kitchen.

1. Review Recipe and Canning Procedures
Read through the recipe and review the canning procedures for the type of preserved food you will be making.

2. Assemble Ingredients and Equipment
Double-check to be sure that you have on hand all of the ingredients, equipment, jars and lids to make the recipe. Gather all of the tools and utensils that you will need to complete the preserved food.

3. Wash Jars and Lids
Wash the jars in a dishwasher or by hand in hot, soapy water and rinse well. Keep the jars hot until ready to use. Wash the lids and screw rings in hot, soapy water. Rinse them thoroughly and dry well.

4. Prepare the Canner
If using a water bath canner, place a rack in the bottom of the canner and fill the pan with water. Cover and begin heating over medium-high to high heat.

If using a pressure canner, inspect all parts of the canner, including the gauge. Place the rack in the bottom of the pan. Fill the canner with 2 to 3 inches of water and begin heating over low heat.

5. Prepare and Measure Produce
Rinse the fruit or vegetables thoroughly with cool, clean water and drain well. Prepare and

measure the fruit or vegetables according to the recipe directions.

For crushed fruit, use a vegetable masher or the back of a large spoon to crush the fruit, 1 cup at a time, in the bottom of a large flat-bottomed bowl or pan.

6. Heat Lids

Drop the lids, one at a time, into a small pan of water that has been brought to a simmer and removed from the heat. Cover the pan and allow the lids to heat for at least 10 minutes. Keep the lids hot until needed.

7. Prepare Preserved Food

Prepare the food to be preserved according to the recipe directions. Check the recipe chapters for special techniques and advice for preparing each type of preserved food.

8. Skim Foam and Fill Jars

Skim off any foam that has formed on the surface of the soft spread or other preserved food as it cooked. Using a ladle and a canning funnel, fill the hot jars quickly, leaving the amount of headspace indicated in the recipe.

9. Remove Air Bubbles

Use a nonmetallic knife, spatula or bubble freer (see page 29) to carefully release any air bubbles trapped inside the jars.

10. Wipe Jar Rims

Using a clean, damp cloth, thoroughly wipe the rim of the jar, inside the top of the jar and the outside screw threads to remove any spilled or sloshed food or liquid. Do not use a sponge to wipe the jar rims.

11. Cover and Seal Jars

Use a lid wand (see page 22) to remove the lids one at a time from the hot water. Position the lids on top of the jars, adjusting the lids until they are centered on the rims. Screw the rings onto the jars and tighten them snugly by hand. Do not use force or tighten the rings too firmly.

12. Place Jars in Canner

Using a jar lifter (see page 21), carefully place the hot, filled jars in the water bath canner, leaving 1 inch of space between each jar. Be sure there are 1 to 2 inches of space between the top of pan and the water and at least 1 to 2 inches of water covering the top of the jars. If necessary, add more hot water to cover the jars. Cover the pan and heat the water to the temperature indicated in the recipe.

If you are processing low-acid preserved foods in a pressure canner, use a jar lifter to carefully lower the jars into the pan, setting them on the rack in the bottom of the canner. Place the lid on the canner and fasten it securely. Be sure to follow the manufacturer's instructions to lock down the lid.

13. Process Jars

Use a canning or candy thermometer to check the water temperature in the water bath canner. Process the jars at the temperature and for the amount of time specified in the recipe. Do not shorten the processing time, or any bacteria in the jars may not be killed and the lids may not seal properly.

If using a pressure canner, vent the air from the canner for 10 minutes, then close the petcock or attach the weighted gauge to the vent and bring the canner up to pressure. Process the jars at the pressure and for the amount of time specified in the recipe. When the processing is complete, remove the canner from the heat and allow the pressure to reduce to 0 before opening the canner.

14. Remove Jars from Canner

Use a jar lifter to remove the hot jars from the canner, being careful not to tip the jars. Never handle hot jars with your bare hands! Place the jars on a wire rack, wooden board or dish towels to cool. Leave at least 1 inch of space between jars for air circulation. Use a clean, absorbent towel to carefully blot any standing water from the tops of the jars. Allow the jars to cool for 12 to 24 hours. Listen for the pinging sound made by the lids as the jars cool and seal.

15. Check Seals

In 24 hours, check all jars to be sure that they are sealed. Press down in the center of the lid. If the lid remains down, the jar is sealed and safe for storage. If the center of the lid pops up, the jar is not sealed. The contents may be emptied back into a pan, heated and reprocessed in a clean jar with a new lid. Or you may store the jar in the refrigerator and use the contents within one month.

16. Wash, Label and Store Jars

Remove the screw rings and wash the jars in warm, soapy water, being careful not to tip jars. Rinse and dry the jars. Label the jars, indicating their contents and canning date. Store the jars in a cool, dry, dark location.

The World of Fair Competitions

For many home canners, their competitive ambitions begin when a friend or family member raves over a special homemade jam or jelly and encourages the cook to enter it at a local, county or state fair because they are "sure to win first place." That ambition ends for some when they receive the fair's competitive handbook and read the preserved foods rules and entry requirements. Others are discouraged from ever entering again when their first exhibits receive low marks from the judges and fail to win any ribbons.

The rules and judging criteria for fair competitions can seem daunting and mystifying. But they are there for a reason. Each one has a specific purpose, and each rule must be followed in order to win top awards. The judges are looking for perfection, and perfection is what you must give them if you want to win blue ribbons.

It is not as hard as it sounds. Creating award-winning preserved foods is not that difficult. It takes paying attention to a few details, using the finest ingredients you can find and having a little patience when preparing your preserved foods. Once you learn the ins and outs of preserved foods competitions and the important steps to getting high marks, you will have the knowledge necessary to compete effectively the first time and every time you enter, dramatically increasing your chances of winning awards.

If you are considering entering your preserved foods into competition at a fair, read through this chapter before you begin canning. Otherwise, you may find that your wonderful preserved foods were canned in the wrong type of jars, improperly filled or inadequately processed, thus making them ineligible for competition.

A BRIEF HISTORY OF FAIRS

In 1811, gentleman farmer and businessman Elkanah Watson of Albany, New York, organized America's first rural agricultural fair, the Berkshire County Fair, in Pittsfield, Massachusetts. He was concerned that Americans were quickly falling behind the Europeans in farming and animal husbandry. Watson realized that attention needed to be focused on these areas to improve both quality and production.

To encourage new innovations and spark local and national pride, he invited the area farmers to enter their animals in competitions to select the best livestock raised in the county. Crop and produce competitions quickly followed. Two years later, Watson rallied the women in the county to enter their homespun cloth, tatting and needlework in an effort to increase interest in using American-made products rather than depending on European goods. In 1819, he convinced the New York legislature to provide $10,000 a year for 6 years to provide premium awards for exhibitors of agricultural products and products made in the home, including preserved foods.

His ideas rapidly spread to neighboring counties and across the country. As these county fairs expanded to include additional areas of competition, such as home canning and baking, and incorporated displays of new products and equipment to make farming more productive, they quickly became the social event of the year. For many rural families, several days of excitement each year revolved around fair preparations, travel and the many fair activities and festivities for all members of the family.

AN INTRODUCTION TO FAIR COMPETITIONS

Entering into preserved foods competitions at fairs can be an exhilarating and rewarding experience. It can also be intimidating and frustrating if you have never entered before or do not understand and comply with the rules. Paying careful attention to the details is important and can mean the difference between your entry winning a blue ribbon or not placing at all.

At each year's fair competitions, I am amazed by how many entrants do not give their preserved foods the opportunity to win. They frequently fail to follow the rules or ignore the simple details that will influence the judges and increase an entry's score.

If you are interested in entering your preserved foods into competition at a fair, be sure to contact the specific fair and request a competitive exhibits handbook. You will find the addresses for most of the major state and county fairs in the country in the back of this book (pages 339–347). When the handbook arrives, read through it carefully. It will contain all the rules and requirements needed for entries at that fair. Read the handbook thoroughly every year, as the rules can change from what they were the previous year and new exhibit requirements or entry classes may have been added. Follow the rules to the letter; they are mandatory requirements, not merely suggestions. Make special note of the entry, delivery and pickup schedules, dates and times.

Fair Awards and Premiums
Do not expect to be able to retire on your winnings from fair competitions. Most fairs can only afford to pay a small or modest cash premium to the winners. Exhibitors compete for the thrill, the challenge, the ribbons and the joy of victory. And

best of all, they earn the bragging rights until next year's fair.

All fairs award ribbons, and the majority of them will also give a cash prize. For special awards, the winner may receive a large ribbon or a trophy, a certificate of achievement or perhaps a donated prize from the sponsor. When it comes to winning cash awards, the goal is to earn back enough money to cover your entry fees and the cost of gasoline or postage needed to deliver your exhibits to the fair.

Special Awards

Special awards are given to entries of superior merit. As the judging process progresses, exceptional entries, the cream of the crop, stand out above the rest of the competition. These exhibits continue to work their way up the competitive ladder, vying for special awards and top honors. Almost every fair now offers the following special awards.

BEST OF CLASS: All of the first-place-winning entries in each class that scored 100 points shall be considered for Best of Class awards. If no entries earned a perfect score of 100 points, then the Best of Class will be determined from the highest-scoring exhibits. This award is presented at fairs using the Danish System of judging (see page 52). In the American System of judging (see page 52), each first-place award is usually considered to be the equivalent of a Best of Class award.

BEST OF DIVISION: All of the Best of Class winners in each division shall be considered for the Best of Division awards. The award is presented by fairs using either the American System or the Danish System of judging.

BEST OF SHOW: All of the Best of Division winners in each show shall be considered for the Best of Show awards. This award is presented by fairs using either the American System or the Danish System of judging.

SWEEPSTAKES AWARD: Most larger fairs will commonly present a sweepstakes award to the competitor who earns the most blue ribbons, or total points, within each individual division or to the exhibitor who wins the most blue ribbons in the entire preserved foods competition. There is usually an intense competition among the exhibitors to see who will receive the sweepstakes award, as this award is the most highly coveted and sought-after prize among the fair participants. It carries a high honor and greatly enhances the reputation of the recipient.

Sponsor Awards and Special Contests

Special contests or awards may be sponsored by the manufacturers of canning jars, pectins, sugar, vinegar and other ingredients, or by the growers of a particular kind of fruit or other produce. These contests and awards will vary from fair to fair. Some fairs may have quite a number of special awards, and others may have none. The American System of judging is used to determine the winners of special awards and contests.

Exhibits must meet very specific criteria to qualify for entry in a special contest or to receive sponsor awards. You are usually required to use the sponsor's product in creating your preserved foods entry. Be honest when entering a contest or in stating your eligibility for a sponsor award. Please do not claim to have used the sponsor's product when you really didn't. It would be unfair to the sponsor and the other competitors.

Some special contests limit entries to only those made using original recipes. In most cases, the exhibitor must be the one who developed the recipe and the recipe must not have been published before in any form. This includes local newspapers, newsletters and community or charity cookbooks, or by any electronic means such as the Internet. Also be aware that the recipes for the winning entries, and sometimes all of the entries in a special contest, may become the property of the sponsor and/or the fair and cannot be published without their permission. These conditions, if they apply, will be clearly stated in the exhibit handbook. If you are unwilling to surrender the ownership rights of an original recipe you have developed, do not enter it in a contest or fair that requires you to do so.

The awards given to the winners of a special contest may include a special ribbon or trophy, a gift certificate, cash premium award and/or free products donated by the sponsor. If you win a special contest or sponsor award, be sure to write a thank you letter to the sponsor thanking them for supporting the fair. The address and name of the contact person for the company may be printed in the handbook or can be obtained from the fair.

Entry Divisions
Shows

Many fairs divide their preserved foods competitions into separate areas of competition, or shows. A preserved foods division may consist of one show, with all of the entries being judged on the same day. Or the competition may be divided into parts, with different shows being held and judged either on the same day or on different days.

For example, jam and jelly divisions may be judged on the same day in the same show. Preserves, marmalades, butters and conserves may be judged in a second show, which may be held that same day or on another day. The judging for fruits, vegetables, pickles and sauces may be on a different day than for the soft spreads.

Divisions and Classes

Divisions are categories within a show. Jams, jellies, fruits, vegetables, sauces and pickles are all examples of divisions. Classes are categories of competition within a division. Strawberry jam, mixed fruit jam, grape jelly, orange marmalade and dill pickles are all examples of classes.

A number of fairs include classes for special collections. A special collection is usually a set of three to six different varieties of a particular preserved food, such as jam or fruit, entered as one exhibit. Each variety must be canned in the same size and type of jar to qualify. Collections are usually judged on appearance only. If you make several different types of a particular preserved food, check the handbook to see if the fair has an entry class for a special collection in that division. At some fairs, a collection may consist of one jar of preserved food from each of four or more divisions. For example, a jar each of jam, fruit, vegetables and pickles would make up a collection. A mixed collection of this type usually does not require that the preserved foods be canned in matching, same-size jars.

Entries

Entry limits and requirements vary from fair to fair. Some limit the number of exhibits a competitor may enter in each division. Others allow you to enter as many exhibits as you want in each division, only placing restrictions on the number of entries per class. Most fairs permit a competitor to enter only one exhibit per class. Under the American System of judging, if you were to enter more than one exhibit in a class, you would be competing against yourself. Fairs using the Danish System of judging may allow two exhibits to be entered in the same class because entries are judged against a standard, not each other.

Delivery of Entries

Entries for the preserved foods divisions are usually all delivered on the same day and display jars picked up together at the end of the fair. However, depending on the fair, entries for different shows may have to be delivered on consecutive days. This practice is sometimes seen at large fairs that conduct an open judging held during the run of the fair or for special contests. The requirement to deliver entries on separate days requires time and dedication on the part of the exhibitor and can cause some competitors to limit the number of shows that they choose to enter.

For example:

First Day: Show 1: Jams and jellies

Second Day: Show 2: Marmalades, preserves and other soft spreads

Third Day: Show 3: Fruits and juices

Fourth Day: Show 4: Pickles, sauces, vegetables and vinegars

If you live within a reasonable driving distance of the fair you are entering, personally hand-delivering your jars is the best way to ensure that the entries arrive in perfect condition for judging.

When delivering your preserved foods entries to a fair, it is best to transport them in the original boxes that the jars were packed in when purchased. These boxes contain cardboard dividers to separate the jars and protect them from banging into each other and possibly breaking. Keep the boxes and jars upright at all times so that the contents of the jars do not shift. When I see exhibitors show up at a fair to proudly deliver their jars of preserved foods, which are attractively arranged and lying on their sides in a decorated basket, it becomes obvious that they are inexperienced competitors who do not realize the important role that proper jar handling plays in the scores given for preserved foods. Worse yet, are the competitors who transport their entries in plastic grocery bags with the jumble of jars all pointing in different directions, some even upside down.

If you live some distance away from the fairgrounds, most fairs will accept delivery of preserved foods entries by mail. This can get expensive for the exhibitor who decides to enter several divisions or classes. There is also no guarantee that your jars will remain upright during shipping and arrive in the same condition they were in when mailed. I have had entries arrive at some fairs in excellent condition, while others were so full of bubbles it looked like the boxes had been turned end over end during shipping. If you decide to ship your entries, pack them in the original jar boxes with padding to keep the jars from shifting, then place the box of jars inside a larger shipping box and pack it well with lots of padding. Be sure to enclose a copy of your entry form and an inventory of the box contents. Also indicate if you have shipped more than one box of entries to the fair. Label the shipping box as fragile and mark the side of the box as to which end is up. Then ship your box and hope for the best.

Pick Up of Entries
Open Tasting Jars

A specific date or dates and time will be designated for the pick up of the tasting jars that were opened by the judges. Any jars remaining after that date and time will be disposed of at the discretion of the fair. Some fairs choose to dispose of the contents, wash the jars and then return the empty jars to the exhibitor. On very rare occasion, a fair will choose not to return any of the open tasting jars to the participants, usually citing health concerns and potential contamination as the reasons.

Nonwinning Jars

Most fairs will place all of the preserved foods entries, whether they win an award or not, on display for the full run of the fair to be viewed by the fair visitors and competitors. A few fairs have only a limited amount of display space, or receive so many entries that they cannot showcase all of them, and will only display the exhibits that win awards. In this case, the fair will require the exhibitors to pick up all nonwinning entries by a specific date and time.

Display Jars

All exhibits winning an award must remain on display for the duration of the fair. The display jars can be claimed by the exhibitor at the end of the fair. Any jars that are not picked up on the specified date will be disposed of at the fair's discretion. Many fairs will not return ship to the exhibitor any jars that were entered by mail. These entries must be picked up in person by the exhibitor, or their representative; otherwise the jars and their contents will be disposed of by the fair.

Following the Rules

One of the primary reasons a jar of preserved foods does not win an award or receives a reduced placing, is because the exhibitor failed to follow the rules. Entries that do not comply with the rules will have points automatically deducted from their score, or the noncompliance may even result in the exhibit being disqualified from the competition.

Read the Exhibit Handbook

Competition rules may change slightly from year to year, while new classes, divisions and contests continue to be added. Read each year's handbook carefully for any changes from the previous year. Comply with the rules exactly or you run the risk of being disqualified.

Exhibitor Eligibility

As a general rule, the preserved foods competitions at fairs are only open to amateurs, and each entry must be the sole work of the individual in whose name the exhibit is entered. Rarely will a fair permit an exhibit to be created and entered by more than one person. An amateur is defined as a person who engages in an activity or event as a hobby or pastime.

In regards to fairs, the term "professional" usually denotes a person who sells their craft or product or anyone who accepts payment for their work. Paid food preparers or food professionals, such as cooks, chefs, bakers, caterers, cake decorators, home economics instructors and professional recipe developers, are usually considered ineligible to enter the preserved foods or baked foods divisions of most fairs. A person who teaches classes or conducts workshops or seminars on home canning and is paid for their efforts will be classified as a professional by most fairs. Separate divisions for professional competitors are offered by only a very few fairs.

It is common for participation in fair competitions to be restricted to only the residents of that specific county, district or state. Nonresidents are frequently ineligible to enter. However there are fairs, such as the Los Angeles County Fair and the State Fair of Texas, that open their competitive exhibits to the world. Anyone who meets the exhibitor qualifications, no matter where they live, is invited to enter.

Entry Forms and Fees

Fair rules may require exhibitors to use only original entry forms on which to enter their preserved foods exhibits. A competitor who has several entries in the preserved foods divisions may need to obtain additional entry forms from the fair. Other fairs will accept photocopies of the entry form, allowing the exhibitors to make as many copies as they need for their entries. Check the handbook and the entry form for any restrictions on submitting photocopies of the forms. If original entry forms are required and you will need more than were sent to you with the exhibit handbook, be sure to request the additional forms early so that you will not run the risk of missing the entry deadline.

With a few exceptions, entry fees for exhibits usually range from $.50 to $2.00 per entry. Some fairs will charge a flat entry fee and permit the exhibitor to enter up to a specified number of entries for that fee. A few fairs do not charge an entry fee for competitive exhibits.

Entry fees must accompany the completed entry forms and the fees and forms must be postmarked or received by the fair on or before the specified deadline or the entry will not be accepted. There are only a handful of fairs that do not require pre-registration of entries prior to delivering the exhibits for competition.

Exhibit Requirements

The vast majority of fairs require that entries must have been canned within 1 year of the opening day of the fair, while a few will accept preserved foods that have been prepared within the past 2 years. Check the competitive exhibits handbook of your fair for their specific requirement. Do not think you can fool the judges by entering a product that is older than allowed. Trust me, an experienced judge can easily tell the difference between a preserve that was canned within the allowed time and one that is older. The date stamped on the lid indicates the year the lid was manufactured and will not be used by the fair judges to determine when the preserves were canned.

Nearly all fairs now require that every canned preserved foods entry must have been processed in a water bath or pressure canner. Not only does this requirement encourage people to use the correct methods and safety procedures when canning, it is also essential to protect the judges. Any

entry that a judge feels has not been properly processed will be immediately disqualified from competition.

Although the rules are very clear, some stubborn competitors continue to ignore the rules and still enter exhibits that have not been properly processed. While a few may get away with it, the risks of contamination and disqualification are not worth taking. Not only do they take the chance of having their entries disqualified from competition, there is the serious concern of potential contamination, which can endanger the health of the judges.

Standard Entry Requirements for Jars

Although the standard requirements for canning jars are the same at most fairs, the specific exhibit requirements for individual jar sizes and labeling can vary from fair to fair.

Unless otherwise specified in the fair handbook, an entry will consist of one Mason-type or standard canning jar sealed with a new lid and new screw ring. If an exhibit is to consist of two identical jars, it will be stated in the exhibit handbook. Fairs that run for more than a week, or fairs that conduct the judging well in advance of opening day, usually require two jars: one to be used for judging and the other one for display during the fair. In the case of special collections, or any other entry class that is to be judged on appearance only without the jars being opened and tasted by the judges, only one jar of each preserved food is usually required.

When two jars are required to be submitted for each entry the size, shape and brand of the jar, as well as the brand of the lid used, must be exactly the same for both jars. The jars must contain the same food and must be packed identically. Failure to submit identical jars will result in a disqualification. The fair will sometimes permit the exhibitor to designate which jar they want the judge to open and sample. In most occurrences though, the judge will examine both of the jars entered and then select the one they want to open.

Always enter the best jars you have of each preserved food. Do this even when you must submit two identical jars and are allowed to select which jar the judge will open. Sometimes the jars get mixed by the fair workers, or occasionally something will happen that will make it necessary for the judge to open the display jar instead of the

STANDARD JAR SIZES

The following jar sizes are generally required by most fairs. Check the exhibitor handbook for your fair for their specific requirements.

Jams, Jellies, Other Soft Spreads and Syrups: Clear glass, standard or sculptured jars, usually 8 to 16 ounces in size (may also be denoted as half-pint and pint jars). The 8-ounce jars are the most common and are accepted by all fairs. A growing number of fairs now allow the entry of exhibits that have been canned in the smaller 4-ounce jars. This small size jar is actually the best one to submit for judging because less jam is wasted, they are lighter in weight and they are easier to mail.

Fruits, Vegetables and Juices: Clear glass standard or sculptured jars, usually pint or quart size. Some fairs will accept 8-ounce jars or even 4-ounce jars.

Pickles, Relishes and Sauces: Clear glass standard or sculptured jars, usually pint or quart size. Some fairs will accept 8-ounce jars or even 4-ounce jars.

Vinegars: 8- to 16-ounce clear glass bottle with a long neck, sealed with a new cork or screw-on cap. Colored bottles are usually prohibited.

one designated for judging. Every now and then a jar may be accidentally dropped or broken by a fair worker or judge. (This has happened to me three times in 11 years of competition.) Be sure you give yourself every opportunity to win by submitting only the best jars out of each batch of preserves.

Jars that are not specifically manufactured for home canning, such as mayonnaise jars, baby food jars or commercial jam jars, and jars that are sealed with paraffin or a one-piece screw-on-type lid instead of a standard two-piece home-canning lid will not be accepted for exhibit and will be disqualified from the competition. All entries must have been processed in a water bath or pressure canner for at least the minimum amount of time recommended by the USDA, or as stated in the fair handbook, for the specific type of preserved food. Only a few smaller fairs still do not make this a mandatory requirement.

Labeling Jars

Each fair has its own specific requirements regarding the labeling of jars, so be sure to follow the rules. The judges will disqualify a mislabeled jar automatically without even tasting the contents.

Unless otherwise instructed, most fairs permit jars to be labeled as to the contents only. No names or distinguishing marks are allowed on the labels. Contents labels may be placed on the lids, sides or bottoms of the jars, unless otherwise indicated in the handbook.

In some cases, the exhibitor may be required to attach a label to the side of the jar listing all of the ingredients used in preparing the preserved food. Or you may be required to submit the complete recipe along with the entry so the judge can verify the ingredients and methods used to prepare the food. One of the purposes of this label or recipe requirement is to enable judges who have a food allergy to avoid tasting a product containing

JAR LABELS

A word about labeling the contents of jars: Be careful about identifying any product, such as a salsa or pepper jelly, as "hot," "mild" or "spicy." When you make this distinction, the judge expects the product to be as labeled and will score it accordingly. Your definition of "hot" may not be the same as the judge's. If you label the contents as hot and the salsa is not fiery hot, you will be marked down on your score because the product did not live up to its billing. Unless you are certain that the entry qualifies as hot to someone who loves spicy foods, it is better not to specify its heat. On the other hand, if your salsa is likely to create a three-alarm fire in the judge's mouth, by all means warn them on the label. But also keep in mind that judges usually do not go for extremes in heat when giving awards.

ingredients that may cause them to have a severe reaction. Or the ingredients list and preparation methods may be used to determine the standard by which the contents will be judged, for example, jams made with pectin and those made without.

Many fairs will provide their own identification labels for the jars, indicating the exhibitor's name or identification number along with the division and class entered. Other fairs may require the exhibitor to provide this information on his or her own label and attach it to the bottom of the jar. Check the fair handbook for specific labeling requirements and restrictions.

If you are considering entering your preserved foods into competition, keep a list of the dates on which each product was canned. This information is a mandatory labeling requirement by many fairs. Failure to include this information as instructed will result in an immediate disqualification by the judge.

JUDGING SYSTEMS

Fair competitions can be both exciting and daunting, not to mention nerve-wracking, especially for the first-time exhibitor. With rules and requirements that can often seem confusing and intimidating, producing winning entries can be a bewildering challenge. How entries are judged can be the most mystifying part of a home canner's fair experience. What exactly are the judges looking for in each type of preserved food and what was right or wrong with each individual entry are questions that often go unanswered.

Closed Judgings

Fairs predominantly conduct what is called a closed judging. Entries are delivered to the fair well in advance of the event's opening date. The judges inspect, sample and score the exhibits and determine the awards for the various preserved foods entries. This is done in private, without an audience or observers. The exhibits are arranged in the display cases prior to the opening of the fair to await the arrival of eager exhibitors and fair visitors.

It is quite common for exhibitors to have to wait until the fair actually opens to learn if their entries received any awards. Competitors are rarely notified of their judging results until well after the fair is over, so they must visit the fair in person to discover the fate of their entries and those of the other exhibitors. While few things can compare with the excitement and exhilaration of walking up to a display case to find a blue ribbon hanging on your jar of preserved food, the long wait can be excruciating.

Open Judgings

If the fair conducts an open judging, entries are delivered to the fair either before opening day or during the fair, and exhibitors are invited to watch the actual judging process and listen to the judges' comments and awards. Sometimes a fair will even provide the exhibitors with complimentary admission tickets to be used for this purpose or to visit the fair later and view the exhibits at their leisure.

At an open judging, exhibitors have the difficult task of silently trying to identify their entries as the jars are brought forward for the judges to examine. This can be a real challenge, especially if you have entered a class such as strawberry jam and there are forty other entries canned in the same size and type of canning jar and lid that you used.

The event is conducted as a blind judging, where the judges do not know whose entry they are examining and tasting. Names of the winners are not usually disclosed until after the day's judging is complete, and then often only the names of the exhibitors who win Bests of Class, Bests of Division, Best of Show or any other special awards are announced. You may have to wait until the next day, when the winning jars have been placed in the exhibit case for display, to discover or confirm your awards.

Open judgings can be both fascinating and rewarding. You get the chance to watch the judges in action and see their facial reactions as they examine each entry and then take their first taste from the jar. A large angled mirror is often suspended over the judging table so the audience can view the actual process the judges go through when examining an entry.

Some of my fondest memories of fair competition have occurred during the open judgings at the California State Fair. One was as a judge opened and scored a jar of raspberry jelly. I could tell it was my jar the moment he held it up to the light and I saw the deep, jewel color. As the judge opened the jar, then placed a spoonful of the shimmering jelly on his plate, I watched intently. My efforts were rewarded by his surprised reac-

tion and silent mouthing of the words, "Oh, wow!" when he tasted the first bite of jelly.

The judge next to him was intrigued by his reaction. When she tasted the sample offered to her by the first judge, her eyes grew wide and she nodded her approval. Judges have to taste so many entries in a day that they leave a good portion of each preserve sample on their plate. But these judges did not. They ate up every last little bit, even scraping the plate clean with their spoons. I knew right then that I had earned 100 points, even before the jelly's perfect score was officially announced.

My favorite memory though, was when my strawberry preserves competed for Best of Show honors against all of the other division winners. My highest compliment for flavor came when one of the judges who had not yet tasted my preserves during the class and division competitions did so, then turned to the preserves division judge and exclaimed in amazement, "Some of those strawberries are still alive!" If I had not attended the judging in person, I would never have known of the judges' high praise. On the judges' scorecard, in addition to listing the awards, was written the simple statement, "Excellent job!"

Moments and memories like these are as important as all the ribbons and trophies hanging on my wall. If your fair holds an open judging, I strongly encourage you to attend. You will be surprised by how much you can learn from observing the judging process, listening to the judges' comments and seeing the number of entries where competitors have repeatedly made the same simple mistakes.

Danish and American Systems of Judging

There are two different systems of judging used by fairs to determine the placings and awards given in the preserved foods divisions, the

Danish System and the American System. If a fair does not specify in the handbook which judging system it uses, entries will most likely be judged according to the American System. To be sure, contact the fair and ask which system of judging they use for the preserved foods divisions, or any other areas of competition you plan to enter.

Danish System of Judging

In the Danish System, all entries are judged against a standard, with a perfect score being 100 points. At the discretion of the judge, points are deducted for criteria that do not meet the perfect standard, such as a jam that is set too firm or a jelly that is too soft and does not hold its shape. Placings are determined by an exhibit's total score with multiple first-, second- and third-placings being awarded in each class.

Based on their scores, exhibits will receive the following award placings:

100 to 90 points earns a first-place award
89 to 80 points earns a second-place award
79 to 70 points earns a third-place award
Below 70 points earns no award

For an entry to continue on to the next level of competition, Best of Class, it really must receive a perfect score from the judges. Although a handbook may state that all first-place-winning entries will compete for Best of Class honors, in actuality, it is only the exhibits that earn the highest score that are considered for this special award.

American System of Judging

Unlike the Danish System, in the American System of judging, the judges compare exhibits against each other to determine the placings. Although there may be ten entries that are worthy of a first-place award, only one will be selected to receive that coveted blue ribbon. There will only be one second, third and fourth award given out as well. This makes winning first place even more of a challenge and brings with it higher prestige and satisfaction in achieving that goal. Under the American System, each first-place award is equivalent to a Best of Class.

The number of the classes for competition will be greater and more diverse at a fair that uses the American System of judging to determine the placings. However, it is also more difficult to win ribbons when the American System is used because only one entry in each class will be awarded first place.

Judge's Scorecard

The judge's scorecard rates the qualities of the preserved food entered and may include brief written comments or observations about the entry. If you are lucky, the fair you enter will release the judges' scorecards to the exhibitors. However, that is not always a common practice. In the American System of judging, scorecards or comment cards are rarely used since exhibits compete directly against one another.

If you do receive the scorecards, pay careful attention to any comments that a judge may have written. Use these comments to improve the quality of your preserved foods to earn higher scores the following year.

PRESERVED FOODS JUDGING STANDARDS

What Do the Judges Look For?

A judge considers several factors when determining an entry's placement and award. When examining jams, jellies and other soft spreads, the judge is looking for the flavor, texture, appearance, color, clarity and consistency of the spread; headspace and the condition of the container.

When examining fruit and pickles, the judge looks for the flavor, texture, appearance, color and clarity of the food; the consistency, shape and appropriate and uniform size of the pieces; the pack, headspace, amount of liquid, clarity of the liquid (clear versus cloudy) and the condition of the container. With pickles, the judge is also looking for the degree of crispness of the pickled food.

Because of the potential for bacterial contamination that can occur in low-acid foods that are not properly processed, judges frequently do not open vegetable jars, and judge them based on their appearance only. If the judges do open the jars, they will do so only to examine the product and will not sample the food inside. When scoring jars of vegetables, the judges will look for the appearance, color, clarity, consistency, shape, appropriate and uniform size of the pieces, pack, headspace, amount of liquid, clarity of the liquid (clear versus cloudy) and condition of the container.

These individual judging criteria, and what they mean, will be discussed in more detail in the next sections.

Although there are certain specific criteria used to determine the awarding of points and placings of preserved foods, remember that judging is still subjective. Even though the judges do their best to remain impartial and judge according to the standard, it still comes down to a matter of personal taste. Some judges like exotic flavors, while others tend to be traditionalists. It is often the luck of the draw as to which judge will examine your entry and whether his or her individual tastes and preferences will match with the product you have created and chosen to exhibit at that particular fair.

Every 2 or 3 years, to keep the judging fair and impartial, most fairs will usually select an entirely new judging panel or at least a different combination of judges for the preserved foods divisions. The types of preserved foods and the flavors that elicit the top awards from this year's judges may not be the same ones that will appeal to next year's judges.

What Makes a Winning Entry?

In determining the placings and awards, the judges examine each entry, looking for the very best examples of home preserved foods. To win first place and have a chance to advance on to higher awards, the preserved food must be of excellent quality with the right flavor, texture, color and appearance. The presentation must be perfect, in clean jars with the proper headspace and have a good, tight seal.

Attention to detail is extremely important. Little imperfections can mean the difference between a jar of preserved food winning a top award and earning no award at all. Two or three minor errors may drop an exhibit from first place to second place under the Danish System of judging, while with the American System, even one of those same small mistakes will result in the entry's complete exclusion from the awards given for that class.

When it comes to selecting the Best of Class, Best of Division and Best of Show winners, the judges will often consider the degree of difficulty involved in preparing each particular type of preserved food as they determine the placings and final outcome of the competition. Which entry was more difficult to make? Which preserved food required more skill in preparation to achieve perfection?

CONTAINER: Jars must be of the correct size, clean and sparkling with tightly sealed lids. When two jars are required, they must be identical in size, shape, brand and lid. Screw rings must be new with no signs of wear, rust or food particles, and they must be able to be unscrewed easily. All jars must be labeled in accordance with the requirements listed in the fair's competitive exhibits handbook. Noncompliance with these criteria will result in a disqualification or substantial reduction in score.

Before entering your preserved foods into a competition, remove the screw rings from the sealed jars and gently wash the jars in warm, soapy water, being careful not to tip the jars. After rinsing, wipe the jars with a clean cloth dipped in vinegar to make the jars sparkle. Dry the jars with a lint-free cloth or towel. When the jars are completely dry, lightly screw on new rings and label the jars according to the fair's rules. Be sure all labels are firmly attached to the jars so they won't accidentally come loose and fall off during storage, transport or handling at the fair. Self-stick labels, rubber cement or clear tape all work well for this purpose.

HEADSPACE: The headspace in the jar must be of the appropriate height for the type of preserved food. No more, no less. If you are not good at visually determining the accurate height of the headspace, use a small ruler to measure it when filling the jars. By carefully measuring the headspace as you fill the jars, you can greatly improve the chances of your entry winning an award.

- ¼-inch headspace is required for jams, jellies, marmalades, preserves, conserves, butters and curds.

- ½-inch headspace is required for fruits, juices, pickles, relishes, sauces, vinegars, pie fillings and toppings.

- 1-inch headspace is required for vegetables.

APPEARANCE: The preserved food should be free from bubbles and have a good color that is consistent with that of a standard cooked and/or processed product. Fruits, vegetables and pickles should be of uniform size, whether whole, halves, quarters or pieces.

Because vegetables are usually judged on appearance only, special care should be taken when filling the jars to arrange the pieces in an attractive manner. While a few fairs specify "no fancy packs," at most fairs, the blue ribbon winners are the jars of vegetables that have been carefully hand-packed with all the pieces arranged uniformly or in a decorative pattern. This is also true for fruit and pickles, where appearance of the pack can make the difference between a first-place ribbon and a second-place ribbon, or even no award at all.

TEXTURE: The proper texture of an entry demonstrates the home-canner's skill and their use of correct and modern preserving techniques. It is a testament to the home-canner's abilities in creating superior preserved foods. Texture is crucial to earning a good score. If the texture of a preserved food is wrong, the entry is in serious trouble.

Each type of preserved food has its own distinct texture criteria. Different techniques are required to attain the proper texture for each preserved food variety. The judges look for specific characteristics as they evaluate the texture of each individual exhibit. Only those entries that meet the highest texture standards will earn the top awards.

- Jams should mound up in a spoon and hold their shape without being either too stiff or too thin. They are made from crushed or finely chopped fruit, not pureed, and there should be no separation of the fruit and juice.

- Jellies should be tender, cut easily and retain their shape without being rubbery or runny.

They should quiver and be crystal clear and free of bubbles.

- Marmalades should have small pieces of fruit and thin pieces of peel evenly suspended in a clear jelly or thick syrup. They should spread easily and be similar in texture to jams.

- Preserves should contain whole or large pieces of fruit that retain their shape and are evenly suspended in a clear jelly or thick syrup. The jelly or syrup should be neither too thin nor too firm.

- Conserves should be jamlike in consistency and contain two or more kinds of crushed or chopped fruit. A true conserve also contains nuts and raisins or other dried fruit.

- Butters should be made from a fine fruit pulp puree and cooked to a smooth spreading consistency. There should be no separation of the fruit and juice, and the butter should be free of lumps or pieces of fruit.

- Curds should be smooth and spreadable yet retain their shape and mound up in a spoon. There should be no separation of the eggs and juice, and the eggs should not show any signs of curdling.

- Fruits and vegetables should be completely free of defects and perfectly ripe, neither overripe nor underripe, and tender, not soft, mushy or crunchy.

- Juices should be smooth and free from large pieces or excessive pulp, in accordance with the specific type of product.

- Pickles and relishes should be firm and crisp yet tender.

- Sauces should have a definite texture and a smooth pouring quality that is neither too thick nor too thin.

- Syrups should be clear and smooth with a pouring texture that is neither too thick nor too thin.

FLAVOR: Flavor counts the most in rating preserved foods, and creating outstanding flavor is the key to grabbing the judge's attention. The judge will first examine the jar and then the preserved food's appearance and texture. If a preserved food earns high marks in these areas, then the flavor becomes the selling point. When the flavor really zings, the judge will be convinced and give the entry a top score. If the flavor falls flat, the judge will be disappointed, feel let down and lower the score. The flavor can make or break the final score, and it separates the cream of the crop from the rest of the pack.

To create preserved foods that pack a flavor punch, you need to use the freshest and finest-quality ingredients available and select produce at the peak of ripeness. If your entry fails to pack a fresh flavor wallop that makes a judge's taste buds stand up and pay attention, you can say goodbye to any chance of picking up a top award.

What Lowers a Score?

While a jar of preserved food may be of excellent quality, with outstanding flavor and texture, minor errors in presentation may reduce its placing or even prevent the preserve from winning an award. Small flaws can make the difference of the 1 or 2 points that separate the winners from the losers. Simple mistakes can take an otherwise perfect preserve out of the running for first place or even Best of Class. While these errors are rarely severe enough to result in a disqualification, they can dramatically reduce an entry's score and may lead to a conclusion of "no award."

HEADSPACE: The most common error that competitors make is in failing to fill the jars to the proper height. The correct amount of headspace is important to ensure a tight seal. Too much headspace and the jar may not have a tight seal. Too little headspace and food may be forced between the jar and the lid, causing a seal to weaken or fail.

Some judges are so precise in examining the headspace in a jar that they will use a ruler or a marked piece of paper to measure the exact height. If the headspace is off by more than a $\frac{1}{16}$ of an inch, sometimes even a $\frac{1}{32}$ of an inch if the competition is really close, the entry will be marked down. This minor error in the headspace measurement when filling the jars can make the difference between competing for awards and being removed from the running at the very start.

If there is food on the inside of the jar in the headspace area, or if there is food stuck on the underside of the lid, it indicates that the jar has been poorly handled and will result in a substantial reduction in the entry's score or placing. This shifting of the food can result in large gaps or bubbles at the top of the jar. These are considered major errors and the score can be drastically reduced, eliminating the preserved food from competition.

CONTAINER: The second most common mistake made by exhibitors is in failing to wash the outside of their preserved food jars before entering them into competition. This simple step is absolutely essential to earning a top score from the judges.

Even though the jar rims and threads are wiped down before sealing the jars, small amounts of sugar or jam may remain on the outside of the jars after processing. When handled with sticky hands, a common occurrence when making preserved foods, filled and cooled jars may also become slightly sticky. During the water bath processing, mineral deposits often form on the outside of the jars, lids and screw rings.

Sticky jars, or jars that have product under the screw ring, and those showing signs of mineral deposits and water marks automatically receive a mandatory deduction in score. At highly competitive fairs, a sticky jar can mean the difference between winning first place and receiving no award at all.

Why force the judge to lower your score before the jar is even opened? Impress the judges with the outside of your jars, and they are more willing to be impressed by the preserved food inside your jars.

BUBBLES: In soft spreads, especially jellies, bubbles trapped in the spread will lead to a major deduction. Even just one or two small bubbles can cause a score to be lowered. To avoid bubbles, ladle the preserves quickly into the jars. Pouring the mixture into the jar too slowly allows air bubbles to become trapped in the soft spread.

Air bubbles in jars of fruits, vegetables, pickles, sauces and other preserved foods are a sign of poor packing and are a reason for a judge to make a substantial reduction in the entry's score, usually eliminating the exhibit from having a chance of receiving any award. Before applying the lids, use a bubble freer or plastic knife to release any trapped bubbles from the jar.

PRODUCT UNDER THE RING: When a judge finds preserved food under the screw ring, it indicates poor handling of the jar and will result in a deduction. Always wipe the jar rim and screw threads carefully after filling the jar and before applying the lid. After processing and cooling the jars, carefully wash and dry the jars and screw rings.

PRESENTATION OF PACK: While it is not necessary to spend hours creating a fancily packed jar of fruit, vegetables or pickles, and some judges will actually take off points when a jar is too perfectly packed, the contents of the jar should be neat and attractive. Arrange the product so that it has a pleasing look, not a hodgepodge.

After processing, fruit, vegetables and pickles may tend to slightly float in the jar, especially if they were packed raw. This is a normal occurrence for a raw pack product. However, the jar should not have 2 inches of empty liquid at the bottom with all the fruit or vegetables floating toward the top. This indicates either poor packing, with too much liquid in proportion to the fruit, or the vegetables or fruit contained too much air and should have been packed hot. To avoid floating preserves, fill the jars as snugly as you can without overpacking, crushing or bruising the produce.

APPEARANCE: Discolored fruit or soft spreads, cloudy liquid in fruit, vegetables or pickles and a lack of uniformity in the size of the pieces in the jar will all result in mandatory deductions. Separation of the fruit and juice in soft spreads or floating fruit in marmalades and preserves demonstrate poor canning methods and the lack of experience and skill of the home canner. Cloudy jellies will also receive reduced scores.

Some fairs prohibit the use of food coloring in any preserved food, even in a product like mint jelly, which would be an unappetizing shade of yellow-brown without the addition of a little green coloring. Read the exhibit handbook carefully for any food coloring restrictions.

TEXTURE: Soft or mushy pickles, fruit or vegetables will have points deducted from their score for poor texture. Soft spreads, juices, sauces and syrups that are too thick or too thin will also receive deductions and fail to win awards. Weeping jellies and graininess or sugar crystals in preserved foods are all signs of poor canning techniques and will result in lower scores and no

awards. Jams made from pureed fruit or large or uneven-sized pieces of fruit will be judged as having poor texture resulting from improper fruit preparation.

FLAVOR: Flavor is the most important quality of all. If a preserved food entry has a poor or bland flavor, it will not win an award.

Reasons for Disqualification

Most preserved foods disqualifications occur before the judge even opens the jar. There are several reasons why an entry may be disqualified from competition and all are easily preventable. Most disqualifications are a result of the home canner's own carelessness or failure to follow proper canning techniques. There is no excuse for an exhibitor earning a disqualification.

UNSEALED JARS OR JARS WITH POOR SEALS: Unsealed jars run the serious risk of mold growth, invisible bacterial contamination and spoilage. Any unsealed or poorly sealed jar will be immediately disqualified and removed from the competition.

Jars of high-acid foods that are inverted after being filled, instead of being safely processed in a water bath, will fail to seal properly. Inverting the jars is an old-fashioned and unsafe method that is, unfortunately, still recommended in many current home-canning cookbooks. It was once thought that inverting jars of high-acid foods would create a vacuum in the jars and cause the lids to seal and that this was an acceptable alternative to water bath processing the jars. This theory has been proven to be false and can lead to serious contamination of the food. Instead of inverting the jars, they should always be processed in a water bath canner to ensure a tight seal.

Inverting jars immediately after water bath processing in an attempt to redistribute floating fruit in jars of marmalades or preserves is not a good idea and is strongly discouraged. The soft spread can be forced between the rim of the jar and the lid, causing the seal to fail. Also, food that sticks to the inside of the lid will impair the head-space, causing air pockets in the jar and preventing the jar from sealing properly. This displaced spread will obscure and impair the judge's ability to visually observe and measure the headspace between the product and the lid. It can also encourage spoilage after the jar has been opened. Never invert jars after filling or processing.

FAILURE TO PROCESS JARS: Almost all fairs now require that jars of preserved foods be properly processed and sealed in either a water bath canner or a pressure canner.

If a fair judge believes a high-acid preserved food entry was not water bath processed, or was processed for too short of a time, the judge may, at his or her own discretion, choose to disqualify the entry without even opening the jar. Judges will not sample the preserved food from any jar that they suspect has not been handled or processed in a safe manner. Never lie and claim that an unprocessed jar of preserved food has been processed. You may be putting the judges' health at risk.

All jars of low-acid preserved foods, such as vegetables, must be processed in a pressure canner to ensure safety. Failure to process the jars correctly will cause them to be disqualified from competition.

JARS SEALED WITH PARAFFIN: The use of paraffin is not an accepted method for sealing jars, as it encourages mold and bacteria growth. The preserved food in jars sealed with paraffin is no longer considered safe to eat. Paraffin seals are ineligible at all fairs, and jars with these seals will be disqualified from the competition.

IMPROPER TYPE OF JAR: A disqualification will occur if the size of the jars used is not the same as that specified in the exhibit handbook for that particular type of preserved food. Entries will also be disqualified if they are canned in any type of jar other than standard home-canning jars. All jars must be sealed with standard canning lids and screw rings. Jars entered into competition must include the screw ring or they will be disqualified.

MISMATCHED JARS OR LIDS: When the rules require the submission of two identical jars, the jars must be identical in size, shape, type, appearance and brand. This criteria applies to the lids as well. Both must be the same size and made by the same manufacturer. Be sure that both of the jars have either a standard opening or a wide-mouth opening. Entering one of each will result in a disqualification.

INCORRECT LABELS: If jars are not correctly labeled as required in the exhibit handbook, or if the labels have fallen off, the entry may be disqualified. Some fairs are more strict about this rule than others. Permanent self-stick labels work well, although they can be difficult to remove from the jars after the fair. Rubber cement or clear tape are both acceptable and effective means of attaching nonpermanent labels.

JARS UNABLE TO BE OPENED: If the screw ring cannot be removed without excessive force, the entry will be disqualified. This is usually an indication that the jar rim was not wiped clean after filling or that the jar was inverted and food has seeped out under the lid, gluing the screw ring to the jar. It also means that the exhibitor failed to remove the rings and wash the jars after they had been removed from the water bath and cooled.

DIRTY JARS OR RUST ON THE LID: If there is rust on the lid or signs of dried food on the outside of the lid or jar, it indicates that the jar has not been properly handled, cleaned and dried. It may also be a sign that the jars were inverted rather than processed or that the jars were stored in a location that was too warm or damp. The food inside the jar may be contaminated. Rusty lids invariably lead to the entry being disqualified.

MOLD OR FOREIGN MATTER: Entries that show any hint of mold or spoilage will be immediately disqualified. If the entry has an unusual, unpleasant or "off" smell, the jar will be disqualified without being sampled. Steadily rising air bubbles in fruits, vegetables or pickles are a sign of fermentation and spoilage and will result in an immediate disqualification of the entry without opening the jar.

Any foreign matter, such as hairs and insects, or any unidentifiable objects found in a jar will result in an immediate disqualification. At one fair, an exhibitor entered two jars of tequila jelly, each complete with a real worm from the liquor bottle. The judges liked the idea of the jelly flavor but were not amused by the worms. The entry was disqualified without being opened.

Advice for the First-Time Exhibitor

Follow the rules carefully, and pay special attention to the small details in making your preserved foods and preparing your jars for entry into competition. If you win a blue ribbon in your first competition, that's terrific! If you don't, con-sider it a learning experience, make a few changes in your preserving techniques and improve your chances of winning the following year.

Winning blue ribbons and other awards is a wonderful feeling. It can become intoxicating—almost addictive. Each new competition is an adventure. As individual competitors become more successful at winning and better known at their particular fair, friendly rivalries frequently develop. Exhibitors will try to outdo each other in the number of entries they submit for judging and the creativity of the recipes they use.

While successful exhibitors are often willing to share advice or offer suggestions to new entrants, they also tend to guard their special recipes and tricks to winning ribbons. Be aware that many recipes printed in fair cookbooks may be missing a special ingredient or an important step in the directions because a competitor does not want to risk giving away their secrets to success and being beaten the next year by a rival. The recipes and instructions you will find in the following chapters include all of the methods and techniques I developed and used to create my award-winning preserved foods that have earned so many blue ribbons and special accolades.

Whether you plan to enter your preserved foods in your state, local or county fair, give the jars away as gifts or simply enjoy them at home, patience and preparation are the keys to success. Most of all, relax, have fun and enjoy the whole fair experience, as nothing else can quite compare to it. And remember, if you give the judges the very best, you will be rewarded with blue ribbons of your own.

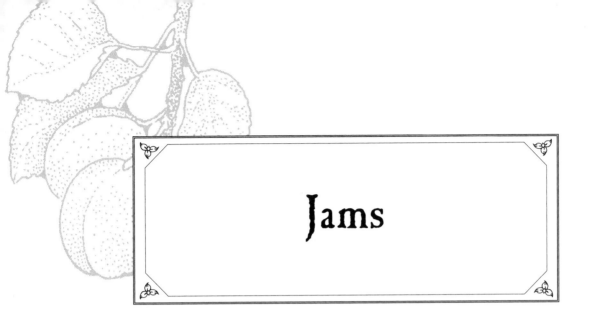

Jams

WHAT IS A JAM?

Of all the different types of soft spreads, jams are the most commonly known variety. They are made from one or more kinds of crushed or chopped fruits that are cooked with sugar to create a delightful preserve. A perfectly textured jam should round up in a spoon, be firm and hold its shape, yet be smooth and spread easily. The small pieces of fruit should be evenly distributed throughout the spread, and there should be no separation of the fruit and juice.

Have you ever seen a jar of homemade jam in which all of the fruit has risen to the top half of the jar and the bottom half of the jar contains only a semiclear jelly? This is a jam where separation between the fruit and juice has occurred and is a sure sign of poor jam-making skill and technique. It is also a jam that will receive very low marks from any judge at a fair competition.

A top-quality jam should have a brilliant color that is natural to the fruit and should have a shimmery translucence. Spreads that have a dull or faded color and look murky scream that they have been made with poor technique, been cooked too long, overprocessed, improperly sealed or stored in a warm location.

Jams may be made from a single fruit, or two or more fruits may be combined to create an exciting blend. In a mixed fruit jam, one fruit flavor should not dominate over the other. Each fruit should be distinct and identifiable, yet blended together to create a new fruit flavor with characteristics of its own. The intensity of the fruit flavors needs to be perfectly balanced with each other and the sugar to produce that special jam.

Traditionally served with breakfast fare or with tea and scones in the afternoon, new flavors of jams are expanding the limits of their use. Tantalizing Garlic and Onion Jam and Zesty Salsa Jam are perfect served with meat or chicken, as well as on fancy crackers for gourmet appetizers. Many sweet jams make wonderful fillings for cakes and cookies or exquisite toppings for elegant cheese-cakes. And of course, any heavenly flavor of homemade jam spread on a slice of toast can make the morning, or turn a late-night snack into something extra special.

MAKING JAM

Soft spreads, such as jams, jellies, marmalades and preserves, are all made from a balanced combination of four ingredients: fruit, sugar, pectin and acid. The correct proportion of each of these ingredients in relation to the others is required to achieve the right consistency or set. Too little sugar, acid or pectin in proportion to the fruit and the spread will remain liquid. Too much sugar, acid or pectin and the spread will end up as stiff as rubber and have about as much flavor.

Jams are the easiest type of soft spread to make. Unlike jellies, marmalades and butters, the fruit for a jam requires very little preparation and cooking time. Because little time is lost between the preparation of the fruit and the point when the finished spread is ladled into the jars and processed, the fresh fruit flavor of the jam remains intense.

For speed and convenience, some home canners choose to crush or chop their fruit in a food processor or a blender. This is an unwise decision that can lead to serious problems with the finished spread. A food processor yields fruit that is chopped into uneven-sized pieces, or worse, fruit that has been pureed. Processing fruit in a blender produces pureed fruit filled with air bubbles that will cause excessive foaming during cooking. Pureed fruits should not be used when making jam, as a good-quality jam should contain small pieces of fruit. Pureeing the fruit or chopping it too finely in a food processor or blender will release too much juice from the fruit, upsetting the recipe balance. Jams made with pureed fruit will contain too much liquid, require extra cooking time and frequently fail to set properly. Because of this excess liquid, pureed jams also run a high risk of having the fruit separate from the juice and rise to the top of the jar. If you prefer a perfectly smooth spread, try making butters, curds or jellies, as these preserves use sieved fruits or pure fruit juice.

Grinding the fruit for a jam instead of chopping or crushing it by hand will also produce an inferior spread. Jams made from ground fruit have many of the same problems as those made from pureed fruit. Too much juice released from the fruit by grinding it can produce a jam containing too much liquid that will set soft. Ground jams are more likely to separate and have a poor texture. Many canners grind up the skins and peels along with the fruit, impairing the fresh flavor, shimmering color and smooth texture of the jam.

The lack of small fruit pieces in pureed and ground jams causes them to receive low scores from most fair judges because the spreads fail to meet the basic definition of a jam. While an occasional jam made from pureed or ground fruit may win a blue ribbon, it is a rare event for a qualified judge to let such a variation slip through without a serious deduction in points.

Always measure the fruit and other ingredients carefully and accurately when making jam or any other preserves. The fruit and other ingredients should be measured in individual batch quantities only. Never double a batch of jam because there will be an insufficient surface area in the pan to allow for the proper amount of liquid to evaporate during cooking. Jam made in double batches frequently fails to set and often separates as it cools.

Do not combine together the fruit with the lemon juice or sugar for more than one batch. The proportions of the ingredients will not be correct when divided later and the jam may fail to set.

The amount of sugar or acid called for in the recipe should not be altered, as the spread will fail to set. To make a jam with less sugar, purchase a pectin designed specifically for this purpose and follow the directions that come inside the package. Unless a fair offers a special entry class for reduced-sugar jams, it is not recommended that a low-sugar spread be entered in a regular class of competition. The low-sugar spread will not compete well against the superior texture and full flavor of a regular jam.

Special Equipment and Techniques

Very few special tools are needed to make homemade jams and most of those are already in your kitchen. A small paring knife, a chef's knife and a cutting board will make chopping the fruit quick and easy. A vegetable or potato masher is handy for crushing fruit, while a stainless steel food mill or a sieve is useful to remove excess seeds from a berry jam. To skim any foam from the top of the jam, a large slotted spoon with small holes comes in handy. With some other standard canning equipment, such as a ladle, a wide-mouth funnel, jars and lids, a jar lifter, a couple of pans and a water bath canner, you will be all set to start creating your own fabulous homemade jams.

Although many standard jam recipes found in other cookbooks call for leaving the skins on such fruits as apricots, pears, plums and tomatoes, I always remove the peels. I prefer the smooth, silky texture that can only be achieved by removing the skins from these fruits. When the skins are removed, the jam develops a pure, full fruit flavor and uniform texture without any of the annoying chewy or tough bits of the peel. Jams made with the skins, particularly plum, often have a bitter taste. This unpleasant flavor, which has never appealed to me, led me to try removing the skins from some fruits when making soft spreads.

While some fair judges are sticklers for following the traditional preparation methods, I have found that most judges appreciate new techniques that improve the quality and flavor of preserved foods. When my Santa Rosa Plum Jam took top honors at the California State Fair and also won the intensely competitive Sure-Jell Jam Competition, the judging sheets included the comments, "Incredible color, outstanding flavor and perfect texture!" and "You peeled it! How wonderful!" The judges agreed that removing the peels from the plums produced a jam of superior quality, flavor and texture.

Peeling Apricots, Peaches, Nectarines and Tomatoes

To easily remove the skins from these fruits dip them into boiling water for 30 seconds, then plunge them into ice water for 1 minute to stop the cooking process and loosen the skin. Drain the fruit well, then use a small paring knife to gently slip off the skin. Plums and pears, which do not slip their skins well using the hot water method, should simply be peeled by hand using a sharp paring knife.

Selecting Fruit

The quality and the ripeness of the fruit used to make a jam or other preserve are the two most important elements in producing an intensely flavorful jam or other soft spread. Because the flavor of the jam is directly related to the condition of the fruit selected, use only top-quality fruit at the peak of ripeness when making a jam. Despite what many cooks may tell you, making jam is not the time to use up underripe, overripe, bruised, ground or otherwise inferior fruit. Top-quality fruit may cost more or be harder to find, but if you insist on using field run, seconds or leftover fruit, you may as well save yourself the trouble and just go buy a jar of jam off the grocery store shelf. If you want to create a great-tasting jam and win awards for your efforts, you must use the best fruit.

Preparing Fruit

Prepare only enough fruit at one time to make one batch of jam. Quickly rinse the fruit two to three times in cool, clean water to remove any dirt, changing water between each rinsing. With a soft brush, gently scrub citrus fruits to remove dirt and any vegetable wax. Drain the fruit well and dry it completely on paper towels. Excess water on the fruit can affect the ingredient ratios, preventing a jam from setting properly, resulting in a spread that may be too soft or runny. Do not allow the fruit to sit in the rinse water, or the fruit will absorb some of the water into its cells, diluting the flavor of the fruit. Exposing most fruits, other than citrus, to water for more than a minute will speed up the natural deterioration process of the fruit. This is especially true with fragile berries, which can degrade rapidly if left to soak in water. Berries should be rinsed quickly in small batches and then used immediately before they begin to deteriorate.

For best results, peel, cut and crush or chop the fruit just before cooking the jam. Fruit that is allowed to stand may release too much juice, which can cause the fruit and juice to separate in the finished jam. Crushed fruit that is allowed to stand for more than 5 minutes or so can begin to foam, requiring more skimming during cooking. This extra skimming can reduce the quantity of spread the recipe will yield or remove too much liquid and produce a tough or very firm jam. Prepared fruit also deteriorates quickly and can lose its delicate fresh flavor, texture and intense color if not used immediately.

Crush berries and other fruits in small quantities in the bottom of a flat bowl or pan. The fruit should only be one layer thick. Always transfer the crushed fruit to a measuring cup before crushing the next layer. If crushed fruit is left in the bottom of the pan and more fruit is added on top, the fruit will not be crushed to a uniform texture. Part of the fruit will end up being in large pieces, while some of the fruit will be nearly pureed. This uneven preparation of the fruit will result in a jam with a very poor texture.

Raspberries, which contain a high proportion of seeds, should be pressed through a food mill or sieve to remove a substantial quantity of the seeds. Sieving at least half of the berries will produce a smoother-textured jam with far fewer seeds. The flavor of the jam will be improved by the replacement of seeds with fruit pulp, because a large quantity of seeds can give the jam a bitter taste. Otherwise, the jam will be very seedy, which will dramatically decrease the quality of both the flavor and the texture of the spread. For entry in a fair competition, it is advisable to remove at least ⅔ to ¾ of the seeds when making a raspberry jam or the entry will have points deducted for being too seedy.

Removing all of the seeds from a berry jam to make a seedless berry jam will change the texture of the spread, as the fruit will become nearly smooth rather than still containing some crushed fruit. The removed seeds are replaced by liquid and pulp, thus changing the texture and balance of the ingredients in the recipe and resulting in a very soft spread. If you want to make a seedless jam, use the Seedless Berry Jam recipe in this chapter. The ingredients have been balanced to account for the extra liquid in the fruit and to produce a seedless spread with a better texture and set.

It is easier to remove the seeds from the berries if you gently heat part or all of the crushed berries over low heat just until they are soft, then press them through the food mill or sieve to remove part of the seeds—or all of the seeds if you are making a seedless jam. Crush any remaining berries and add them to the sieved fruit. Always measure the quantity of crushed fruit needed for a recipe after the portion of seeds have been removed.

Seedless berry jams should not be entered into fair competitions unless there is a specific class for seedless jams. Otherwise, the jam will probably be marked down significantly for having a texture that may be too soft and for being made from a puree that does not contain crushed fruit or small pieces of fruit. Judges sometimes draw a fine line between a berry jam that has too many seeds and one that does not contain enough crushed fruit.

Cooking the Jam

Heat the fruit over low heat until warm before adding the sugar. This simple step will help the sugar dissolve faster and also reduce the possibility that, over high heat, some of the sugar may scorch on the bottom of the pan before it can dissolve. Continue heating the fruit over low heat until the sugar is completely dissolved, then increase the heat and bring the mixture to a boil. This method will prevent the chance of crystals forming in the finished jam. Crystallization can occur if there is too much sugar in the jam or if the fruit is brought to a boil before the sugar is completely dissolved.

As soon as the fruit and sugar mixture reaches a full rolling boil (a boil that cannot be stirred down), add the liquid pectin. Additional boiling before adding the pectin will evaporate too much liquid from the mixture and can cause the fruit to lose its fresh flavor. When the liquid pectin is added, be sure to squeeze the pouch to remove the entire contents. Stir the fruit mixture constantly to distribute the pectin evenly throughout the jam. When the mixture returns to a full rolling boil, set a timer for 1 minute. Boil the jam, stirring constantly, for exactly 1 minute, and remove the pan from the heat. Cooking the jam longer will allow too much liquid to evaporate, and the finished jam will set too firm and be difficult to spread.

Cooking times for jams should be strictly adhered to, as overcooking may lead to a thick, burnt-tasting mass, while undercooking can result in a thin syrup that may contain sugar crystals. Cooking the jam for several minutes after the pectin has been added will expose the pectin to heat for too long a period of time, causing the pectin to break down and the jam to either seize into a large, rubbery mass or return to a soft liquid state.

Filling the Jars

Use a wide-mouth canning funnel and a ladle to fill the jars. This will make the job of filling the jars easier and a lot less messy. All jams require a ¼-inch headspace between the jam and the top of the jar rim. This space is necessary to create a vacuum in the jar and form a strong seal between the lid and the jar during water bath processing. Never fill a jar to the brim or leave only ⅛-inch headspace. During processing, the spread will be forced between the lid and the rim of an overfilled jar, preventing a tight seal and providing the opportunity for bacteria to enter the jar, contaminating the contents. Too much headspace will keep a vacuum from forming in the jar and weaken the seal. Excessive headspace can also cause the jam in the top part of the jar to darken from exposure to air.

After filling the jars and checking the headspace depth, use a clean, damp cloth to wipe down the jar rim, screw threads and any spills inside the jar in the headspace area. Apply the hot lids and then the screw bands, tightening snugly but not too firmly. Jars should then be properly processed in a water bath to complete the seals.

It is no longer considered safe to preserve jams or other soft spreads using the open-kettle method. Using this method, sterilized jars were filled with hot jam, lids and screw rings were applied and the jars were then turned upside down for 5 minutes to complete the seals. Instead of sealing the jars, this old-fashioned method actually allows the jam to seep between the lid and the jar rim, preventing a tight seal from forming and encouraging bacteria growth in the jar. It also shifts the contents in the jar, causing the jam to stick to the lid, cloud the headspace and trap air

bubbles throughout the spread. All jars of jam and other soft spreads should be processed in a water bath to ensure safety. Most fairs will disqualify from competition any jar that is even suspected of not having been properly processed by approved methods.

Soft spreads will thicken as they cool. Most jams will set within 24 hours, although some may take a few days to complete the jelling process. If a jam has not set by the end of a week, it is unlikely that it ever will. An unset jam may be reheated with additional sugar, acid and pectin and then reprocessed (see Troubleshooting, page 324), or it may be used as an ice-cream or dessert topping or served over pancakes or waffles.

Apricot Jam

Traditional apricot jam recipes advise leaving the peels on the fruit. While some longtime jam makers may scoff, as may a few judges, I find that removing the peels results in a smoother-textured jam with a much more intense flavor. The apricot jam recipes may be prepared with or without removing the peels, but for superior results, I strongly recommend removing them.

MAKES ABOUT 6 HALF-PINT JARS

4 cups pitted, peeled and crushed or
    finely chopped ripe apricots
6 tablespoons strained fresh lemon
    juice
6 cups sugar
½ teaspoon unsalted butter
1 (3-ounce) pouch liquid pectin

In an 8-quart pan, combine the apricots and lemon juice. Stir in about half of the sugar. Cover and let stand 1 hour.

Remove the cover and stir in the remaining sugar. Over medium-low heat, stirring constantly, heat the mixture until the sugar is completely dissolved. Increase the heat to medium-high and bring the apricot mixture to a boil. Boil for 2 minutes, stirring gently. Remove the pan from the heat and skim off the foam.

Return the pan to the heat and bring to a boil. Boil for 1 minute, stirring constantly. Remove the pan from the heat and skim off the foam.

Stir in the butter. Over medium-high heat, bring the mixture to a full rolling boil, stirring constantly. Stir in the entire contents of the pectin pouch. Return the mixture to a full rolling boil, stirring constantly. Boil, stirring constantly, for 1 minute. Remove the pan from the heat. Skim off any foam.

To prevent the jam from separating in the jars, allow the jam to cool 5 minutes before filling the jars. Gently stir the jam every minute or so to distribute the fruit. Ladle the hot jam into hot jars, leaving ¼-inch headspace. Wipe the jar rims and threads with a clean, damp cloth. Cover with hot lids and apply screw rings. Process half-pint jars in a 200F (93C) water bath for 10 minutes, pint jars for 15 minutes.

Tip

Apricots, cherries and plums each tend to produce a lot of foam during cooking. Extra care should be taken with these fruits to remove as much of the foam as possible during the skimming process.

Apricot-Pineapple Jam

This jam is a traditional favorite, bound to please most everyone. Check the crushed pineapple for any large chunks, and cut any you find into small pieces before adding it to the apricot mixture.

MAKES ABOUT 7 HALF-PINT JARS

2½ cups pitted, peeled and crushed ripe
    apricots
6 tablespoons strained fresh lemon
    juice
1 cup drained crushed pineapple
5¾ cups sugar
½ teaspoon unsalted butter
1 (3-ounce) pouch liquid pectin

 In an 8-quart pan, combine the apricots and lemon juice. Add the pineapple, then stir in the sugar and butter.

Over medium-low heat, stirring constantly, heat the mixture until the sugar is completely dissolved. Increase the heat to medium-high and bring the mixture to a full rolling boil, stirring constantly. Stir in the entire contents of the pectin pouch. Return the mixture to a full rolling boil, stirring constantly. Boil, stirring constantly, for 1 minute. Remove the pan from the heat. Skim off any foam.

To prevent the jam from separating in the jars, allow the jam to cool 5 minutes before filling the jars. Gently stir the jam every minute or so to distribute the fruit. Ladle the hot jam into hot jars, leaving ¼-inch headspace. Wipe the jar rims and threads with a clean, damp cloth. Cover with hot lids and apply screw rings. Process half-pint jars in a 200F (93C) water bath for 10 minutes, pint jars for 15 minutes.

Apricot-Plum Jam

This delightful jam has won blue ribbons all across the country. Fair judges love this jam's beautiful color and great flavor.

MAKES ABOUT 7 HALF-PINT JARS

2½ cups pitted, peeled and crushed or
    finely chopped ripe apricots
1½ cups pitted, peeled and crushed ripe
    Santa Rosa or other plums
2 tablespoons strained fresh lemon juice

7 cups sugar

½ teaspoon unsalted butter

1 (3-ounce) pouch liquid pectin

In an 8-quart pan, combine the apricots, plums and lemon juice. Stir in the sugar. Cover and let stand 30 minutes.

Remove the cover. Over medium-low heat, stirring constantly, heat the mixture until the sugar is completely dissolved. Increase the heat to medium-high and bring the mixture to a boil. Boil for 2 minutes, stirring gently. Remove the pan from the heat and skim off the foam.

Return the pan to the heat and bring to a boil. Boil for 1 minute, stirring constantly. Remove the pan from the heat and skim off the foam.

Stir in the butter. Over medium-high heat, bring the mixture to a full rolling boil, stirring constantly. Stir in the entire contents of the pectin pouch. Return the mixture to a full rolling boil, stirring constantly. Boil, stirring constantly, for 1 minute. Remove the pan from the heat. Skim off any foam.

To prevent the jam from separating in the jars, allow the jam to cool 5 minutes before filling the jars. Gently stir the jam every minute or so to distribute the fruit. Ladle the hot jam into hot jars, leaving ¼-inch headspace. Wipe the jar rims and threads with a clean, damp cloth. Cover with hot lids and apply screw rings. Process half-pint jars in a 200F (93C) water bath for 10 minutes, pint jars for 15 minutes.

Banana-Pineapple Jam

For the best flavor, be sure to use bananas that are fully ripe. They should be golden yellow in color and flecked with brown spots.

MAKES ABOUT 5 HALF-PINT JARS

2¾ cups peeled and diced ripe bananas (about 7 medium)

⅓ cup bottled lemon juice

1 teaspoon antioxidant crystals or ascorbic acid crystals

1 cup drained canned crushed pineapple

5 cups sugar

½ teaspoon unsalted butter

1 (3-ounce) pouch liquid pectin

In an 8-quart pan, combine the bananas, lemon juice and antioxidant crystals. Add the pineapple and stir in the sugar and butter.

Over medium-low heat, stirring constantly, heat the mixture until the sugar is completely dissolved. Increase the heat to medium-high and bring the mixture to a full rolling boil, stirring constantly. Stir in the entire contents of the pectin pouch. Return the mixture to a full rolling boil, stirring constantly. Boil, stirring constantly, for 1 minute. Remove the pan from the heat. Skim off any foam.

To prevent the jam from separating in the jars, allow the jam to cool 5 minutes before filling the jars. Gently stir the jam every minute or so to distribute the fruit. Ladle the hot jam into hot jars, leaving ¼-inch headspace. Wipe the jar rims and threads with a clean, damp cloth. Cover with hot lids and apply screw rings. Process half-pint jars in a 200F (93C) water bath for 10 minutes, pint jars for 15 minutes.

Banana-Rum Jam

An exotic pairing of flavors makes for a truly tropical jam. Stir the jam gently during cooking to prevent the finished jam from being filled with tiny air bubbles.

MAKES ABOUT 5 HALF-PINT JARS

3¾ cups peeled and diced ripe bananas
    (about 10 medium)
6 tablespoons bottled lemon juice
1 teaspoon antioxidant crystals or ascorbic
    acid crystals
5 cups sugar
½ teaspoon unsalted butter
1 (3-ounce) pouch liquid pectin
1½ to 2 teaspoons rum extract

❧ In an 8-quart pan, combine the bananas, lemon juice and antioxidant crystals. Stir in the sugar and butter.

Over medium-low heat, stirring constantly, heat the mixture until the sugar is completely dissolved. Increase the heat to medium-high and bring the mixture to a full rolling boil, stirring constantly. Stir in the entire contents of the pectin pouch. Return the mixture to a full rolling boil, stirring constantly. Boil, stirring constantly, for 1 minute. Remove the pan from the heat. Skim off any foam. Stir in the rum extract to taste.

To prevent the jam from separating in the jars, allow the jam to cool 5 minutes before filling the jars. Gently stir the jam every minute or so to distribute the fruit. Ladle the hot jam into hot jars, leaving ¼-inch headspace. Wipe the jar rims and threads with a clean, damp cloth. Cover with hot lids and apply screw rings. Process half-pint jars in a 200F (93C) water bath for 10 minutes, pint jars for 15 minutes.

Banberry Jam

Strawberries and bananas make a great pairing of flavors and a great jam.

MAKES ABOUT 7 HALF-PINT JARS

2¼ cups hulled and crushed ripe
    strawberries
1¾ cups peeled and mashed ripe bananas
2 tablespoons bottled lemon juice
7 cups sugar
½ teaspoon unsalted butter
1 (3-ounce) pouch liquid pectin

❧ In an 8-quart pan, combine the strawberries, bananas, lemon juice, sugar and butter.

Over medium-low heat, stirring constantly, heat the mixture until the sugar is completely dissolved. Increase the heat to medium-high and bring the mixture to a full rolling boil, stirring constantly. Stir in the entire contents of the pectin pouch. Return the mixture to a full rolling boil, stirring constantly. Boil, stirring constantly, for 1 minute. Remove the pan from the heat. Skim off any foam.

To prevent the jam from separating in the jars, allow the jam to cool 5 minutes before filling the jars. Gently stir the jam every minute or so to distribute the fruit. Ladle the hot jam into hot jars, leaving ¼-inch headspace. Wipe the jar rims and threads with a clean, damp cloth. Cover with hot lids and apply screw rings. Process half-pint jars in a 200F (93C) water bath for 10 minutes, pint jars for 15 minutes.

Blackberry Jam

Frozen blackberries will also make a very good jam. I have won first-place awards with this jam made from both fresh and frozen berries. If using frozen berries, you will need 2 to 3 (16-ounce) bags. Do not rinse frozen berries before defrosting, and be sure to add all of the released juice to the pan, or the jam will be too thick.

To reduce the quantity of seeds in the jam, sieve about ¼ of the berry pulp before measuring.

MAKES ABOUT 8 HALF-PINT JARS

4 cups crushed fresh, ripe blackberries
   (8 to 9 pint baskets)
7 cups sugar
½ teaspoon unsalted butter
1 (3-ounce) pouch liquid pectin

In an 8-quart pan, combine the blackberries, sugar and butter.

Over medium-low heat, stirring constantly, heat the mixture until the sugar is completely dissolved. Increase the heat to medium-high and bring the mixture to a full rolling boil, stirring constantly. Stir in the entire contents of the pectin pouch. Return the mixture to a full rolling boil, stirring constantly. Boil, stirring constantly, for 1 minute. Remove the pan from the heat. Skim off any foam.

To prevent the jam from separating in the jars, allow the jam to cool 5 minutes before filling the jars. Gently stir the jam every minute or so to distribute the fruit. Ladle the hot jam into hot jars, leaving ¼-inch headspace. Wipe the jar rims and threads with a clean, damp cloth. Cover with hot lids and apply screw rings. Process half-pint jars in a 200F (93C) water bath for 10 minutes, pint jars for 15 minutes.

Tip

After cooking a blackberry, boysenberry, loganberry or olallieberry jam, the center white cores of the berries, to which the individual seeds were attached, will rise to the surface of the jam. As I stir the jam during the 5-minute standing period before ladling it into the jars, I skim off as many of these cores as I can find. While this step is purely optional, it creates a more attractive jam with a smoother texture. If you plan to enter your berry jam in a fair competition, I strongly recommended removing the cores.

Blueberry Jam

Adding a small amount of lemon juice to blueberry jam heightens the flavor of the berries, giving the jam an extra pizzazz. Judges have remarked on the great color, flavor and texture of this jam.

Frozen blueberries may also be used for this recipe. A 16-ounce bag of frozen blueberries will yield about 2 cups of crushed fruit.

MAKES ABOUT 9 HALF-PINT JARS

5 cups crushed fresh, ripe blueberries
2 tablespoons strained fresh lemon juice
7 cups sugar
½ teaspoon unsalted butter
2 (3-ounce) pouches liquid pectin
¼ teaspoon ground cinnamon (optional)

In an 8-quart pan, combine the blueberries, lemon juice, sugar and butter.

Over medium-low heat, stirring constantly, heat the mixture until the sugar is completely dissolved. Increase the heat to medium-high and bring the mixture to a full rolling boil, stirring constantly. Stir in the entire contents of both pectin pouches. Return the mixture to a full rolling boil, stirring constantly. Boil, stirring constantly, for 1 minute. Remove the pan from the heat. Skim off any foam. Stir in the cinnamon, if desired.

To prevent the jam from separating in the jars, allow the jam to cool 5 minutes before filling the jars. Gently stir the jam every minute or so to distribute the fruit. Ladle the hot jam into hot jars, leaving ¼-inch headspace. Wipe the jar rims and threads with a clean, damp cloth. Cover with hot lids and apply screw rings. Process half-pint jars in a 200F (93C) water bath for 10 minutes, pint jars for 15 minutes.

Boysenberry Jam

When my patch of boysenberries ripens, I usually make several batches of jam. If I do not have time to use up all of the berries, I freeze some and make jam later when I have more time. My boysenberry jams, made with fresh or frozen berries, have won multiple blue ribbons for their excellent texture, flavor and color.

To reduce the quantity of seeds in the jam, sieve about ¼ of the berry pulp before measuring.

MAKES ABOUT 8 HALF-PINT JARS

4 cups crushed fresh, ripe boysenberries (8 to 9 pint baskets)

7 cups sugar

½ teaspoon unsalted butter

1 (3-ounce) pouch liquid pectin

 In an 8-quart pan, combine the boysenberries, sugar and butter.

Over medium-low heat, stirring constantly, heat the mixture until the sugar is completely dissolved. Increase the heat to medium-high and bring the mixture to a full rolling boil, stirring constantly. Stir in the entire contents of the pectin pouch. Return the mixture to a full rolling boil, stirring constantly. Boil, stirring constantly, for 1 minute. Remove the pan from the heat. Skim off any foam.

To prevent the jam from separating in the jars, allow the jam to cool 5 minutes before filling the jars. Gently stir the jam every minute or so to distribute the fruit. Ladle the hot jam into hot jars, leaving ¼-inch headspace. Wipe the jar rims and threads with a clean, damp cloth. Cover with hot lids and apply screw rings. Process half-pint jars in a 200F (93C) water bath for 10 minutes, pint jars for 15 minutes.

Cantaloupe Jam

Cantaloupes make a beautiful melon jam with a bright, clear orange color. Cantaloupe and honeydew cross-bred melons, such as honeyloupe or cantadew, also make a nice jam that is slightly less sweet. Select melons that are ripe, but avoid very ripe melons or the jam will be cloyingly sweet.

MAKES ABOUT 5 HALF-PINT JARS

3 cups seeded, peeled, crushed, lightly drained firm, ripe cantaloupe (about 2 large)

½ cup strained fresh lemon juice

5¾ cups sugar

½ teaspoon unsalted butter

2 (3-ounce) pouches liquid pectin

In an 8-quart pan, combine the cantaloupe, lemon juice, sugar and butter.

Over medium-low heat, stirring constantly, heat the mixture until the sugar is completely dissolved. Increase the heat to medium-high and bring the mixture to a full rolling boil, stirring constantly. Stir in the entire contents of both pectin pouches. Return the mixture to a full rolling boil, stirring constantly. Boil, stirring constantly, for 1 minute. Remove the pan from the heat. Skim off any foam.

To prevent the jam from separating in the jars, allow the jam to cool 5 minutes before filling the jars. Gently stir the jam every minute or so to distribute the fruit. Ladle the hot jam into hot jars, leaving ¼-inch headspace. Wipe the jar rims and threads with a clean, damp cloth. Cover with hot lids and apply screw rings. Process half-pint jars in a 200F (93C) water bath for 10 minutes, pint jars for 15 minutes.

Bing Cherry Jam

This jam is a multiple blue ribbon winner and a favorite among family and friends. When selecting the jam to receive the Best of Division award, the judges remarked, "A beautiful cherry jam. Your excellent canning skills shine through. The color, texture and delicious Bing cherry flavor were a delight to judge. An outstanding product!" For the best flavor, cherries should be used within 3 days of harvesting.

MAKES ABOUT 6 HALF-PINT JARS

4 cups pitted and chopped, fresh, ripe Bing cherries (about 3 pounds)

½ cup strained fresh lemon juice

5 cups sugar

½ teaspoon unsalted butter

1 (3-ounce) pouch liquid pectin

1 teaspoon pure almond extract

In an 8-quart pan, combine the cherries, lemon juice, sugar and butter.

Over medium-low heat, stirring constantly, heat the mixture until the sugar is completely dissolved. Increase the heat to medium-high and bring the mixture to a full rolling boil, stirring constantly. Stir in the entire contents of the pectin pouch. Return the mixture to a full rolling boil, stirring constantly. Boil, stirring constantly, for 1 minute. Remove the pan from the heat. Skim off any foam. Stir in the almond extract.

To prevent the jam from separating in the jars, allow the jam to cool 5 minutes before filling the jars. Gently stir the jam every minute or so to distribute the fruit. Ladle the hot jam into hot jars, leaving ¼-inch headspace. Wipe the jar rims and threads with a clean, damp cloth. Cover with hot lids and apply screw rings. Process half-pint jars in a 200F (93C) water bath for 10 minutes, pint jars for 15 minutes.

Sour Cherry Jam

Tart pie cherries make a tangy jam with a bright color. Fresh-picked cherries make the best jam.

MAKES ABOUT 6 HALF-PINT JARS

4 cups pitted and chopped, fresh, tart pie
    cherries (about 3½ pounds)
1 tablespoon strained fresh lemon juice
5 cups sugar
½ teaspoon unsalted butter
1 (3-ounce) pouch liquid pectin

In an 8-quart pan, combine the cherries, lemon juice, sugar and butter.

Over medium-low heat, stirring constantly, heat the mixture until the sugar is completely dissolved. Increase the heat to medium-high and bring the mixture to a full rolling boil, stirring constantly. Stir in the entire contents of the pectin pouch. Return the mixture to a full rolling boil, stirring constantly. Boil, stirring constantly, for 1 minute. Remove the pan from the heat. Skim off any foam.

To prevent the jam from separating in the jars, allow the jam to cool 5 minutes before filling the jars. Gently stir the jam every minute or so to distribute the fruit. Ladle the hot jam into hot jars, leaving ¼-inch headspace. Wipe the jar rims and threads with a clean, damp cloth. Cover with hot lids and apply screw rings. Process half-pint jars in a 200F (93C) water bath for 10 minutes, pint jars for 15 minutes.

Fig Jam

My friend Sandra Manning provides me with the most wonderful little Ruby Nectar figs that she grows in her orchard in Northern California. They make a shimmering red jam, almost the color of strawberries.

MAKES ABOUT 8 HALF-PINT JARS

4 cups stemmed and finely chopped fresh
    black figs or other flavorful variety
½ cup strained fresh lemon juice
6 cups sugar
½ cup water
½ teaspoon unsalted butter
1 (3-ounce) pouch liquid pectin

In an 8-quart pan, combine the figs, lemon juice and about ⅓ of the sugar. Stir well to combine, and let stand for 10 minutes. Stir in the water.

Over medium-low heat, stirring constantly, heat the mixture until the sugar begins to dissolve. Gradually stir in the remaining sugar and add the butter. Heat the mixture, stirring constantly, until the sugar is completely dissolved. Increase the heat to medium-high and bring the mixture to a full rolling boil, stirring constantly. Stir in the entire contents of the pectin pouch. Return the mixture to a full rolling boil, stirring constantly. Boil, stirring constantly, for 1 minute. Remove the pan from the heat. Skim off any foam.

To prevent the jam from separating in the jars, allow the jam to cool 5 minutes before filling the jars. Gently stir the jam every minute or so to distribute the fruit. Ladle the hot jam into hot jars, leaving ¼-inch headspace. Wipe the jar rims and threads with a clean, damp cloth. Cover with hot lids and apply screw rings. Process half-pint jars in a 200F (93C) water bath for 10 minutes, pint jars for 15 minutes.

Garlic and Onion Jam

This unusual jam is surprisingly good. Serve it alongside beef or chicken, or spoon small quantities onto fancy crackers for a gourmet appetizer to serve at parties.

MAKES 5 TO 6 HALF-PINT JARS

2 tablespoons unsalted butter
2 tablespoons vegetable oil
5 cups peeled and finely chopped onions
    (2 to 3 pounds)
8 large cloves garlic, peeled and chopped
4 cups sugar
2 cups white wine
1 tablespoon strained fresh lemon juice
2 (3-ounce) pouches liquid pectin

In a large heavy skillet over low heat, combine the butter and vegetable oil. Add the onions and sauté gently, stirring frequently, for 10 minutes. Do not allow the onions to brown or the jam will have a tough texture. Add the garlic and ½ cup of the sugar. Sauté, stirring frequently, for 5 minutes. Do not allow the onions and garlic to brown. Remove the pan from the heat.

Transfer the mixture to an 8-quart stainless steel pan. Add the wine, lemon juice and the remaining sugar.

Over low heat, stirring constantly, heat the mixture until the sugar is completely dissolved.

Increase the heat to medium-high and bring the mixture to a full rolling boil, stirring constantly. Stir in the entire contents of both pectin pouches. Return the mixture to a full rolling boil, stirring constantly. Boil, stirring constantly, for 1 minute. Remove the pan from the heat.

To prevent the jam from separating in the jars, allow the jam to cool 5 minutes before filling the jars. Gently stir the jam every minute or so to distribute the fruit. Ladle the hot jam into hot jars, leaving ¼-inch headspace. Wipe the jar rims and threads with a clean, damp cloth. Cover with hot lids and apply screw rings. Process half-pint jars in a 200F (93C) water bath for 10 minutes, pint jars for 15 minutes.

Concord Grape Jam

Select fully ripe grapes that are still firm, and make the jam within 2 days of harvest. Keep the grapes in a cool location until you are ready to make the jam. The judges enjoyed the excellent color, flavor and texture of this jam.

MAKES ABOUT 10 HALF-PINT JARS

4½ pounds Concord grapes
½ cup water
¾ cup Concord grape juice or water
7½ cups sugar
½ teaspoon unsalted butter
1 (3-ounce) pouch liquid pectin

Remove the grapes from the stems and rinse them in cool water. Drain well. Remove the skins from the grapes and finely chop the skins. Gently crush the pulp and set aside.

In a 4-quart stainless steel pan, combine the grape skins and water. Over medium heat, bring the skin mixture to a boil. Reduce the heat and simmer for 20 minutes, stirring occasionally to prevent sticking. Remove the pan from the heat.

In an 8-quart stainless steel pan, combine the grape pulp and the grape juice. Over medium heat, bring the pulp to a boil. Reduce the heat and simmer for 5 to 7 minutes, stirring occasionally to prevent sticking. Remove the pan from the heat.

Press the grape pulp through a food mill or fine-meshed sieve. Discard the seeds. Combine the pulp and the skins and measure 5½ cups.

Place the grape mixture in the 8-quart pan and add the sugar and butter. Over low heat, stirring constantly, heat the mixture until the sugar is completely dissolved. Increase the heat to medium-high and bring the mixture to a full rolling boil, stirring constantly. Stir in the entire contents of the pectin pouch. Return the mixture to a full rolling boil, stirring constantly. Boil, stirring constantly, for 1 minute. Remove the pan from the heat. Skim off any foam.

To prevent the jam from separating in the jars, allow the jam to cool 5 minutes before filling the jars. Gently stir the jam every minute or so to distribute the fruit. Ladle the hot jam into hot jars, leaving ¼-inch headspace. Wipe the jar rims and threads with a clean, damp cloth. Cover with hot lids and apply screw rings. Process half-pint jars in a 200F (93C) water bath for 10 minutes, pint jars for 15 minutes.

Kiwi Jam

A tomato corer or a grapefruit spoon makes easy work of removing the center core from the kiwis. Peel the kiwis, then cut in half lengthwise and remove the core. All or part of the seeds may be removed, depending on your personal preference.

MAKES ABOUT 9 HALF-PINT JARS

5 cups peeled, cored, seeded and gently
    crushed kiwifruit (about 30 medium)
2 tablespoons strained fresh lemon juice
7 cups sugar
½ teaspoon unsalted butter
1 (3-ounce) pouch liquid pectin

In an 8-quart pan, combine the kiwifruit, lemon juice and sugar. Cover and let stand for 2 hours.

Remove the cover. Over medium-low heat, stirring constantly, heat the mixture until the sugar is completely dissolved. Stir in the butter. Increase the heat to medium-high and bring the mixture to a full rolling boil, stirring constantly. Stir in the entire contents of the pectin pouch. Return the mixture to a full rolling boil, stirring constantly. Boil, stirring constantly, for 1 minute. Remove the pan from the heat. Skim off any foam.

To prevent the jam from separating in the jars, allow the jam to cool 5 minutes before filling the jars. Gently stir the jam every minute or so to distribute the fruit. Ladle the hot jam into hot jars, leaving ¼-inch headspace. Wipe the jar rims and threads with a clean, damp cloth. Cover with hot lids and apply screw rings. Process half-pint jars in a 200F (93C) water bath for 10 minutes, pint jars for 15 minutes.

Loganberry Jam

Loganberries are a cross between a blackberry and a boysenberry and make an excellent jam. This jam won first place every year I entered it in competition. Olallieberries, which are a cross between a blackberry and a loganberry, also make a great jam.

To reduce the quantity of seeds in the jam, sieve about ¼ of the berry pulp before measuring.

MAKES ABOUT 8 HALF-PINT JARS

4 cups crushed fresh, ripe loganberries (8 to
    9 pint baskets)
7 cups sugar
½ teaspoon unsalted butter
1 (3-ounce) pouch liquid pectin

In an 8-quart pan, combine the loganberries, sugar and butter.

Over medium-low heat, stirring constantly, heat the mixture until the sugar is completely dissolved. Increase the heat to medium-high and bring the mixture to a full rolling boil, stirring constantly. Stir in the entire contents of the pectin pouch. Return the mixture to a full rolling boil, stirring constantly. Boil, stirring constantly, for 1 minute. Remove the pan from the heat. Skim off any foam.

To prevent the jam from separating in the jars, allow the jam to cool 5 minutes before filling the jars. Gently stir the jam every minute or so to distribute the fruit. Ladle the hot jam into hot jars, leaving ¼-inch headspace. Wipe the jar rims and threads with a clean, damp cloth. Cover with hot lids and apply screw rings. Process half-pint jars in a 200F (93C) water bath for 10 minutes, pint jars for 15 minutes.

Mango Jam

Mangoes make a wonderful jam with a vibrant yellow-orange color.

MAKES ABOUT 7 HALF-PINT JARS

4½ cups pitted, peeled and crushed ripe
    mangoes (about 8 medium)
2 tablespoons strained fresh lemon juice
1 tablespoon strained fresh orange juice
7 cups sugar
½ teaspoon unsalted butter
1 (3-ounce) pouch liquid pectin

In an 8-quart pan, combine the mangoes, lemon juice, orange juice and sugar. Cover and let stand for 2 to 3 hours.

Remove the cover. Over medium-low heat, stirring constantly, heat the mixture until the sugar is completely dissolved. Stir in the butter. Increase the heat to medium and bring the mixture to a boil. Reduce the heat and simmer, stirring constantly, for 2 to 3 minutes.

Increase the heat to medium-high and bring the mixture to a full rolling boil, stirring constantly. Stir in the entire contents of the pectin pouch. Return the mixture to a full rolling boil, stirring constantly. Boil, stirring constantly, for 1 minute. Remove the pan from the heat. Skim off any foam.

To prevent the jam from separating in the jars, allow the jam to cool 5 minutes before filling the jars. Gently stir the jam every minute or so to distribute the fruit. Ladle the hot jam into hot jars, leaving ¼-inch headspace. Wipe the jar rims and threads with a clean, damp cloth. Cover with hot lids and apply screw rings. Process half-pint jars in a 200F (93C) water bath for 10 minutes, pint jars for 15 minutes.

Tip

Preparing Mangoes To pit, peel and chop a mango, use a knife to cut through the skin and flesh on the side of the mango until the knife hits the pit. Continue cutting around the mango until you have made a circular cut all the way around the fruit. Holding the mango in the palm of your hand and using a thin-bowled tablespoon, slide the spoon into the cut from the end of the mango. Guide the spoon up and over the pit, sliding the spoon back and forth to the sides until the mango half is separated from the pit. Slide the spoon under the pit and remove the pit from the other half of the mango. With a sharp knife, cut a multiple cross-hatch pattern all the way through the mango flesh, being careful not to cut through the skin. Holding the outer edges of the mango half with your fingers, use your thumbs to push against the center of the skin to gently turn the mango inside out. Slice the mango from the peel in chunks.

Nectarine Jam

White nectarines have a mild flavor and are not recommended for making jam. Cut the fruit in quarters and remove the red fibers from the center before crushing the fruit.

MAKES ABOUT 8 HALF-PINT JARS

4 cups peeled, pitted and crushed ripe
    yellow nectarines (3½ to 4 pounds)
¼ cup strained fresh lemon juice

7½ cups sugar
½ teaspoon unsalted butter
1 (3-ounce) pouch liquid pectin

In an 8-quart pan, combine the nectarines and lemon juice. Stir in about half of the sugar. Cover the pan and let stand for 20 minutes.

Remove the cover. Stir in the remaining sugar and the butter. Over medium-low heat, stirring constantly, heat the mixture until the sugar is completely dissolved. Increase the heat to medium-high and bring the mixture to a full rolling boil, stirring constantly. Remove the pan from the heat and skim off the foam.

Return the pan to the heat and bring the mixture to a full rolling boil. Stir in the entire contents of the pectin pouch. Return the mixture to a full rolling boil, stirring constantly. Boil, stirring constantly, for 1 minute. Remove the pan from the heat. Skim off any foam.

To prevent the jam from separating in the jars, allow the jam to cool 5 minutes before filling the jars. Gently stir the jam every minute or so to distribute the fruit. Ladle the hot jam into hot jars, leaving ¼-inch headspace. Wipe the jar rims and threads with a clean, damp cloth. Cover with hot lids and apply screw rings. Process half-pint jars in a 200F (93C) water bath for 10 minutes, pint jars for 15 minutes.

Onion Jam

This remarkable jam has a delicate herb flavor.

MAKES ABOUT 7 HALF-PINT JARS

2 cups peeled, quartered and thinly sliced
    small red onions
1 cup peeled, quartered and thinly sliced
    small Spanish or brown onions
1½ cups apple juice
¾ cup red wine vinegar
½ teaspoon rubbed ground sage
¼ teaspoon freshly ground black pepper
4½ cups granulated sugar
1 cup firmly packed light brown sugar
½ teaspoon unsalted butter
1 (3-ounce) pouch liquid pectin

❧ In an 8-quart stainless steel pan, combine all ingredients except the pectin.

Over medium-low heat, stirring constantly, heat the mixture until the sugars are completely dissolved. Increase the heat to medium and bring the mixture to a boil. Boil and stir for 5 minutes.

Increase the heat to medium-high and bring the mixture to a full rolling boil, stirring constantly. Stir in the entire contents of the pectin pouch. Return the mixture to a full rolling boil, stirring constantly. Boil and stir for 2 minutes. Remove the pan from the heat.

To prevent the jam from separating in the jars, allow the jam to cool 5 minutes before filling the jars. Gently stir the jam every minute or so to distribute the fruit. Ladle the hot jam into hot jars, leaving ¼-inch headspace. Wipe the jar rims and threads with a clean, damp cloth. Cover with hot lids and apply screw rings. Process half-pint jars in a 200F (93C) water bath for 10 minutes, pint jars for 15 minutes.

Orange Jam

This jam is similar to a marmalade but without the citrus peel. Do not use navel oranges for this recipe; they will become tough and chewy when cooked.

MAKES ABOUT 5 HALF-PINT JARS

15 to 20 medium Valencia oranges
2 tablespoons strained fresh lemon juice
5 cups sugar
½ teaspoon unsalted butter
1 (3-ounce) pouch liquid pectin

❧ Scrub the oranges with a vegetable brush to remove any dirt. Rinse well in cool water and drain.

Using a sharp knife, remove all of the colored peel and outer white membrane. Cut along each side of the tough white connective membrane that separates the fruit segments so they will fall away cleanly. Discard the fibrous white membrane. Remove any seeds from the citrus segments. Discard the seeds. Chop the fruit into small pieces with a sharp knife, saving the juice. Measure 3 cups of fruit and juice.

In an 8-quart stainless steel pan, combine the oranges, lemon juice, sugar and butter.

Over medium-low heat, stirring constantly, heat the mixture until the sugar is completely dissolved. Increase the heat to medium-high and bring the mixture to a boil. Reduce the heat and simmer gently for 5 minutes, stirring frequently.

Increase the heat to medium-high and bring the mixture to a full rolling boil, stirring constantly. Stir in the entire contents of the pectin pouch. Return the mixture to a full rolling boil,

stirring constantly. Boil, stirring constantly, for 1 minute. Remove the pan from the heat.

To prevent the jam from separating in the jars, allow the jam to cool 5 minutes before filling the jars. Gently stir the jam every minute or so to distribute the fruit. Ladle the hot jam into hot jars, leaving ¼-inch headspace. Wipe the jar rims and threads with a clean, damp cloth. Cover with hot lids and apply screw rings. Process half-pint jars in a 200F (93C) water bath for 10 minutes, pint jars for 15 minutes.

Papaya Jam

This tropical jam is a wonderful treat on toast or biscuits.

MAKES 7 TO 8 HALF-PINT JARS

4 cups seeded, peeled and crushed ripe
    papayas (about 8 medium)
2 tablespoons strained fresh lemon juice
1 tablespoon strained fresh orange juice
7 cups sugar
½ teaspoon unsalted butter
1 (3-ounce) pouch liquid pectin

In an 8-quart pan, combine the papayas, lemon juice, orange juice, sugar and butter.

Over medium-low heat, stirring constantly, heat the mixture until the sugar is completely dissolved. Increase the heat to medium-high and bring the mixture to a full rolling boil, stirring constantly. Stir in the entire contents of the pectin pouch. Return the mixture to a full rolling boil, stirring constantly. Boil, stirring constantly, for 1

minute. Remove the pan from the heat. Skim off any foam.

To prevent the jam from separating in the jars, allow the jam to cool 5 minutes before filling the jars. Gently stir the jam every minute or so to distribute the fruit. Ladle the hot jam into hot jars, leaving ¼-inch headspace. Wipe the jar rims and threads with a clean, damp cloth. Cover with hot lids and apply screw rings. Process half-pint jars in a 200F (93C) water bath for 10 minutes, pint jars for 15 minutes.

Tip

Peeling Papayas Here is a quick and easy way to peel a papaya. Rinse and dry the papaya. Cut the papaya in half and use a spoon to remove the seeds. With a sharp knife, cut a multiple cross-hatch pattern all the way through the papaya flesh, being careful not to cut through the skin. Holding the outer edges of the papaya half with your fingers, use your thumbs to push against the center of the skin to gently turn the papaya inside out. Slice the papaya from the peel in chunks.

Peach Jam

When preparing the peaches, cut the fruit in quarters and remove the red fibers from the center before crushing the fruit. The fibers can be tough and stringy when cooked, and the red streaks in the jam can detract from its appearance.

MAKES ABOUT 8 HALF-PINT JARS

4 cups peeled, pitted and crushed ripe
    yellow peaches (3½ to 4 pounds)
¼ cup strained fresh lemon juice

7½ cups sugar

½ teaspoon unsalted butter

1 (3-ounce) pouch liquid pectin

In an 8-quart pan, combine the peaches and lemon juice. Stir in about half of the sugar. Cover the pan and let stand for 20 minutes.

Remove the cover. Stir in the remaining sugar and the butter. Over medium-low heat, stirring constantly, heat the mixture until the sugar is completely dissolved. Increase the heat to medium-high and bring the mixture to a full rolling boil, stirring constantly. Remove the pan from the heat and skim off the foam.

Return the pan to the heat and bring the mixture to a full rolling boil. Stir in the entire contents of the pectin pouch. Return the mixture to a full rolling boil, stirring constantly. Boil, stirring constantly, for 1 minute. Remove the pan from the heat. Skim off any foam.

To prevent the jam from separating in the jars, allow the jam to cool 5 minutes before filling the jars. Gently stir the jam every minute or so to distribute the fruit. Ladle the hot jam into hot jars, leaving ¼-inch headspace. Wipe the jar rims and threads with a clean, damp cloth. Cover with hot lids and apply screw rings. Process half-pint jars in a 200F (93C) water bath for 10 minutes, pint jars for 15 minutes.

Peach-Apricot Jam

A perfectly balanced flavor and a warm, sunny color are two of the highlights of this combined fruit jam.

MAKES ABOUT 7 HALF-PINT JARS

2 cups peeled, pitted and crushed ripe peaches

1¾ cups peeled, pitted and crushed ripe apricots

5 tablespoons strained fresh lemon juice

6⅔ cups sugar

½ teaspoon unsalted butter

1 (3-ounce) pouch liquid pectin

In an 8-quart pan, combine the peaches, apricots and lemon juice. Stir in about half of the sugar. Cover the pan and let stand for 20 minutes.

Remove the cover. Stir in the remaining sugar and the butter. Over medium-low heat, stirring constantly, heat the mixture until the sugar is completely dissolved. Increase the heat to medium-high and bring the mixture to a full rolling boil, stirring constantly. Remove the pan from the heat and skim off the foam.

Return the pan to the heat and bring the mixture to a full rolling boil. Stir in the entire contents of the pectin pouch. Return the mixture to a full rolling boil, stirring constantly. Boil, stirring constantly, for 1 minute. Remove the pan from the heat. Skim off any foam.

To prevent the jam from separating in the jars, allow the jam to cool 5 minutes before filling the jars. Gently stir the jam every minute or so to distribute the fruit. Ladle the hot jam into hot jars, leaving ¼-inch headspace. Wipe the jar rims and threads with a clean, damp cloth. Cover with hot lids and apply screw rings. Process half-pint jars in a 200F (93C) water bath for 10 minutes, pint jars for 15 minutes.

Peach Melba Jam

An exquisite blending of flavors creates a jam of exceptional quality. This recipe earned the first-place Alltrista Premium Food Preservation Award for soft spreads.

MAKES ABOUT 7 HALF-PINT JARS

3 cups peeled, pitted and crushed ripe
    peaches (about 3 pounds)
3 tablespoons strained fresh lemon juice
7¼ cups sugar
1 cup crushed and seeded raspberry pulp
½ teaspoon unsalted butter
1 (3-ounce) pouch liquid pectin

In an 8-quart pan, combine the peaches and lemon juice. Stir in about half of the sugar. Cover the pan and let stand for 20 minutes.

Remove the cover. Stir in the raspberry pulp, remaining sugar and the butter. Over medium-low heat, stirring constantly, heat the mixture until the sugar is completely dissolved. Increase the heat to medium-high and bring the mixture to a full rolling boil, stirring constantly. Remove the pan from the heat and skim off the foam.

Return the pan to the heat and bring the mixture to a full rolling boil. Stir in the entire contents of the pectin pouch. Return the mixture to a full rolling boil, stirring constantly. Boil, stirring con-

stantly, for 1 minute. Remove the pan from the heat. Skim off any foam.

To prevent the jam from separating in the jars, allow the jam to cool 5 minutes before filling the jars. Gently stir the jam every minute or so to distribute the fruit. Ladle the hot jam into hot jars, leaving ¼-inch headspace. Wipe the jar rims and threads with a clean, damp cloth. Cover with hot lids and apply screw rings. Process half-pint jars in a 200F (93C) water bath for 10 minutes, pint jars for 15 minutes.

Pear Jam

Prepare the pears just before making the jam and immediately combine the crushed fruit with the lemon juice to prevent the pears from turning brown.

MAKES ABOUT 8 HALF-PINT JARS

4 cups peeled, cored and crushed ripe
    Bartlett pears (3½ to 4 pounds)
¼ cup strained fresh lemon juice
7½ cups sugar
½ teaspoon unsalted butter
1 (3-ounce) pouch liquid pectin

In an 8-quart pan, combine the pears and lemon juice. Stir in about half of the sugar. Cover the pan and let stand for 20 minutes.

Remove the cover. Stir in the remaining sugar and the butter. Over medium-low heat, stirring constantly, heat the mixture until the sugar is completely dissolved. Increase the heat to medium-high and bring the mixture to a full rolling boil, stirring constantly. Remove the pan from the heat and skim off the foam.

Return the pan to the heat and bring the mixture to a full rolling boil. Stir in the entire contents of the pectin pouch. Return the mixture to a full rolling boil, stirring constantly. Boil, stirring constantly, for 1 minute. Remove the pan from the heat. Skim off any foam.

To prevent the jam from separating in the jars, allow the jam to cool 5 minutes before filling the jars. Gently stir the jam every minute or so to distribute the fruit. Ladle the hot jam into hot jars, leaving ¼-inch headspace. Wipe the jar rims and threads with a clean, damp cloth. Cover with hot lids and apply screw rings. Process half-pint jars in a 200F (93C) water bath for 10 minutes, pint jars for 15 minutes.

Mixed-Pepper Jam

A rainbow of colors makes this lively jam as pretty as it is tasty.

MAKES ABOUT 6 HALF-PINT JARS

1 cup seeded, deribbed and finely chopped red bell peppers (about 2 medium)
¾ cup seeded, deribbed and finely chopped green bell peppers (about 1 large)
¾ cup seeded, deribbed and finely chopped yellow or orange bell peppers (about 1 large)
½ cup seeded and finely chopped jalapeño chile peppers

1 cup cider vinegar
5¼ cups sugar
½ teaspoon unsalted butter
1 (3-ounce) pouch liquid pectin

 In an 8-quart pan, combine the bell peppers, jalapeño peppers, cider vinegar and sugar.

Over medium-low heat, stirring constantly, heat the mixture until the sugar is completely dissolved. Stir in the butter. Increase the heat to medium and bring the mixture to a boil. Reduce the heat and simmer, stirring constantly, for 1 to 2 minutes.

Increase the heat to medium-high and bring the mixture to a full rolling boil, stirring constantly. Stir in the entire contents of the pectin pouch. Return the mixture to a full rolling boil, stirring constantly. Boil, stirring constantly, for 1 minute. Remove the pan from the heat. Skim off any foam.

To prevent the jam from separating in the jars, allow the jam to cool 5 minutes before filling the jars. Gently stir the jam every minute or so to distribute the peppers. Ladle the hot jam into hot jars, leaving ¼-inch headspace. Wipe the jar rims and threads with a clean, damp cloth. Cover with hot lids and apply screw rings. Process half-pint jars in a 200F (93C) water bath for 10 minutes, pint jars for 15 minutes.

Fresh Pineapple Jam

Depending on the juice content of the pineapple, this jam can have a slightly softer set than most and also makes a wonderful ice-cream topping.

MAKES 6 TO 7 HALF-PINT JARS

4 cups pared, cored and finely chopped
    fresh, ripe pineapple (about 5 pounds)
6 cups sugar
2 tablespoons stained fresh lemon juice
½ teaspoon unsalted butter
1 (3-ounce) pouch liquid pectin

❦ In an 8-quart pan, combine the pineapple, sugar and lemon juice. Cover and let stand 1 hour.

Remove the cover. Over medium-low heat, stirring constantly, heat the mixture until the sugar is completely dissolved. Stir in the butter. Increase the heat to medium-high and bring the mixture to a gentle boil. Reduce the heat and cook for 10 minutes, stirring occasionally to prevent sticking.

Increase the heat to medium-high and bring the mixture to a full rolling boil, stirring constantly. Stir in the entire contents of the pectin pouch. Return the mixture to a full rolling boil, stirring constantly. Boil, stirring constantly, for 1 minute. Remove the pan from the heat. Skim off any foam.

To prevent the jam from separating in the jars, allow the jam to cool 5 minutes before filling the jars. Gently stir the jam every minute or so to distribute the fruit. Ladle the hot jam into hot jars, leaving ¼-inch headspace. Wipe the jar rims and threads with a clean, damp cloth. Cover with hot lids and apply screw rings. Process half-pint jars in a 200F (93C) water bath for 10 minutes, pint jars for 15 minutes.

Santa Rosa Plum Jam

I like to use Santa Rosa plums, which have a full plum flavor and exquisite jewel-tone color, although other plum varieties could be used in this recipe. Plum jam recipes traditionally call for leaving the skins on the plums, but I prefer the silky-smooth texture achieved by removing the peels.

This jam has earned several blue ribbons and perfect scores, impressing the judges with its beautiful color and wonderful flavor. It was the unanimous choice of the judges, above all other jam entries, as the winner of the first-place award in the prestigious Sure-Jell Jam Competition at the California State Fair.

MAKES 8 TO 9 HALF-PINT JARS

4½ cups pitted, peeled and crushed ripe
    Santa Rosa plums
7½ cups sugar
½ teaspoon unsalted butter
1 (3-ounce) pouch liquid pectin

❦ In an 8-quart pan, combine the plums and sugar. Cover and let stand 20 minutes.

Remove the cover. Over medium-low heat, stirring constantly, heat the mixture until the sugar is completely dissolved. Increase the heat to medium-high and bring the plum mixture to a boil. Boil for 2 minutes, stirring gently. Remove the pan from the heat and skim off the foam.

Return the pan to the heat and bring to a boil. Boil for 1 minute, stirring constantly. Remove the pan from the heat and skim off the foam.

Stir in the butter. Over medium-high heat, bring the mixture to a full rolling boil, stirring constantly. Stir in the entire contents of the pectin pouch. Return the mixture to a full rolling boil,

stirring constantly. Boil, stirring constantly, for 1 minute. Remove the pan from the heat. Skim off any foam.

To prevent the jam from separating in the jars, allow the jam to cool 5 minutes before filling the jars. Gently stir the jam every minute or so to distribute the fruit. Ladle the hot jam into hot jars, leaving ¼-inch headspace. Wipe the jar rims and threads with a clean, damp cloth. Cover with hot lids and apply screw rings. Process half-pint jars in a 200F (93C) water bath for 10 minutes, pint jars for 15 minutes.

Raspberry Jam

Before measuring the raspberries, sieve about ¾ of the crushed fruit to remove the seeds or the finished jam will be mostly seeds. While fresh raspberries usually make the best jam, frozen berries also produce a very good jam. A 12-ounce bag of frozen raspberries will yield about 1½ cups of crushed fruit or about 1 cup of seedless pulp.

MAKES ABOUT 7 HALF-PINT JARS

4 cups crushed fresh, ripe raspberries (6 to 8 pint baskets)
1 tablespoon strained fresh lemon juice
6½ cups sugar
½ teaspoon unsalted butter
1 (3-ounce) pouch liquid pectin

In an 8-quart pan, combine the raspberries, lemon juice, sugar and butter.

Over medium-low heat, stirring constantly, heat the mixture until the sugar is completely dis-

solved. Increase the heat to medium-high and bring the mixture to a full rolling boil, stirring constantly. Stir in the entire contents of the pectin pouch. Return the mixture to a full rolling boil, stirring constantly. Boil, stirring constantly, for 1 minute. Remove the pan from the heat. Skim off any foam.

To prevent the jam from separating in the jars, allow the jam to cool 5 minutes before filling the jars. Gently stir the jam every minute or so to distribute the fruit. Ladle the hot jam into hot jars leaving, ¼-inch headspace. Wipe the jar rims and threads with a clean, damp cloth. Cover with hot lids and apply screw rings. Process half-pint jars in a 200F (93C) water bath for 10 minutes, pint jars for 15 minutes.

Raspberry-Blueberry Jam

Crush the raspberries and press them through a fine-meshed sieve to remove the seeds before measuring.

MAKES ABOUT 7 HALF-PINT JARS

2 cups crushed and seeded raspberry pulp
1¼ cups crushed blueberries
1 tablespoon strained fresh lemon juice
5¼ cups sugar
½ teaspoon unsalted butter
1 (3-ounce) pouch liquid pectin

In an 8-quart pan, combine the raspberry pulp, blueberries, lemon juice, sugar and butter.

Over medium-low heat, stirring constantly, heat the mixture until the sugar is completely dissolved. Increase the heat to medium-high and bring the mixture to a full rolling boil, stirring constantly. Stir in the entire contents of the pectin pouch. Return the mixture to a full rolling boil, stirring constantly. Boil, stirring constantly, for 1 minute. Remove the pan from the heat. Skim off any foam.

To prevent the jam from separating in the jars, allow the jam to cool 5 minutes before filling the jars. Gently stir the jam every minute or so to distribute the fruit. Ladle the hot jam into hot jars, leaving ¼-inch headspace. Wipe the jar rims and threads with a clean, damp cloth. Cover with hot lids and apply screw rings. Process half-pint jars in a 200F (93C) water bath for 10 minutes, pint jars for 15 minutes.

Salsa Jam

I created this recipe for family members and friends who wanted a jam with more zip and zing. This festive spread earned first place in the Sure-Jell Jam Competition at the 2000 California State Fair when the judges declared it "An A+ jam!" It will liven up your breakfast toast and is also great served on crackers spread with cream cheese.

MAKES ABOUT 5 HALF-PINT JARS

2 cups peeled, seeded and chopped ripe
    plum tomatoes
⅔ cup chopped red onion
⅔ cup tomato sauce
3 tablespoons seeded and finely chopped
    jalapeño chile peppers
3 tablespoons strained fresh lime juice

1½ teaspoons finely minced lime zest
¼ teaspoon Tabasco sauce or other hot
    pepper sauce
5 cups sugar
1 (3-ounce) pouch liquid pectin

In an 8-quart stainless steel pan, combine the tomatoes, onion, tomato sauce and peppers.

Over medium heat, stirring constantly, bring the mixture to a boil. Reduce the heat and simmer gently for 5 minutes, stirring frequently to prevent sticking. Add in the lime juice, zest and hot pepper sauce. Gradually stir in the sugar.

Over medium-low heat, stirring constantly, heat the mixture until the sugar is completely dissolved. Increase the heat to medium-high and bring the mixture to a full rolling boil, stirring constantly. Stir in the entire contents of the pectin pouch. Return the mixture to a full rolling boil, stirring constantly. Boil, stirring constantly, for 1 minute. Remove the pan from the heat.

To prevent the jam from separating in the jars, allow the jam to cool 5 minutes before filling the jars. Gently stir the jam every minute or so to distribute the salsa. Ladle the hot jam into hot jars, leaving ¼-inch headspace. Wipe the jar rims and threads with a clean, damp cloth. Cover with hot lids and apply screw rings. Process half-pint jars in a 200F (93C) water bath for 10 minutes, pint jars for 15 minutes.

Seedless Berry Jam

This recipe, which may produce a slightly softer set jam, will work well for most varieties of seeded berries, such as blackberries, boysenberries and loganberries.

MAKES 6 TO 7 HALF-PINT JARS

4 cups crushed and seeded fresh, ripe
    berries (6 to 8 pint baskets)
6¾ cups sugar
½ teaspoon unsalted butter
1 (3-ounce) pouch liquid pectin

❧ In an 8-quart pan, combine the berries, sugar and butter.

Over medium-low heat, stirring constantly, heat the mixture until the sugar is completely dissolved. Increase the heat to medium-high and bring the mixture to a full rolling boil, stirring constantly. Stir in the entire contents of the pectin pouch. Return the mixture to a full rolling boil, stirring constantly. Boil, stirring constantly, for 1 minute. Remove the pan from the heat. Skim off any foam.

Ladle the hot jam into hot jars, leaving ¼-inch headspace. Wipe the jar rims and threads with a clean, damp cloth. Cover with hot lids and apply screw rings. Process half-pint jars in a 200F (93C) water bath for 10 minutes, pint jars for 15 minutes.

Strawberry Jam

This delightful favorite is the winner of multiple blue ribbons and specialty awards.

Use strawberries as soon after harvest as possible and always on the same day. If you must wait a few hours after picking before you can use them, cover the unwashed berries with a piece of waxed paper and store them in the refrigerator. Wash the berries just before using. Chop the berries, then lightly crush them in small batches. Do not thoroughly mash or puree the berries, just crush the pieces enough to release the juice.

MAKES ABOUT 9 HALF-PINT JARS

4 cups hulled and crushed ripe strawberries
    (about 2 quarts whole berries)
2 tablespoons strained fresh lemon juice
7 cups sugar
½ teaspoon unsalted butter
1 (3-ounce) pouch liquid pectin

❧ In an 8-quart pan, combine the strawberries, lemon juice and sugar. Cover and let stand for 2 hours.

Remove the cover. Over medium-low heat, stirring constantly, heat the mixture until the sugar is completely dissolved. Stir in the butter. Increase the heat to medium-high and bring the mixture to a full rolling boil, stirring constantly. Stir in the entire contents of the pectin pouch. Return the mixture to a full rolling boil, stirring constantly. Boil, stirring constantly, for 1 minute. Remove the pan from the heat. Skim off any foam.

To prevent the jam from separating in the jars, allow the jam to cool 5 minutes before filling the jars. Gently stir the jam every minute or so to distribute the fruit. Ladle the hot jam into hot jars, leaving ¼-inch headspace. Wipe the jar rims and threads with a clean, damp cloth. Cover with hot lids and apply screw rings. Process half-pint jars in a 200F (93C) water bath for 10 minutes, pint jars for 15 minutes.

Strawberry-Pineapple Jam

This jam has a great combination of flavors. Be sure to check the crushed pineapple for any large chunks and cut any you find into small pieces before adding it to the strawberry mixture.

MAKES ABOUT 8 HALF-PINT JARS

3 cups hulled and crushed ripe strawberries
  (about 1½ quarts whole berries)
1 cup drained canned crushed pineapple
6½ cups sugar
½ teaspoon unsalted butter
1 (3-ounce) pouch liquid pectin

In an 8-quart pan, combine the strawberries, pineapple, sugar and butter.

Over medium-low heat, stirring constantly, heat the mixture until the sugar is completely dissolved. Increase the heat to medium-high and bring the mixture to a full rolling boil, stirring constantly. Stir in the entire contents of the pectin pouch. Return the mixture to a full rolling boil, stirring constantly. Boil, stirring constantly, for 1 minute. Remove the pan from the heat. Skim off any foam.

To prevent the jam from separating in the jars, allow the jam to cool 5 minutes before filling the

jars. Gently stir the jam every minute or so to distribute the fruit. Ladle the hot jam into hot jars, leaving ¼-inch headspace. Wipe the jar rims and threads with a clean, damp cloth. Cover with hot lids and apply screw rings. Process half-pint jars in a 200F (93C) water bath for 10 minutes, pint jars for 15 minutes.

Strawberry-Raspberry Jam

The ruby jewel-tone color and strong berry flavors make this jam a winner.

MAKES 7 TO 8 HALF-PINT JARS

2 cups hulled and crushed ripe strawberries
2 cups crushed and seeded raspberry pulp
1 tablespoon strained fresh lemon juice
6¾ cups sugar
½ teaspoon unsalted butter
1 (3-ounce) pouch liquid pectin

In an 8-quart pan, combine the strawberries, raspberry pulp, lemon juice, sugar and butter.

Over medium-low heat, stirring constantly, heat the mixture until the sugar is completely dissolved. Increase the heat to medium-high and bring the mixture to a full rolling boil, stirring constantly. Stir in the entire contents of the pectin pouch. Return the mixture to a full rolling boil, stirring constantly. Boil, stirring constantly, for 1 minute. Remove the pan from the heat. Skim off the foam.

To prevent the jam from separating in the jars, allow the jam to cool 5 minutes before filling the jars. Gently stir the jam every minute or so to distribute the fruit. Ladle the hot jam into hot jars, leaving ¼-inch headspace. Wipe the jar rims and threads with a clean, damp cloth. Cover with hot lids and apply screw rings. Process half-pint jars in a 200F (93C) water bath for 10 minutes, pint jars for 15 minutes.

Tropical Sunrise Jam

An exotic blending of fruits, this jam is bursting with flavor.

MAKES ABOUT 7 HALF-PINT JARS

1¾ cups peeled, pitted and crushed ripe
    apricots
2 tablespoons fresh lemon juice
¾ cup pitted, peeled and crushed Santa
    Rosa or other red plums
¾ cup pitted, peeled and crushed mangoes
¾ cup drained canned crushed pineapple
5¾ cups sugar
½ teaspoon unsalted butter
1 (3-ounce) pouch liquid pectin

In an 8-quart pan, combine the apricots and lemon juice. Stir in the plums, mangoes, pineapple, sugar and butter.

Over medium-low heat, stirring constantly, heat the mixture until the sugar is completely dissolved. Increase the heat to medium-high and bring the mixture to a full rolling boil, stirring constantly. Stir in the entire contents of the pectin pouch. Return the mixture to a full rolling boil, stirring constantly. Boil, stirring constantly, for 1 minute. Remove the pan from the heat. Skim off the foam.

To prevent the jam from separating in the jars, allow the jam to cool 5 minutes before filling the jars. Gently stir the jam every minute or so to distribute the fruit. Ladle the hot jam into hot jars, leaving ¼-inch headspace. Wipe the jar rims and threads with a clean, damp cloth. Cover with hot lids and apply screw rings. Process half-pint jars in a 200F (93C) water bath for 10 minutes, pint jars for 15 minutes.

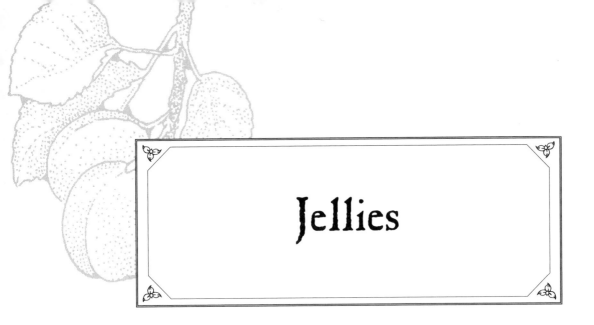

Jellies

WHAT IS A JELLY?

Jellies are translucent spreads that are made from strained or filtered fruit juice. High-quality jellies are crystal clear and shimmering with a vibrant color. Jellies should be firm, cut easily and cleanly with a knife and hold their shape, yet still be tender and spread easily.

Making Jelly

A perfect jelly is not difficult to create, but it does require both time and patience. Jelly-making is the most time-consuming of all the soft spreads. Cutting corners and rushing the straining process will only lead to disappointing results and an inferior jelly. Making jelly is a two-step process. Before you can make jelly, the juice must first be extracted from the fruit and filtered to make it perfectly clear. In the second step, the juice is heated and combined with the sugar, pectin and acid. When finished, the juice mixture will be transformed into a wonderful jelly.

Because of the amount of preparation involved in making jellies, they require more time to can than other soft spreads. The jelly-making process is best spread out over 2 days. Extract the juice from the fruit, strain and filter it on one day, let any sediment in the juice settle to the bottom overnight in the refrigerator. On the second day, filter the juice again and make the jelly.

Recipes should not be doubled when making jelly. Doubling the volume of jelly cooked in the pan does not allow enough surface area for evaporation and may result in a jelly that does not set. This is a common mistake made by many home canners and is often the reason some cooks believe that making jelly or other soft spreads is too difficult. While some canners may be able to get a double batch of jam to set well enough, jelly is not very forgiving in this area. In other words, instead of jars of perfectly set jelly, you may end up with a double-size batch of syrup.

For any home canner, the truest test of his or her ability, patience and skill is the clarity of the canner's jellies. Many homemade jellies appear cloudy because the juice was not filtered to remove the minute particles that prevent a clear jelly. To test the clarity of a jelly, hold it up to the light. The jelly should sparkle, and you should be able to see through the jar. If the jelly is hazy or cloudy, some of the fine particulate matter was not filtered from the juice before making the jelly, or the jelly was not handled properly when filling the jars. While the jelly may taste great and is fine for sharing with family and friends, it would not earn a perfect score from fair judges.

Jelly competitions at fairs can be intense, and the flavor, texture and clarity must be exceptional to win top awards. I was delighted when out of the hundreds of jelly entries at the Los Angeles County Fair, my special collection of jellies was chosen as the Best of Division winner for jelly. The judges decided that it was far more difficult to produce six different outstanding, crystal-clear jellies, than it was to make any single variety of jelly. The judges' comments included "Exceptional jellies" and "Amazing clarity." It was the only time a Best of Division has ever been awarded to a special collection competing against the individual class entries. It is a feat that will never be repeated, because the following year the Los Angeles County Fair grouped special collections of preserved foods into their own separate division.

Special Equipment and Techniques
Jelly Bag or Cheesecloth-Lined Sieve

A fabric mesh bag usually suspended from a metal stand, a jelly bag is commonly used in jelly-making to separate the fruit juice from the pulp. But commercially produced jelly bags do not work very well. Most of these jelly bags are too small to hold all of the fruit needed to be strained for a batch of jelly. Because of their cone-shaped design, the juice must travel a long way to the bottom of the bag before it can drip into the bowl below. The fruit pulp clogs the pores of the bag and slows down the straining. This makes for a very slow process, often taking more than 24 hours to obtain enough juice to make jelly.

The tightness of the weave of the jelly bags varies greatly depending on the manufacturer. Some bags have a more open weave that allows the juice to flow through more rapidly, but also increases the amount of fine pulp that remains in the juice, leading to cloudy jelly. Other bags are woven so tightly that they quickly become clogged with pulp and stop working. The bag must be emptied, rinsed out, refilled and the process started again. Often the blockage will have to be cleared several times during straining. This becomes very frustrating and many home canners start squeezing the bag to speed up the extraction process. The result, again, is juice containing fine pulp that makes for a cloudy jelly.

Another problem with jelly bags is that the metal frame that holds the bag is designed to attach to the top rim of a bowl or pan. This means that the juice has a long way to drip. When the juice hits the bottom of the bowl it splashes back up, often out of the bowl and onto the counter or table. This is not only messy, but precious juice is lost as well.

Instead of a commercial jelly bag, I prefer to use a large sieve lined with cheesecloth to separate the fruit pulp from the juice. I find it allows the juice to flow freer and faster while producing a clearer juice, which results in a clearer jelly. Cheesecloth should always be dampened before use to minimize the amount of juice that is absorbed by the fabric.

When using cheesecloth for jelly-making,

select a sturdy cloth with a tight weave. The best brand that I have found and highly recommend is made by Norpro. It has a tight, uniform weave and is made of top-quality material. Best of all, it is less expensive than most of the large-meshed, lesser-quality cheesecloths found in grocery and hardware stores. If you have difficulty finding Norpro cheesecloth in your local stores, it can be ordered by mail (see Mail-Order Sources, page 337). Should you decide to use a cheesecloth with a loose, open weave, use several layers and do not unfold it or much of the small fruit pulp will slip through the weave and into the juice, making the jelly cloudy.

Cloudy Jelly

Cloudy jelly can also result from poor juice extraction techniques, cooking the fruit too long before straining off the juice or from using underripe or green fruit. Unripe fruit, especially apples, contain a high level of starch that can cause a clear jelly to turn cloudy within weeks after canning. Because of this starch content, homemade pectins, which are primarily made from unripe apples, should not be used to make jellies or other soft spreads.

While adding a small amount of butter to other soft spreads can help to reduce the amount of foaming that occurs during cooking and can add richness to the flavor, butter should not be added to jellies, as it will make them cloudy.

Selecting Fruit for Jellies

Always use fully ripe fruit when making jelly. Fruit that is completely ripe will yield a larger quantity of juice with a more intense flavor. Underripe fruit will produce less juice with a weaker flavor, while the use of overripe fruit will result in a jelly that tastes overripe or spoiled.

Fresh fruit is usually preferred for making jelly because frozen fruit is frequently underripe and yields a poor flavor. The exception is frozen berries. They can be used to make great jelly. The freezing and defrosting process breaks down the delicate cell structure in berries such as raspberries, boysenberries, blackberries and blueberries, increasing both the quantity and clarity of the juice obtained from the fruit. Frozen strawberries will also produce a greater amount of clear juice, but the fruit is usually frozen substantially underripe and therefore has far less flavor. I prefer using only the fresh, fully ripe strawberries that I purchase directly from a local field stand, the same morning they are harvested, for making my strawberry jellies, jams and preserves.

Preparing Fruit

Rinse the fruit in clear, cool water, being sure to remove all dirt, dust or sand. Drain the fruit well on paper towels and dry completely. Excess water on the fruit will dilute the flavor strength of the juice and the taste of the finished jelly. Do not allow delicate, soft-skinned fruits to stand in the water. Their fragile cell structure will break down quickly and their quality will rapidly decrease. Water will be absorbed into the fruit, diluting the strength of its flavor and forcing some of the precious, flavorful juice out into the rinse water. The extracted fruit juice will be watered down, lacking a full, rich flavor.

Jelly is the one soft spread that is the exception to the rule of only preparing the fruit for one batch of preserves at a time. Because of the lengthy extraction process, the quantities of fruit prepared may be doubled and the fruit for two batches of the same flavor of jelly extracted and strained together. After the juice is filtered, it should be measured into individual batch quantities and then each batch of jelly made separately.

If you will be doing a lot of jelly-making at one time, the juice for two or more different kinds of jelly may be prepared one day, refrigerated and the jellies made the next day. However, the juice should not be kept for more than 2 days before being turned into jelly because it can begin to deteriorate and lose its intense, fresh flavor. Juices kept for several days can also develop mold spores, leading to spoilage.

Extracting Juice for Jelly

When making jelly, do not puree or thoroughly crush the fruit, as minute particles of pulp or sediment will remain in the juice after filtering, causing the finished jelly to be cloudy. To release the juice from the cells of the fruit, chop or gently crush and heat the fruit as instructed in the individual recipe. Place a large fine-meshed sieve over a large bowl or pan. Carefully pour or spoon the heated fruit and juice into the sieve. Allow the juice to drain from the fruit. This may take 1 to 2 hours or more, depending on the juiciness of the fruit used.

If the dripping process dramatically slows down after a while or even stops before the extraction of juice is completed, a layer of drained pulp has probably built up against the inside of the sieve. To release more juice, the fruit in the center of the sieve may be gently stirred with a small spoon or knife. Be careful not to scrape the sides of the sieve or press any of the pulp through the sieve, as this will cause the juice to be cloudy.

Another method of straining the juice from the fruit is to line the sieve with the 2 layers of fine-meshed, damp cheesecloth, but leave several extra inches of the fabric overhanging the edges of the sieve. Spoon the fruit and juice into the sieve. Tie the ends of the cheesecloth together securely, making sure that no fruit can escape, yet not tying it so snugly that you squeeze the fruit inside. Slip a strong wooden spoon or long stainless steel utensil under the knot and suspend the cheesecloth bag over the pan or bowl, leaving ample room for the juice to drip. Let the fruit drip for at least 3 to 4 hours before checking the quantity of juice. Be careful in handling the cheesecloth bag so that the bag does not rest up against any surface. To prevent cloudy jelly, do not squeeze the cheesecloth to extract the juice or to speed up the process.

After the juice has been separated from the fruit during the initial straining process, tiny bits of pulp will still remain, suspended in the juice, giving it a somewhat murky appearance. This remaining pulp will cause the finished jelly to appear cloudy. Most, if not all, of this pulp can be removed, improving the clarity of both the juice and the jelly.

Strain the juice again by slowly pouring it through a sieve lined with 4 layers of damp, fine-meshed cheesecloth. If the juice is particularly cloudy or contains a lot of fine pulp, the process will gradually slow and the juice will not flow freely through the cheesecloth. This reduced flow will be caused by a layer of "sludge" developing in the bottom of the cheesecloth. Stop straining and pour the unstrained juice back into your container. Rinse the cheesecloth under cool running water to remove the sludge. Squeeze out the excess water from the cheesecloth after rinsing so that the cheesecloth is lightly damp but not dripping. Reline the sieve with the cheesecloth and begin straining again. Repeat this procedure as needed until all of the juice has been strained.

Filtering the Juice

When the extraction and straining process is complete, measure the amount of juice obtained. You should have at least 1 cup more juice than the final measurement called for in the recipe. Each step in the filtering process will slightly reduce the amount of juice, and this extra quantity will allow you to filter the juice for perfect clarity. If the quantity of juice extracted from the fruit is insufficient to allow for filtering, prepare and extract juice from additional fruit. Or you can combine 1 cup of water with the remaining fruit pulp and strain it again through 2 layers of clean, damp cheesecloth to produce more juice. Be aware that this will weaken the flavor of the juice and, consequently, the finished jelly and should only be done as a last resort. It is much better to prepare additional fruit and extract the juice than to water down the flavor. Jelly may be made without filtering the juice, but be aware that the jelly will be cloudy.

While filtering the juice is not absolutely necessary, it is highly recommended, especially if you intend to enter your jelly into competition at a fair. A blue ribbon quality jelly, in addition to having great flavor, perfect texture and a beautiful color, must also be crystal clear and shimmering. It should be so clear that you can see through it when the jar is held up to the light. Many fair judges use the light test to determine the clarity of the jellies that pass before them.

To filter juice for crystal-clear jelly, line a small sieve with a paper coffee filter. Place the sieve over a large, clean bowl or pan. Using a measuring cup, pour part of the strained juice into the filter. Cover the sieve loosely with a piece of plastic wrap and let the juice drip undisturbed. When the dripping stops, pour any unfiltered juice back into the measuring cup, replace the filter with a new one and pour more juice into the lined sieve. Continue this process until all of the juice has been filtered. You may need to replace the paper filter several times to strain all of the juice. I usually speed up the process by using 2 or 3 sieves lined with coffee filters, each placed over a separate bowl or pan.

After all of the juice has been filtered, refrigerate it for several hours or overnight to allow any sediment to settle to the bottom. Filter the juice again through 2 layers of paper coffee filters stacked together in a sieve placed over a clean bowl or pan. Pour or ladle the juice into the lined sieve, being careful not to disturb any sediment resting on the bottom of the container. Discard the sediment. Replace the paper filters when the dripping stops. For the clearest jelly, filter juice again through 4 layers of paper coffee filters.

If you are an experienced jelly maker and have never taken the time to filter the juice before making a jelly, you may be quite surprised by the difference in clarity achieved by following this procedure. Filtering not only improves the clarity of the jelly but the texture and color as well. A filtered jelly is smooth, without any graininess, and the jewel-tone colors shimmer and dance in the light. It does take extra time to filter the juice, but it is worth the effort. You will impress your friends, family and the fair judges as well with the superior quality and clarity of your jellies.

Cooking Jelly

Heat the filtered juice over low heat until warm. Add the sugar and stir until it is completely dissolved. Any particles of undissolved sugar that remain in the juice may cause crystals to form in the finished jelly. Crystallization can occur if too much sugar is used or if the juice is brought to a boil before the sugar is completely dissolved.

Undissolved sugar can also cause the jelly to weep (when some of the juice separates from the set spread and accumulates on the top of the jelly and also between the jelly and the sides of the jar). Weeping can also result from storing the jelly in a location that is too warm. Any signs of weeping will have a significant impact on the score of a jelly entered into competition.

When the sugar is dissolved, increase the heat and bring the juice to a full rolling boil. As soon as the juice and sugar mixture reaches a full rolling boil, add the entire contents of the liquid pectin pouch. Additional boiling before adding the pectin will cause too much liquid to evaporate, and the finished jelly may turn into a rubbery mass. After adding the pectin, return the mixture to a full rolling boil, stirring constantly to distribute the pectin evenly throughout the jelly. When the mixture returns to a full rolling boil, set a timer for 1 minute. Boil the jelly, stirring constantly, for exactly 1 minute, then remove the pan from the heat.

Filling the Jars

After filtering the juice, filling the jars is the next most crucial step in making jelly. Before adding the pectin to the jelly, set the hot jars right side up on the counter, ready to be filled. Stir the pectin into the juice and cook and stir as indicated in the recipe. Remove the pan from the heat and quickly skim off any foam. IMMEDIATELY ladle the jelly into the jars, filling all jars before wiping the rims and sealing with lids.

Do not allow the jelly to stand in the pan for even a moment or the top surface of the jelly will quickly cool and set, forming a thin skin. This skin is extremely difficult to skim off and will break up when the jelly is stirred or ladled into the jars. The result will be small, wispy strands of skin suspended in the jars of otherwise clear jelly.

Pour the hot jelly into the jars quickly, keeping the ladle close to the funnel. Pouring the jelly slowly into the jars or from a height above the funnel can trap air bubbles in the jelly. Attempting to remove these air bubbles can also lead to wispy strands developing in the jars. While these small imperfections will not affect the taste of the spread, they will severely impact the overall appearance of the jelly. They will also result in reduced scores for exhibits in fair competitions.

Never tip the pan and pour the jelly directly from the pan into the jars. Any undissolved sugar clinging to the side of the pan will be picked up by the jelly and form hard crystals in the jelly as it cools. Always use a ladle and a canning funnel to transfer the jelly from the pan to the jars.

When the jars have all been filled, wipe the jar rims and threads with a clean, damp cloth and apply the hot lids and screw rings. Process all jars of jelly in a water bath canner. Using paraffin is no longer an acceptable method for sealing jars of jelly or any other soft spread. When lowering the jars into the water bath, use a jar lifter and keep the jars upright. Tipping the jars may cause the surface skin on the jelly to break and become suspended in the jelly.

Apple Jelly

Select unblemished apples that are fully ripe. Choose a variety with a good flavor, such as Granny Smith, McIntosh or Gravenstein. The wonderful clarity and great flavor of this jelly impressed the judges.

MAKES 8 TO 9 HALF-PINT JARS

Apple Juice
5 pounds fully ripe tart apples, cored and chopped
4 cups water

Jelly Ingredients
5 cups apple juice
7½ cups sugar
1 (3-ounce) pouch liquid pectin

To extract the juice: In an 8-quart pan, combine the apples and water. Over medium-high heat, bring the mixture to a boil. Reduce the heat, cover and simmer gently until soft, 20 to 30 minutes. Remove the pan from the heat. Let stand for 30 minutes.

Place a sieve over a large pan or bowl. Ladle the cooked apples into the sieve and strain the juice from the pulp. Discard the pulp. Rinse the sieve thoroughly and line it with 3 to 4 layers of clean, damp cheesecloth. Strain the juice through the cheesecloth 2 times, rinsing the cheesecloth between each straining. Line the sieve with a paper coffee filter and strain the juice again. Cover the juice and refrigerate for several hours or overnight.

Ladle or pour the juice into another container, being careful not to disturb or pick up any of the sediment from the bottom of the original container. Discard the sediment. Place a fine-meshed sieve over a pan or bowl. Line the sieve with a paper coffee filter and strain the juice. For a crystal-clear jelly, strain the juice through 2 or 3 layered paper coffee filters. Measure 5 cups of juice.

To make the jelly: In an 8-quart pan, over medium heat, heat the juice until warm. Add the sugar and heat, stirring constantly, until the sugar is completely dissolved. Increase the heat to medium-high and bring the mixture to a full rolling boil, stirring constantly. Stir in the entire contents of the pectin pouch. Return the mixture to a full rolling boil, stirring constantly. Boil, stirring constantly, for 1 minute. Remove the pan from the heat.

Quickly skim off any foam and immediately ladle the hot jelly into hot jars, leaving ¼-inch headspace. Wipe the jar rims and threads with a clean, damp cloth. Cover with hot lids and apply screw rings. Process half-pint jars in a 200F (93C) water bath for 10 minutes, pint jars for 15 minutes.

Easy Apple Cider Jelly

Here is an apple jelly that is quick and easy to make. I have won blue ribbons with this recipe as well.

MAKES 7 TO 8 HALF-PINT JARS

3¾ cups bottled apple cider
7 cups sugar
2 (3-ounce) pouches liquid pectin

Place a sieve over a large pan or bowl. Line the sieve with a paper coffee filter and strain the cider.

In an 8-quart pan, over medium heat, heat the cider until warm. Add the sugar and heat, stirring constantly, until the sugar is completely dissolved. Increase the heat to medium-high and bring the mixture to a full rolling boil, stirring constantly. Stir in the entire contents of both pectin pouches. Return the mixture to a full rolling boil, stirring constantly. Boil, stirring constantly, for 1 minute. Remove the pan from the heat.

Quickly skim off any foam and immediately ladle the hot jelly into hot jars, leaving ¼-inch headspace. Wipe the jar rims and threads with a clean, damp cloth. Cover with hot lids and apply screw rings. Process half-pint jars in a 200F (93C) water bath for 10 minutes, pint jars for 15 minutes.

Apricot Jelly

This is a beautiful orange-colored jelly with a pleasant apricot flavor.

MAKES 5 TO 6 HALF-PINT JARS

Apricot Juice
5 cups peeled, pitted and chopped fresh ripe apricots
1½ cups water

Jelly Ingredients
3 cups apricot juice
⅓ cup filtered fresh lemon juice
5¾ cups sugar
2 (3-ounce) pouches liquid pectin

To extract the juice: In a 4-quart stainless steel pan, combine the apricots and water. Over medium-high heat, bring the mixture to a boil. Reduce the heat, cover and simmer gently for 5 minutes. Remove the pan from the heat. Skim off any foam. Let stand, covered, for 20 minutes.

Place a sieve over a large pan or bowl. Ladle the cooked apricots into the sieve and strain the juice from the pulp. Discard the pulp. Rinse the sieve thoroughly and line it with 3 to 4 layers of clean, damp cheesecloth. Strain the juice through the cheesecloth two times, rinsing the cheesecloth between each straining. Line the sieve with a paper coffee filter and strain the juice again. Cover the juice and refrigerate for several hours or overnight.

Ladle or pour the juice into another container, being careful not to disturb or pick up any of the sediment from the bottom of the original container. Discard the sediment. Place a fine-meshed sieve over a pan or bowl. Line the sieve with a paper coffee filter and strain the juice. For a clearer jelly, strain the juice through 2 or 3 layered paper coffee filters. Measure 3 cups of juice.

To make the jelly: In an 8-quart pan, combine the apricot juice and lemon juice.

Over medium heat, heat the juice until warm. Add the sugar and heat, stirring constantly, until the sugar is completely dissolved. Increase the heat to medium-high and bring the mixture to a full rolling boil, stirring constantly. Stir in the entire contents of both pectin pouches. Return the mixture to a full rolling boil, stirring constantly. Boil, stirring constantly, for 1 minute. Remove the pan from the heat.

Quickly skim off any foam and immediately ladle the hot jelly into hot jars, leaving ¼-inch headspace. Wipe the jar rims and threads with a clean, damp cloth. Cover with hot lids and apply screw rings. Process half-pint jars in a 200F (93C) water bath for 10 minutes, pint jars for 15 minutes.

Blackberry Jelly

Frozen blackberries also make very good jelly.
MAKES ABOUT 8 HALF-PINT JARS

Blackberry Juice
3 quarts ripe blackberries
½ cup water

Jelly Ingredients
5 cups blackberry juice
7½ cups sugar
2 (3-ounce) pouches liquid pectin

To extract the juice: Gently rinse the blackberries in cool water and drain well. If using frozen berries, defrost the berries, but do not rinse them. In a flat-bottomed bowl or pan, use a vegetable masher or large spoon to gently crush the blackberries, one batch at a time, to release the juice.

In an 8-quart stainless steel pan, combine the crushed blackberries and water. Over medium-low heat, bring the mixture to 180F (82C) and heat the berries for 5 minutes. Do not allow the berry mixture to boil. Remove the pan from the heat, cover and let stand for 20 minutes.

Place a fine-meshed sieve over a pan or bowl. Ladle the blackberry pulp and juice into the sieve to separate the pulp from the juice. Discard the pulp and seeds. Rinse the sieve and line it with 4 layers of clean, damp cheesecloth. Strain the juice through the cheesecloth 2 times, rinsing the cheesecloth between each straining. Line the sieve with a paper coffee filter and strain the juice again. Cover the juice and refrigerate several hours or overnight.

Ladle or pour the juice into another container, being careful not to disturb or pick up any of the sediment from the bottom of the original container. Discard the sediment. Place a fine-meshed sieve over a pan or bowl. Line the sieve with a paper coffee filter and strain the juice. For a crystal-clear jelly, strain the juice through 2 or 3 layered paper coffee filters. Measure 5 cups of juice.

To make the jelly: In an 8-quart pan, over medium heat, heat the juice until warm. Add the sugar and heat, stirring constantly, until the sugar is completely dissolved. Increase the heat to medium-high and bring the mixture to a full rolling boil, stirring constantly. Stir in the entire contents of both pectin pouches. Return the mixture to a full rolling boil, stirring constantly. Boil, stirring constantly, for 1 minute. Remove the pan from the heat.

Quickly skim off any foam and immediately ladle the hot jelly into hot jars, leaving ¼-inch headspace. Wipe the jar rims and threads with a clean, damp cloth. Cover with hot lids and apply screw rings. Process half-pint jars in a 200F (93C) water bath for 10 minutes, pint jars for 15 minutes.

Blueberry Jelly

While wild blueberries make the most intense and flavorful jellies, any type of blueberry may be used to make a great jelly. Frozen blueberries also make an excellent jelly.
MAKES ABOUT 8 HALF-PINT JARS

Blueberry Juice
3 quarts frozen or fresh blueberries
1½ cups water

Jelly Ingredients
5 cups blueberry juice
7½ cups sugar
2 (3-ounce) pouches liquid pectin

❦ To extract the juice: Remove any stems from the blueberries and rinse in cool water. Drain well. If using frozen berries, defrost the berries, but do not rinse them. In a flat-bottomed bowl or pan, use a vegetable masher or large spoon to gently crush the blueberries, one batch at a time, to release the juice.

In an 8-quart stainless steel pan, combine the crushed blueberries and water. Over medium-low heat, bring the mixture to 180F (82C) and heat the berries for 5 minutes. Do not allow the berry mixture to boil. Remove the pan from the heat, cover and let stand for 20 minutes.

Place a fine-meshed sieve over a pan or bowl. Ladle the blueberry pulp and juice into the sieve to separate the pulp from the juice. Discard the pulp and seeds. Rinse the sieve and line it with 4 layers of clean, damp cheesecloth. Strain the juice through the cheesecloth two times, rinsing the cheesecloth between each straining. Line the sieve with a paper coffee filter and strain the juice again. Cover the juice and refrigerate several hours or overnight.

Ladle or pour the juice into another container, being careful not to disturb or pick up any of the sediment from the bottom of the original container. Discard the sediment. Place a fine-meshed sieve over a pan or bowl. Line the sieve with a paper coffee filter and strain the juice. For a crystal-clear jelly, strain the juice through 2 or 3 layered paper coffee filters. Measure 5 cups of juice.

To make the jelly: In an 8-quart pan, over medium heat, heat the juice until warm. Add the sugar and heat, stirring constantly, until the sugar is completely dissolved. Increase the heat to medium-high and bring the mixture to a full rolling boil, stirring constantly. Stir in the entire contents of both pectin pouches. Return the mixture to a full rolling boil, stirring constantly. Boil, stirring constantly, for 1 minute. Remove the pan from the heat.

Quickly skim off any foam and immediately ladle the hot jelly into hot jars, leaving ¼-inch headspace. Wipe the jar rims and threads with a clean, damp cloth. Cover with hot lids and apply screw rings. Process half-pint jars in a 200F (93C) water bath for 10 minutes, pint jars for 15 minutes.

Boysenberry Jelly

This incredibly clear jelly has an intense berry flavor. I have won blue ribbons with jellies made from frozen boysenberries as well as jellies made from fresh berries.

MAKES ABOUT 8 HALF-PINT JARS

Boysenberry Juice
3 quarts ripe boysenberries
½ cup water

Jelly Ingredients
5 cups boysenberry juice
7½ cups sugar
2 (3-ounce) pouches liquid pectin

❦ To extract the juice: Gently rinse the boysenberries in cool water and drain well. If using frozen berries, defrost the berries, but do not rinse them. In a flat-bottomed bowl or pan, use a vegetable masher or large spoon to gently crush the boysenberries, one batch at a time, to release the juice.

In an 8-quart stainless steel pan, combine the crushed boysenberries and water. Over medium-low heat, bring the mixture to 180F (82C) and heat the berries for 5 minutes. Do not allow the berry mixture to boil. Remove the pan from the heat, cover and let stand for 20 minutes.

Place a fine-meshed sieve over a pan or bowl. Ladle the boysenberry pulp and juice into the sieve to separate the pulp from the juice. Discard the pulp and seeds. Rinse the sieve and line it with 4 layers of clean, damp cheesecloth. Strain the juice through the cheesecloth 2 times, rinsing the cheesecloth between each straining. Line the sieve with a paper coffee filter and strain the juice again. Cover the juice and refrigerate several hours or overnight.

Ladle or pour the juice into another container, being careful not to disturb or pick up any of the sediment from the bottom of the original container. Discard the sediment. Place a fine-meshed sieve over a pan or bowl. Line the sieve with a paper coffee filter and strain the juice. For a crystal-clear jelly, strain the juice through 2 or 3 layered paper coffee filters. Measure 5 cups of juice.

To make the jelly: In an 8-quart pan, over medium heat, heat the juice until warm. Add the sugar and heat, stirring constantly, until the sugar is completely dissolved. Increase the heat to medium-high and bring the mixture to a full rolling boil, stirring constantly. Stir in the entire contents of both pectin pouches. Return the mixture to a full rolling boil, stirring constantly. Boil, stirring constantly, for 1 minute. Remove the pan from the heat.

Quickly skim off any foam and immediately ladle the hot jelly into hot jars, leaving ¼-inch headspace. Wipe the jar rims and threads with a clean, damp cloth. Cover with hot lids and apply screw rings. Process half-pint jars in a 200F (93C) water bath for 10 minutes, pint jars for 15 minutes.

Cherry Jelly

I make cherry jelly using a combination of both sour and sweet cherries. The sour cherries provide the traditional tang, while the sweet cherries intensify the flavor and give the jelly a beautiful color. This jelly has earned multiple blue ribbons, a first place Alltrista Premium Food Preservation Award for soft spreads and a Best of Show award.

MAKES ABOUT 7 TO 8 HALF-PINT JARS

Cherry Juice
4 pounds sour cherries
2 pounds Bing or other sweet cherries
1 cup water

Jelly Ingredients
3¾ cups cherry juice
2 tablespoons filtered fresh lemon juice
7 cups sugar
2 (3-ounce) pouches liquid pectin

To extract the juice: Stem the cherries, rinse in cool water and drain well. Remove the pits from the cherries. Using a vegetable masher, gently crush the cherries to release the juice.

In a 6- to 8-quart pan, combine the cherries and water. Over medium heat, bring the cherry mixture to a gentle boil. Reduce the heat, cover and simmer gently for 10 minutes. Remove the pan from the heat. Let stand for 20 minutes.

Place a fine-meshed sieve over a pan or bowl. Ladle the cherry pulp and juice into the sieve to separate the pulp from the juice. Discard the pulp. Rinse the sieve and line it with 4 layers of clean, damp cheesecloth. Strain the juice through the cheesecloth 2 times, rinsing the cheesecloth between each straining. Line the sieve with a paper coffee filter and strain the juice again. Cover the juice and refrigerate several hours or overnight.

Ladle or pour the juice into another container, being careful not to disturb or pick up any of the sediment from the bottom of the original container. Discard the sediment. Place a fine-meshed sieve over a pan or bowl. Line the sieve with a paper coffee filter and strain the juice. For a crystal-clear jelly, strain the juice through 2 or 3 layered paper coffee filters. Measure 3¾ cups of juice.

To make the jelly: In an 8-quart pan, combine the cherry juice and lemon juice.

Over medium heat, heat the juice until warm. Add the sugar and heat, stirring constantly, until the sugar is completely dissolved. Increase the heat to medium-high and bring the mixture to a full rolling boil, stirring constantly. Stir in the entire contents of both pectin pouches. Return the mixture to a full rolling boil, stirring constantly. Boil, stirring constantly, for 2 minutes. Remove the pan from the heat.

Quickly skim off any foam and immediately ladle the hot jelly into hot jars, leaving ¼-inch headspace. Wipe the jar rims and threads with a clean, damp cloth. Cover with hot lids and apply screw rings. Process half-pint jars in a 200F (93C) water bath for 10 minutes, pint jars for 15 minutes.

Variations

Sour Cherry Jelly: Increase the amount of sour cherries to 6½ pounds and omit the Bing cherries and lemon juice.

Sweet Cherry Jelly: Omit the sour cherries, increase the Bing cherries or other sweet cherries to 5½ pounds and increase the lemon juice to ¼ cup.

Cherry Cider Jelly

Cherry cider can be found in many gourmet and specialty stores. This recipe has won multiple blue ribbons and earned the first-place Alltrista Premium Food Preservation Award for soft spreads.

MAKES 7 TO 8 HALF-PINT JARS

4 cups bottled cherry cider
7 cups sugar
2 (3-ounce pouches) liquid pectin

Place a sieve over a large pan or bowl. Line the sieve with a paper coffee filter and strain the cider.

In an 8-quart pan, over medium heat, heat the cider until warm. Add the sugar and heat, stirring constantly, until the sugar is completely dissolved. Increase the heat to medium-high and bring the mixture to a full rolling boil, stirring constantly. Stir in the entire contents of both pectin pouches. Return the mixture to a full rolling boil, stirring constantly. Boil, stirring constantly, for 1 minute. Remove the pan from the heat.

Quickly skim off any foam and immediately ladle the hot jelly into hot jars, leaving ¼-inch headspace. Wipe the jar rims and threads with a clean, damp cloth. Cover with hot lids and apply screw rings. Process half-pint jars in a 200F (93C) water bath for 10 minutes, pint jars for 15 minutes.

Cranberry Jelly

A beautiful jelly with a tangy flavor, this is great served with biscuits or spread on a turkey sandwich.

MAKES ABOUT 7 HALF-PINT JARS

Cranberry Juice
5 cups fresh or frozen unblemished whole
    cranberries
4½ cups water

Jelly Ingredients
4 cups cranberry juice
6 cups sugar
1 (3-ounce) pouch liquid pectin

To extract the juice: Remove any stems from the cranberries. Rinse in cool water and drain well.

In a 4-quart stainless steel pan, combine the cranberries and water. Over medium-high heat, bring to a boil. Reduce the heat, cover and boil gently for 15 minutes or until all of the berries have popped their skins and turned soft. Remove the pan from the heat, cover and let stand for 1 hour.

Place a fine-meshed sieve over a pan or bowl. Ladle the cranberry pulp and juice into the sieve to separate the pulp from the juice. Discard the pulp and seeds. Rinse the sieve and line it with 4 layers of clean, damp cheesecloth. Strain the juice through the cheesecloth 2 times, rinsing the cheesecloth between each straining. Line the sieve with a paper coffee filter and strain the juice again. Cover the juice and refrigerate several hours or overnight.

Ladle or pour the juice into another container, being careful not to disturb or pick up any of the sediment from the bottom of the original container. Discard the sediment. Place a fine-meshed sieve over a pan or bowl. Line the sieve with a paper coffee filter and strain the juice. For a crystal-clear jelly, strain the juice through 2 or 3 layered paper coffee filters. Measure 4 cups of juice.

To make the jelly: In an 8-quart pan, over medium heat, heat the juice until warm. Add the sugar and heat, stirring constantly, until the sugar is completely dissolved. Increase the heat to medium-high and bring the mixture to a full rolling boil, stirring constantly. Stir in the entire contents of the pectin pouch. Return the mixture to a full rolling boil, stirring constantly. Boil, stirring constantly, for 1 minute. Remove the pan from the heat.

Quickly skim off any foam and immediately ladle the hot jelly into hot jars, leaving ¼-inch headspace. Wipe the jar rims and threads with a clean, damp cloth. Cover with hot lids and apply screw rings. Process half-pint jars in a 200F (93C) water bath for 10 minutes, pint jars for 15 minutes.

Feijoa Jelly

Feijoas, also known as pineapple guavas, make a beautiful golden to pale pink jelly. To preserve the delicate flavor and aroma of the fruit, feijoa jelly should be made within 2 days of harvest.

MAKES ABOUT 7 HALF-PINT JARS

Feijoa Juice
4½ pounds fully ripe feijoas
4½ cups water

Jelly Ingredients
3½ cups feijoa juice
½ cup filtered fresh lemon juice
6 cups sugar
1 (3-ounce) pouch liquid pectin

To extract the juice: Rinse the feijoas in cool water and drain well. Slice ⅛-inch off both the stem and blossom ends of each fruit. Slice fruit thinly.

In a 4-quart pan, combine the sliced feijoas and water. Over medium heat, bring the feijoa mixture to a gentle boil. Reduce the heat, cover and simmer gently for 30 minutes. Remove the pan from the heat. Let stand for 30 minutes.

Place a fine-meshed sieve over a pan or bowl. Ladle the feijoa pulp and juice into the sieve to separate the pulp from the juice. Discard the pulp. Rinse the sieve and line it with 4 layers of clean, damp cheesecloth. Strain the juice through the cheesecloth 2 times, rinsing the cheesecloth between each straining. Line the sieve with a paper coffee filter and strain the juice again. Cover the juice and refrigerate several hours or overnight.

Ladle or pour the juice into another container, being careful not to disturb or pick up any of the sediment from the bottom of the original container. Discard the sediment. Place a fine-meshed sieve over a pan or bowl. Line the sieve with a paper coffee filter and strain the juice. For a crystal-clear jelly, strain the juice through 2 or 3 layered paper coffee filters. Measure 3½ cups of juice.

To make the jelly: In an 8-quart pan, combine the feijoa juice and lemon juice.

Over medium heat, heat the juice until warm. Add the sugar and heat, stirring constantly, until the sugar is completely dissolved. Increase the heat to medium-high and bring the mixture to a full rolling boil, stirring constantly. Stir in the entire contents of the pectin pouch. Return the mixture to a full rolling boil, stirring constantly. Boil, stirring constantly, for 1 minute. Remove the pan from the heat.

Quickly skim off any foam and immediately ladle the hot jelly into hot jars, leaving ¼-inch headspace. Wipe the jar rims and threads with a clean, damp cloth. Cover with hot lids and apply screw rings. Process half-pint jars in a 200F (93C) water bath for 10 minutes, pint jars for 15 minutes.

Garlic Jelly

This exotic jelly is heaven for garlic lovers. Spread a small spoonful on a cracker for a great snack or appetizer.

MAKES ABOUT 7 HALF-PINT JARS

Garlic Vinegar
3 cups white wine vinegar
¾ cup peeled and very thinly sliced fresh
    garlic (about 50 cloves)

Jelly Ingredients
2 cups garlic vinegar
2 cups white wine
6 cups sugar
2 (3-ounce) pouches liquid pectin

To prepare the garlic vinegar: In a medium stainless steel saucepan, combine the wine vinegar and garlic. Over medium heat, bring the garlic mixture to a gentle boil. Reduce the heat, cover and simmer for 15 minutes. Remove the pan from the heat.

Pour the garlic and vinegar into a 1½-quart clean glass jar, or divide evenly between 2 (1-quart) jars, then set aside to cool. When the mixture is cool, cover the jar opening with 2 layers of plastic wrap, then screw on the lid or ring. Let stand at room temperature for 24 hours.

Place a fine-meshed sieve over a pan or bowl. Ladle the garlic pulp and vinegar into the sieve to separate the pulp from the vinegar. Discard the garlic pulp. Rinse the sieve and line it with 4 layers of clean, damp cheesecloth. Strain the vinegar through the cheesecloth 2 times, rinsing the cheesecloth between each straining. Line the sieve with a paper coffee filter and strain the vinegar

again. Cover the vinegar and let stand several hours or overnight.

Ladle or pour the vinegar into another container, being careful not to disturb or pick up any sediment from the bottom of the original container. Discard any sediment. Place a fine-meshed sieve over a pan or bowl. Line the sieve with a paper coffee filter and strain the vinegar. For a clearer jelly, strain the vinegar through 2 or 3 layered paper coffee filters. Measure 2 cups of vinegar.

To make the jelly: In an 8-quart pan, combine the garlic vinegar and white wine.

Over medium heat, heat the mixture until warm. Add the sugar and heat, stirring constantly, until the sugar is completely dissolved. Increase the heat to medium-high and bring the mixture to a full rolling boil, stirring constantly. Stir in the entire contents of both pectin pouches. Return the mixture to a full rolling boil, stirring constantly. Boil, stirring constantly, for 1 minute. Remove the pan from the heat.

Quickly skim off any foam and immediately ladle the hot jelly into hot jars, leaving ¼-inch headspace. Wipe the jar rims and threads with a clean, damp cloth. Cover with hot lids and apply screw rings. Process half-pint jars in a 200F (93C) water bath for 10 minutes, pint jars for 15 minutes.

Variation
Garlic Chive Jelly: Add ½ cup finely chopped fresh chives to the jar before adding the hot garlic and vinegar mixture.

Ginger Jelly

A hot-sweet Asian jelly, this has an assertive flavor. Use fresh, firm hands of ginger that do not show any signs of wrinkling.

MAKES ABOUT 4 HALF-PINT JARS

Ginger Juice
3 cups water
2 cups peeled and thinly sliced fresh ginger

Jelly Ingredients
2 cups ginger juice
3 tablespoons filtered fresh lemon juice
2½ tablespoons rice vinegar
4 cups sugar
1 (3-ounce) pouch liquid pectin

To prepare the ginger juice: In a medium saucepan, combine the water and ginger. Over low heat, heat the mixture just until hot. Remove the pan from the heat. Cover and let stand for 30 minutes.

Place a sieve over a large pan or bowl. Line the sieve with 3 to 4 layers of clean, damp cheesecloth. Strain the juice through the lined sieve. Line the sieve with a paper coffee filter and strain the juice again. Cover the juice and refrigerate for several hours or overnight.

Ladle or pour the juice into another container, being careful not to disturb any sediment on the bottom of the container. Discard the sediment. Line the sieve with a paper coffee filter and strain the juice. For a clearer jelly, strain the juice through 2 or 3 layered paper coffee filters. Measure 2 cups of juice.

To make the jelly: In a 4-quart pan, combine the ginger juice, lemon juice and vinegar.

Over medium heat, heat the mixture until warm. Add the sugar and heat, stirring constantly, until the sugar is completely dissolved. Increase the heat to medium-high and bring the mixture to a full rolling boil, stirring constantly. Stir in the entire contents of the pectin pouch. Return the mixture to a full rolling boil, stirring constantly. Boil, stirring constantly, for 1 minute. Remove the pan from the heat.

Quickly skim off any foam and immediately ladle the hot jelly into hot jars, leaving ¼-inch headspace. Wipe the jar rims and threads with a clean, damp cloth. Cover with hot lids and apply screw rings. Process half-pint jars in a 200F (93C) water bath for 10 minutes, pint jars for 15 minutes.

Concord Grape Jelly

This classic jelly is a favorite of adults as well as kids and has earned multiple awards including Best of Division. Grapes are fragile and should be used within a day or 2 of harvest to achieve the best flavor.

MAKES ABOUT 7 HALF-PINT JARS

Grape Juice
4½ pounds fresh, fully ripe Concord grapes
¾ cup water

Jelly Ingredients
4 cups Concord grape juice
7 cups sugar
1 (3-ounce) pouch liquid pectin

To extract the juice: Remove the grapes from the stems. Rinse the grapes 2 to 3 times in cool water and drain well.

In an 8-quart stainless steel pan, combine the grapes and water. Over medium-low heat, bring the grape mixture just to simmer. Reduce the heat, cover and simmer gently for 8 to 10 minutes, or until all of the grapes have popped their skins and turned soft. Do not allow the mixture to boil or the juice may lose its flavor. Remove the pan from the heat, cover and let stand for 20 minutes.

Place a fine-meshed sieve over a pan or bowl. Ladle the grape pulp and juice into the sieve to separate the pulp from the juice. Discard the pulp and seeds. Rinse the sieve and line it with 4 layers of clean, damp cheesecloth. Strain the juice through the cheesecloth 2 times, rinsing the cheesecloth between each straining. Line the sieve with a paper coffee filter and strain the juice again. Cover the juice and refrigerate several hours or overnight.

Ladle or pour the juice into another container, being careful not to disturb or pick up any of the sediment from the bottom of the original container. Discard the sediment. Place a fine-meshed sieve over a pan or bowl. Line the sieve with a paper coffee filter and strain the juice. For a crystal-clear jelly, strain the juice through 2 or 3 layered paper coffee filters. Measure 4 cups of juice.

To make the jelly: In an 8-quart pan, over medium heat, heat the juice until warm. Add the sugar and heat, stirring constantly, until the sugar is completely dissolved. Increase the heat to medium-high and bring the mixture to a full rolling boil, stirring constantly. Stir in the entire contents of the pectin pouch. Return the mixture to a full rolling boil, stirring constantly. Boil, stir-

ring constantly, for 1 minute. Remove the pan from the heat.

Quickly skim off any foam and immediately ladle the hot jelly into hot jars, leaving ¼-inch headspace. Wipe the jar rims and threads with a clean, damp cloth. Cover with hot lids and apply screw rings. Process half-pint jars in a 200F (93C) water bath for 10 minutes, pint jars for 15 minutes.

Easy Grape Jelly

This quick recipe makes a wonderful, blue ribbon jelly that you can prepare any time of year. Both white and red grape juice also work well for this jelly.

MAKES 7 TO 8 HALF-PINT JARS

4 cups bottled Concord grape juice
7 cups sugar
2 (3-ounce pouches) liquid pectin

Place a sieve over a large pan or bowl. Line the sieve with a paper coffee filter and strain the juice.

In an 8-quart pan, over medium heat, heat the juice until warm. Add the sugar and heat, stirring constantly, until the sugar is completely dissolved. Increase the heat to medium-high and bring the mixture to a full rolling boil, stirring constantly. Stir in the entire contents of both pectin pouches. Return the mixture to a full rolling boil, stirring constantly. Boil, stirring constantly, for 1 minute. Remove the pan from the heat.

Quickly skim off any foam and immediately ladle the hot jelly into hot jars, leaving ¼-inch headspace. Wipe the jar rims and threads with a clean, damp cloth. Cover with hot lids and apply screw rings. Process half-pint jars in a 200F (93C) water bath for 10 minutes, pint jars for 15 minutes.

Horseradish Jelly

This jelly is wonderful served alongside roast beef or spread on a sandwich.

MAKES ABOUT 7 HALF-PINT JARS

Horseradish Vinegar

3 cups white wine vinegar

1 cup peeled and very thinly sliced fresh
　　horseradish root

Jelly Ingredients

2 cups horseradish vinegar

2 cups white wine

6 cups sugar

2 (3-ounce) pouches liquid pectin

To prepare the horseradish vinegar: In a medium stainless steel saucepan, over medium heat, heat the vinegar until hot. Remove the pan from the heat.

Place the horseradish into a 1½-quart clean glass jar, or divide evenly between 2 (1-quart) jars. Pour the hot vinegar into the jar, or divide evenly between the 2 jars, then set aside to cool. When the mixture is cool, cover the jar opening with 2 layers of plastic wrap, then screw on the lid or ring. Let stand at room temperature for 24 hours.

Place a fine-meshed sieve over a pan or bowl. Ladle the horseradish pulp and vinegar into the sieve to separate the pulp from the vinegar. Discard the horseradish pulp. Rinse the sieve and line it with 4 layers of clean, damp cheesecloth. Strain the vinegar through the cheesecloth 2 times, rinsing the cheesecloth between each straining. Line the sieve with a paper coffee filter and strain the vinegar again. Cover the vinegar and let stand several hours or overnight.

Ladle or pour the vinegar into another container, being careful not to disturb or pick up any sediment from the bottom of the original container. Discard any sediment. Place a fine-meshed sieve over a pan or bowl. Line the sieve with a paper coffee filter and strain the vinegar. For a clearer jelly, strain the vinegar through 2 or 3 layered paper coffee filters. Measure 2 cups of vinegar.

To make the jelly: In an 8-quart pan, combine the horseradish vinegar and white wine.

Over medium heat, heat the mixture until warm. Add the sugar and heat, stirring constantly, until the sugar is completely dissolved. Increase the heat to medium-high and bring the mixture to a full rolling boil, stirring constantly. Stir in the entire contents of both pectin pouches. Return the mixture to a full rolling boil, stirring constantly. Boil, stirring constantly, for 1 minute. Remove the pan from the heat.

Quickly skim off any foam and immediately ladle the hot jelly into hot jars, leaving ¼-inch headspace. Wipe the jar rims and threads with a clean, damp cloth. Cover with hot lids and apply screw rings. Process half-pint jars in a 200F (93C) water bath for 10 minutes, pint jars for 15 minutes.

Jalapeño Jelly

Fiery jalapeño pepper jelly is a gourmet delight. Serve it on crackers spread with cream cheese as an appetizer at parties and watch it disappear! This jelly earned Best of Show at the MontanaFair.

MAKES ABOUT 5 HALF-PINT JARS

Jalapeño Juice
1¾ cups white wine vinegar
1¼ cups water
1⅔ cups stemmed, seeded and finely chopped jalapeño chile peppers (about 35 medium)

Jelly Ingredients
2 cups jalapeño pepper juice
2 to 3 drops green or red food coloring (optional)
5 cups sugar
1 (3-ounce) pouch liquid pectin

To extract the juice: In a 4-quart stainless steel pan, combine the vinegar, water and peppers. Over medium heat, bring the mixture to a boil. Reduce the heat, cover and simmer for 15 minutes. Remove the pan from the heat and let stand 15 minutes.

Place a fine-meshed sieve over a pan or bowl. Remove the lid from the pan, being careful to turn your face away from the pepper fumes. Ladle the pepper pulp and juice into the sieve to separate the pulp from the juice. Discard the pulp. Rinse the sieve and line it with 4 layers of clean, damp cheesecloth. Strain the juice through the cheesecloth 2 times, rinsing the cheesecloth between each straining. Line the sieve with a paper coffee filter and strain the juice again. Cover the juice and refrigerate several hours or overnight.

Ladle or pour the juice into another container, being careful not to disturb or pick up any of the sediment from the bottom of the original container. Discard the sediment. Place a fine-meshed sieve over a pan or bowl. Line the sieve with a paper coffee filter and strain the juice. For a crystal-clear jelly, strain the juice through 2 or 3 layered paper coffee filters. Measure 2 cups of juice.

To make the jelly: In an 8-quart pan, combine the pepper juice and food coloring.

Over medium heat, heat the juice until warm. Add the sugar and heat, stirring constantly, until the sugar is completely dissolved. Increase the heat to medium-high and bring the mixture to a full rolling boil, stirring constantly. Stir in the entire contents of the pectin pouch. Return the mixture to a full rolling boil, stirring constantly. Boil, stirring constantly, for 1 minute. Remove the pan from the heat.

Quickly skim off any foam and immediately ladle the hot jelly into hot jars, leaving ¼-inch headspace. Wipe the jar rims and threads with a clean, damp cloth. Cover with hot lids and apply screw rings. Process half-pint jars in a 200F (93C) water bath for 10 minutes, pint jars for 15 minutes.

Kiwi Jelly

Kiwi jelly tends to be a very pale yellow-green in color, but a couple drops of green food coloring may be added to the juice to give it a more attractive appearance.

MAKES ABOUT 7 HALF-PINT JARS

Kiwifruit Juice

8 cups peeled, seeded and crushed ripe
    kiwifruits (35 to 40 large)
1 cup water

Jelly Ingredients

4½ cups kiwifruit juice
¼ cup filtered fresh lemon juice
2 to 3 drops green food coloring (optional)
7½ cups sugar
2 (3-ounce) pouches liquid pectin

To extract the juice: In an 8-quart pan, combine the crushed kiwifruits and water. Over medium heat, bring the mixture to a boil. Reduce the heat, cover and simmer gently for 10 minutes. Remove the pan from the heat and let stand for 20 minutes.

Place a fine-meshed sieve over a pan or bowl. Ladle the kiwifruit pulp and juice into the sieve to separate the pulp from the juice. Discard the pulp. Rinse the sieve and line it with 4 layers of clean, damp cheesecloth. Strain the juice through the cheesecloth 2 times, rinsing the cheesecloth between each straining. Line the sieve with a paper coffee filter and strain the juice again. Cover the juice and refrigerate several hours or overnight.

Ladle or pour the juice into another container, being careful not to disturb or pick up any of the sediment from the bottom of the original container. Discard the sediment. Place a fine-meshed sieve over a pan or bowl. Line the sieve with a paper coffee filter and strain the juice. For a clearer jelly, strain the juice through 2 or 3 layered paper coffee filters. Measure 4½ cups of juice.

To make the jelly: In an 8-quart pan, combine the kiwi juice and lemon juice. Stir in food coloring.

Over medium heat, heat the juice until warm. Add the sugar and heat, stirring constantly, until

the sugar is completely dissolved. Increase the heat to medium-high and bring the mixture to a full rolling boil, stirring constantly. Stir in the entire contents of both pectin pouches. Return the mixture to a full rolling boil, stirring constantly. Boil, stirring constantly, for 1 minute. Remove the pan from the heat.

Quickly skim off any foam and immediately ladle the hot jelly into hot jars, leaving ¼-inch headspace. Wipe the jar rims and threads with a clean, damp cloth. Cover with hot lids and apply screw rings. Process half-pint jars in a 200F (93C) water bath for 10 minutes, pint jars for 15 minutes.

Meyer Lemon Jelly

A tangy jelly with an intense flavor and a shimmering translucence, this jelly is not perfectly clear in appearance. Meyer lemons have an excellent color and flavor and are recommended for this jelly, although other lemons may be used as well. Filter the lemon juice through 1 or 2 paper coffee filters before measuring.

MAKES 7 TO 8 HALF-PINT JARS

4 cups filtered fresh lemon juice, preferably
    from Meyer lemons
7 cups sugar
2 (3-ounce) pouches liquid pectin

In an 8-quart stainless steel pan, over medium heat, heat the juice until warm. Add the sugar and heat, stirring constantly, until the sugar is completely dissolved. Increase the heat to medium-high and bring the mixture to a full rolling boil, stirring constantly. Stir in the entire contents of both pectin pouches. Return the mixture to a full rolling boil, stirring constantly. Boil, stirring constantly, for 1 minute. Remove the pan from the heat.

Quickly skim off any foam and immediately ladle the hot jelly into hot jars, leaving ¼-inch headspace. Wipe the jar rims and threads with a clean, damp cloth. Cover with hot lids and apply screw rings. Process half-pint jars in a 200F (93C) water bath for 10 minutes, pint jars for 15 minutes.

Mango-Papaya Jelly

Bottled mango juice and papaya juice can sometimes be found in specialty food stores, making this an easy jelly to prepare. If you use bottled juice, select a juice that is unsweetened, otherwise the proportions of fruit, sugar, acid and pectin will be unbalanced and the jelly may fail to set.

MAKES ABOUT 7 HALF-PINT JARS

Mango-Papaya Juice
4 large ripe mangoes
1 cup water
4 large ripe papayas
1 cup water

Jelly Ingredients
2 cups mango juice
2 cups papaya juice
2 tablespoons filtered fresh lemon juice
7 cups sugar
1 (3-ounce) pouch liquid pectin

To extract the juices: Rinse and dry the mangoes. Using a sharp a knife, cut through the skin and flesh on the side of the mango until the knife hits the pit. Continue cutting around the mango until you have made a circular cut all the way around the fruit. Holding the mango in the palm of your hand and using a thin-bowled tablespoon, slide the spoon into the cut from the end of the mango. Guide the spoon up and over the pit, sliding the spoon back and forth to the sides, until the mango half is separated from the pit. Slide the spoon under the pit and remove the pit from the other half of the mango. Cut a multiple cross-hatch pattern all the way through the mango flesh, being careful not to cut through the skin. Holding the outer edges of the mango half with your fingers, use your thumbs to push against the center of the skin to gently turn the mango inside out. Slice the mango from the peel in chunks. Repeat with remaining mangoes.

In a medium saucepan, using a vegetable masher or large spoon, lightly crush the mangoes. Stir in 1 cup water. Over medium heat, bring the mixture to a boil. Reduce the heat, cover and simmer for 5 minutes. Remove the pan from the heat and let stand for 20 minutes.

Rinse and dry the papayas. Cut the papayas in half and use a spoon to remove the seeds. Peel the papayas the same way as the mangoes.

In a medium saucepan, using a vegetable masher or large spoon, lightly crush the papayas. Stir in 1 cup water. Over medium heat, bring the mixture to a boil. Reduce the heat, cover and simmer for 5 minutes. Remove the pan from the heat and let stand for 20 minutes.

Place a fine-meshed sieve over a pan or bowl. Ladle the mango pulp and juice into the sieve to separate the pulp from the juice. Discard the pulp.

Rinse the sieve and line it with 4 layers of clean, damp cheesecloth. Strain the juice through the cheesecloth 2 times, rinsing the cheesecloth between each straining. Line the sieve with a paper coffee filter and strain the juice again. Cover the juice and refrigerate several hours or overnight.

Strain the papaya juice in the same way as the mango juice. Cover the juice and refrigerate several hours or overnight.

Ladle or pour the mango juice into another container, being careful not to disturb or pick up any of the sediment from the bottom of the original container. Discard the sediment. Place a fine-meshed sieve over a pan or bowl. Line the sieve with a paper coffee filter and strain the juice. For a clearer jelly, strain the juice through 2 or 3 layered paper coffee filters.

Filter the papaya juice in the same as the mango juice. Measure 2 cups of each juice.

To make the jelly: In an 8-quart pan, combine the mango juice, papaya juice and lemon juice.

Over medium heat, heat the juice until warm. Add the sugar and heat, stirring constantly, until the sugar is completely dissolved. Increase the heat to medium-high and bring the mixture to a full rolling boil, stirring constantly. Stir in the entire contents of the pectin pouch. Return the mixture to a full rolling boil, stirring constantly. Boil, stirring constantly, for 1 minute. Remove the pan from the heat.

Quickly skim off any foam and immediately ladle the hot jelly into hot jars, leaving ¼-inch headspace. Wipe the jar rims and threads with a clean, damp cloth. Cover with hot lids and apply screw rings. Process half-pint jars in a 200F (93C) water bath for 10 minutes, pint jars for 15 minutes.

Maple Jelly

This is an easy jelly to make, and its flavor is an unusual one for a jelly. In addition to serving the jelly with biscuits for breakfast, try using it as a glaze for ham or pork chops. Choose a high-quality maple syrup with a wonderful, rich flavor.

MAKES ABOUT 2 HALF-PINT JARS

1¾ cups pure maple syrup
4 teaspoons filtered lemon juice
2 (3-ounce) pouches liquid pectin

In a medium saucepan, combine the maple syrup and lemon juice. Over medium heat, bring the syrup mixture to a simmer. Remove the pan from the heat and stir in the entire contents of both pectin pouches until completely dissolved.

Immediately ladle the hot jelly into hot jars, leaving ¼-inch headspace. Wipe the jar rims and threads with a clean, damp cloth. Cover with hot lids and apply screw rings. Process half-pint jars in a 200F (93C) water bath for 10 minutes, pint jars for 15 minutes.

Margarita Jelly

A delightfully refreshing jelly, serve it any time of day. Make the jelly immediately after juicing the limes to keep the juice from developing a bitter taste.

MAKES ABOUT 5 HALF-PINT JARS

1¼ cups water
1 cup filtered fresh lime juice
½ cup tequila
¼ cup Triple Sec
4½ cups sugar
1 (3-ounce) pouch liquid pectin

❧ In a 6- to 8-quart stainless steel pan, combine the water, lime juice, tequila and Triple Sec.

Over medium heat, gently heat the mixture until warm. Add the sugar and heat, stirring constantly, until the sugar is completely dissolved. Increase the heat to medium-high and bring the mixture to a full rolling boil, stirring constantly. Stir in the entire contents of the pectin pouch. Return the mixture to a full rolling boil, stirring constantly. Boil, stirring constantly, for 1 minute. Remove the pan from the heat. Skim off any foam.

Immediately ladle the hot jelly into hot jars, leaving ¼-inch headspace. Wipe the jar rims and threads with a clean, damp cloth. Cover with hot lids and apply screw rings. Process half-pint jars in a 200F (93C) water bath for 10 minutes, pint jars for 15 minutes.

Mint Jelly

Mint jelly is wonderful served with roasted or grilled lamb. For chocolate-mint fans, try spreading the jelly on warm chocolate cake layers before icing. Any variety of mint may be used to make jelly, but spearmint and lemon mint give the best, truest mint flavor. This jelly is a multiple blue ribbon winner across the country.

MAKES 6 TO 7 HALF-PINT JARS

Mint Juice
6 cups stemmed and lightly packed whole
    mint leaves
4½ cups water

Jelly Ingredients
3½ cups mint juice
¼ cup filtered fresh lemon juice
A few drops green and blue food coloring
    (optional)
7 cups sugar
2 (3-ounce) pouches liquid pectin

❧ To extract the juice: Carefully remove the mint leaves from the stems. Rinse thoroughly in cool water to remove any dirt or sand. Gently blot the leaves with paper towels to remove excess water.

Using a food processor or a sharp knife, finely chop the mint leaves. Measure 3 cups firmly packed chopped mint leaves.

In a 4-quart stainless steel pan, combine the mint leaves and water. Over medium-high heat, bring the mixture to a boil. Remove the pan from the heat. Cover and let stand 30 minutes.

Place a fine-meshed sieve over a pan or bowl. Ladle the mint pulp and juice into the sieve to separate the pulp from the juice. Discard the pulp. Rinse the sieve and line it with 4 layers of clean, damp cheesecloth. Strain the juice through the cheesecloth 3 times, rinsing the cheesecloth between each straining. Line the sieve with a paper coffee filter and strain the juice again. Cover the juice and refrigerate several hours or overnight.

Ladle or pour the juice into another container, being careful not to disturb or pick up any of the sediment from the bottom of the original container. Discard the sediment. Place a fine-meshed sieve over a pan or bowl. Line the sieve with a paper coffee filter and strain the juice. For a crystal-clear jelly, strain the juice through 2 or 3 layered paper coffee filters. Measure 3½ cups of juice.

To make the jelly: In an 8-quart pan, combine the mint juice and lemon juice. Add the green and blue food coloring to reach the desired shade of green. The color will lighten after the addition of the sugar.

Over medium heat, heat the juice until warm. Add the sugar and heat, stirring constantly, until the sugar is completely dissolved. Increase the heat to medium-high and bring the mixture to a full rolling boil, stirring constantly. Stir in the entire contents of both pectin pouches. Return the mixture to a full rolling boil, stirring constantly. Boil, stirring constantly, for 1 minute. Remove the pan from the heat.

Quickly skim off any foam and immediately ladle the hot jelly into hot jars, leaving ¼-inch headspace. Wipe the jar rims and threads with a clean, damp cloth. Cover with hot lids and apply screw rings. Process half-pint jars in a 200F (93C) water bath for 10 minutes, pint jars for 15 minutes.

Orange Jelly

Even though this jelly is not perfectly clear, it is still a lovely spread. Filter the fresh citrus juices through 1 or 2 paper coffee filters before measuring. Make the jelly immediately after extracting the juices to prevent the orange juice from turning bitter from exposure to the air.

MAKES 7 TO 8 HALF-PINT JARS

3¾ cups filtered fresh orange juice
¼ cup filtered fresh lemon juice
7 cups sugar
2 (3-ounce) pouches liquid pectin

In an 8-quart stainless steel pan, over medium heat, heat the orange juice and lemon juice until warm. Add the sugar and heat, stirring constantly, until the sugar is completely dissolved. Increase the heat to medium-high and bring the mixture to a full rolling boil, stirring constantly. Stir in the entire contents of both pectin pouches. Return the mixture to a full rolling boil, stirring constantly. Boil, stirring constantly, for 1 minute. Remove the pan from the heat.

Quickly skim off any foam and immediately ladle the hot jelly into hot jars, leaving ¼-inch headspace. Wipe the jar rims and threads with a clean, damp cloth. Cover with hot lids and apply screw rings. Process half-pint jars in a 200F (93C) water bath for 10 minutes, pint jars for 15 minutes.

Peach Jelly

This softly colored jelly has a delicate, fragrant peach scent.

MAKES ABOUT 8 HALF-PINT JARS

Peach Juice
6 pounds fresh ripe yellow peaches, pitted, peeled and crushed or finely chopped
1½ cups water

Jelly Ingredients
3½ cups peach juice
¼ cup filtered fresh lemon juice
7½ cups sugar
2 (3-ounce) pouches liquid pectin

 To extract the juice: In an 8-quart stainless steel pan, combine the peaches and water. Over medium-high heat, bring the mixture to a boil. Reduce the heat, cover and simmer gently for 5 minutes. Remove the pan from the heat. Skim off any foam. Let stand, covered, for 20 minutes.

Place a sieve over a large pan or bowl. Ladle the cooked peaches into the sieve and strain the juice from the pulp. Discard the pulp. Rinse the sieve thoroughly and line it with 3 to 4 layers of clean, damp cheesecloth. Strain the juice through the cheesecloth 2 times, rinsing the cheesecloth between each straining. Line the sieve with a paper coffee filter and strain the juice again. Cover the juice and refrigerate for several hours or overnight.

Ladle or pour the juice into another container, being careful not to disturb or pick up any of the sediment from the bottom of the original container. Discard the sediment. Place a fine-meshed sieve over a pan or bowl. Line the sieve with a paper coffee filter and strain the juice. For a clearer jelly, strain the juice through 2 or 3 layered paper coffee filters. Measure 3½ cups of juice.

To make the jelly: In an 8-quart pan, combine the peach juice and lemon juice.

Over medium heat, heat the juice until warm. Add the sugar and heat, stirring constantly, until the sugar is completely dissolved. Increase the heat to medium-high and bring the mixture to a full rolling boil, stirring constantly. Stir in the entire contents of both pectin pouches. Return the mixture to a full rolling boil, stirring constantly. Boil, stirring constantly, for 1 minute. Remove the pan from the heat.

Quickly skim off any foam and immediately ladle the hot jelly into hot jars, leaving ¼-inch headspace. Wipe the jar rims and threads with a clean, damp cloth. Cover with hot lids and apply screw rings. Process half-pint jars in a 200F (93C) water bath for 10 minutes, pint jars for 15 minutes.

Bartlett Pear Jelly

Bottled pear juice may be used in this recipe. Pure Bartlett pear juice can be found in some gourmet, specialty and health food stores.

MAKES 7 TO 8 HALF-PINT JARS

Pear Juice
6 pounds fresh, fully ripe Bartlett pears, cored, peeled and crushed or finely chopped
2 cups water

Jelly Ingredients

4 cups pear juice

2 tablespoons filtered fresh lemon juice

7 cups sugar

2 (3-ounce) pouches liquid pectin

❧ To extract the juice: In an 8-quart stainless steel pan, combine the pears and water. Over medium-high heat, bring the mixture to a boil. Reduce the heat, cover and simmer gently for 5 minutes. Remove the pan from the heat. Skim off any foam. Let stand, covered, for 20 minutes.

Place a sieve over a large pan or bowl. Ladle the cooked pears into the sieve and strain the juice from the pulp. Discard the pulp. Rinse the sieve thoroughly and line it with 3 to 4 layers of clean, damp cheesecloth. Strain the juice through the cheesecloth 2 times, rinsing the cheesecloth between each straining. Line the sieve with a paper coffee filter and strain the juice again. Cover the juice and refrigerate for several hours or overnight.

Ladle or pour the juice into another container, being careful not to disturb or pick up any of the sediment from the bottom of the original container. Discard the sediment. Place a fine-meshed sieve over a pan or bowl. Line the sieve with a paper coffee filter and strain the juice. For a clearer jelly, strain the juice through 2 or 3 layered paper coffee filters. Measure 4 cups of juice.

To make the jelly: In an 8-quart pan, combine the pear juice and lemon juice.

Over medium heat, heat the juice until warm. Add the sugar and heat, stirring constantly, until the sugar is completely dissolved. Increase the heat to medium-high and bring the mixture to a full rolling boil, stirring constantly. Stir in the entire contents of both pectin pouches. Return the mixture to a full rolling boil, stirring con-

stantly. Boil, stirring constantly, for 1 minute. Remove the pan from the heat.

Quickly skim off any foam and immediately ladle the hot jelly into hot jars, leaving ¼-inch headspace. Wipe the jar rims and threads with a clean, damp cloth. Cover with hot lids and apply screw rings. Process half-pint jars in a 200F (93C) water bath for 10 minutes, pint jars for 15 minutes.

Pineapple Jelly

Pineapple juice makes a lovely jelly with a delicate flavor. Select a premium pineapple juice to produce a jelly of high quality.

MAKES 7 TO 8 HALF-PINT JARS

4 cups bottled or canned pineapple juice

2 tablespoons filtered fresh lemon juice

7 cups sugar

2 (3-ounce) pouches liquid pectin

❧ Place a sieve over a large pan or bowl. Line the sieve with a paper coffee filter and strain the juice.

In an 8-quart pan, combine the pineapple juice and lemon juice.

Over medium heat, heat the juice until warm. Add the sugar and heat, stirring constantly, until the sugar is completely dissolved. Increase the heat to medium-high and bring the mixture to a full rolling boil, stirring constantly. Stir in the entire contents of both pectin pouches. Return the mixture to a full rolling boil, stirring constantly. Boil, stirring constantly, for 1 minute. Remove the pan from the heat.

Quickly skim off any foam and immediately ladle the hot jelly into hot jars, leaving ¼-inch headspace. Wipe the jar rims and threads with a clean, damp cloth. Cover with hot lids and apply screw rings. Process half-pint jars in a 200F (93C) water bath for 10 minutes, pint jars for 15 minutes.

Santa Rosa Plum Jelly

Santa Rosa plums have a wonderful sweet and tangy flavor and make a beautiful shimmering soft pink jelly. If Santa Rosa plums are not available in your area, almost any other variety of plum may be used instead. I like to remove the peels before extracting the juice from the fruit, as the peels tend to give the jelly a slightly bitter taste. It is a little more work, but well worth the effort. This jelly is a multiple blue ribbon winner and has earned the Alltrista Premium Food Preservation Award for soft spreads.

MAKES ABOUT 7 HALF-PINT JARS

Plum Juice
6 pounds ripe Santa Rosa plums, pitted, peeled and crushed or finely chopped
1 cup water

Jelly Ingredients
4 cups Santa Rosa plum juice
6½ cups sugar
1 (3-ounce) pouch liquid pectin

To extract the juice: In an 8-quart stainless steel pan, combine the plums and water. Over medium-high heat, bring the mixture to a boil. Reduce the heat, cover and simmer gently for 10 minutes. Remove the pan from the heat. Skim off any foam. Let stand, covered, for 20 minutes.

Place a sieve over a large pan or bowl. Ladle the cooked plums into the sieve and strain the juice from the pulp. Discard the pulp. Rinse the sieve thoroughly and line it with 3 to 4 layers of clean, damp cheesecloth. Strain the juice through the cheesecloth 2 times, rinsing the cheesecloth between each straining. Line the sieve with a paper coffee filter and strain the juice again. Cover the juice and refrigerate for several hours or overnight.

Ladle or pour the juice into another container, being careful not to disturb or pick up any of the sediment from the bottom of the original container. Discard the sediment. Place a fine-meshed sieve over a pan or bowl. Line the sieve with a paper coffee filter and strain the juice. For a crystal-clear jelly, strain the juice through 2 or 3 layered paper coffee filters. Measure 4 cups of juice.

To make the jelly: In an 8-quart pan, over medium heat, heat the juice until warm. Add the sugar and heat, stirring constantly, until the sugar is completely dissolved. Increase the heat to medium-high and bring the mixture to a full rolling boil, stirring constantly. Stir in the entire contents of the pectin pouch. Return the mixture to a full rolling boil, stirring constantly. Boil, stirring constantly, for 1 minute. Remove the pan from the heat.

Quickly skim off any foam and immediately ladle the hot jelly into hot jars, leaving ¼-inch headspace. Wipe the jar rims and threads with a clean, damp cloth. Cover with hot lids and apply screw rings. Process half-pint jars in a 200F (93C) water bath for 10 minutes, pint jars for 15 minutes.

Pomegranate Jelly

The color, clarity and flavor of this deep pink jelly are quite remarkable. Wearing rubber or latex gloves while juicing the pomegranates is highly recommended, as the juice will stain skin and clothing. Removing the seeds from the pomegranates underwater helps prevent the juice from spattering.

Be sure to remove all of the white pith from the fleshy seeds before crushing. A reamer should not be used to extract the juice, as the pith will also be squeezed and will make the juice very bitter. Be careful not to crush the hard center of the seeds, as it is also very bitter.

MAKES ABOUT 7 HALF-PINT JARS

Pomegranate Juice
10 large pomegranates
½ cup water

Jelly Ingredients
4 cups pomegranate juice
¼ cup filtered fresh lemon juice
7 cups sugar
1 (3-ounce) pouch liquid pectin

To extract the juice: With a sharp knife, score the pomegranates into quarters, cutting just through the outside skin and being careful not to damage the seeds. Submerge the pomegranates in a large bowl or basin filled with water. Break the fruit apart along the score lines.

Using your fingers, gently remove seeds from the white pith, being careful not to break the seeds. The white pith will rise to the surface of the water, while the seeds will sink to the bottom of the bowl or basin. Skim the pith from the top of the water. Be sure to remove all of the white pith from the seeds, as it is very bitter and will

give the jelly a bad flavor. Carefully transfer the seeds to a colander. Gently rinse the seeds and drain well.

In a flat-bottomed bowl or pan, using a vegetable masher or the back of a large spoon, gently crush the seeds, in small batches, to release their juice. Take care not to crush the hard center of the seeds.

In an 8-quart stainless steel pan, combine the crushed pomegranates and water. Over medium-low heat, bring the mixture to 180F (82C) and heat for 5 minutes. Do not allow the pomegranate mixture to boil. Remove the pan from the heat, cover and let stand for 20 minutes.

Place a fine-meshed sieve over a pan or bowl. Ladle the pomegranate pulp and juice into the sieve to separate the pulp from the juice. Discard the pulp and seeds. Rinse the sieve and line it with 4 layers of clean, damp cheesecloth. Strain the juice through the cheesecloth 2 times, rinsing the cheesecloth between each straining. Line the sieve with a paper coffee filter and strain the juice again. Cover the juice and refrigerate several hours or overnight.

Ladle or pour the juice into another container, being careful not to disturb or pick up any of the sediment from the bottom of the original container. Discard the sediment. Place a fine-meshed sieve over a pan or bowl. Line the sieve with a paper coffee filter and strain the juice. For a crystal-clear jelly, strain the juice through 2 or 3 layered paper coffee filters. Measure 4 cups of juice.

To make the jelly: In an 8-quart pan, combine the pomegranate juice and lemon juice.

Over medium heat, heat the juice until warm. Add the sugar and heat, stirring constantly, until the sugar is completely dissolved. Increase the heat to medium-high and bring the mixture to a full rolling boil, stirring constantly. Stir in the entire contents of the pectin pouch. Return the mixture to a full rolling boil, stirring constantly. Boil, stirring constantly, for 1 minute. Remove the pan from the heat.

Quickly skim off any foam and immediately ladle the hot jelly into hot jars, leaving ¼-inch headspace. Wipe the jar rims and threads with a clean, damp cloth. Cover with hot lids and apply screw rings. Process half-pint jars in a 200F (93C) water bath for 10 minutes, pint jars for 15 minutes.

Raspberry Jelly

The exquisite jewel-tone color, crystal-clear clarity and amazing flavor of this jelly have earned it multiple blue ribbons at fairs across the country. It has also won Best of Class, Best of Division and has been selected as a judge's special choice for Sweepstakes Award for best overall entry in preserved foods.

Frozen raspberries make an excellent jelly. The frozen berries often yield a larger quantity of juice, with a more intense flavor, than that produced by fresh berries. You will need about 4 (16-ounce) bags of frozen berries to yield 4 cups of juice. If you live in an area of the country where black raspberries are plentiful, you may use them in place of the red raspberries.

MAKES ABOUT 8 HALF-PINT JARS

Raspberry Juice
3½ quarts frozen or fresh red raspberries

Jelly Ingredients
4 cups raspberry juice
7½ cups sugar
2 (3-ounce) pouches liquid pectin

To extract the juice: Gently rinse the fresh raspberries in cool water and drain well. If using frozen berries, defrost the berries, but do not rinse them. In a flat-bottomed bowl or pan, use a vegetable masher or large spoon to gently crush the raspberries, one batch at a time, to release the juice.

In an 8-quart stainless steel pan, over medium heat, bring the crushed raspberries to a simmer. Reduce the heat, cover and simmer gently for 5 minutes. Remove the pan from the heat. Remove the cover and skim off any foam. Replace the cover and let stand for about 20 minutes.

Place a fine-meshed sieve over a pan or bowl. Ladle the raspberry pulp and juice into the sieve to separate the pulp from the juice. Discard the pulp and seeds. Rinse the sieve and line it with 4 layers of clean, damp cheesecloth. Strain the juice through the cheesecloth 2 times, rinsing the cheesecloth between each straining. Line the sieve with a paper coffee filter and strain the juice again. Cover the juice and refrigerate several hours or overnight.

Ladle or pour the juice into another container, being careful not to disturb or pick up any of the sediment from the bottom of the original container. Discard the sediment. Place a fine-meshed sieve over a pan or bowl. Line the sieve with a paper coffee filter and strain the juice. For a crystal-clear jelly, strain the juice through 2 or 3 layered paper coffee filters. Measure 4 cups of juice.

To make the jelly: In an 8-quart pan, over medium heat, heat the juice until warm. Add the sugar and heat, stirring constantly, until the sugar is completely dissolved. Increase the heat to medium-high and bring the mixture to a full rolling boil, stirring constantly. Stir in the entire contents of both pectin pouches. Return the mixture to a full rolling boil, stirring constantly. Boil, stirring constantly, for 1 minute. Remove the pan from the heat.

Quickly skim off any foam and immediately ladle the hot jelly into hot jars, leaving ¼-inch headspace. Wipe the jar rims and threads with a clean, damp cloth. Cover with hot lids and apply screw rings. Process half-pint jars in a 200F (93C) water bath for 10 minutes, pint jars for 15 minutes.

Raspberry-Strawberry Jelly

A wonderful blend of berry flavors makes this beautiful red jelly special. It has earned blue ribbons at fairs across the country and a Best of Division award. The judges gave high praise to the jelly, stating, "Your jelly is beautiful! Very pure, clean and sparkling! Delicious fresh taste. Keep up the good work!"

MAKES 7 TO 8 HALF-PINT JARS

Raspberry-Strawberry Juice
7 cups ripe strawberries
7 cups fresh or frozen red raspberries
½ cup water

Jelly Ingredients
4 cups berry juice
2 tablespoons filtered fresh lemon juice
7½ cups sugar
2 (3-ounce) pouches liquid pectin

 To extract the juice: Gently rinse the strawberries and raspberries in cool water and drain well. If using frozen raspberries, defrost the berries, but do not rinse them. Remove the stems from the strawberries and cut the berries into quarters. In a flat-bottomed bowl or pan, use a vegetable masher or large spoon to gently crush the strawberries and raspberries, one batch at a time, to release the juice.

In an 8-quart pan, combine the crushed strawberries, raspberries and water. Over medium heat, bring the mixture to a boil. Reduce the heat, cover and simmer gently for 10 minutes. Remove the pan from the heat. Remove the cover and skim off any foam. Replace the cover and let stand for 20 minutes.

Place a fine-meshed sieve over a pan or bowl. Ladle the berry pulp and juice into the sieve to separate the pulp from the juice. Discard the pulp. Rinse the sieve and line it with 4 layers of clean, damp cheesecloth. Strain the juice through the cheesecloth 2 times, rinsing the cheesecloth between each straining. Line the sieve with a paper coffee filter and strain the juice again. Cover the juice and refrigerate several hours or overnight.

Ladle or pour the juice into another container, being careful not to disturb or pick up any of the sediment from the bottom of the original container. Discard the sediment. Place a fine-meshed sieve over a pan or bowl. Line the sieve with a paper coffee filter and strain the juice. For a crystal-clear jelly, strain the juice through 2 or 3 layered paper coffee filters. Measure 4 cups of juice.

To make the jelly: In an 8-quart pan, combine the berry juice and lemon juice.

Over medium heat, heat the juice until warm. Add the sugar and heat, stirring constantly, until the sugar is completely dissolved. Increase the heat to medium-high and bring the mixture to a full rolling boil, stirring constantly. Stir in the entire contents of both pectin pouches. Return the mixture to a full rolling boil, stirring constantly. Boil, stirring constantly, for 1 minute. Remove the pan from the heat.

Quickly skim off any foam and immediately ladle the hot jelly into hot jars, leaving ¼-inch headspace. Wipe the jar rims and threads with a clean, damp cloth. Cover with hot lids and apply screw rings. Process half-pint jars in a 200F (93C) water bath for 10 minutes, pint jars for 15 minutes.

may develop an unpleasant, tannic flavor. Remove the pan from the heat.

Thoroughly stir in the entire contents of both pectin pouches until completely dissolved. Quickly skim off any foam.

Immediately ladle the hot jelly into hot jars, leaving ¼-inch headspace. Wipe the jar rims and threads with a clean, damp cloth. Cover with hot lids and apply screw rings. Process half-pint jars in a 200F (93C) water bath for 10 minutes, pint jars for 15 minutes.

Sangria Jelly

This is an enticing jelly with a beautiful color. Select a nicely flavored, mellow wine that is not too tannic.

MAKES 7 TO 8 HALF-PINT JARS

3 cups Burgundy wine
½ cup filtered fresh orange juice
¼ cup filtered fresh lemon juice
¼ cup Cointreau
6 cups sugar
2 (3-ounce) pouches liquid pectin

 In an 8-quart stainless steel pan, combine the wine, orange juice, lemon juice and Cointreau.

Over medium heat, gently heat the wine mixture until slightly warm. Stir in the sugar. Heat, stirring constantly, until the sugar is completely dissolved and the wine comes to just below simmering. (Tiny bubbles will form on the bottom of the pan.) Do not allow the wine to boil or the jelly

Strawberry Jelly

This delightful berry jelly has won multiple first-place awards and the Alltrista Premium Food Preservation Award for soft spreads. The judges were impressed by the jelly's exceptional clarity and excellent flavor.

MAKES ABOUT 7 HALF-PINT JARS

Strawberry Juice
3½ quarts ripe strawberries
1 cup water

Jelly Ingredients
4½ cups strawberry juice
¼ cup filtered fresh lemon juice
7½ cups sugar
2 (3-ounce) pouches liquid pectin

 To extract the juice: Gently rinse the strawberries in cool water and drain well. Remove the stems and cut the berries into quarters. In a flat-bottomed bowl or pan, use a vegetable masher or

large spoon to gently crush the strawberries, one batch at a time, to release the juice.

In an 8-quart pan, combine the crushed strawberries and water. Over medium heat, bring the mixture to a boil. Reduce the heat, cover and simmer gently for 10 minutes. Remove the pan from the heat. Remove the cover and skim off any foam. Replace the cover and let stand for 20 minutes.

Place a fine-meshed sieve over a pan or bowl. Ladle the strawberry pulp and juice into the sieve to separate the pulp from the juice. Discard the pulp. Rinse the sieve and line it with 4 layers of clean, damp cheesecloth. Strain the juice through the cheesecloth 2 times, rinsing the cheesecloth between each straining. Line the sieve with a paper coffee filter and strain the juice again. Cover the juice and refrigerate several hours or overnight.

Ladle or pour the juice into another container, being careful not to disturb or pick up any of the sediment from the bottom of the original container. Discard the sediment. Place a fine-meshed sieve over a pan or bowl. Line the sieve with a paper coffee filter and strain the juice. For a crystal-clear jelly, strain the juice through 2 or 3 layered paper coffee filters. Measure 4½ cups of juice.

To make the jelly: In an 8-quart pan, combine the strawberry juice and lemon juice.

Over medium heat, heat the juice until warm. Add the sugar and heat, stirring constantly, until the sugar is completely dissolved. Increase the heat to medium-high and bring the mixture to a full rolling boil, stirring constantly. Stir in the entire contents of both pectin pouches. Return the mixture to a full rolling boil, stirring constantly. Boil, stirring constantly, for 1 minute. Remove the pan from the heat.

Quickly skim off any foam and immediately ladle the hot jelly into hot jars, leaving ¼-inch headspace. Wipe the jar rims and threads with a clean, damp cloth. Cover with hot lids and apply screw rings. Process half-pint jars in a 200F (93C) water bath for 10 minutes, pint jars for 15 minutes.

Tangerine Jelly

Citrus juices contain minute particles that are difficult to filter out without weakening the flavor of the jelly. A little cloudiness is a small price to pay for great flavor. Make the jelly immediately after extracting the juices to prevent the tangerine juice from turning bitter from exposure to the air.

MAKES 7 TO 8 HALF-PINT JARS

3⅔ cups filtered fresh tangerine juice
⅓ cup filtered fresh lemon juice
7 cups sugar
2 (3-ounce) pouches liquid pectin

In an 8-quart stainless steel pan, over medium heat, heat the tangerine juice and lemon juice until warm. Add the sugar and heat, stirring constantly, until the sugar is completely dissolved. Increase the heat to medium-high and bring the mixture to a full rolling boil, stirring constantly. Stir in the entire contents of both pectin pouches. Return the mixture to a full rolling boil, stirring constantly. Boil, stirring constantly, for 1 minute. Remove the pan from the heat.

Quickly skim off any foam and immediately ladle the hot jelly into hot jars, leaving ¼-inch headspace. Wipe the jar rims and threads with a clean, damp cloth. Cover with hot lids and apply screw rings. Process half-pint jars in a 200F (93C) water bath for 10 minutes, pint jars for 15 minutes.

Thyme and Garlic Jelly

The subtle fusion of herbs and wine produces an aromatic jelly with a pleasing flavor.

MAKES ABOUT 7 HALF-PINT JARS

Thyme Juice
2 to 3 cups stemmed fresh thyme leaves
6 cloves garlic, peeled and chopped
3 cups water

Jelly Ingredients
2 cups thyme juice
1½ cups white wine
¼ cup filtered fresh lemon juice
7 cups sugar
2 (3-ounce) pouches liquid pectin

To extract the juice: Carefully remove the thyme leaves from the stems. Rinse thoroughly in cool water to remove any dirt or sand. Gently blot the leaves with paper towels to remove excess water. Measure 2 cups thyme leaves.

In a 4-quart stainless steel pan, combine the thyme leaves, garlic and water. Over medium-high heat, bring the mixture to a boil. Remove the pan from the heat. Cover and let stand 30 minutes.

Place a fine-meshed sieve over a pan or bowl. Ladle the thyme pulp and juice into the sieve to separate the pulp from the juice. Discard the pulp. Rinse the sieve and line it with 4 layers of clean, damp cheesecloth. Strain the juice through the cheesecloth 3 times, rinsing the cheesecloth between each straining. Line the sieve with a paper coffee filter and strain the juice again. Cover the juice and refrigerate several hours or overnight.

Ladle or pour the juice into another container, being careful not to disturb or pick up any of the sediment from the bottom of the original container. Discard the sediment. Place a fine-meshed sieve over a pan or bowl. Line the sieve with a paper coffee filter and strain the juice. For a crystal-clear jelly, strain the juice through 2 or 3 layered paper coffee filters. Measure 2 cups of juice.

To make the jelly: In an 8-quart pan, combine the thyme juice, white wine and lemon juice.

Over medium heat, heat the juice until warm. Add the sugar and heat, stirring constantly, until the sugar is completely dissolved. Increase the heat to medium-high and bring the mixture to a full rolling boil, stirring constantly. Stir in the entire contents of both pectin pouches. Return the mixture to a full rolling boil, stirring constantly. Boil, stirring constantly, for 1 minute. Remove the pan from the heat.

Quickly skim off any foam and immediately ladle the hot jelly into hot jars, leaving ¼-inch headspace. Wipe the jar rims and threads with a clean, damp cloth. Cover with hot lids and apply screw rings. Process half-pint jars in a 200F (93C) water bath for 10 minutes, pint jars for 15 minutes.

Variation
Rosemary-Garlic Jelly: Replace the thyme leaves with 2 cups chopped fresh rosemary leaves and increase the garlic to 8 cloves.

Wine Jelly

You will need two bottles of the same variety of wine for this recipe. Select a red, white or blush wine with good flavor and color. Choose a dry or semi-dry wine, otherwise the jelly will be too sweet. Chardonnay, Rosé of Cabernet and Cabernet Sauvignon are a few good possibilities, as well as a White Zinfandel that is not too sweet. Use a full-flavored champagne or sparkling wine to make champagne jelly.

I have won multiple blue ribbons with this recipe, using a variety of wines. This intoxicating jelly, made with a full-bodied blush wine, also earned the first place Alltrista Premium Food Preservation Award for soft spreads.

MAKES ABOUT 7 HALF-PINT JARS

4 cups wine
6 cups sugar
2 (3-ounce) pouches liquid pectin

In an 8-quart stainless steel pan, over medium heat, gently heat the wine until slightly warm. Stir in the sugar. Heat, stirring constantly, until the sugar is completely dissolved and the wine comes to just below simmering. (Tiny bubbles will form on the bottom of the pan.) Do not allow the wine to boil or the jelly may develop an unpleasant, tannic flavor. Remove the pan from the heat.

Thoroughly stir in the entire contents of both pectin pouches until completely dissolved. Quickly skim off any foam.

Immediately ladle the hot jelly into hot jars, leaving ¼-inch headspace. Wipe the jar rims and threads with a clean, damp cloth. Cover with hot lids and apply screw rings. Process half-pint jars in a 200F (93C) water bath for 10 minutes, pint jars for 15 minutes.

Marmalades

WHAT IS A MARMALADE?

Marmalades are some of my favorite soft spreads, and they have done very well for me with the judges at both state and county fair competitions. During canning season, friends and family line up to be on my list of "official marmalade tasters."

The name "marmalade" comes from the Portuguese word for quince, *marmelo,* the fruit from which this preserve was originally made. The first English recipe for quince marmalade, based on the Portuguese preserve of this firm and sour fruit, appeared in a 1524 cookbook. Recipes for bitter orange marmalades began appearing in England as early as the 1600s. In the eighteenth century, it was Scotsman James Keiller and his wife who were the first to have the idea of adding thin strips of citrus peel to the orange jamlike preserve. It was their recipe that popularized the preserve, and orange quickly became England's marmalade flavor of choice. Traditionally made from tangy citrus fruits, marmalades are now frequently made with a wide variety of fruits and flavor combinations.

Marmalades are actually a cross between jams and jellies. They have the translucent quality and consistency of a jelly and the texture and structure of a jam. A marmalade contains small pieces of soft fruit and peel that are evenly suspended in a transparent jelly.

If you like citrus but are not a marmalade fan, it is probably because the marmalades you have tasted in the past were bitter. This is a common problem with many store-bought marmalades and those made by home canners who are unwilling to put forth the extra effort to make an excellent marmalade. Try the rich flavor and superior texture of a high-quality marmalade, however, and I think you will change your mind.

When all the pith has been removed from the fruit, leaving only the fruit segments, juice and zest, the sweet, tangy, pure flavor of the citrus comes through. Although there are some people who like their marmalades to have a bitter taste, most fair judges usually mark scores down for bitterness in marmalades. Even in classes specifically designed for bitter marmalades, the sharp, unpleasant flavor of the pith can reduce scores.

Marmalades may also be made from citrus combined with a variety of other fruits, such as apricots, blueberries or strawberries. The citrus gives the spread a slight tang and brings out the flavor of the other fruits. These fruit marmalades are great for people who prefer a marmalade with less of a citrus flavor.

A gleaming jar of homemade marmalade makes a wonderful surprise gift and is always well received. Keep a few extra jars on hand for holidays, birthdays and unexpected guests. They also make great hostess gifts.

Making Marmalades

While marmalades may look complicated and tricky, they are actually not that difficult to make. They do require a fair amount of preparation time, though. If you do not have enough time available to both prepare and can your marmalade on the same day, or if you plan to make several batches of marmalade at one time, the process can easily be spread out over two days.

The fruit and peels for one or more batches of marmalade can be prepared on one day, tightly covered and refrigerated overnight and then cooked and canned the next day. If you refrigerate the peels overnight, add about ⅔ cup water to the zest before refrigerating it or it will dry out. The next day, drain off and discard the water shortly before cooking. It is not necessary to soak the peels again, so eliminate the 1 cup of water used for soaking from the recipe and proceed with cooking the peel and fruit. For best results, prepared fruit and peels should be used within 24 hours.

The amount of sugar used in the recipes should not be decreased. The correct balance of fruit, sugar, acid and pectin is necessary for the marmalade to jell, or set properly. Reducing the quantity of sugar, even by a small amount, will result in a thin, runny spread. Batches of marmalade should not be doubled, as doubling does not permit enough of the liquid to evaporate during cooking and will yield marmalades that fail to set.

Citrus marmalades can be a little more unpredictable than other varieties of soft spreads, with the possible exception of curds. Occasionally, despite your best effort, a batch of marmalade may refuse to set properly. Don't look on this as a failure. The marmalade can be returned to the pan and boiled again with additional pectin to make it set and then reprocessed. Or, do what I do: Serve it over French toast spread with a layer of cream cheese for a special breakfast or brunch treat. Offer it to company and they will be thoroughly impressed and sing your praises.

Special Equipment and Techniques

There are two tools that I find indispensable when making marmalades. My favorite is a zester. This wonderful little tool quickly slices the colored peel off of the citrus fruit, dramatically reducing the preparation time. The zester does all the work for you. In one motion, it removes the outer colored zest from the fruit without taking any of the bitter white pith beneath, and cuts it into thin, uniform strips that are just perfect for making delicate marmalades. The zester I like to use has five small holes across the blade, each about ⅛ inch in diameter; it removes five perfectly sized strips of peel at a time.

The other helpful tool is a small paring knife

with a curved blade, usually called a peeling knife or fruit knife. The curved blade makes it easy to peel the membrane from the citrus fruit and then remove the fruit segments with a minimum of effort. If you plan to make several batches of marmalade, I strongly recommend that you spend a few dollars for these tools. I wouldn't make a marmalade without either one of them.

There are two basic quality levels of homemade marmalade—standard and premium. Which you choose to make will depend on how much time and effort you want to invest and the finished quality of marmalade you desire. If you plan to exhibit your marmalade at fairs, or really want to impress your family and friends, it is worth taking the extra time to make a premium marmalade.

The primary differences between the two are in using only the pure zested peel in the premium marmalade and in the way the fruit is prepared after the zest and pith have been removed. For a standard marmalade, the fruit is simply chopped. When making a premium marmalade, the fruit is sectioned and removed from the white membrane and then finely chopped. Although this is a simple procedure, it does require a little more time, and more fruit will be needed.

I like marmalades that are smooth-textured, without any of the chewy white pith or tough membrane. When a marmalade is made with only the best parts of the fruit, that is what you will taste—pure fruit. Premium marmalades also go over well with judges, who recognize the extra effort and techniques that go into making a top-quality marmalade. All of my marmalade blue ribbons, Best of Class and Best of Division awards were earned with quality premium marmalades.

Crystallization can occur when the sugar is added to the fruit and the mixture is brought to a boil before the sugar is completely dissolved. As the marmalade cools, the sugar crystals can re-form in the spread. It is very important to dissolve the sugar completely before bringing the fruit mixture to a boil. Sugar crystals will cause judges to give a marmalade low scores, and the spread will fail to win any awards.

A small quantity of unsalted butter is a frequent ingredient in marmalade recipes. The addition of the butter reduces the amount of foam in the marmalade. Foam is the air bubbles that become trapped in the fruit and juice during cooking and rise to the surface. This foam must be removed from the pan after cooking to prevent it from forming tiny air bubbles in the jars or causing the marmalade to appear cloudy. By adding a little butter, the foam produced is limited and the amount of skimming necessary before the jars can be filled is reduced. Always use unsalted butter for home canning. Salted butter can give preserved foods an unusual flavor and unpleasant aftertaste.

Peeling Peaches and Apricots

Some fruits, such as peaches and apricots, should be peeled for use in marmalade recipes. These fruits will slip out of their skins easily using the boiling water method. Rinse and drain the fruit well, then place small batches of fruit into a large pan of gently boiling water. Leave the fruit in the water for about 30 to 45 seconds, depending on the size of the fruit. Using a slotted spoon, quickly remove the fruit from the boiling water and immediately plunge it into a bowl of ice water to stop the cooking process. Allow the fruit to cool in the ice water for at least 1 minute. Then remove the fruit from the water and drain it well in a strainer. Using your hands or a small paring knife, carefully slip the loose skins from the fruit. If the skin remains tightly attached to a piece of fruit, repeat the above process. If the skin still remains firmly attached and will not release easily, the fruit is probably underripe or immature and should be discarded.

Selecting Fruit

Whenever possible, use homegrown fruit or fruit you purchase directly from the growers, farmers' markets or produce stands. Tree-ripened fruit has a better flavor than fruit picked green and shipped to grocery stores or markets. This is particularly true of lemons, which do not develop their full flavor or sweetness when harvested green. The difference can be tasted in the finished spread. Growers and vendors can also tell you whether the fruit was organically grown or if pesticides were used.

Select medium to large citrus fruit that is fully ripe but firm, not overripe, and has a fragrant aroma natural to the type of fruit. The peel should be smooth and have a deep color. The smoother the peel, the thinner the white pith layer will be and the larger the actual usable amount of fruit the citrus will yield. In my experience, citrus fruits with smoother peels also tend to be sweeter.

If you are making orange marmalade and the Valencia oranges you are using have skins that are rather pale or yellow in color, select a few dark oranges of another good-colored variety such as navels, using the navels for the peel and the Valencias for the fruit. Do not use navel oranges for the fruit part of the marmalade, as they tend to be a little tougher and the finished texture of the cooked fruit will not be nearly as tender.

Preparing Citrus Peel

Store-bought citrus fruits are usually coated with a tasteless, nontoxic vegetable wax designed to enhance their color and shine and to inhibit mold growth during shipping. This wax should be removed before making marmalade, as too much wax may affect the texture and set of the finished spread. Gently and thoroughly scrub the fruit with a soft-bristle brush and rinse well under cool running water. Be careful not to scrub so hard that you release too much of the citrus oil

from the peels. Dry the fruit well before zesting or removing the peel.

The easiest and best way to remove the citrus peel is with a zester. Working from stem to blossom end, glide the zester down the side of the fruit. Use a light pressure to remove several thin strips of peel at a time. If you do not have a zester, use a sharp paring knife to carefully cut only the colored part of the peel from the fruit. A swivel-bladed vegetable peeler may also be used to remove the zest. Be sure to remove all of the white pithy membrane from the back of the peel, otherwise it will make the marmalade taste bitter. Slice the peel into very thin strips of an even width no more than 1/8 inch wide.

The recipes in this chapter call for briefly soaking the citrus peels in water before cooking. This step will help remove any remaining bitterness from the peels and should not be omitted, especially if you use a paring knife or vegetable peeler to remove the peels and any of the white pith remains on the zest. Before preparing the marmalade, discard the water used for soaking the peels.

When cooking the zest with the water and juice, simmer it gently. Peels that are cooked at a rapid boil tend to become tough and chewy. A small amount of baking soda added to the water and juice in which the peels are cooked heightens the color of the zest and keeps its bright color from fading.

Preparing Citrus Fruit

After zesting or cutting away the outer part of the peels, cut a slice off the top and bottom of each piece of fruit. Stand the fruit, bottom-side down, on a stable cutting board. Using a sharp knife and starting at the top, cut the remaining white pith and the membrane just beneath it from the fruit in strips. Be careful not to cut away too much of the fruit.

Peeling the fruit in this manner gives you more control. It is also physically less stressful for your hands and wrists. Peeling the fruit by holding it in your hand and cutting away the pith with a paring knife can cause your hand to cramp and puts repetitive strain on your wrist. These stresses can lead to pain and stiffness, particularly for anyone with arthritis or carpal tunnel problems. Placing the fruit on a cutting board is also safer, with less risk of cutting yourself while peeling the fruit.

At this point, you will need to decide which quality level of marmalade you want to make. For a premium marmalade, the citrus fruit is carefully segmented and removed from the white membrane. This requires more fruit to attain the measured amount. The quantities of fruit indicated in the recipes in this section include the extra amount needed for making premium marmalade. For a standard marmalade, the fruit is simply chopped without removing the membrane. Less fruit will be required to make a standard marmalade. Standard is faster. Premium tastes better. I strongly recommend taking the time to make a premium-quality marmalade. The results are more than worth the extra effort.

Premium Marmalade

After removing the peel, the white pith and the outer membrane, use a peeling knife with a curved blade or a small paring knife to segment the fruit. Cut along each side of the tough white connective membrane that separates the fruit sections so that the segments will fall away cleanly. This method of preparing citrus fruit is known as "supreming" the fruit. Discard the fibrous white membrane. Remove any seeds from the citrus segments and chop the fruit into small pieces with a sharp knife. Drain the fruit lightly, saving the juice.

Fill a measuring container with chopped fruit to the level called for in the specific marmalade recipe. Do not pack the fruit down. Add the reserved juice to displace the air bubbles, and measure the fruit and juice to exactly 3 cups. This will take ½ to 1 cup of juice, depending on the recipe and the type of fruit used. Proceed as instructed in the selected marmalade recipe.

Standard Marmalade

Slice the peeled fruit in half lengthwise, and, using a sharp paring knife, remove the center white core. Finely chop the fruit with a sharp knife and remove any seeds. Drain the fruit lightly, saving the juice.

Fill a measuring container with chopped fruit to the level called for in the specific marmalade recipe. Do not pack the fruit down. Add the reserved juice to displace the air bubbles, and measure the fruit and juice to exactly 3 cups. This will take ½ to 1 cup of juice, depending on the recipe and the type of fruit used. Proceed as instructed in the selected marmalade recipe.

Filling Jars

To reduce the chances of the fruit and peel floating to the top of the jars as the marmalade cools, after cooking, remove the pan from the heat and allow the marmalade to cool for 5 minutes before filling jars. Gently stir the marmalade every minute or so to distribute the fruit and peel in the pan. Ladle the marmalade into hot jars, leaving ¼-inch headspace. When all of the jars have been filled, use a plastic knife to gently distribute the fruit and peel throughout the jar, pushing some of the pieces to the bottom of the jar. Wipe the jar rims and threads with a clean, damp cloth, then cover and seal with the hot lids and rings.

Always process jars of marmalade in a water bath canner.

Floating Fruit

After removing the jars from the water bath, if you notice that some of the fruit is floating to the tops of the jars, resist the temptation to invert the jars (turning them upside down) or to shake the jars to redistribute the fruit. While you may succeed in balancing the fruit throughout the jar, there is also a strong probability that you will weaken or damage the seals and allow spoilage agents to enter the jars. Inverting or shaking the jars can also cause the headspace to become obscured, air bubbles to be trapped in the marmalade and the spread to stick to the inside of the lid. All of these can have a serious impact on the quality and safe storage ability of the marmalade. These flaws will also result in significant score reductions should you choose to enter your marmalades into a fair competition. Judges will either disqualify or dramatically reduce the score of any entry that they suspect has been inverted, either after or in place of, water bath canning.

Marmalades will continue to thicken as they cool. Most marmalades will set within 24 hours, although some may take a few days to completely gel. If the marmalade has not set after about a week, it probably will not set any firmer. The marmalade may be used soft or it may be reprocessed with additional sugar, pectin and acid. An unset marmalade should not be entered into a fair competition, as it will be marked down considerably for having a poor texture.

Apricot Marmalade

This marmalade is a delightful spread for people who are not fond of citrus marmalades—and for the rest of us, too. The orange and apricot flavors complement each other well and make this marmalade a multiple blue ribbon winner.

MAKES ABOUT 5 HALF-PINT JARS

2 medium Valencia oranges
¼ cup water
3½ cups peeled, pitted and finely chopped
    ripe apricots (about 3 pounds)
¼ cup strained fresh lemon juice
½ cup water
½ teaspoon unsalted butter
5½ cups sugar
1 (3-ounce) pouch liquid pectin

Using a zester, remove only the outer colored peel of the oranges. Or, with a sharp paring knife, thinly slice off the zest, then cut it into fine strips. Peel the fruit, removing all of the white pith. Separate the orange segments from the white membrane and remove any seeds. Discard the membrane and seeds. Finely chop the fruit and set aside.

In a small bowl, combine the orange peel and ¼ cup water. Let soak for 10 minutes. Drain the peel and discard the water.

In a medium bowl, combine the chopped apricots and lemon juice. Stir gently until the apricots are completely coated with lemon juice.

In an 8-quart pan, combine the drained peel, chopped oranges and ½ cup water. Over medium heat, bring the mixture to a boil. Reduce the heat, cover and simmer for 15 minutes.

Add the apricots and butter to the citrus mixture and simmer, uncovered, for 5 minutes. Stir frequently to prevent sticking. Gradually stir in the sugar. Heat, stirring constantly, until the sugar is completely dissolved.

Increase the heat to medium-high. Bring the mixture to a full rolling boil, stirring constantly. Stir in the entire contents of the pectin pouch. Return the mixture to a full rolling boil, stirring constantly. Boil, stirring constantly, for 1 minute. Remove the pan from the heat. Skim off any foam.

To prevent floating fruit, allow the marmalade to cool 5 minutes before filling jars. Gently stir the marmalade to distribute the fruit. Ladle the marmalade into hot jars, leaving ¼-inch headspace. Wipe the jar rims and threads with a clean, damp cloth. Cover with hot lids and apply screw rings. Process half-pint jars in a 200F (93C) water bath for 10 minutes, pint jars for 15 minutes.

Bittersweet Orange Marmalade

Do you or a friend have an orange tree that produces sour oranges? If so, they're perfect for this tantalizing marmalade, traditionally made from Seville oranges from Spain, which are too sour to be eaten on their own. This marmalade has earned several first-place awards.

MAKES ABOUT 6 HALF-PINT JARS

1 cup zested or thinly sliced orange peel (do not pack)
1 cup water
½ cup strained fresh orange juice
¾ cup water
⅛ teaspoon baking soda
2¾ cups supremed and finely chopped orange segments plus enough reserved juice to equal 3 cups (16 to 20 tart or sour oranges)
5 cups sugar
½ teaspoon unsalted butter
1 (3-ounce) pouch liquid pectin

In a small bowl, combine the peel and 1 cup water. Let soak for 10 minutes. Drain the peel and discard the water.

In an 8-quart pan, combine the peel with the orange juice, ¾ cup water and baking soda. Over medium-high heat, bring to a full boil. Reduce the heat, cover and simmer for 10 minutes, stirring occasionally. Stir in the fruit. Cover and simmer 10 minutes more.

Remove the cover and stir in the sugar and butter. Heat, stirring constantly, until the sugar is completely dissolved.

Increase the heat to medium-high and bring the mixture to a full rolling boil, stirring constantly. Stir in the entire contents of the pectin pouch. Return the mixture to a full rolling boil, stirring constantly. Boil, stirring constantly, for 1 minute. Remove the pan from the heat. Skim off any foam.

To prevent floating fruit, allow the marmalade to cool 5 minutes before filling jars. Gently stir the marmalade to distribute the fruit. Ladle the marmalade into hot jars, leaving ¼-inch headspace. Wipe the jar rims and threads with a clean, damp cloth. Cover with hot lids and apply screw rings. Process half-pint jars in a 200F (93C) water bath for 10 minutes, pint jars for 15 minutes.

Wild Blueberry Marmalade

Deep color and flavor are the trademarks of this marmalade. The citrus flavors blend very nicely with the blueberries. This is a great spread for biscuits or toast.

MAKES ABOUT 5 HALF-PINT JARS

1 large Valencia orange
1 lemon
¼ cup water
¼ cup strained fresh orange juice
¼ cup strained fresh lemon juice
½ cup water
4 cups wild or cultivated blueberries,
    fresh or frozen (2 to 3 pint baskets
    fresh berries)
½ teaspoon unsalted butter
5 cups sugar
1 (3-ounce) pouch liquid pectin

❧ Using a zester, remove only the outer colored peel of the orange and lemon. Or, with a sharp paring knife, thinly slice off the zest, then cut it into fine strips. Peel the fruit, removing all of the white pith. Separate the orange and lemon segments from the white membrane and remove any

seeds. Discard the membrane and seeds. Finely chop the fruit and set aside.

In a small bowl, combine the orange and lemon peel and ¼ cup water. Let soak for 10 minutes. Drain the peel and discard the water.

In an 8-quart pan, combine the drained peel, chopped citrus fruit, orange juice, lemon juice and ½ cup water. Over medium heat, bring the mixture to a boil. Reduce the heat, cover, and simmer for 15 minutes.

Sort, stem and rinse the blueberries. If using frozen blueberries, do not defrost.

Add the blueberries and butter to the citrus mixture and simmer, uncovered, for 3 minutes. Stir frequently to prevent sticking. Gradually stir in the sugar. Heat, stirring constantly, until the sugar is completely dissolved.

Increase the heat to medium-high. Bring the mixture to a full rolling boil, stirring constantly. Stir in the entire contents of the pectin pouch. Return the mixture to a full rolling boil, stirring constantly. Boil, stirring constantly, for 1 minute. Remove the pan from the heat. Skim off any foam.

To prevent floating fruit, allow the marmalade to cool 5 minutes before filling jars. Gently stir the marmalade to distribute the fruit. Ladle the marmalade into hot jars, leaving ¼-inch headspace. Wipe the jar rims and threads with a clean, damp cloth. Cover with hot lids and apply screw rings. Process half-pint jars in a 200F (93C) water bath for 10 minutes, pint jars for 15 minutes.

Cherry Marmalade

This beautiful marmalade has a wonderful sweet and tangy flavor. Measure the cherries after pitting and before cutting them.

MAKES ABOUT 5 HALF-PINT JARS

2 large Valencia oranges
Zested or thinly sliced peel of 1 lemon
¼ cup water
4 cups pitted tart cherries, quartered
2 tablespoons strained fresh lemon juice
¼ cup strained fresh orange juice
¼ cup water
½ teaspoon unsalted butter
4 cups sugar
1 (3-ounce) pouch liquid pectin

Using a zester, remove only the outer colored peel of the oranges. Or, with a sharp paring knife, thinly slice off the zest, then cut it into fine strips. Peel the fruit, removing all of the white pith. Separate the orange segments from the white membrane and remove any seeds. Discard the membrane and seeds. Finely chop the fruit and set aside.

In a small bowl, combine the orange and lemon peels and ¼ cup water. Let soak for 10 minutes. Drain the peel and discard the water.

In a medium bowl, combine the cherries and lemon juice. Stir gently until the cherries are completely coated with lemon juice.

In an 8-quart pan, combine the drained peel, chopped oranges, orange juice and ¼ cup water. Over medium heat, bring the mixture to a boil. Reduce the heat, cover and simmer for 15 minutes.

Add the cherries and butter to the citrus mixture and simmer, uncovered, for 5 minutes. Stir frequently to prevent sticking. Gradually stir in the sugar. Heat, stirring constantly, until the sugar is completely dissolved.

Increase the heat to medium-high. Bring the mixture to a full rolling boil, stirring constantly. Stir in the entire contents of the pectin pouch. Return the mixture to a full rolling boil, stirring constantly. Boil, stirring constantly, for 1 minute. Remove the pan from the heat. Skim off any foam.

To prevent floating fruit, allow the marmalade to cool 5 minutes before filling jars. Gently stir the marmalade to distribute the fruit. Ladle the marmalade into hot jars, leaving ¼-inch headspace. Wipe the jar rims and threads with a clean, damp cloth. Cover with hot lids and apply screw rings. Process half-pint jars in a 200F (93C) water bath for 10 minutes, pint jars for 15 minutes.

Citrus Marmalade

The delicate blending of flavors creates an excellent marmalade. Either pink or white grapefruit may be used with equally good results.

MAKES ABOUT 6 HALF-PINT JARS

¾ cup zested or thinly sliced orange peel
　(do not pack)
¼ cup zested or thinly sliced lemon peel
　(do not pack)
1 cup water
½ cup strained fresh orange juice
¾ cup water

⅛ teaspoon baking soda

1⅓ cups supremed and finely chopped orange segments plus enough reserved juice to equal 1½ cups (8 to 10 Valencia oranges)

⅞ cup supremed and finely chopped grapefruit segments plus enough reserved juice to equal 1 cup (2 to 3 large grapefruit)

½ cup prepared lemons (supremed and finely chopped segments and juice of 3 to 4 lemons)

5 cups sugar

½ teaspoon unsalted butter

1 (3-ounce) pouch liquid pectin

In a small bowl, combine the orange and lemon peels and 1 cup water. Let soak for 10 minutes. Drain the peel and discard the water.

In an 8-quart pan, combine the peel with the orange juice, ¾ cup water and baking soda. Over medium-high heat, bring to a full boil. Reduce the heat, cover and simmer for 10 minutes, stirring occasionally. Stir in the citrus fruits. Cover and simmer 10 minutes more.

Remove the cover and stir in the sugar and butter. Heat, stirring constantly, until the sugar is completely dissolved.

Increase the heat to medium-high and bring the mixture to a full rolling boil, stirring constantly. Stir in the entire contents of the pectin pouch. Return the mixture to a full rolling boil, stirring constantly. Boil, stirring constantly, for 1 minute. Remove the pan from the heat. Skim off any foam.

To prevent floating fruit, allow the marmalade to cool 5 minutes before filling jars. Gently stir the marmalade to distribute the fruit. Ladle the marmalade into hot jars, leaving ¼-inch head-

space. Wipe the jar rims and threads with a clean, damp cloth. Cover with hot lids and apply screw rings. Process half-pint jars in a 200F (93C) water bath for 10 minutes, pint jars for 15 minutes.

Grapefruit Marmalade

Either white or pink grapefruit may be used in this recipe, depending on your personal taste. White grapefruit produce a stronger flavor, while pink or ruby red grapefruit are milder but create a gorgeous color. I like to use a combination of white and pink grapefruit to enhance both the flavor and color of the marmalade. I use half white and half pink peels and a ratio of ¾ white fruit to ¼ pink fruit in my measured ingredients. The addition of fresh orange juice heightens the flavor of the marmalade.

MAKES ABOUT 6 HALF-PINT JARS

1 cup zested or thinly sliced grapefruit peel (do not pack)

1 cup water

½ cup strained fresh grapefruit juice

¾ cup water

⅛ teaspoon baking soda

2¾ cups supremed and finely chopped grapefruit segments plus enough fresh orange juice to equal 3 cups (8 to 10 medium to large grapefruit)

5 cups sugar

½ teaspoon unsalted butter

1 (3-ounce) pouch liquid pectin

In a small bowl, combine the peel and 1 cup water. Let soak for 10 minutes. Drain the peel and discard the water.

In an 8-quart pan, combine the peel with the grapefruit juice, ¾ cup water and baking soda. Over medium-high heat, bring to a full boil. Reduce the heat, cover and simmer for 10 minutes, stirring occasionally. Stir in the fruit. Cover and simmer 10 minutes more.

Remove the cover and stir in the sugar and butter. Heat, stirring constantly, until the sugar is completely dissolved.

Increase the heat to medium-high and bring the mixture to a full rolling boil, stirring constantly. Stir in the entire contents of the pectin pouch. Return the mixture to a full rolling boil, stirring constantly. Boil, stirring constantly, for 1 minute. Remove the pan from the heat. Skim off any foam.

To prevent floating fruit, allow the marmalade to cool 5 minutes before filling jars. Gently stir the marmalade to distribute the fruit. Ladle the marmalade into hot jars, leaving ¼-inch headspace. Wipe the jar rims and threads with a clean, damp cloth. Cover with hot lids and apply screw rings. Process half-pint jars in a 200F (93C) water bath for 10 minutes, pint jars for 15 minutes.

Kumquat Marmalade

This is a beautifully colored marmalade with a distinctive flavor. The texture is not quite as smooth as the other citrus marmalades, but this is still an excellent preserve.

MAKES ABOUT 6 HALF-PINT JARS

4 to 6 medium Valencia oranges
3 cups seeded, thinly sliced kumquats
　(do not pack)
½ cup strained fresh orange juice
¾ cup water
⅛ teaspoon baking soda
5 cups sugar
½ teaspoon unsalted butter
1 (3-ounce) pouch liquid pectin

Peel the oranges, removing all of the white pith. Separate the orange segments from the white membrane and remove any seeds. Discard the membrane and seeds. Finely chop the oranges, saving the juice. Combine the fruit and enough of the reserved juice to measure 1 cup. Set aside.

In an 8-quart pan, combine the sliced kumquats with the ½ cup orange juice, water and baking soda. Over medium-high heat, bring to a full boil. Reduce the heat, cover and simmer for 10 minutes, stirring occasionally. Stir in the chopped oranges. Cover and simmer 10 minutes more.

Remove the cover and stir in the sugar and butter. Heat, stirring constantly, until the sugar is completely dissolved.

Increase the heat to medium-high and bring the mixture to a full rolling boil, stirring constantly. Stir in the entire contents of the pectin pouch. Return the mixture to a full rolling boil,

stirring constantly. Boil, stirring constantly, for 1 minute. Remove the pan from the heat. Skim off any foam.

To prevent floating fruit, allow the marmalade to cool 5 minutes before filling jars. Gently stir the marmalade to distribute the fruit. Ladle the marmalade into hot jars, leaving ¼-inch headspace. Wipe the jar rims and threads with a clean, damp cloth. Cover with hot lids and apply screw rings. Process half-pint jars in a 200F (93C) water bath for 10 minutes, pint jars for 15 minutes.

Meyer Lemon Marmalade

I am fortunate to have an abundant supply of Meyer lemons growing in my backyard, because they make the most wonderfully flavorful marmalade. Store-bought lemons may be substituted for the Meyer lemons, but the marmalade will be tarter. Because they are usually harvested green, let store-bought lemons sit on the counter for at least a week to develop more flavor before making the marmalade.

A multiple blue ribbon winner, this marvelously tangy marmalade has also been named Best of Class twice and earned two Best of Division awards.

MAKES ABOUT 6 HALF-PINT JARS

1 cup zested or thinly sliced Meyer lemon peel (do not pack)
1 cup water
½ cup strained fresh Meyer lemon juice
1 cup water

⅛ teaspoon baking soda
2½ cups supremed and finely chopped lemon segments plus enough reserved juice to equal 3 cups (20 to 25 Meyer lemons)
5 cups sugar
½ teaspoon unsalted butter
1 (3-ounce) pouch liquid pectin

In a small bowl, combine the peel and 1 cup water. Let soak for 10 minutes. Drain the peel and discard the water.

In an 8-quart pan, combine the peel with the lemon juice, 1 cup water and baking soda. Over medium-high heat, bring to a full boil. Reduce the heat, cover and simmer for 10 minutes, stirring occasionally. Stir in the fruit. Cover and simmer 10 minutes more.

Remove the cover and stir in the sugar and butter. Heat, stirring constantly, until the sugar is completely dissolved.

Increase the heat to medium-high and bring the mixture to a full rolling boil, stirring constantly. Stir in the entire contents of the pectin pouch. Return the mixture to a full rolling boil, stirring constantly. Boil, stirring constantly, for 1 minute. Remove the pan from the heat. Skim off any foam.

To prevent floating fruit, allow the marmalade to cool 5 minutes before filling jars. Gently stir the marmalade to distribute the fruit. Ladle the marmalade into hot jars, leaving ¼-inch headspace. Wipe the jar rims and threads with a clean, damp cloth. Cover with hot lids and apply screw rings. Process half-pint jars in a 200F (93C) water bath for 10 minutes, pint jars for 15 minutes.

Lime Marmalade

This special marmalade has a strong, vibrant flavor. Select large limes that have dark green skins. A few drops of green food coloring stirred into the water before adding it to the pan with the fruit and peel will enhance the color and appearance of the marmalade. It is a multiple blue ribbon winner.

MAKES ABOUT 6 HALF-PINT JARS

1 cup zested or thinly sliced lime peel
   (do not pack)
1 cup water
¼ cup strained fresh lime juice
1 cup water
⅛ teaspoon baking soda
2½ cups supremed and finely chopped lime
   segments plus enough reserved juice to
   equal 3 cups (22 to 26 large limes)
5 cups sugar
½ teaspoon unsalted butter
Green food coloring (optional)
1 (3-ounce) pouch liquid pectin

In a small bowl, combine the peel and 1 cup water. Let soak for 10 minutes. Drain the peel and discard the water.

In an 8-quart pan, combine the peel with the lime juice. Stir 2 or 3 drops food coloring if using into the 1 cup water. Add water and baking soda to the pan. Over medium-high heat, bring to a full boil. Reduce the heat, cover and simmer for 10 minutes, stirring occasionally. Stir in the fruit. Cover and simmer 10 minutes more.

Remove the cover and stir in the sugar and butter. Heat, stirring constantly, until the sugar is completely dissolved.

Increase the heat to medium-high and bring the mixture to a full rolling boil, stirring constantly. Stir in the entire contents of the pectin pouch. Return the mixture to a full rolling boil, stirring constantly. Boil, stirring constantly, for 1 minute. Remove the pan from the heat. Skim off any foam.

To prevent floating fruit, allow the marmalade to cool 5 minutes before filling jars. Gently stir the marmalade to distribute the fruit. Ladle the marmalade into hot jars, leaving ¼-inch headspace. Wipe the jar rims and threads with a clean, damp cloth. Cover with hot lids and apply screw rings. Process half-pint jars in a 200F (93C) water bath for 10 minutes, pint jars for 15 minutes.

Orange Marmalade

Orange marmalade is still the most popular of all marmalades. This tangy-sweet spread is great on toast, pancakes, waffles or just about anything else. It also makes a wonderful peanut butter and marmalade sandwich. Spoon some on top of vanilla ice cream for a simple and elegant dessert. This delightful marmalade has earned multiple first-place awards.

MAKES ABOUT 6 HALF-PINT JARS

1 cup zested or thinly sliced orange peel (do
   not pack)
1 cup water
½ cup strained fresh orange juice
¾ cup water
⅛ teaspoon baking soda
2¾ cups supremed and finely chopped
   orange segments plus enough reserved
   juice to equal 3 cups (16 to 20 Valencia
   oranges)

5 cups sugar

½ teaspoon unsalted butter

1 (3-ounce) pouch liquid pectin

❧ In a small bowl, combine the peel and 1 cup water. Let soak for 10 minutes. Drain the peel and discard the water.

In an 8-quart pan, combine the peel with the orange juice, ¾ cup water and baking soda. Over medium-high heat, bring to a full boil. Reduce the heat, cover and simmer for 10 minutes, stirring occasionally. Stir in the fruit. Cover and simmer 10 minutes more.

Remove the cover and stir in the sugar and butter. Heat, stirring constantly, until the sugar is completely dissolved.

Increase the heat to medium-high and bring the mixture to a full rolling boil, stirring constantly. Stir in the entire contents of the pectin pouch. Return the mixture to a full rolling boil, stirring constantly. Boil, stirring constantly, for 1 minute. Remove the pan from the heat. Skim off any foam.

To prevent floating fruit, allow the marmalade to cool 5 minutes before filling jars. Gently stir the marmalade to distribute the fruit. Ladle the marmalade into hot jars, leaving ¼-inch headspace. Wipe the jar rims and threads with a clean, damp cloth. Cover with hot lids and apply screw rings. Process half-pint jars in a 200F (93C) water bath for 10 minutes, pint jars for 15 minutes.

Orange-Tangerine Marmalade

The subtle blending of citrus flavors gives this sunny marmalade a wonderful flavor.

MAKES ABOUT 6 HALF-PINT JARS

1 cup zested or thinly sliced orange and tangerine peels (do not pack)

1 cup water

½ cup strained fresh tangerine juice

¾ cup water

⅛ teaspoon baking soda

2¾ cups supremed and finely chopped fruit segments plus enough reserved tangerine juice to equal 3 cups (7 Valencia oranges and 14 tangerines)

5 cups sugar

½ teaspoon unsalted butter

1 (3-ounce) pouch liquid pectin

❧ In a small bowl, combine the peel and 1 cup water. Let soak for 10 minutes. Drain the peel and discard the water.

In an 8-quart pan, combine the peel with the tangerine juice, ¾ cup water and baking soda. Over medium-high heat, bring to a full boil. Reduce the heat, cover and simmer for 10 minutes, stirring occasionally. Stir in the fruit. Cover and simmer 10 minutes more.

Remove the cover and stir in the sugar and butter. Heat, stirring constantly, until the sugar is completely dissolved.

Increase the heat to medium-high and bring the mixture to a full rolling boil, stirring constantly. Stir in the entire contents of the pectin pouch. Return the mixture to a full rolling boil,

stirring constantly. Boil, stirring constantly, for 1 minute. Remove the pan from the heat. Skim off any foam.

To prevent floating fruit, allow the marmalade to cool 5 minutes before filling jars. Gently stir the marmalade to distribute the fruit. Ladle the marmalade into hot jars, leaving ¼-inch headspace. Wipe the jar rims and threads with a clean, damp cloth. Cover with hot lids and apply screw rings. Process half-pint jars in a 200F (93C) water bath for 10 minutes, pint jars for 15 minutes.

Peach Marmalade

A glorious spread for toast or biscuits, this marmalade has a lovely golden color and fresh fruit flavor.

MAKES 5 TO 6 HALF-PINT JARS

2 medium Valencia oranges
1 lemon
¼ cup water
3½ cups peeled, pitted and finely chopped
    ripe peaches (about 3 pounds)
¼ cup strained fresh lemon juice
½ cup water
½ teaspoon unsalted butter
5½ cups sugar
1 (3-ounce) pouch liquid pectin

Using a zester, remove only the outer colored peel of the oranges and lemon. Or, with a sharp paring knife, thinly slice off the zest, then cut into fine strips. Peel the fruit, removing all of the white pith. Separate the orange and lemon segments from the white membrane and remove any seeds. Discard the membrane. Chop the fruit and set aside.

In a small bowl, combine the peels and ¼ cup water. Let soak for 10 minutes. Drain the peel and discard the water.

In a medium bowl, combine the chopped peaches and lemon juice. Stir gently until the peaches are completely coated with lemon juice.

In an 8-quart pan, combine the drained peel, chopped oranges and lemon and ½ cup water. Over medium heat, bring the mixture to a boil. Reduce the heat, cover and simmer for 15 minutes.

Add the peaches and butter to the citrus mixture and simmer, uncovered, for 5 minutes, stirring frequently to prevent sticking. Gradually stir in the sugar. Heat, stirring constantly, until the sugar is completely dissolved.

Increase the heat to medium-high. Bring the mixture to a full rolling boil, stirring constantly. Stir in the entire contents of the pectin pouch. Return the mixture to a full rolling boil, stirring constantly. Boil, stirring constantly, for 1 minute. Remove the pan from the heat. Skim off any foam.

To prevent floating fruit, allow the marmalade to cool 5 minutes before filling jars. Gently stir the marmalade to distribute the fruit. Ladle the marmalade into hot jars, leaving ¼-inch headspace. Wipe the jar rims and threads with a clean, damp cloth. Cover with hot lids and apply screw rings. Process half-pint jars in a 200F (93C) water bath for 10 minutes, pint jars for 15 minutes.

Bartlett Pear Marmalade

This unique marmalade makes a wonderful gift for holidays and special occasions. The oranges give a light, pleasing tang to the pears.

MAKES 7 TO 8 HALF-PINT JARS

3½ cups peeled, cored and finely
    chopped ripe Bartlett pears
    (about 3½ pounds)
¼ cup strained fresh lemon juice
2 medium Valencia oranges
¼ cup water
½ cup water
1 (8¼-ounce) can juice packed crushed
    pineapple, lightly drained
½ teaspoon unsalted butter
6 cups sugar
1 (3-ounce) pouch liquid pectin

In a medium bowl, combine chopped pears and lemon juice. Stir gently until pears are completely coated with lemon juice. Set aside.

Using a zester, remove only the outer colored peel of the oranges. Or, with a sharp paring knife, thinly slice off the zest, then cut into fine strips. Peel the fruit, removing all of the white pith. Separate the orange segments from the white membrane and remove any seeds. Discard the membrane. Chop the fruit and set aside.

In a small bowl, combine the orange peel and ¼ cup water. Let soak for 10 minutes. Drain the peel and discard the water.

In an 8-quart pan, combine the drained peel, chopped oranges and ½ cup water. Over medium heat, bring the mixture to a boil. Reduce the heat, cover and simmer for 15 minutes.

Add the pears, pineapple and butter to the citrus mixture and simmer, uncovered, for 5 minutes. Stir frequently to prevent sticking. Gradually stir in the sugar. Heat, stirring constantly, until the sugar is completely dissolved.

Increase the heat to medium-high. Bring the mixture to a full rolling boil, stirring constantly. Stir in the entire contents of the pectin pouch. Return the mixture to a full rolling boil, stirring constantly. Boil, stirring constantly, for 1 minute. Remove the pan from the heat.

To prevent floating fruit, allow the marmalade to cool 5 minutes before filling jars. Gently stir the marmalade to distribute the fruit. Ladle the marmalade into hot jars, leaving ¼-inch headspace. Wipe the jar rims and threads with a clean, damp cloth. Cover with hot lids and apply screw rings. Process half-pint jars in a 200F (93C) water bath for 10 minutes, pint jars for 15 minutes.

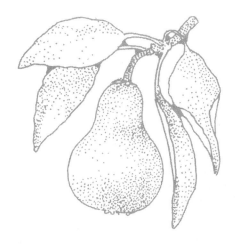

Pineapple-Papaya Marmalade

This exotic marmalade is like a tropical breeze— sweet, fragrant and tantalizing. Mango may be substituted for papaya, or use some of each for a pineapple, papaya and mango marmalade!

MAKES ABOUT 4 HALF-PINT JARS

2 cups pared, cored, finely diced and lightly drained fresh, ripe pineapple (about 3 pounds)

6 cups sugar

2 tablespoons strained fresh lemon juice

3 tablespoons zested or thinly sliced lemon peel

¼ cup water

2 cups peeled, seeded and diced fresh, ripe papaya

½ teaspoon unsalted butter

1 (3-ounce) pouch liquid pectin

In an 8-quart pan, combine the pineapple, sugar and lemon juice. Cover and let stand 1 hour.

In a small bowl, combine the lemon peel and water. Let soak for 10 minutes. Drain the peel and discard the water.

Add the papaya, drained lemon peel and butter to the pineapple mixture. Stir gently until well combined. Over medium heat, stirring constantly, heat until the sugar is completely dissolved. Bring the mixture to a gentle boil, stirring occasionally to prevent sticking. Cook and stir occasionally for 10 minutes.

Increase the heat to medium-high and bring the mixture to a full rolling boil, stirring constantly. Stir in the entire contents of the pectin pouch. Return the mixture to a full rolling boil,

stirring constantly. Boil, stirring constantly, for 1 minute. Remove the pan from the heat. Skim off any foam.

To prevent floating fruit, allow the marmalade to cool 5 minutes before filling jars. Gently stir the marmalade to distribute the fruit. Ladle the marmalade into hot jars, leaving ¼-inch headspace. Wipe the jar rims and threads with a clean, damp cloth. Cover with hot lids and apply screw rings. Process half-pint jars in a 200F (93C) water bath for 10 minutes, pint jars for 15 minutes.

Strawberry Marmalade

This marmalade has a beautiful ruby color and a strong strawberry flavor—a winner by any standard.

MAKES ABOUT 8 HALF-PINT JARS

2 medium Valencia oranges

1 lemon

¼ cup water

½ cup water

3½ cups crushed strawberries (about 1 quart)

2 tablespoons strained fresh lemon juice

½ teaspoon unsalted butter

7 cups sugar

1 (3-ounce) pouch liquid pectin

Using a zester, remove only the outer colored peel of the oranges and lemon. Or, with a sharp paring knife, thinly slice off the zest, then cut into fine strips. Peel the fruit, removing all of the white pith. Separate the orange and lemon segments from the white membrane and remove any seeds. Discard the membrane. Chop the fruit and set aside.

In a small bowl, combine the orange and lemon peels and ¼ cup water. Let soak for 10 minutes. Drain the peel and discard the water.

In an 8-quart pan, combine the drained peel, chopped oranges and lemon and ½ cup water. Over medium heat, bring the mixture to a boil. Reduce the heat, cover and simmer for 15 minutes.

Add the strawberries, lemon juice and butter to the citrus mixture. Gradually stir in the sugar. Heat, stirring constantly, until the sugar is completely dissolved.

Increase the heat to medium-high. Bring the mixture to a full rolling boil, stirring constantly. Stir in the entire contents of the pectin pouch. Return the mixture to a full rolling boil, stirring constantly. Boil, stirring constantly, for 1 minute. Remove the pan from the heat. Skim off any foam.

To prevent floating fruit, allow the marmalade to cool 5 minutes before filling jars. Gently stir the marmalade to distribute the fruit. Ladle the marmalade into hot jars, leaving ¼-inch headspace. Wipe the jar rims and threads with a clean, damp cloth. Cover with hot lids and apply screw rings. Process half-pint jars in a 200F (93C) water bath for 10 minutes, pint jars for 15 minutes.

Sunrise Marmalade

The unique flavor combinations in this marmalade are quite a treat. Make an extra batch of this beautiful and unusual preserve to give as special holiday gifts.

MAKES ABOUT 6 HALF-PINT JARS

6 medium Valencia oranges
½ cup water
2 cups peeled, pitted and finely chopped
    ripe apricots (about 1½ pounds)
¼ cup strained fresh lemon juice
½ cup water
½ teaspoon unsalted butter
¾ cup drained crushed canned pineapple
6 cups sugar
1 (3-ounce) pouch liquid pectin

Using a zester, remove only the outer colored peel of the oranges. Or, with a sharp paring knife, thinly slice off the zest, then cut into fine strips. Peel the fruit, removing all of the white pith. Separate the orange segments from the white membrane and remove any seeds. Discard the membrane. Chop the fruit and set aside.

In a small bowl, combine the orange peel and ½ cup water. Let soak for 10 minutes. Drain the peel and discard the water.

In a medium bowl, combine the apricots and lemon juice. Stir gently until the apricots are completely coated with lemon juice.

In an 8-quart pan, combine the drained peel, chopped oranges and ½ cup water. Over medium heat, bring the mixture to a boil. Reduce the heat, cover and simmer for 15 minutes.

Add the apricots and butter to the citrus mixture and simmer, uncovered, for 5 minutes. Stir frequently to prevent sticking. Stir in the pineapple. Gradually stir in the sugar. Heat, stirring constantly, until the sugar is completely dissolved.

Increase the heat to medium-high. Bring the mixture to a full rolling boil, stirring constantly. Stir in the entire contents of the pectin pouch. Return the mixture to a full rolling boil, stirring constantly. Boil, stirring constantly, for 1 minute. Remove the pan from the heat. Skim off any foam.

To prevent floating fruit, allow the marmalade to cool 5 minutes before filling jars. Gently stir the marmalade to distribute the fruit. Ladle the marmalade into hot jars, leaving ¼-inch headspace. Wipe the jar rims and threads with a clean, damp cloth. Cover with hot lids and apply screw rings. Process half-pint jars in a 200F (93C) water bath for 10 minutes, pint jars for 15 minutes.

Tangerine Marmalade

Opening a jar of this sweet, fragrant marmalade is like opening a jar of sunshine. I prefer to use Minneola tangelos, which are sweet, flavorful and rich in color, but most any variety of tangerine may be used.

MAKES ABOUT 6 HALF-PINT JARS

1 cup zested or thinly sliced tangerine peel
   (do not pack)
1 cup water
½ cup strained fresh tangerine juice

¾ cup water
⅛ teaspoon baking soda
2¾ cups supremed and finely chopped fruit
   plus enough reserved juice to equal 3
   cups (18 to 24 tangerines)
5 cups sugar
½ teaspoon unsalted butter
1 (3-ounce) pouch liquid pectin

In a small bowl, combine the peel and 1 cup water. Let soak for 10 minutes. Drain the peel and discard the water.

In an 8-quart pan, combine the peel with the tangerine juice, ¾ cup water and baking soda. Over medium-high heat, bring to a full boil. Reduce the heat, cover and simmer for 10 minutes, stirring occasionally. Stir in the fruit. Cover and simmer 10 minutes more.

Remove the cover and stir in the sugar and butter. Heat, stirring constantly, until the sugar is completely dissolved.

Increase the heat to medium-high and bring the mixture to a full rolling boil, stirring constantly. Stir in the entire contents of the pectin pouch. Return the mixture to a full rolling boil, stirring constantly. Boil, stirring constantly, for 1 minute. Remove the pan from the heat. Skim off any foam.

To prevent floating fruit, allow the marmalade to cool 5 minutes before filling jars. Gently stir the marmalade to distribute the fruit. Ladle the marmalade into hot jars, leaving ¼-inch headspace. Wipe the jar rims and threads with a clean, damp cloth. Cover with hot lids and apply screw rings. Process half-pint jars in a 200F (93C) water bath for 10 minutes, pint jars for 15 minutes.

Preserves

WHAT IS A PRESERVE?

While the term "preserves" is loosely applied to any form of preserved foods, it is also the name of one particular type and method of preserved food. Preserves are soft spreads made from small whole fruit, such as strawberries or cherries, or larger fruit, such as peaches and apricots, that are cut into large pieces. The fruit is distributed throughout the jar, evenly suspended in a translucent jelly or a clear, thick syrup. True preserves are prepared in a way that maintains the natural shape of the whole fruit or the pieces, resulting in a spread that is clear and shiny with fruit that is plump and tender.

Preserves are the soft spread of choice for many people because of the whole pieces of fruit they contain. While jams contain bits of fruit and jellies are made from clear fruit juices, preserves are packed with big chunks of fruit that mound up on a piece of toast or a fresh scone. When you bite into the fruit in preserves, your mouth is treated to an intense flavor experience.

Making Preserves

Making preserves can be both rewarding and challenging. The biggest mistake home canners make when preparing preserves is that they either partially crush the fruit or chop it into very small pieces. From this simple action, their soft spreads immediately go from being a preserve to being nothing more than a jam with a fancy name. Most people do not realize that preserves must contain whole fruit or large chunks of fruit to truly be classified as a preserve. A number of home-canning cookbooks, both old and new, give recipes for preserves that call for finely chopping, grinding or even pureeing the fruit. These recipes just add to the continuing confusion for a number of home canners. Many a fair entry has been disqualified or failed to win an award because it was entered as a preserve when it was really a jam.

To make exceptional preserves, the fruit must be fresh and of the highest quality. In order to preserve its optimum texture and flavor, the fruit should be canned on the same day it is harvested or the moment it becomes fully ripe. Once the fruit begins to soften, it will be difficult for the fruit to maintain its shape when cooked and may break apart during the continuous stirring necessary to prevent the preserves from scorching.

The best fruit to use for making preserves is fruit that you harvest at the peak of ripeness from your own or a friend's garden, or fruit that you pick yourself at a u-pick orchard or berry patch. Fruit may also be obtained on the same day as harvested from roadside stands set up alongside orchards and growing fields. Some growers will also harvest their produce and transport it to local farmers' markets for sale on the same day. On rare occasion, prime, unblemished fruit may also be obtained from produce markets and grocery stores.

For my blue ribbon berry preserves, I use fruit harvested within a few hours of canning. The boysenberries come from my own garden, where I have a prolific patch of hardy and abundantly producing vines. Blackberries come from the vines of friends, and strawberries from a local field where my family has bought berries for over 20 years. For blueberry preserves, I buy wild berries from a nearby specialty food store. The quality of the fruit does make a difference, and these berry preserves consistently win blue ribbons each year.

Fortunate preserve makers are those who have berry vines growing in their own backyards, or those who have friends with berry vines. If you do not have any, cultivate a few—both vines and friends with vines. A jar of homemade jam will go a long way to securing access to future harvests.

My Bing Cherry Preserves are the most popular preserves among family and friends and are the first jars to fly off my shelves. I am very fortunate to live within 2 hours' driving distance from Leona Valley, which is great cherry-growing country for both sweet cherries and tart pie cherries. Every June, I get up before dawn and make the trek to Bright's Ranch to hand-pick sweet Bing cherries straight from the trees in Ron Bright's well-tended orchard. Some people think I am a bit crazy to drive nearly 200 miles round-trip on a Saturday morning just to pick cherries. Then they taste the incredible cherries that I bring back! People are amazed by the difference in the taste and quality of these superior, fresh-from-the-orchard cherries over the fruit available in the grocery and produce stores. When they clamor for more cherries, I give them directions to the orchard so they can go out and pick their own.

This extra effort in obtaining the best-quality fruit pays off in making preserves. My Bing Cherry Preserves have earned first place in every fair competition I have entered them in across the country. At a recent fair, the judge rewarded me with special words of praise: "Your sweet cherry preserves are exquisite, containing whole cherries, not chopped or halved like most do, and perfectly ripe fruit with exceptional flavor." A judge at another fair was equally kind: "These are by far the best cherry preserves I have ever tasted. Keep making preserves!"

Selecting Fruit

Because preserves are made from whole fruit or large pieces of fruit, the fruit chosen must be of the highest quality and free of blemishes. Even tiny blemishes or imperfections can compromise the quality of whole-fruit preserves. Small surface blemishes may be removed from fruit that is to be cut into pieces, but do not use fruit that is bruised or shows any signs of spoilage. The cell structure of bruised fruit, even when the bruises are cut out, will tend to break down, soften and sometimes turn mushy during the cooking of the preserves. Fruit with even small spoiled spots can harbor harmful bacteria.

Fruit selected for use in making preserves should be fully ripe but still firm. Soft or overripe fruit will fall apart during cooking, and the resulting spread will be more like jam rather than a high-quality preserve packed with pieces of fruit. Underripe fruit will not absorb enough sugar and will remain firm after cooking. Preserves made with underripe fruit will have poor texture, may not set, will be weak instead of intense in flavor and the fruit will have a greater tendency to float in the jars.

Lemon Juice

Except for when making preserves containing tomatoes, only fresh lemon juice should be used when the juice is called for in the recipe ingredients. Lemon juice is added to protect the natural color of the fruit, enhance the flavor and increase the acid level so the preserves will set properly. Fresh lemon juice has a much better flavor than commercially bottled lemon juice, which can taste very sour. When making tomato preserves, however, bottled lemon juice must be added to ensure that the acid level of the preserves is high enough to permit safe canning. While the acid level can vary in fresh lemons, commercially produced bottled lemon juice has a consistent acid content. Never substitute fresh lemon juice for bottled lemon juice when preserving tomatoes. A little extra sugar added to tomato recipes offsets the tart flavor of the bottled lemon juice.

Special Techniques

Because the fruit is left whole or in large pieces, the key to successful preserves is to replace the air and part of the liquid in the cells of the fruit with sugar. Dense fruits or fruits cut into large pieces are usually combined with sugar and set aside to macerate for a few hours. By this process, the fruit absorbs some of the sugar and releases juice. When cooked, the sugar-loaded fruit softens and becomes transparent. The whole fruit or pieces of fruit will remain plump and will retain their natural shape without becoming too soft or mushy.

A small quantity of unsalted butter is a frequent ingredient in many preserves recipes. The addition of the butter reduces the amount of foam (air that becomes trapped in the juice during cooking and rises to the surface) which is created by some fruits, particularly apricots and plums. This foam must be removed from the pan after cooking to prevent it from forming tiny air bubbles in the jars or causing the preserves to appear cloudy. A little butter limits the amount of foam produced, and the amount of skimming necessary before the jars can be filled is reduced. Always use unsalted butter for home canning. Salted butter can give preserved foods an unpleasant flavor and aftertaste.

Preparing Fruit

Each batch of preserves should be prepared separately to achieve the proper set and texture. Do not combine the fruit and sugar in quantities larger than that called for in the recipe, as the proportions of fruit and sugar will not be correct when divided later. Batches of preserves should not be doubled, as doubling does not permit enough of the liquid to evaporate during cooking and will result in preserves that fail to set.

Depending on the recipe, the instructions may call for the fruit to be pitted and left whole, halved, quartered or chopped into pieces about 1/2 inch to 3/4 inch in size. All large fruit that is to be halved, quartered or chopped, such as apricots, peaches, tomatoes, plums and pears, should be peeled first.

Peeling Peaches, Nectarines, Apricots and Tomatoes

These fruits slip out of their skins easily using the boiling water method. Rinse and drain the fruit well. Place small batches of fruit into a large pan of gently boiling water. Leave the fruit in the water for 30 to 45 seconds, depending on the size of the fruit. Using a slotted spoon, quickly remove the fruit from the boiling water and immediately plunge it into a bowl of ice water to stop the cooking process. Allow the fruit to cool in the ice water for at least 1 minute. Remove the fruit from the water and drain it well in a strainer. Using your hands or a paring knife, carefully slip the loose skins from the fruit. If the skin remains tightly attached to a piece of fruit, repeat the above process. If the skin still remains firmly attached and will not release easily, the fruit is underripe or immature and should be discarded.

Peeling Plums, Pears and Apples

Plums and pears, which do not slip their skins easily, should be peeled by hand using a paring knife to maintain their shape. Apples cook best when peeled, cored and cut into slices that are about 3/8 inch thick. It is important to peel the apples because apple peels become very tough and chewy when cooked and can produce a preserve with a very poor texture.

Antioxidant Solutions

Because light-colored fruits, such as apples, peaches, pears and apricots, have a tendency to turn brown when exposed to air, some recipes in this chapter recommend soaking the fruit in an antioxidant solution before canning. Commercial antioxidants are available where most canning supplies are sold, or you may use ascorbic acid crystals, which can be purchased in health food stores. Prepare a bowl of antioxidant solution according to the recipe or the manufacturer's directions. As you peel each piece of fruit, gently drop it into the solution. Make sure that the fruit is completely covered by the solution. Do not leave the fruit in the solution for more than 20 minutes, as it can absorb too much of the solution and develop a tart flavor. Rinse and drain the fruit thoroughly before proceeding with the recipe.

Cooking Preserves

When making preserves in which the fruit has not been combined with the sugar and macerated first, such as cherry or blackberry, a few simple steps should be followed to prevent the sugar from sticking to the bottom of the pan and scorching or caramelizing during cooking. First, layer the fruit and about half of the measured sugar in the pan. Place the pan over low heat. As the fruit heats, it will begin to release juice. Stir gently and often to prevent the fruit and sugar from scorching. As the sugar dissolves in the juice, gradually add the remaining sugar 1 cup at a time, stirring gently after each addition until the sugar is completely absorbed into the juice. Increase the heat and follow the recipe directions for cooking the preserves.

For fruit that has been combined with sugar and set aside to macerate for several hours, gradually heat the fruit and sugar mixture over low to medium heat and, stirring gently, heat until the sugar is completely dissolved. Increase the heat and follow the recipe directions for cooking the preserves.

Crystallization can occur if the preserves are brought to a boil before the sugar is completely dissolved. As the preserves cool, the sugar crystals can re-form. It is very important to dissolve the sugar completely before bringing the fruit mixture to a boil. Preserves containing sugar crystals will receive serious score reductions and fail to win awards in the highly competitive world of fair competitions.

Filling Jars

To reduce the chances of the fruit floating to the top of the jars as the preserves cool, remove the pan from the heat and allow the preserves to cool for 5 minutes before filling the jars. Gently stir the preserves every minute or so to distribute the fruit in the pan. Ladle the preserves into hot jars, leaving ¼-inch headspace. When all of the jars have been filled, use a plastic knife to gently distribute the fruit throughout the jar, pushing some of the pieces to the bottom of the jar. Wipe the jar rims and threads with a clean, damp cloth, then cover and seal with the hot lids and rings. Always process jars of preserves in a water bath canner.

Floating Fruit

After removing the jars from the water bath, if you notice that some of the fruit is floating to the tops of the jars, resist the temptation to invert the jars (turning them upside down) or to shake the jars to redistribute the fruit. While you may succeed in balancing the fruit throughout the jar, there is also a strong probability that you will weaken or damage the seals and allow spoilage agents to enter the jars. Inverting or shaking the jars can also cause the headspace to become obscured, air bubbles to be trapped in the preserves and the spread to stick to the inside of the lid. All of these can have a serious impact on the quality and safe storage ability of the preserves. These flaws will also result in significant score reductions should you choose to enter your preserves into a fair competition.

Apple Preserves

Apple pie fans will love these preserves. The scents of nutmeg and cinnamon fill the house as they cook. Be sure to stir gently or the finished preserves may be full of tiny air bubbles. This preserve recipe has won multiple blue ribbons.

MAKES ABOUT 6 HALF-PINT JARS

7 cups cored, peeled and sliced ¼-inch-thick
    tart apples, such as Granny Smith
    (7 to 9 large apples)
1 cup apple juice
2 tablespoons strained fresh lemon juice
½ teaspoon unsalted butter

5 cups sugar
1 (3-ounce) pouch liquid pectin
1 teaspoon ground nutmeg
¼ teaspoon ground cinnamon

In an 8-quart pan, combine the apples, apple juice, lemon juice and butter. Over medium heat, bring the apple mixture to a boil. Reduce the heat and simmer, covered, until the apples are tender, about 8 to 10 minutes.

Remove the cover and add the sugar, 1 cup at a time, stirring gently between each addition. Heat, stirring constantly, until the sugar is completely dissolved. Increase the heat to medium-high and bring the mixture to a full rolling boil, stirring constantly. Stir in the entire contents of the pectin pouch. Return to a full rolling boil, stirring constantly. Boil, stirring constantly, 1 minute. Remove the pan from the heat. Skim off any foam. Gently stir in the nutmeg and cinnamon until well combined.

To prevent floating fruit, allow the preserves to cool 5 minutes before filling the jars. Gently stir the preserves to distribute the fruit. Ladle the preserves into hot jars, leaving ¼-inch headspace. Wipe the jar rims and threads with a clean, damp cloth. Cover hot lids and apply screw rings. Process half-pint jars in a 200F (93C) water bath for 10 minutes, pint jars for 15 minutes.

Apricot Preserves

These vibrant preserves are packed with fresh apricot flavor. Use apricots that are fully ripe but have not yet turned soft, otherwise the fruit will fall apart during cooking and the finished spread will be more like a jam rather than a preserve. Some minor discoloration on the outside of the fruit may occur during preparation. This is normal and will disappear during cooking.

MAKES ABOUT 5 HALF-PINT JARS

5 cups pitted, peeled and halved firm, ripe apricots
⅔ cup strained fresh lemon juice
4 cups sugar
½ teaspoon unsalted butter
1 (3-ounce) pouch liquid pectin

In a large bowl, combine the apricots with the lemon juice, stirring gently to coat the fruit.

In an 8-quart pan, alternately layer the apricots and sugar. Cover and let stand at least 4 to 5 hours.

Remove the cover. Over medium-low heat, gradually heat the apricot mixture, stirring constantly and gently, until the sugar is completely dissolved. Stir in the butter. Increase the heat to medium-high and bring the mixture to a boil. Reduce the heat and simmer gently for 8 to 10 minutes, stirring occasionally to prevent sticking.

Increase the heat to medium-high. Bring the mixture to a full rolling boil, stirring constantly but gently. Stir in the entire contents of the pectin pouch. Return the mixture to a full rolling boil, stirring constantly. Boil, stirring constantly, for 1 minute. Remove the pan from the heat. Skim off any foam.

To prevent floating fruit, allow the preserves to cool 5 minutes before filling the jars. Gently stir the preserves to distribute the fruit. Ladle the preserves into hot jars, leaving ¼-inch headspace. Wipe the jar rims and threads with a clean, damp cloth. Cover with hot lids and apply screw rings. Process half-pint jars in a 200F (93C) water bath for 10 minutes, pint jars for 15 minutes.

Blackberry Preserves

This excellent preserve is loaded with lots of flavorful berries. This recipe is a multiple first-place winner.

MAKES 6 TO 7 HALF-PINT JARS

7 cups whole firm, ripe fresh or frozen
    blackberries
6½ cups sugar
½ teaspoon unsalted butter
1 (3-ounce) pouch liquid pectin

❧ Gently rinse the fresh blackberries in cool water. Drain well. If using frozen berries, do not defrost or rinse.

In an 8-quart pan, alternately layer the blackberries and about half of the sugar. Let stand for 30 minutes.

Over medium-low heat, stirring frequently to prevent sticking, gradually heat the mixture until the sugar is mostly dissolved. Add the remaining sugar, 1 cup at a time, stirring gently between each addition. Heat until the sugar is completely dissolved. Stir in the butter.

Increase the heat to medium-high and bring the mixture to a full rolling boil, stirring constantly. Stir in the entire contents of the pectin pouch. Return the mixture to a full rolling boil, stirring constantly. Boil, stirring constantly, for 1 minute. Remove the pan from the heat. Skim off any foam.

To prevent floating fruit, allow the preserves to cool 5 minutes before filling the jars. Gently stir the preserves to distribute the fruit. Ladle the preserves into hot jars, leaving ¼-inch headspace. Wipe the jar rims and threads with a clean, damp cloth. Cover with hot lids and apply screw rings. Process half-pint jars in a 200F (93C) water bath for 10 minutes, pint jars for 15 minutes.

Wild Blueberry Preserves

The hint of cinnamon enhances the natural flavor of the blueberries, and the enticing aroma evokes visions of fresh homemade blueberry pie. Wild blueberries have a wonderful flavor and make the best preserves, but the cultivated blueberries found in most grocery stores also work well. Fresh or frozen blueberries may be used with equally good results.

Unsalted butter, added at the end of the cooking process, gives these preserves a rich flavor and luxurious texture. It has helped this recipe to become a multiple blue ribbon winner.

MAKES ABOUT 7 HALF-PINT JARS

6 cups whole wild blueberries
    (4 to 5 dry pint baskets)
½ cup water
7 cups sugar
1 (3-ounce) pouch liquid pectin
2 tablespoons unsalted butter
½ teaspoon ground cinnamon

❧ Remove the stems from the blueberries and gently rinse the berries in cool water. Drain well. If using frozen blueberries, do not defrost or rinse.

In an 8-quart pan, alternately layer the blueberries, water and about half of the sugar. Over medium-low heat, stirring frequently to prevent sticking, gradually heat the mixture until the sugar is mostly dissolved. Add the remaining sugar, 1 cup at a time, stirring gently between each addition. Heat until the sugar is completely dissolved.

Increase the heat to medium-high and bring the mixture to a full rolling boil, stirring constantly. Stir in the entire contents of the pectin pouch. Return the mixture to a full rolling boil, stirring constantly. Boil, stirring constantly, for 1 minute. Remove the pan from the heat. Skim off any foam. Gently stir in the butter and cinnamon until well combined.

To prevent floating fruit, allow the preserves to cool 5 minutes before filling the jars. Gently stir the preserves to distribute the fruit. Ladle the preserves into hot jars, leaving ¼-inch headspace. Wipe the jar rims and threads with a clean, damp cloth. Cover with hot lids and apply screw rings. Process half-pint jars in a 200F (93C) water bath for 10 minutes, pint jars for 15 minutes.

Boysenberry Preserves

This is the perfect berry preserve! It is almost like boysenberry pie in a jar. These preserves have earned blue ribbons across the country.

MAKES ABOUT 7 HALF-PINT JARS

7 cups whole firm, ripe fresh or frozen
    boysenberries
6½ cups sugar
½ teaspoon unsalted butter
1 (3-ounce) pouch liquid pectin

Gently rinse the fresh boysenberries in cool water. Drain well. If using frozen berries, do not defrost or rinse.

In an 8-quart pan, alternately layer the boysenberries and about half of the sugar. Let stand for 30 minutes.

Over medium-low heat, stirring frequently to prevent sticking, gradually heat the mixture until

the sugar is mostly dissolved. Add the remaining sugar, 1 cup at a time, stirring gently between each addition. Heat until the sugar is completely dissolved. Stir in the butter.

Increase the heat to medium-high and bring the mixture to a full rolling boil, stirring constantly. Stir in the entire contents of the pectin pouch. Return the mixture to a full rolling boil, stirring constantly. Boil, stirring constantly, for 1 minute. Remove the pan from the heat. Skim off any foam.

To prevent floating fruit, allow the preserves to cool 5 minutes before filling the jars. Gently stir the preserves to distribute the fruit. Ladle the preserves into hot jars, leaving ¼-inch headspace. Wipe the jar rims and threads with a clean, damp cloth. Cover with hot lids and apply screw rings. Process half-pint jars in a 200F (93C) water bath for 10 minutes, pint jars for 15 minutes.

Bing Cherry Preserves

Every June for the past 25 years, my family and I have gotten up at 4:30 in the morning and made the 100-mile trek to our favorite u-pick cherry orchard on opening day. We hand-select between 50 and 100 pounds of sweet cherries, depending on the quality of that year's crop. Once I had experienced the sweet, full flavor of these tree-ripened gems, I have never settled for a store-bought cherry again.

These incredible preserves are a multiple first-place winner and Best of Division winner and a family favorite. The preserves can also be made with tart pie cherries. If using pie cherries, omit the lemon juice.

MAKES ABOUT 5 HALF-PINT JARS

5 cups pitted sweet cherries
2 tablespoons strained fresh lemon juice
4 cups sugar
½ cup light corn syrup
½ teaspoon unsalted butter
1 (3-ounce) pouch liquid pectin

❧ In an 8-quart pan, alternately layer the cherries, lemon juice, about half of the sugar and the corn syrup. Let stand for 20 minutes.

Over medium-low heat, gradually heat the mixture until the sugar is mostly dissolved; gently shake the pan occasionally to prevent sticking. Add the remaining sugar, 1 cup at a time, stirring gently between each addition. Heat until the sugar is completely dissolved. Stir in the butter. Increase the heat to medium and simmer gently for 5 minutes, stirring occasionally to prevent sticking.

Increase the heat to medium-high and bring the mixture to a full rolling boil, stirring constantly. Stir in the entire contents of the pectin pouch. Return the mixture to a full rolling boil, stirring constantly. Boil, stirring constantly, for 1 minute. Remove the pan from the heat. Skim off any foam.

To prevent floating fruit, allow the preserves to cool 5 minutes before filling the jars. Gently stir the preserves to distribute the fruit. Ladle the preserves into hot jars, leaving ¼-inch headspace. Wipe the jar rims and threads with a clean, damp cloth. Cover with hot lids and apply screw rings. Process half-pint jars in a 200F (93C) water bath for 10 minutes, pint jars for 15 minutes.

Kumquat Preserves

Jars filled with tangy-sweet, plump kumquats are a delightful sight to see and a treat for the senses.

MAKES 5 TO 6 HALF-PINT JARS

5 cups small whole kumquats, stems removed
1½ teaspoons baking soda
2 cups water
3½ cups sugar
2 tablespoons strained fresh lemon juice
1 (3-ounce) pouch liquid pectin

❧ In an 8-quart stainless steel pan, combine the kumquats and baking soda. Add just enough water to the pan to cover the kumquats. Over medium-high heat, bring the mixture to a boil. Reduce the heat and boil gently for 5 minutes. Remove the pan from the heat and let stand for 15 minutes.

Drain the kumquats and rinse thoroughly under cool water. Drain well. With a sharp paring knife, remove ¹⁄₁₆ inch from the blossom end of each kumquat. Set kumquats aside.

In an 8-quart stainless steel pan, combine the 2 cups water and sugar. Over medium-low heat, stirring constantly, heat until the sugar is completely dissolved. Increase the heat to medium-high and bring the syrup to a boil. Reduce the heat and boil the syrup for 5 minutes. Add the kumquats and the lemon juice and simmer gently for 15 minutes. Remove the pan from the heat. Cover and let the kumquats stand in the syrup overnight to plump, stirring occasionally.

Remove the cover. Over medium-high heat, bring the mixture to a full rolling boil, stirring constantly. Stir in the entire contents of the pectin pouch. Return the mixture to a full rolling boil,

stirring constantly. Boil, stirring constantly, for 1 minute. Remove the pan from the heat. Skim off any foam.

To prevent floating fruit, allow the preserves to cool 5 minutes before filling the jars. Gently stir the preserves to distribute the fruit. Ladle the preserves into hot jars, leaving ¼-inch headspace. Wipe the jar rims and threads with a clean, damp cloth. Cover with hot lids and apply screw rings. Process half-pint jars in a 200F (93C) water bath for 10 minutes, pint jars for 15 minutes.

Nectarine Preserves

The nectarines add a delightful tang that makes these preserves special.

MAKES ABOUT 4 HALF-PINT JARS

5 cups pitted, peeled and sliced or chopped
    firm, ripe nectarines
¼ cup strained fresh lemon juice
4 cups sugar
½ teaspoon unsalted butter
1 (3-ounce) pouch liquid pectin

In a large bowl, combine the nectarines with the lemon juice, stirring gently to coat the fruit.

In an 8-quart pan, alternately layer the nectarines and sugar. Cover and let stand for 3 to 4 hours.

Remove the cover. Over medium-low heat, gradually heat the nectarine mixture, stirring constantly and gently, until the sugar is completely

dissolved. Stir in the butter. Increase the heat to medium-high and bring the mixture to a boil. Reduce the heat and simmer gently for 5 minutes, stirring occasionally to prevent sticking.

Increase the heat to medium-high. Bring the mixture to a full rolling boil, stirring constantly and gently. Stir in the entire contents of the pectin pouch. Return the mixture to a full rolling boil, stirring constantly. Boil, stirring constantly, for 1 minute. Remove the pan from the heat. Skim off any foam.

To prevent floating fruit, allow the preserves to cool 5 minutes before filling the jars. Gently stir the preserves to distribute the fruit. Ladle the preserves into hot jars, leaving ¼-inch headspace. Wipe the jar rims and threads with a clean, damp cloth. Cover with hot lids and apply screw rings. Process half-pint jars in a 200F (93C) water bath for 10 minutes, pint jars for 15 minutes.

Papaya Preserves

Papayas make a tropical preserve with exceptional flavor.

MAKES ABOUT 4 HALF-PINT JARS

5 cups seeded, peeled and cubed ripe
    papaya
2 tablespoons strained fresh lemon
    juice
4 cups sugar
½ teaspoon unsalted butter
1 (3-ounce) pouch liquid pectin

In a large bowl, combine the papaya with the lemon juice, stirring gently to coat the fruit.

In an 8-quart pan, alternately layer the papaya and sugar. Cover and let stand 4 hours.

Remove the cover. Over medium-low heat, gradually heat the papaya mixture, stirring constantly and gently, until the sugar is completely dissolved. Stir in the butter. Increase the heat to medium-high and bring the mixture to a boil. Reduce the heat and simmer gently for 5 to 7 minutes, stirring occasionally to prevent sticking.

Increase the heat to medium-high. Bring the mixture to a full rolling boil, stirring constantly, but gently. Stir in the entire contents of the pectin pouch. Return the mixture to a full rolling boil, stirring constantly. Boil, stirring constantly, for 1 minute. Remove the pan from the heat. Skim off any foam.

To prevent floating fruit, allow the preserves to cool 5 minutes before filling the jars. Gently stir the preserves to distribute the fruit. Ladle the preserves into hot jars, leaving 1/4-inch headspace. Wipe the jar rims and threads with a clean, damp cloth. Cover with hot lids and apply screw rings. Process half-pint jars in a 200F (93C) water bath for 10 minutes, pint jars for 15 minutes.

Peach Preserves

This pleasant, fruity preserve has a delicate peach flavor.

MAKES ABOUT 5 HALF-PINT JARS

**5 cups pitted, peeled and sliced or chopped
  firm, ripe peaches**
1/4 cup strained fresh lemon juice
4 cups sugar
1/2 teaspoon unsalted butter
1 (3-ounce) pouch liquid pectin

In a large bowl, combine the peaches with the lemon juice, stirring gently to coat the fruit.

In an 8-quart pan, alternately layer the peaches and sugar. Cover and let stand 3 to 4 hours.

Remove the cover. Over medium-low heat, gradually heat the peach mixture, stirring constantly and gently, until the sugar is completely dissolved. Stir in the butter. Increase the heat to medium-high and bring the mixture to a boil. Reduce the heat and simmer gently for 5 minutes, stirring occasionally to prevent sticking.

Increase the heat to medium-high. Bring the mixture to a full rolling boil, stirring constantly and gently. Stir in the entire contents of the pectin pouch. Return the mixture to a full rolling boil, stirring constantly. Boil, stirring constantly, for 1 minute. Remove the pan from the heat. Skim off any foam.

To prevent floating fruit, allow the preserves to cool 5 minutes before filling the jars. Gently stir the preserves to distribute the fruit. Ladle the preserves into hot jars, leaving 1/4-inch headspace. Wipe the jar rims and threads with a clean, damp cloth. Cover with hot lids and apply screw rings. Process half-pint jars in a 200F (93C) water bath for 10 minutes, pint jars for 15 minutes.

Peach-Pineapple Preserves

A pleasant blending of peach and pineapple flavors makes a special preserve. Apricots may also be used in place of the peaches for a classic taste combination.

MAKES ABOUT 6 HALF-PINT JARS

4 cups pitted, peeled and chopped firm, ripe peaches
3 tablespoons strained fresh lemon juice
5 cups sugar
½ teaspoon unsalted butter
1 (20-ounce) can crushed pineapple packed in heavy syrup, well drained
1 (3-ounce) pouch liquid pectin

In a large bowl, combine the peaches with the lemon juice, stirring gently to coat the fruit.

In an 8-quart pan, alternately layer the peaches and sugar. Cover and let stand 4 hours.

Remove the cover. Over medium-low heat, gradually heat the peach mixture, stirring constantly and gently, until the sugar is completely dissolved. Stir in the butter. Increase the heat to medium-high and bring the mixture to a boil. Reduce the heat and simmer gently for 5 minutes, stirring occasionally to prevent sticking. Stir in the drained pineapple.

Increase the heat to medium-high. Bring the mixture to a full rolling boil, stirring constantly, but gently. Stir in the entire contents of the pectin pouch. Return the mixture to a full rolling boil, stirring constantly. Boil, stirring constantly, for 1 minute. Remove the pan from the heat. Skim off any foam.

To prevent floating fruit, allow the preserves to cool 5 minutes before filling the jars. Gently stir the preserves to distribute the fruit. Ladle the preserves into hot jars, leaving ¼-inch headspace. Wipe the jar rims and threads with a clean, damp cloth. Cover with hot lids and apply screw rings. Process half-pint jars in a 200F (93C) water bath for 10 minutes, pint jars for 15 minutes.

Pear Preserves

A delightfully different preserve, it's sure to please any pear fan. If Bartlett pears are not available, another firm variety of pear that will hold its shape when cooked may be substituted.

MAKES ABOUT 5 HALF-PINT JARS

5 cups cored, peeled and sliced firm, ripe Bartlett pears
¼ cup strained fresh lemon juice
4 cups sugar
½ teaspoon unsalted butter
1 (3-ounce) pouch liquid pectin

In a large bowl, combine the pears with the lemon juice, stirring gently to coat the fruit.

In an 8-quart pan, alternately layer the pears and sugar. Cover and let stand 3 to 4 hours.

Remove the cover. Over medium-low heat, gradually heat the pear mixture, stirring constantly and gently, until the sugar is completely dissolved. Stir in the butter. Increase the heat to medium-high and bring the mixture to a boil. Reduce the heat and simmer gently for 5 minutes, stirring occasionally to prevent sticking.

Increase the heat to medium-high. Bring the mixture to a full rolling boil, stirring constantly and gently. Stir in the entire contents of the pectin pouch. Return the mixture to a full rolling boil, stirring constantly. Boil, stirring constantly, for 1 minute. Remove the pan from the heat. Skim off any foam.

To prevent floating fruit, allow the preserves to cool 5 minutes before filling the jars. Gently stir the preserves to distribute the fruit. Ladle the preserves into hot jars, leaving ¼-inch headspace. Wipe the jar rims and threads with a clean, damp cloth. Cover with hot lids and apply screw rings. Process half-pint jars in a 200F (93C) water bath for 10 minutes, pint jars for 15 minutes.

Plum Preserves

Intense flavor and gorgeous color make this exceptional preserve a multiple first-place winner. Although I prefer Santa Rosa plums for making preserves, another variety of firm plum may be substituted.

MAKES ABOUT 8 HALF-PINT JARS

6¾ cups pitted, peeled and sliced firm, ripe
    Santa Rosa plums, drained
6 cups sugar
½ teaspoon unsalted butter
1 (3-ounce) pouch liquid pectin

In an 8-quart pan, alternately layer the plums and about half of the sugar. Let stand for 30 minutes.

Over medium-low heat, stirring frequently to prevent sticking, gradually heat the mixture until the sugar is mostly dissolved. Add the remaining sugar, 1 cup at a time, stirring gently between

each addition. Heat until the sugar is completely dissolved. Stir in the butter. Increase the heat to medium-high and bring the mixture to a boil. Reduce the heat and boil gently for 5 minutes, stirring occasionally to prevent sticking. Remove the pan from the heat and skim off foam.

Return the pan to the heat and increase the heat to medium-high. Bring the mixture to a full rolling boil, stirring constantly. Stir in the entire contents of the pectin pouch. Return the mixture to a full rolling boil, stirring constantly. Boil, stirring constantly, for 1 minute. Remove the pan from the heat. Skim off any foam.

To prevent floating fruit, allow the preserves to cool 5 minutes before filling the jars. Gently stir the preserves to distribute the fruit. Ladle the preserves into hot jars, leaving ¼-inch headspace. Wipe the jar rims and threads with a clean, damp cloth. Cover with hot lids and apply screw rings. Process half-pint jars in a 200F (93C) water bath for 10 minutes, pint jars for 15 minutes.

Pomegranate Preserves

This unusual preserve has a vibrant red color. Wear rubber or latex gloves and an apron when handling pomegranates, as the juice will stain both clothing and skin.

MAKES ABOUT 6 HALF-PINT JARS

7 to 8 large pomegranates
6½ cups sugar
1 tablespoon strained fresh lemon juice
½ teaspoon unsalted butter
1 (3-ounce) pouch liquid pectin

With a sharp knife, score the pomegranates into quarters, cutting just through the outside skin and being careful not to damage the seeds. Submerge the pomegranates in a large bowl or basin filled with water. Break the fruit apart along the score lines.

Using your fingers, gently remove seeds from the white pith, being careful not to break the seeds. The white pith will rise to the surface of the water, while the seeds will sink to the bottom of the bowl or basin. Skim the pith from the top of the water. Be sure to remove all of the white pith from the seeds, as it is very bitter and will give the preserves a bitter flavor. Carefully transfer the seeds to a colander. Gently rinse the seeds and drain well. Measure 6 cups of pomegranate seeds.

In an 8-quart pan, alternately layer the pomegranate seeds, sugar and the lemon juice. Let stand for 1 hour.

Over low heat, stirring very gently to prevent sticking, gradually heat the mixture until the sugar is dissolved. Stir in the butter. Increase the heat to medium-high and bring the mixture to a boil. Stir in the entire contents of the pectin pouch. Return the mixture to a full rolling boil, stirring gently and constantly. Boil, stirring constantly, for 1 minute. Remove the pan from the heat. Skim off any foam.

To prevent floating fruit, allow the preserves to cool 5 minutes before filling the jars. Gently stir the preserves to distribute the fruit. Ladle the preserves into hot jars, leaving ¼-inch headspace. Wipe the jar rims and threads with a clean, damp cloth. Cover with hot lids and apply screw rings. Process half-pint jars in a 200F (93C) water bath for 10 minutes, pint jars for 15 minutes.

Strawberry Preserves Supreme

This is my absolute favorite soft spread. It has earned 12 blue ribbons at fairs across the country, a Best of Class, a Best of Division, an Alltrista Premium Food Preservation Award and three other special awards of merit. The glorious color and exceptional flavor have earned high praise from judges.

These preserves are best when made at the peak of strawberry season, when the berries have developed their fullest flavor. Use a medium-firm type of berry, such as Chandler or other full-flavored variety. A tomato corer is the perfect tool for removing the strawberry stems.

MAKES ABOUT 9 HALF-PINT JARS

9 cups small whole unblemished
    strawberries
¼ cup strained fresh lemon juice
8 cups sugar
½ teaspoon unsalted butter
1 (3-ounce) pouch liquid pectin

Gently rinse the strawberries in cool water and drain well. Using a sharp paring knife or tomato corer, remove the stems. Discard any hollow berries.

In a large bowl, combine the strawberries with the lemon juice, stirring gently to coat the berries.

In an 8-quart pan, alternately layer the strawberries and sugar. Cover and let stand 4 to 5 hours.

Remove the cover. Over medium-low heat, gradually heat the strawberry mixture, stirring constantly and gently, until the sugar is dissolved.

Stir in the butter. Increase the heat to medium-high and bring the mixture to a boil. Reduce the heat and boil gently for 10 minutes, stirring occasionally to prevent sticking.

Increase the heat to medium-high. Bring the mixture to a full rolling boil, stirring constantly and gently. Stir in the entire contents of the pectin pouch. Return the mixture to a full rolling boil, stirring constantly. Boil, stirring constantly, for 1 minute. Remove the pan from the heat. Skim off any foam.

To prevent floating fruit, allow the preserves to cool 5 minutes before filling the jars. Gently stir the preserves to distribute the fruit. Ladle the preserves into hot jars, leaving ¼-inch headspace. Wipe the jar rims and threads with a clean, damp cloth. Cover with hot lids and apply screw rings. Process half-pint jars in a 200F (93C) water bath for 10 minutes, pint jars for 15 minutes.

Tomato Preserves

An old-fashioned preserve with a modern method makes for a winning combination. Be sure to use bottled lemon juice in this recipe to ensure the acid level is high enough for safe water bath processing.

MAKES ABOUT 6 HALF-PINT JARS

7 cups peeled, cored, quartered and seeded
    plum tomatoes (about 4 pounds)
7 cups sugar, divided use
¼ cup bottled lemon juice
½ teaspoon unsalted butter
2 (3-ounce) pouches liquid pectin

In an 8-quart pan, alternately layer the tomatoes and 2 cups of the sugar. Cover and let stand 4 to 5 hours.

Remove the cover. Drain the tomatoes. Add the remaining 5 cups sugar and lemon juice. Over medium-low heat, gradually heat the tomato mixture, stirring constantly and gently, until the sugar is dissolved. Stir in the butter. Increase the heat to medium-high and bring the mixture to a boil. Reduce the heat and simmer gently for 5 minutes, stirring occasionally to prevent sticking.

Increase the heat to medium-high. Bring the mixture to a full rolling boil, stirring constantly and gently. Stir in the entire contents of both pectin pouches. Return the mixture to a full rolling boil, stirring constantly. Boil, stirring constantly, for 1 minute. Remove the pan from the heat. Skim off any foam.

To prevent floating fruit, allow the preserves to cool 5 minutes before filling the jars. Gently stir the preserves to distribute the fruit. Ladle the preserves into hot jars, leaving ¼-inch headspace. Wipe the jar rims and threads with a clean, damp cloth. Cover with hot lids and apply screw rings. Process half-pint jars in a 200F (93C) water bath for 10 minutes, pint jars for 15 minutes.

Conserves, Butters and Curds

Conserves, butters and curds are three types of old-fashioned soft spreads that are once again gaining in popularity. Fair competition classes are expanding to include a wider variety of flavors as home canners experiment with new and traditional flavor combinations. Each spread has its own unique characteristics and taste appeal. Try an array of them to see which types of spread you, your family and your friends like best.

WHAT IS A CONSERVE?

Conserves have a soft, jamlike consistency and are made from a combination of two or more fruits, one of them traditionally being a citrus fruit. Conserves may be made with two or more fresh fruits or a combination of fresh and dried fruits. A true conserve will contain both nuts and raisins or other dried fruits. It may contain spices as well and is usually made with slightly less sugar in proportion to the fruit than a jam.

Making Conserves

Conserves are made in the same way as jams, by using crushed or finely chopped fruits, but have a slightly softer set than jams. A true conserve contains both nuts and raisins, but many home canners choose to leave these out. When the nuts and raisins are omitted, the conserve basically becomes a soft, mixed fruit jam and no longer classifies as a true, classic conserve.

If you are planning to enter your conserves into a fair competition, check the fair's entry handbook for their specific exhibit requirements. Many fairs require conserves to contain either nuts or raisins, and sometimes both, while other fairs make the addition of these ingredients optional. Realize that, even though the rules say they are optional, many judges will still look for the inclusion of nuts and raisins or other dried fruit when giving high scores. As a true conserve contains two or more different kinds of fruit, check the fair entry handbook for any specific rules regarding the number of fruits a conserve must contain to be eligible to compete in their exhibition.

Feel free to change the dried fruits in the conserve recipes to suit your personal taste. If you do not like raisins, try dried apricots, cherries, dates, cranberries or even blueberries. Select a dried fruit that will harmonize and blend well with the other flavors used in the recipe. If you prefer, when making conserves for family use, you may omit the nuts, raisins or dried fruit.

Special Techniques

As with making jams, a smoother-textured, better-tasting conserve is achieved by peeling most types of fruit rather than leaving the skins on the fruit. Removing the peels gives the conserve a fuller fruit flavor without any of the tough or chewy bits of the peel getting in the way. If you are short on time and want to prepare a conserve with unpeeled fruit you may, but you will sacrifice both flavor and texture for convenience.

If too much sugar is added to the fruit or if the conserve is brought to a boil before the sugar is completely dissolved, sugar crystals can form in the cooled spread. To avoid the development of sugar crystals in the finished conserve, add the sugar and cook the fruit over low heat until the sugar is completely dissolved, then increase the heat and complete the conserve according to the recipe directions.

Toasting and Adding Nuts

Walnuts and pecans provide the best flavor when they are toasted rather than used raw. To quickly and easily toast nuts, place the chopped nuts in a nonstick sauté pan. Over medium-low heat, stir-ring frequently to prevent burning, toast the nuts for about 5 minutes. The nuts will appear dry and develop a nutty aroma when done. Remove the pan from the heat and allow the nuts to cool before use. Nuts may also be toasted on a baking sheet or jelly roll pan in a 350F (175C) oven for about 8 to 10 minutes. Keep a close watch on the nuts, and stir frequently to prevent browning.

To maintain the firm texture of nuts and retain their full flavor, in most cases, the nuts should be added to the conserve after the sugar is completely dissolved and just before stirring the pectin into the fruit mixture. Otherwise the nuts may become soft and mushy or develop a bland or even bitter taste from excessive cooking.

Preparing Fruit

The fruit and other ingredients should be prepared and measured in individual batch quantities only. Never double a batch of conserve because an insufficient amount of liquid will evaporate during cooking, and the conserve may fail to set properly. For best results, crush or chop just enough fruit for one batch and prepare the fruit just before making the conserve. Crushed fruit that is allowed to stand for a length of time can begin to foam and will require more skimming as it cooks to remove the excess foam. Prepared fruit should also be used immediately to prevent the loss of its delicate fresh flavor, texture and intense color.

WHAT IS A BUTTER?

Butters are fine-textured spreads made from pureed or sieved fruit pulp that is cooked with sugar to a smooth, thick, spreadable consistency. Butters should be thick enough to mound up in a spoon without setting firm. Spices are often added to enhance the flavor of the fruit. What would a pumpkin pie be without the heady aromas and flavors of cinnamon, nutmeg and ginger? The same is true for a rich pumpkin butter. In addition to changing the flavor of the butter, spices will also give the spread a dark, warm color.

Making Butters

Fruit butters are made by pressing cooked fruit pulp through a fine sieve or food mill and then cooking the sieved pulp with sugar over low heat until the mixture thickens to a good spreading consistency. Ground spices can be added to butter recipes, with the kind and quantity determined by your individual taste, or they can be omitted.

You can adjust the quantity of spices called for in the recipes to suit your own personal taste. If you like lots of spice, increase or add spices to achieve your desired result. Spices may also be decreased or even omitted if you prefer a more fruity flavor. Be aware that while many fair judges prefer butters that contain small to moderate amounts of spices, heavy use of spices can be too intense, overpowering the natural flavor of the fruit. Spices should enhance the fruit flavor of the butter, not overwhelm it. If all the judge can taste is the spice and not the fruit, the butter's score will drop it out of the running for awards.

The cooking time and number of jars a butter recipe will yield can vary with each batch prepared and depends on the juice content of the fruit. Fruit that is very juicy will require a longer cooking time to reduce to the proper consistency for a butter. As the liquid evaporates, the quantity of the spread in the pan will also reduce. Moderately juicy fruit will require less reducing and thus yield more butter.

Preparing the Fruit

Gently rinse the fruit in clear, cool water, then peel, pit and chop as indicated in the recipe. Place the prepared fruit in a pan, and add a small amount of juice or water to prevent the fruit from sticking while it cooks. Cook the fruit slowly until it is soft, stirring frequently to keep the fruit from sticking to the bottom of the pan and burning.

To create the smoothest of fruit butters, press the cooked fruit through a food mill or sieve to puree the fruit and remove any seeds or skins. Then press the pulp again through a fine sieve to remove any fibrous material or tiny seeds that may remain. This double sieving creates a very smooth, uniform-textured pulp. The sieved fruit will then reduce to a butterlike consistency as it cooks, concentrating the fruit flavor. Double-sieving is recommended for butters that will be entered into a fair's preserved foods competition, where the top prizewinners are set above the rest by both their flavor and their silky-smooth texture.

Pureeing the fruit in a blender or food processor is not recommended, as the fruit pulp can easily become liquefied while trying to remove lumps to achieve a smooth, uniform consistency. When cooked, this liquid pulp will take a long time to reduce and will frequently result in it jelling rather than thickening. A butter should not jell or hold its shape, and you should not be able to cut it with a knife. The other possible result from using a fruit puree is that the butter will have a poor, thin consistency and the spread will separate as it cools. Either extreme can easily happen when using a puree instead of fruit pulp. Both will produce disappointing results and a failure to win awards.

Special Techniques for Cooking Butters

Because most butters are thickened by cooking the pulp slowly over low heat for an extended amount of time, rather than by the addition of pectin as in other spreads, the fruit loses its distinct fresh taste and develops a cooked fruit flavor. Butters should be simmered, not boiled. They will splatter more when boiled, increasing the risk of burns, and the excessive heat under the bottom of the pan greatly increases the possibility of sticking and burning. A butter requires your undivided attention while cooking and must be stirred constantly as it thickens to prevent scorching. This is crucial because even a minimum amount of scorching will cause the entire mixture to taste burned.

When a butter has reached the right consistency, it will be thick enough to mound up in a spoon and it will take on a slightly glossy or shiny appearance. To test the consistency of the spread, place a small amount of the butter on a cool plate. If the butter holds its shape and no separation of juice occurs, the butter is done. If a small puddle of juice forms around the butter, it needs to be cooked for a few more minutes.

WHAT IS A CURD?

Curds are rich, thick, very smooth custardlike spreads made with fruit, sugar, butter and eggs. Usually made from citrus fruits, with lemon being the most common, they have a sweet and tangy flavor. They have a soft translucence, will mound up in a spoon and spread effortlessly. Traditionally English, they are a wonderful treat spread on biscuits or scones or used as fillings for elegant tarts. They can be found in small jars at expensive gourmet shops and served at formal teas in elegant tearooms and fancy hotels.

Making Curds

Curds take relatively little time to prepare and are surprisingly easy to make, yet they make an elegant and superb impression when served to guests. Curds are basically rich egg custards that are extraordinarily smooth and creamy. Recipe quantities for most citrus curds may be doubled or halved, depending on your needs, without sacrificing the quality of the spread. I like to make a double batch of a curd a few days before company

arrives and keep it in the refrigerator, ready for use. Then when it comes time for dessert, I spoon the curd into fresh-baked tartlet shells and top with a spoonful of whipped cream and some fresh zest to create individual servings that are sure to please even the most discriminating gourmet. My lemon curd tarts have also been blue ribbon winners at the Los Angeles County Fair.

Because curds are made with an egg base, they are highly perishable, and it is imperative that they be properly processed in a pressure canner and stored in a cool location. Curds may also be kept in the refrigerator, without processing, for up to a month. For fair entry and shelf storage, they must be pressure canner processed to prevent bacteria growth. To enjoy the best flavor and texture, curds should not be stored for long periods of time and should be used within about 4 months of canning.

Preparing Ingredients

Fresh-squeezed citrus juice that is exposed to air for more than a few minutes can turn quite bitter when heated. Juice the citrus fruit just before making the curd so that the juice does not stand for more than a few minutes time after extraction. If the juice will not be used immediately, cover it tightly with plastic wrap to minimize air exposure and refrigerate. Bring the juice back up to room temperature before using. While this procedure is not recommended, it will produce acceptable results.

Gently scrub store-bought citrus fruits well to remove any vegetable wax that has been applied to make the fruit shine. While nontoxic, this commercial wax can block the zest from releasing its flavorful oils. When you zest the citrus fruit, remove only the colored outer part of the peel from the fruit. The white pith under the colored zest will give the curd a bitter taste. Use a special tool, called a zester, to remove fine strips of colored peel from the citrus fruit. If you do not have a zester, use a vegetable peeler to remove pieces of the outer peel, then slice them into thin strips with a sharp knife. There is no need to grate or mince the zest, as it will be strained from the curd before the curd is ladled into the jars.

Combining the sugar and zest and letting them stand before making the curd allows the sugar to absorb the pungent citrus oil from the zest. When later dissolved in the eggs and juice, the sugar will release the oil and give the curd a stronger citrus flavor. As the mixture heats and cooks, the zest will impart even more flavor to the curd.

Bring the eggs to room temperature before making the curd. Room-temperature eggs will combine better with the other ingredients and will produce a smoother curd. Eggs, however, are easier to separate when they are cold because the yolks are firmer and hold together better. Rich curds require the use of more egg yolks than egg whites. For ease in preparing the ingredients, separate the number of extra egg yolks needed while the eggs are cold. Place the yolks in a small bowl and cover them tightly with plastic wrap. Crack the remaining whole eggs after they reach room temperature and just before making the curd.

Superfine granulated sugar is preferred over regular granulated white sugar because it dissolves faster and will form an emulsion with the eggs and egg yolks. The whole eggs, egg yolks and sugar must be well beaten together before adding the juice, zest and butter, otherwise the eggs will tend to separate from the other ingredients and congeal when heated.

Unsalted butter gives the curd a rich flavor and texture, without the unpleasant aftertaste that can be caused by salted butter. The butter is added cold to help moderate the temperature of the egg mixture as it cooks, preventing the eggs from heating too fast and curdling. Margarine should never be substituted for the unsalted butter in a curd recipe. The margarine will seriously affect the fruit flavor of the curd, and, because of the vegetable oil in the margarine, it does not chill to a temperature that is sufficiently cold enough to slow down the cooking process of the eggs.

Special Equipment and Techniques

Because of the delicate nature of eggs and their tendency to cook unevenly over direct heat, to properly prepare a curd you will need a double boiler. Cooking the curd in the top of a double boiler over gently boiling water will prevent the spread from scorching or overcooking. If you do not have a double boiler, you can improvise by placing a stainless steel bowl over a pan of gently boiling water. Make sure that the water does not touch the bottom of the top pan or bowl. The curd should be cooked by the heat and steam from the gently boiling water, not by direct contact with the water itself.

Extra care should be taken when preparing curds, as they can quickly curdle if cooked to too high of a temperature. They must be stirred constantly or they will scorch or curdle. Curds should be cooked slowly, stirring constantly with a heat-proof rubber spatula, scraping both the sides and the bottom of the pan. The temperature of the custard must be watched closely. The eggs will begin to bond and thicken around 160F (71C). At a temperature of 180F (82C), the eggs will scramble. There is no way to save a curd that has been overcooked; the only solution is to start over again with fresh ingredients. When the curd reaches about 168F (76C), remove the top pan or bowl from over the pan of boiling water and set it on a pot holder or hot pad. The residual heat remaining in the pan should be sufficient to complete the cooking of the curd.

After the curd has finished cooking, it should always be strained through a fine sieve to remove the citrus zest and any small lumps that may have formed in the curd as it cooked. A major element by which a curd is judged is its smooth, creamy texture. Any graininess at all or separation of the eggs and the quality of the curd will be classified as second-rate.

Apple Pie Conserve

Granny Smith apples work very well in this conserve, but you may also use another tart apple variety if you prefer.

MAKES ABOUT 6 HALF-PINT JARS

1 cup apple juice

½ cup golden raisins

3 cups cored, peeled and finely chopped ripe Granny Smith apples

¼ cup strained fresh lemon juice

4 cups granulated sugar

1¼ cups firmly packed light brown sugar

1 teaspoon ground cinnamon

¼ teaspoon ground nutmeg

½ teaspoon unsalted butter

1 (3-ounce) pouch liquid pectin

In a small bowl, combine the apple juice and raisins. Let stand for 1 hour to plump the raisins.

In an 8-quart pan, combine the apples and lemon juice, stirring until the apples are well coated. Stir in the raisin mixture.

In a medium bowl, combine the granulated sugar, brown sugar, cinnamon and nutmeg until well blended. Stir the sugar mixture into the apple mixture in the pan. Add the butter.

Over medium-low heat, heat the apple mixture, stirring constantly, until the sugar is com-pletely dissolved. Increase the heat to medium and bring the mixture to a boil. Reduce the heat and simmer, stirring constantly, for 3 minutes.

Increase the heat to medium-high, and bring the mixture to a full rolling boil, stirring constantly. Stir in the entire contents of the pectin pouch. Return to a full rolling boil, stirring constantly. Boil, stirring constantly, 1 minute. Remove the pan from the heat. Skim off any foam.

To prevent floating fruit, allow the conserve to cool for 5 minutes before filling the jars. Gently stir the conserve to distribute the fruit. Ladle the conserve into hot jars, leaving ¼-inch headspace. Wipe the jar rims and threads with a clean, damp cloth. Cover with hot lids and apply screw rings. Process half-pint jars in a 200F (93C) water bath for 10 minutes, pint jars for 15 minutes.

Apricot-Orange Conserve

The combination of apricots and oranges in this sunny conserve heightens the flavor of both fruits.

MAKES 7 TO 8 HALF-PINT JARS

½ cup golden raisins

½ cup strained fresh orange juice

2½ cups pitted, peeled and crushed ripe apricots

1 cup peeled, segmented and finely chopped Valencia oranges

⅓ cup strained fresh lemon juice

1 tablespoon minced or finely grated fresh orange zest

6 cups sugar

½ teaspoon unsalted butter

½ cup sliced or slivered almonds

2 (3-ounce) pouches liquid pectin

In a small bowl, combine the raisins and orange juice. Let stand for 1 hour to plump the raisins.

In an 8-quart pan, combine the apricots, oranges, lemon juice and orange zest. Drain the raisins. Add the raisins to the pan. Stir in the sugar and butter.

Over medium-low heat, heat the mixture, stirring constantly, until the sugar is completely dissolved. Stir in the almonds.

Increase the heat to medium-high, and bring the mixture to a full rolling boil, stirring constantly. Stir in the entire contents of both pectin pouches. Return to a full rolling boil, stirring constantly. Boil, stirring constantly, 1 minute. Remove the pan from the heat. Skim off any foam.

To prevent floating fruit, allow the conserve to cool for 5 minutes before filling the jars. Gently stir the conserve to distribute the fruit. Ladle the conserve into hot jars, leaving ¼-inch headspace. Wipe the jar rims and threads with a clean, damp cloth. Cover with hot lids and apply screw rings. Process half-pint jars in a 200F (93C) water bath for 10 minutes, pint jars for 15 minutes.

Apricot-Pineapple Conserve

In addition to being a multiple first-place winner, this flavorful conserve earned Best of Class, Best of Division and other special awards.

MAKES ABOUT 6 HALF-PINT JARS

1½ cups finely chopped dried apricots

½ cup golden raisins

1¼ cups strained fresh orange juice

2 tablespoons strained fresh lemon juice

1 (8-ounce) can crushed pineapple

1 tablespoon minced or finely grated fresh orange zest

4 cups sugar

½ teaspoon unsalted butter

½ cup sliced or slivered almonds

1 (3-ounce) pouch liquid pectin

In an 8-quart stainless steel pan, combine the apricots, raisins, orange juice and lemon juice. Let stand for 2 hours to plump the fruit.

Add the undrained pineapple and orange zest to the pan. Stir in the sugar and butter.

Over medium-low heat, heat the mixture, stirring constantly, until the sugar is completely dissolved. Stir in the almonds.

Increase the heat to medium-high, and bring the mixture to a full rolling boil, stirring constantly. Stir in the entire contents of the pectin pouch. Return to a full rolling boil, stirring constantly. Boil, stirring constantly, 1 minute. Remove the pan from the heat. Skim off any foam.

To prevent floating fruit, allow the conserve to cool for 5 minutes before filling the jars. Gently stir the conserve to distribute the fruit. Ladle the conserve into hot jars, leaving ¼-inch headspace. Wipe the jar rims and threads with a clean, damp cloth. Cover with hot lids and apply screw rings. Process half-pint jars in a 200F (93C) water bath for 10 minutes, pint jars for 15 minutes.

Cherry-Almond Conserve

Either finely chopped walnuts or pecans may be substituted for the almonds in this recipe.
MAKES ABOUT 6 HALF-PINT JARS

3 cups pitted and chopped sweet
cherries
¼ cup strained fresh lemon juice
1 tablespoon minced or finely grated
fresh lemon zest
5 cups sugar
½ teaspoon unsalted butter
½ cup sliced or slivered almonds
1 (3-ounce) pouch liquid pectin
½ teaspoon pure almond extract

In an 8-quart stainless steel pan, combine the cherries, lemon juice and lemon zest, stirring until the cherries are well coated. Stir in the sugar and the butter.

Over medium-low heat, heat the mixture, stirring constantly, until the sugar is completely dissolved. Stir in the almonds.

Increase the heat to medium-high, and bring the mixture to a full rolling boil, stirring constantly. Stir in the entire contents of the pectin pouch. Return to a full rolling boil, stirring constantly. Boil, stirring constantly, 1 minute. Remove the pan from the heat. Skim off any foam. Stir in the almond extract.

To prevent floating fruit, allow the conserve to cool for 5 minutes before filling the jars. Gently stir the conserve to distribute the fruit. Ladle the conserve into hot jars, leaving ¼-inch headspace. Wipe the jar rims and threads with a clean, damp cloth. Cover with hot lids and apply screw rings. Process half-pint jars in a 200F (93C) water bath for 10 minutes, pint jars for 15 minutes.

Coconut-Pineapple Conserve

A refreshing tropical spread, it will remind you of warm, sunny days in the islands.

MAKES ABOUT 7 HALF-PINT JARS

2 (20-ounce) cans crushed pineapple, lightly drained
¼ cup bottled lemon juice
5 cups sugar
2 (3-ounce) pouches liquid pectin
1¼ cups shredded or flaked coconut
1 cup chopped roasted macadamia nuts

In an 8-quart stainless steel pan, combine the pineapple and lemon juice. Gradually stir in the sugar. Over medium-low heat, stirring constantly, heat the mixture until the sugar is completely dissolved.

Increase the heat to medium-high and bring the mixture to a full rolling boil, stirring constantly. Stir in the entire contents of both pectin pouches. Return the mixture to a full rolling boil, stirring constantly. Boil, stirring constantly, 1 minute. Remove the pan from the heat. Stir in the coconut and macadamia nuts.

To prevent floating fruit, allow the conserve to cool for 5 minutes before filling the jars. Gently stir the conserve to distribute the fruit. Ladle the conserve into hot jars, leaving ¼-inch headspace. Wipe the jar rims and threads with a clean, damp cloth. Cover with hot lids and apply screw rings. Process half-pint jars in a 200F (93C) water bath for 10 minutes, pint jars for 15 minutes.

Cranberry Conserve

This is an excellent conserve to give as gifts during the holidays.

MAKES ABOUT 7 HALF-PINT JARS

4 cups sorted and stemmed fresh cranberries
1 cup strained fresh orange juice
½ cup water
1 tablespoon minced or finely grated fresh orange zest
6½ cups sugar
½ teaspoon unsalted butter
½ cup finely chopped toasted walnuts (see page 157)
1 (3-ounce) pouch liquid pectin

In an 8-quart stainless steel pan, combine the cranberries, orange juice, water and orange zest.

Over medium heat, bring the mixture to a boil. Reduce the heat, cover and simmer for 8 minutes, stirring occasionally to prevent sticking. Stir in the sugar and butter.

Over medium-low heat, heat the mixture, stirring constantly, until the sugar is completely dissolved. Stir in the walnuts.

Increase the heat to medium-high, and bring the mixture to a full rolling boil, stirring constantly. Stir in the entire contents of the pectin pouch. Return to a full rolling boil, stirring constantly. Boil, stirring constantly, 1 minute. Remove the pan from the heat. Skim off any foam.

To prevent floating fruit, allow the conserve to cool for 5 minutes before filling the jars. Gently stir the conserve to distribute the fruit. Ladle the conserve into hot jars, leaving ¼-inch headspace. Wipe the jar rims and threads with a clean, damp cloth. Cover with hot lids and apply screw rings. Process half-pint jars in a 200F (93C) water bath for 10 minutes, pint jars for 15 minutes.

Golden Conserve

This makes a beautifully colored conserve with a fresh fruit flavor. For a more attractive conserve, remove the red fibers from the center of the nectarines and peaches before crushing.

MAKES ABOUT 8 HALF-PINT JARS

½ cup golden raisins

½ cup strained fresh orange juice

1¾ cups pitted, peeled and crushed ripe nectarines

1½ cups pitted, peeled and crushed ripe peaches

½ cup strained fresh lemon juice

6 cups sugar

1 tablespoon minced or finely grated fresh orange zest

½ teaspoon unsalted butter

1 cup sliced or slivered almonds

2 (3-ounce) pouches liquid pectin

In a small bowl, combine the raisins and orange juice. Let stand for 2 hours to plump the raisins.

In an 8-quart pan, combine the nectarines, peaches and lemon juice, stirring until the fruit is well coated. Drain the raisins. Add the raisins to the pan. Stir in the sugar, orange zest and butter.

Over medium-low heat, heat the mixture, stirring constantly, until the sugar is completely dissolved. Stir in the almonds.

Increase the heat to medium-high, and bring the mixture to a full rolling boil, stirring constantly. Stir in the entire contents of both pectin pouches. Return to a full rolling boil, stirring constantly. Boil, stirring constantly, 1 minute. Remove the pan from the heat. Skim off any foam.

To prevent floating fruit, allow the conserve to cool for 5 minutes before filling the jars. Gently stir the conserve to distribute the fruit. Ladle the conserve into hot jars, leaving ¼-inch headspace. Wipe the jar rims and threads with a clean, damp cloth. Cover with hot lids and apply screw rings. Process half-pint jars in a 200F (93C) water bath for 10 minutes, pint jars for 15 minutes.

Brandy Peach Conserve

Before crushing the peaches, remove the tough red fibers from the center of the fruit. This will produce a conserve with a smoother texture and better appearance.

MAKES ABOUT 8 HALF-PINT JARS

½ cup golden raisins

½ cup strained fresh orange juice

3 cups pitted, peeled and crushed ripe peaches

½ cup strained fresh lemon juice

6 cups sugar

1 tablespoon minced or finely grated fresh orange zest

½ teaspoon unsalted butter

¾ cup sliced or slivered almonds

2 (3-ounce) pouches liquid pectin

⅓ cup brandy (optional)

In a small bowl, combine the raisins and orange juice. Let stand for 2 hours to plump the raisins.

In an 8-quart pan, combine the peaches and lemon juice, stirring until the fruit is well coated. Drain the raisins. Add the raisins to the pan. Stir in the sugar, orange zest and butter.

Over medium-low heat, heat the mixture, stirring constantly, until the sugar is completely dissolved. Stir in the almonds.

Increase the heat to medium-high, and bring the mixture to a full rolling boil, stirring constantly. Stir in the entire contents of both pectin pouches. Return to a full rolling boil, stirring constantly. Boil, stirring constantly, 1 minute. Remove the pan from the heat. Skim off any foam. Stir in the brandy.

To prevent floating fruit, allow the conserve to cool for 5 minutes before filling the jars. Gently stir the conserve to distribute the fruit. Ladle the conserve into hot jars, leaving ¼-inch headspace. Wipe the jar rims and threads with a clean, damp cloth. Cover with hot lids and apply screw rings. Process half-pint jars in a 200F (93C) water bath for 10 minutes, pint jars for 15 minutes.

Tropical Peach Conserve

This conserve has a wonderful combination of flavors. Removing the red fibers from the center of the peaches before crushing will create a superior conserve.

MAKES ABOUT 7 HALF-PINT JARS

3 cups pitted, peeled and crushed ripe peaches

1 (6-ounce) can frozen orange juice concentrate, thawed

2 tablespoons strained fresh lemon juice

6 cups sugar

1 tablespoon minced or finely grated fresh orange zest

½ teaspoon unsalted butter

1¼ cups shredded or flaked coconut

2 (3-ounce) pouches liquid pectin

In an 8-quart pan, combine the peaches, orange juice concentrate and lemon juice. Stir in the sugar, orange zest and butter.

Over medium-low heat, heat the mixture, stirring constantly, until the sugar is completely dissolved. Stir in the coconut.

Increase the heat to medium-high, and bring the mixture to a full rolling boil, stirring constantly. Stir in the entire contents of both pectin pouches. Return to a full rolling boil, stirring constantly. Boil, stirring constantly, 1 minute. Remove the pan from the heat. Skim off any foam.

To prevent floating fruit, allow the conserve to cool for 5 minutes before filling the jars. Gently stir the conserve to distribute the fruit. Ladle the conserve into hot jars, leaving ¼-inch headspace. Wipe the jar rims and threads with a clean, damp cloth. Cover with hot lids and apply screw rings. Process half-pint jars in a 200F (93C) water bath for 10 minutes, pint jars for 15 minutes.

stantly. Stir in the entire contents of the pectin pouch. Return to a full rolling boil, stirring constantly. Boil, stirring constantly, 1 minute. Remove the pan from the heat. Skim off any foam.

To prevent floating fruit, allow the conserve to cool for 5 minutes before filling the jars. Gently stir the conserve to distribute the fruit. Ladle the conserve into hot jars, leaving ¼-inch headspace. Wipe the jar rims and threads with a clean, damp cloth. Cover with hot lids and apply screw rings. Process half-pint jars in a 200F (93C) water bath for 10 minutes, pint jars for 15 minutes.

Variation

Plum-Rum Conserve: Stir ⅓ cup of light rum into the conserve after removing it from the heat and skimming off any foam.

Plum Conserve

This conserve is easy to make and has a rich plum flavor. Almonds or pecans may be substituted for the walnuts.

MAKES ABOUT 6 HALF-PINT JARS

3 cups pitted, peeled and crushed ripe plums
5 cups sugar
1 tablespoon strained fresh lemon juice
½ teaspoon unsalted butter
½ cup finely chopped toasted walnuts (see page 157)
1 (3-ounce) pouch liquid pectin

❧ In an 8-quart pan, combine the plums, sugar, lemon juice and butter.

Over medium-low heat, heat the mixture, stirring constantly, until the sugar is completely dissolved. Stir in the walnuts.

Increase the heat to medium-high, and bring the mixture to a full rolling boil, stirring con-

Apple Butter

This classic butter is packed with old-fashioned goodness and a wonderful apple flavor.

MAKES ABOUT 5 HALF-PINT JARS

4 pounds tart apples, such as Granny Smith
2 cups unsweetened apple juice
2 cups sugar
1¼ teaspoons ground cinnamon
¼ teaspoon grated nutmeg

❧ Rinse apples in cool water and drain well. Core, peel and chop the apples.

In an 8-quart pan, combine the apples and apple juice. Over medium heat, bring the mixture

to a boil. Reduce the heat, cover and simmer until the apples are soft, about 30 minutes. Remove the pan from the heat.

Press the apples and juice through a food mill or fine-meshed sieve. Return the apple pulp to the pan. Stir in the sugar, cinnamon and nutmeg.

Over medium-low heat, heat the mixture, stirring constantly, until the sugar is completely dissolved. Increase the heat to medium and bring the mixture to a simmer, stirring frequently. Reduce the heat and simmer until thick, about 30 minutes. As the butter thickens, stir constantly to prevent sticking or scorching. Remove the pan from the heat. Skim off any foam.

Ladle the hot butter into hot jars, leaving ¼-inch headspace. Wipe the jar rims and threads with a clean, damp cloth. Cover with hot lids and apply screw rings. Process half-pint jars in a 200F (93C) water bath for 10 minutes, pint jars for 15 minutes.

Caramel Apple Butter

The brown sugar in this recipe gives the butter a very special, rich flavor and texture.

MAKES ABOUT 7 HALF-PINT JARS

Apple Pulp
3½ pounds tart apples, cored, peeled
    and chopped
2 cups unsweetened apple juice
1 cup water
¼ cup strained fresh lemon
    juice

Butter Ingredients
4 cups apple pulp
3 cups firmly packed light brown sugar
2⅓ cups granulated sugar
½ teaspoon unsalted butter
1 (3-ounce) pouch liquid pectin

To make the pulp: In a 4-quart pan, combine the apples, apple juice, water and lemon juice.

Over medium heat, bring the mixture to a boil. Reduce the heat, cover and simmer until the apples are soft, about 30 minutes. Remove the pan from the heat.

Press the apples and juice through a food mill or fine-meshed sieve. Return the apple pulp to the pan.

Over medium heat, bring the mixture to a boil. Reduce the heat and simmer gently for 30 minutes. As the apple pulp thickens, stir the mixture frequently to prevent sticking or scorching. Remove the pan from the heat. Measure 4 cups of apple pulp.

To make the butter: In an 8-quart pan, combine the apple pulp, brown sugar, granulated sugar and butter.

Over medium-low heat, heat the mixture, stirring constantly, until the sugar is completely dissolved. Increase the heat to medium-high, and bring the mixture to a full rolling boil, stirring constantly. Stir in the entire contents of the pectin pouch. Return to a full rolling boil, stirring constantly. Boil, stirring constantly, 1 minute. Remove the pan from the heat. Skim off any foam.

Ladle the hot butter into hot jars, leaving ¼-inch headspace. Wipe the jar rims and threads with a clean, damp cloth. Cover with hot lids and apply screw rings. Process half-pint jars in a 200F (93C) water bath for 10 minutes, pint jars for 15 minutes.

Apricot Butter

If you like spiced butters, a small quantity of cinnamon and nutmeg may be added along with the sugar.

MAKES ABOUT 6 HALF-PINT JARS

3 pounds ripe apricots, pitted, peeled and chopped

½ cup apricot nectar or strained fresh orange juice

1 teaspoon antioxidant crystals or ascorbic acid crystals

½ teaspoon unsalted butter

3 cups sugar

2 tablespoons strained fresh lemon juice

In an 8-quart pan, combine the apricots, apricot nectar, antioxidant crystals and butter.

Over medium heat, bring the mixture to a boil. Reduce the heat, cover and simmer until the apricots are soft, about 10 minutes. Stir frequently to prevent sticking. Remove the pan from the heat. Skim off any foam.

Press the apricots and juice through a food mill or fine-meshed sieve. Return the apricot pulp to the pan. Stir in the sugar and lemon juice.

Over medium-low heat, heat the mixture, stirring constantly, until the sugar is completely dissolved. Increase the heat to medium and bring the mixture to a simmer, stirring frequently. Reduce the heat and simmer until thick, about 20 to 30 minutes. As the butter thickens, stir constantly to prevent sticking or scorching. Remove the pan from the heat. Skim off any foam.

Ladle the hot butter into hot jars, leaving ¼-inch headspace. Wipe the jar rims and threads with a clean, damp cloth. Cover with hot lids and apply screw rings. Process half-pint jars in a 200F (93C) water bath for 10 minutes, pint jars for 15 minutes.

Apricot-Orange Butter

A beautiful butter, it has a refreshing orange tang. The antioxidant crystals will help keep the butter from darkening during storage.

MAKES ABOUT 4 HALF-PINT JARS

7 cups ripe apricots, pitted, peeled and chopped (about 2½ pounds)

½ cup apricot nectar or strained fresh orange juice

2 tablespoons strained fresh lemon juice

Zested peel of 1 orange

1 teaspoon antioxidant crystals or ascorbic acid crystals

2 cups sugar

3 tablespoons frozen orange juice concentrate, thawed

In an 8-quart pan, combine the apricots, apricot nectar, lemon juice, orange zest and antioxidant crystals.

Over medium heat, bring the mixture to a boil. Reduce the heat, cover and simmer until the apricots are soft, about 10 minutes. Stir frequently to prevent sticking. Remove the pan from the heat. Skim off any foam.

Press the apricots and juice through a food mill or fine-meshed sieve. Return the apricot pulp to the pan. Stir in the sugar and orange juice concentrate.

Over medium-low heat, heat the mixture, stirring constantly, until the sugar is completely dissolved. Increase the heat to medium and bring the mixture to a simmer, stirring frequently.

Reduce the heat and simmer until thick, about 15 to 25 minutes. As the butter thickens, stir constantly to prevent sticking or scorching. Remove the pan from the heat. Skim off any foam.

Ladle the hot butter into hot jars, leaving ¼-inch headspace. Wipe the jar rims and threads with a clean, damp cloth. Cover with hot lids and apply screw rings. Process half-pint jars in a 200F (93C) water bath for 10 minutes, pint jars for 15 minutes.

Banana Butter

The rum adds a subtle flavor to the butter and both complements and enhances the banana.

MAKES ABOUT 6 HALF-PINT JARS

3½ cups thoroughly mashed bananas
(10 to 12 medium)
⅔ cups bottled lemon juice
1 teaspoon antioxidant crystals or
ascorbic acid crystals
5 cups sugar
½ teaspoon unsalted butter
1 (3-ounce) pouch liquid pectin
1 tablespoon light rum
(optional)

 In an 8-quart pan, combine the bananas, lemon juice and antioxidant crystals. Gradually stir in the sugar and butter.

Over medium-low heat, heat the mixture, stirring constantly, until the sugar is completely dissolved. Increase the heat to medium-high, and bring the mixture to a full rolling boil, stirring constantly. Stir in the entire contents of the pectin pouch. Return to a full rolling boil, stirring constantly. Boil, stirring constantly, 1 minute. Remove the pan from the heat. Skim off any foam. Stir in the rum.

Ladle the hot butter into hot jars, leaving ¼-inch headspace. Wipe the jar rims and threads with a clean, damp cloth. Cover with hot lids and apply screw rings. Process half-pint jars in a 200F (93C) water bath for 10 minutes, pint jars for 15 minutes.

Cranberry Butter

This butter has a deep color and a wonderful, tangy flavor from the cranberries. Either fresh or frozen cranberries may be used for this recipe.

MAKES ABOUT 4 HALF-PINT JARS

2 (12-ounce) packages
cranberries
1 cup water
Zested peel of 1 orange
Zested peel of 1 lemon
3 cups sugar

In an 8-quart pan, combine the cranberries, water, orange zest and lemon zest.

Over medium heat, bring the mixture to a boil. Reduce the heat, cover and simmer until all of the skins pop and the cranberries are soft, about 15 to 20 minutes. Stir frequently to prevent sticking. Remove the pan from the heat. Skim off any foam.

Press the cranberries and juice through a food mill or fine-meshed sieve. Discard the skins and seeds. Rinse and dry the pan. Return the cranberry pulp to the pan. Stir in the sugar.

Over medium-low heat, heat the mixture, stirring constantly, until the sugar is completely dissolved. Increase the heat to medium and bring the mixture to a simmer, stirring frequently. Reduce the heat and simmer until thick, about 10 to 15 minutes. As the butter thickens, stir constantly to prevent sticking or scorching. Remove the pan from the heat. Skim off any foam.

Ladle the hot butter into hot jars, leaving 1/4-inch headspace. Wipe the jar rims and threads with a clean, damp cloth. Cover with hot lids and apply screw rings. Process half-pint jars in a 200F (93C) water bath for 10 minutes, pint jars for 15 minutes.

Mango Butter

Mangoes make a very nice and unusual butter with a tropical flavor.

MAKES ABOUT 4 HALF-PINT JARS

6 cups pitted, peeled and sliced or chopped
    ripe mangoes
1/2 cup strained fresh orange juice
1/2 cup water
2 tablespoons strained fresh lemon juice
1 teaspoon antioxidant crystals or ascorbic
    acid crystals
2 cups sugar

In an 8-quart pan, combine the mangoes, orange juice, water, lemon juice and antioxidant crystals.

Over medium heat, bring the mixture to a boil. Reduce the heat, cover and simmer until the mangoes are soft, about 10 minutes. Stir frequently to prevent sticking. Remove the pan from the heat. Skim off any foam.

Press the mangoes and juice through a food mill or fine-meshed sieve. Return the mango pulp to the pan. Stir in the sugar.

Over medium-low heat, heat the mixture, stirring constantly, until the sugar is completely dissolved. Increase the heat to medium and bring the mixture to a simmer, stirring frequently. Reduce the heat and simmer until thick, about 10 to 20 minutes. As the butter thickens, stir constantly to prevent sticking or scorching. Remove the pan from the heat. Skim off any foam.

Ladle the hot butter into hot jars, leaving 1/4-inch headspace. Wipe the jar rims and threads with a clean, damp cloth. Cover with hot lids and apply screw rings. Process half-pint jars in a 200F (93C) water bath for 10 minutes, pint jars for 15 minutes.

Peach Butter

For a spicy butter, add a touch of ground cinnamon and grated nutmeg.

MAKES ABOUT 6 HALF-PINT JARS

4 pounds ripe peaches, peeled, pitted and chopped
⅓ cup strained fresh orange juice
1 teaspoon antioxidant crystals or ascorbic acid crystals
½ teaspoon unsalted butter
3 cups sugar
2 tablespoons strained fresh lemon juice

In an 8-quart pan, combine the peaches, orange juice, antioxidant crystals and butter.

Over medium heat, bring the mixture to a boil. Reduce the heat, cover and simmer until the peaches are soft, about 10 minutes. Stir frequently to prevent sticking. Remove the pan from the heat. Skim off any foam.

Press the peaches and juice through a food mill or fine-meshed sieve. Return the peach pulp to the pan. Stir in the sugar and lemon juice.

Over medium-low heat, heat the mixture, stirring constantly, until the sugar is completely dissolved. Increase the heat to medium and bring the mixture to a simmer, stirring frequently. Reduce the heat and simmer until thick, about 20 to 30 minutes. As the butter thickens, stir constantly to

prevent sticking or scorching. Remove the pan from the heat. Skim off any foam.

Ladle the hot butter into hot jars, leaving ¼-inch headspace. Wipe the jar rims and threads with a clean, damp cloth. Cover with hot lids and apply screw rings. Process half-pint jars in a 200F (93C) water bath for 10 minutes, pint jars for 15 minutes.

Variation
Nectarine Butter: Substitute ripe yellow-fleshed nectarines for the peaches. Or try using half peaches and half nectarines for a tasty blended butter.

Peach-Mango Butter

A very nice mixed fruit butter, it has a tropical flavor.

MAKES 6 TO 7 HALF-PINT JARS

2¾ cups pitted, peeled and crushed ripe peaches
1½ cups pitted, peeled and crushed ripe mangoes
⅔ cup strained fresh orange juice
2 tablespoons strained fresh lemon juice
½ teaspoon unsalted butter
4½ cups sugar
1 (3-ounce) pouch liquid pectin

In an 8-quart pan, combine the peaches, mangoes, orange juice, lemon juice and butter.

Over medium heat, bring the mixture to a boil. Reduce the heat, cover and simmer gently 5 minutes, stirring frequently to prevent sticking. Remove the pan from the heat. Skim off any foam.

Press the fruit and juice through a food mill or fine-meshed sieve. Return the fruit pulp to the pan. Stir in the sugar.

Over medium-low heat, heat the mixture, stirring constantly, until the sugar is completely dissolved. Increase the heat to medium-high, and bring the mixture to a full rolling boil, stirring constantly. Stir in the entire contents of the pectin pouch. Return to a full rolling boil, stirring constantly. Boil, stirring constantly, 1 minute. Remove the pan from the heat. Skim off any foam.

Ladle the hot butter into hot jars, leaving ¼-inch headspace. Wipe the jar rims and threads with a clean, damp cloth. Cover with hot lids and apply screw rings. Process half-pint jars in a 200F (93C) water bath for 10 minutes, pint jars for 15 minutes.

Pear Butter

This is a smooth butter with a delicate pear flavor.
MAKES ABOUT 6 HALF-PINT JARS

15 medium, ripe Bartlett pears, cored, peeled and chopped
½ cup strained fresh orange juice
1 teaspoon antioxidant crystals or ascorbic acid crystals
Zested peel of 1 orange
Zested peel of 1 lemon
½ teaspoon unsalted butter

3 cups sugar
2 tablespoons strained fresh lemon juice
½ teaspoon grated nutmeg

In an 8-quart pan, combine the pears, orange juice, antioxidant crystals, orange zest, lemon zest and butter.

Over medium heat, bring the mixture to a boil. Reduce the heat, cover and simmer until the pears are soft, about 20 minutes. Stir frequently to prevent sticking. Remove the pan from the heat. Skim off any foam.

Press the pears and juice through a food mill or fine-meshed sieve. Return the pear pulp to the pan. Stir in the sugar and lemon juice.

Over medium-low heat, heat the mixture, stirring constantly, until the sugar is completely dissolved. Increase the heat to medium and bring the mixture to a simmer, stirring frequently. Reduce the heat and simmer until thick, about 25 to 30 minutes. As the butter thickens, stir constantly to prevent sticking or scorching. Remove the pan from the heat. Skim off any foam. Stir in the nutmeg.

Ladle the hot butter into hot jars, leaving ¼-inch headspace. Wipe the jar rims and threads with a clean, damp cloth. Cover with hot lids and apply screw rings. Process half-pint jars in a 200F (93C) water bath for 10 minutes, pint jars for 15 minutes.

Pumpkin Butter

The spicy aroma from this butter conjures up fond memories of Christmases past. If you prefer a spicier butter, the cinnamon may be increased to 2 teaspoons.

MAKES 6 HALF-PINT JARS

3½ cups canned solid pack pumpkin
1½ teaspoons ground cinnamon
½ teaspoon grated nutmeg
¼ teaspoon ground ginger
4 cups granulated sugar
1½ cups firmly packed light brown sugar
½ teaspoon unsalted butter
1 (3-ounce) pouch liquid pectin

In an 8-quart pan, combine the pumpkin, cinnamon, nutmeg and ginger, stirring until smooth and well blended. Gradually stir in the granulated sugar and brown sugar. Add the butter.

Over medium-low heat, heat the mixture, stirring constantly, until the sugar is completely dissolved. Increase the heat to medium-high, and bring the mixture to a full rolling boil, stirring constantly. Stir in the entire contents of the pectin pouch. Return to a full rolling boil, stirring constantly. Boil, stirring constantly, 1 minute. Remove the pan from the heat. Skim off any foam.

Ladle the hot butter into hot jars, leaving ¼-inch headspace. Wipe the jar rims and threads with a clean, damp cloth. Cover with hot lids and apply screw rings. Process half-pint jars in a 200F (93C) water bath for 10 minutes, pint jars for 15 minutes.

Variation

Pumpkin-Pecan Butter: Stir ¾ cup finely chopped toasted pecans into the pumpkin mixture after the sugar is dissolved and before adding the pectin.

Cranberry Curd

The cranberry juice gives this a curd a wonderful tang and a beautiful pink color. Pure, unsweetened cranberry juice can be found in many health food stores and specialty food stores. Do not use a sweetened juice or juice blend, as the curd will be too sweet and may not thicken properly. Reducing the quantity of sugar in the recipe to accommodate the sugar in a sweetened juice will produce a thin custard rather than a thick curd.

MAKES ABOUT 3 HALF-PINT JARS

4 large eggs
8 large egg yolks
2 cups superfine sugar
¾ cup unsweetened cranberry juice
½ cup unsalted butter, chilled, cut into
    10 pieces

Place a medium glass or metal bowl in the refrigerator to chill.

Fill the bottom pan of a double boiler or medium saucepan about ¼ full of water. Over medium-high heat, bring the water to a gentle boil.

In the top pan of a double boiler or a medium metal bowl, lightly beat the eggs and egg yolks. Gradually whisk in the superfine sugar until well blended. Stir in the cranberry juice. Add the butter pieces.

Place the pan or bowl over the pan of boiling water. Make sure the top pan sits well above the water so the curd will be cooked by the steam only, not the boiling water. Reduce the heat to keep the water from boiling too vigorously.

Slowly heat the mixture, stirring constantly with a flexible spatula or a spoon. Stir gently or the curd will be filled with tiny air bubbles. Scrape the bottom of the pan frequently to prevent scorching or curdling. Cook the mixture until it reaches a temperature between 168F and 170F (76C and 77C), about 5 to 7 minutes.

Remove the top pan or bowl from the double boiler and place it on a dish towel. Continue to stir the mixture until the curd thickens and coats the back of a metal spoon, about 5 minutes.

Remove the chilled bowl from the refrigerator. Place a fine-meshed sieve over the bowl. Slowly pour the curd through the sieve and into the chilled bowl to strain the zest and any small lumps from the curd. Gently stir the curd to remove any air bubbles.

Ladle the curd into hot jars, leaving ¼-inch headspace. Using a plastic knife, remove any trapped air bubbles. Wipe the jar rims and threads with a clean, damp cloth. Cover with hot lids and apply screw rings. Process 4-ounce jars and half-pint jars for 10 minutes at 11 pounds of pressure in a dial-gauge pressure canner or at 10 pounds pressure in a weighted-gauge pressure canner.

Grapefruit Curd

Grapefruit curd has a refreshingly crisp flavor. Either white or pink grapefruit may be used in this recipe. Pink grapefruit will give the curd a pretty pale pinkish-orange color.

MAKES ABOUT 3 HALF-PINT JARS

1¾ cups superfine sugar
3 tablespoons fresh grapefruit zest
4 large eggs

7 large egg yolks
1 cup strained fresh grapefruit juice (2 to 3 medium grapefruit)
¾ cup unsalted butter, chilled, cut into 10 pieces

Place a medium glass or metal bowl in the refrigerator to chill.

In a small bowl, combine the superfine sugar and grapefruit zest, stirring until well blended. Let stand for 30 minutes to allow the sugar to pick up the citrus flavor of the zest.

Fill the bottom pan of a double boiler or medium saucepan about ¼ full of water. Over medium-high heat, bring the water to a gentle boil.

In the top pan of a double boiler or a medium metal bowl, lightly beat the whole eggs and egg yolks. Gradually whisk in the sugar and zest until well blended. Stir in the grapefruit juice. Add the butter pieces.

Place the pan or bowl over the pan of boiling water. Make sure the top pan sits well above the water so the curd will be cooked by the steam only, not the boiling water. Reduce the heat to keep the water from boiling too vigorously.

Slowly heat the mixture, stirring constantly with a flexible spatula or a spoon. Stir gently or the curd will be filled with tiny air bubbles. Scrape the bottom of the pan frequently to prevent scorching or curdling. Cook the mixture until it reaches a temperature between 168F and 170F (76C and 77C), about 5 to 7 minutes.

Remove the top pan or bowl from the double boiler and place it on a dish towel. Continue to stir the mixture until the curd thickens and coats the back of a metal spoon, about 5 minutes.

Remove the chilled bowl from the refrigerator. Place a fine-meshed sieve over the bowl. Slowly pour the curd through the sieve and into the chilled bowl to strain the zest and any small lumps from the curd. Gently stir the curd to remove any air bubbles.

Ladle the curd into hot jars, leaving ¼-inch headspace. Using a plastic knife, remove any trapped air bubbles. Wipe the jar rims and threads with a clean, damp cloth. Cover with hot lids and apply screw rings. Process 4-ounce jars and half-pint jars for 10 minutes at 11 pounds of pressure in a dial-gauge pressure canner or at 10 pounds pressure in a weighted-gauge pressure canner.

Meyer Lemon Curd

Lemon is the traditional English flavor for curd and is the most common variety found in specialty stores. This recipe is a multiple blue ribbon winner. It makes a great filling for pies, tarts and cakes, as well as a smooth spread for scones. Meyer Lemon Curd is a popular choice of my friends and family, and I have a hard time keeping up with the demand. One long-time friend, Peg DePiazza, uses jars of my lemon curd to barter for special favors from her children.

The Meyer lemon juice and zest give this curd the intense flavor of a luscious lemon pie filling. If you do not have access to Meyer lemons, regular lemons may be substituted.

MAKES 3 HALF-PINT JARS

2½ cups superfine sugar

½ cup fresh Meyer lemon zest

4 large eggs

7 large egg yolks

1 cup strained fresh Meyer lemon juice
   (6 to 8 medium lemons)

¾ cup unsalted butter, chilled, cut into
   10 pieces

❧ Place a medium glass or metal bowl in the refrigerator to chill.

In a small bowl, combine the superfine sugar and lemon zest, stirring until well blended. Let stand for 30 minutes to allow the sugar to pick up the citrus flavor of the zest.

Fill the bottom pan of a double boiler or medium saucepan about ¼ full of water. Over medium-high heat, bring the water to a gentle boil.

In the top pan of a double boiler or a medium metal bowl, lightly beat the whole eggs and egg yolks. Gradually whisk in the sugar and zest until well blended. Stir in the lemon juice. Add the butter pieces.

Place the pan or bowl over the pan of boiling water. Make sure the top pan sits well above the water so the curd will be cooked by the steam only, not the boiling water. Reduce the heat to keep the water from boiling too vigorously.

Slowly heat the mixture, stirring constantly with a flexible spatula or a spoon. Stir gently or the curd will be filled with tiny air bubbles. Scrape the bottom of the pan frequently to prevent scorching or curdling. Cook the mixture until it reaches a temperature between 168F and 170F (76C and 77C), about 5 to 7 minutes.

Remove the top pan or bowl from the double boiler and place it on a dish towel. Continue to stir the mixture until the curd thickens and coats the back of a metal spoon, about 5 minutes.

Remove the chilled bowl from the refrigerator. Place a fine-meshed sieve over the bowl. Slowly pour the curd through the sieve and into the chilled bowl to strain the zest and any small lumps from the curd. Gently stir the curd to remove any air bubbles.

Ladle the curd into hot jars, leaving ¼-inch headspace. Using a plastic knife, remove any trapped air bubbles. Wipe the jar rims and threads with a clean, damp cloth. Cover with hot lids and apply screw rings. Process 4-ounce jars and half-pint jars for 10 minutes at 11 pounds of pressure in a dial-gauge pressure canner or at 10 pounds pressure in a weighted-gauge pressure canner.

Lime Curd

This curd has a zesty lime flavor that is sure to brighten up any breakfast table or afternoon tea. It also makes an excellent filling for tarts.

MAKES ABOUT 3 HALF-PINT JARS

2 cups superfine sugar

¼ cup fresh lime zest

4 large eggs

7 large egg yolks

1 cup strained fresh lime juice (about
    10 medium limes)

⅔ cup unsalted butter, chilled, cut into
    10 pieces

Place a medium glass or metal bowl in the refrigerator to chill.

In a small bowl, combine the superfine sugar and lime zest, stirring until well blended. Let stand for 30 minutes to allow the sugar to pick up the citrus flavor of the zest.

Fill the bottom pan of a double boiler or medium saucepan about ¼ full of water. Over medium-high heat, bring the water to a gentle boil.

In the top pan of a double boiler or a medium metal bowl, lightly beat the whole eggs and egg yolks. Gradually whisk in the sugar and zest until well blended. Stir in the lime juice. Add the butter pieces.

Place the pan or bowl over the pan of boiling water. Make sure the top pan sits well above the water so the curd will be cooked by the steam only, not the boiling water. Reduce the heat to keep the water from boiling too vigorously.

Slowly heat the mixture, stirring constantly with a flexible spatula or a spoon. Stir gently or the curd will be filled with tiny air bubbles. Scrape the bottom of the pan frequently to prevent scorching or curdling. Cook the mixture until it reaches a temperature between 168F and 170F (76C and 77C), about 5 to 7 minutes.

Remove the top pan or bowl from the double boiler and place it on a dish towel. Continue to stir the mixture until the curd thickens and coats the back of a metal spoon, about 5 minutes.

Remove the chilled bowl from the refrigerator. Place a fine-meshed sieve over the bowl. Slowly pour the curd through the sieve and into the chilled bowl to strain the zest and any small lumps from the curd. Gently stir the curd to remove any air bubbles.

Ladle the curd into hot jars, leaving ¼-inch headspace. Using a plastic knife, remove any trapped air bubbles. Wipe the jar rims and threads with a clean, damp cloth. Cover with hot lids and apply screw rings. Process 4-ounce jars and half-pint jars for 10 minutes at 11 pounds of pressure in a dial-gauge pressure canner or at 10 pounds of pressure in a weighted-gauge pressure canner.

Mango Curd

This special curd has a tropical flavor, soft orange color and a fruity fragrance. Bottled, unsweetened mango juice may be used in place of the fresh mango juice.

MAKES ABOUT 3 HALF-PINT JARS

Mango Juice
2 to 3 large ripe mangoes, pitted, peeled and crushed
⅓ cup water

Curd Ingredients
1⅓ cups superfine sugar
¼ cup fresh orange zest
4 large eggs
7 large egg yolks
¾ cup mango juice
1 tablespoon strained fresh orange juice
1 tablespoon strained fresh lemon juice
½ cup unsalted butter, chilled, cut into 8 pieces

To extract the juice: In a medium saucepan, combine the mangoes and water. Over medium heat, bring the mixture to a boil. Reduce the heat, cover and simmer until the mangoes are soft, about 5 to 10 minutes. Remove the pan from the heat and let stand for 15 minutes.

Place a fine-meshed sieve over a bowl. Ladle the mango pulp and juice into the sieve to separate the juice from the pulp. Discard the pulp. Measure ¾ cup juice.

To make the curd: Place a medium glass or metal bowl in the refrigerator to chill.

In a small bowl, combine the superfine sugar and orange zest, stirring until well blended. Let stand for 30 minutes to allow the sugar to pick up the citrus flavor of the zest.

Fill the bottom pan of a double boiler or medium saucepan about ¼ full of water. Over medium-high heat, bring the water to a gentle boil.

In the top pan of a double boiler or a medium metal bowl, lightly beat the whole eggs and egg yolks. Gradually whisk in the sugar and zest until well blended. Stir in the mango juice, orange juice and lemon juice. Add the butter pieces.

Place the pan or bowl over the pan of boiling water. Make sure the top pan sits well above the water so the curd will be cooked by the steam only, not the boiling water. Reduce the heat to keep the water from boiling too vigorously.

Slowly heat the mixture, stirring constantly with a flexible spatula or a spoon. Stir gently or the curd will be filled with tiny air bubbles. Scrape the bottom of the pan frequently to prevent scorching or curdling. Cook the mixture until it reaches a temperature between 168F and 170F (76C and 77C), about 5 to 7 minutes.

Remove the top pan or bowl from the double boiler and place it on a dish towel. Continue to stir the mixture until the curd thickens and coats the back of a metal spoon, about 5 minutes.

Remove the chilled bowl from the refrigerator. Place a fine-meshed sieve over the bowl. Slowly pour the curd through the sieve and into the chilled bowl to strain the zest and any small lumps from the curd. Gently stir the curd to remove any air bubbles.

Ladle the curd into hot jars, leaving ¼-inch headspace. Using a plastic knife, remove any trapped air bubbles. Wipe the jar rims and threads with a clean, damp cloth. Cover with hot lids and apply screw rings. Process 4-ounce jars and half-pint jars for 10 minutes at 11 pounds of pressure in a dial-gauge pressure canner or at 10 pounds of pressure in a weighted-gauge pressure canner.

Orange Curd

This curd has a delicate orange flavor and soft fragrance.

MAKES ABOUT 3 HALF-PINT JARS

1⅔ cups superfine sugar
⅓ cup fresh orange zest
4 large eggs
8 large egg yolks
1 cup strained fresh orange juice
   (5 to 6 medium oranges)
⅔ cup unsalted butter, chilled, cut into
   10 pieces

Place a medium glass or metal bowl in the refrigerator to chill.

In a small bowl, combine the superfine sugar and orange zest, stirring until well blended. Let stand for 30 minutes to allow the sugar to pick up the citrus flavor of the zest.

Fill the bottom pan of a double boiler or medium saucepan about ¼ full of water. Over medium-high heat, bring the water to a gentle boil.

In the top pan of a double boiler or a medium metal bowl, lightly beat the whole eggs and egg yolks. Gradually whisk in the sugar and zest until well blended. Stir in the orange juice. Add the butter pieces.

Place the pan or bowl over the pan of boiling water. Make sure the top pan sits well above the water so the curd will be cooked by the steam only, not the boiling water. Reduce the heat to keep the water from boiling too vigorously.

Slowly heat the mixture, stirring constantly with a flexible spatula or a spoon. Stir gently or the curd will be filled with tiny air bubbles. Scrape the bottom of the pan frequently to prevent scorching or curdling. Cook the mixture until it reaches a temperature between 168F and 170F (76C and 77C), about 5 to 7 minutes.

Remove the top pan or bowl from the double boiler and place it on a dish towel. Continue to stir the mixture until the curd thickens and coats the back of a metal spoon, about 5 minutes.

Remove the chilled bowl from the refrigerator. Place a fine-meshed sieve over the bowl. Slowly pour the curd through the sieve and into the chilled bowl to strain the zest and any small lumps from the curd. Gently stir the curd to remove any air bubbles.

Ladle the curd into hot jars, leaving ¼-inch headspace. Using a plastic knife, remove any trapped air bubbles. Wipe the jar rims and threads with a clean, damp cloth. Cover with hot lids and apply screw rings. Process 4-ounce jars and half-pint jars for 10 minutes at 11 pounds of pressure in a dial-gauge pressure canner or at 10 pounds of pressure in a weighted-gauge pressure canner.

Raspberry Curd

The red raspberries give this curd a marvelous flavor and a beautiful pink color. Frozen raspberries work better because they release a large quantity of flavorful juice. This recipe should not be doubled because the curd may not thicken.

MAKES ABOUT 3 (4-OUNCE) JARS

Raspberry Juice
1 (10-ounce) package frozen red raspberries

Curd Ingredients
2 large eggs
4 large egg yolks
⅞ cup superfine sugar
½ cup raspberry juice
2 teaspoons strained fresh lemon juice
¼ cup unsalted butter, chilled, cut into 4
   pieces

To extract the juice: Thaw the raspberries. Do not rinse or drain. In a flat-bottomed bowl or pan, using a vegetable masher, crush the raspberries.

Place a fine-meshed sieve over a bowl. Pour the raspberry pulp and juice into the sieve to separate the juice from the pulp and seeds. Gently press the pulp with a spoon to release the juice. Discard the pulp and seeds. Measure 1 cup juice.

To make the curd: Place a medium glass or metal bowl in the refrigerator to chill.

Fill the bottom pan of a double boiler or medium saucepan about ¼ full of water. Over medium-high heat, bring the water to a gentle boil.

In the top pan of a double boiler or a medium metal bowl, lightly beat the eggs and egg yolks.

Gradually whisk in the sugar until well blended. Stir in the raspberry juice and lemon juice. Add the butter pieces.

Place the pan or bowl over the pan of boiling water. Make sure the top pan sits well above the water so the curd will be cooked by the steam only, not the boiling water. Reduce the heat to keep the water from boiling too vigorously.

Slowly heat the mixture, stirring constantly with a flexible spatula or a spoon. Stir gently or the curd will be filled with tiny air bubbles. Scrape the bottom of the pan frequently to prevent scorching or curdling. Cook the mixture until it reaches a temperature between 168F and 170F (76C and 77C), about 5 to 7 minutes.

Remove the top pan or bowl from the double boiler and place it on a dish towel. Continue to stir the mixture until the curd thickens and coats the back of a metal spoon, about 5 minutes.

Remove the chilled bowl from the refrigerator. Place a fine-meshed sieve over the bowl. Slowly pour the curd through the sieve and into the chilled bowl to strain the zest and any small lumps from the curd. Gently stir the curd to remove any air bubbles.

Ladle the curd into hot jars, leaving ¼-inch headspace. Using a plastic knife, remove any trapped air bubbles. Wipe the jar rims and threads with a clean, damp cloth. Cover with hot lids and apply screw rings. Process 4-ounce jars and half-pint jars for 10 minutes at 11 pounds of pressure in a dial-gauge pressure canner or at 10 pounds of pressure in a weighted-gauge pressure canner.

Tangerine Curd

I prefer to use Minneola tangelos in this delightful curd recipe, but any variety of tangerine will work well.

MAKES ABOUT 3 HALF-PINT JARS

1½ cups superfine sugar
⅓ cup fresh tangerine zest
4 large eggs
8 large egg yolks
1 cup strained fresh tangerine juice
   (about 6 medium tangerines)
⅔ cup unsalted butter, chilled, cut into
   10 pieces

Place a medium glass or metal bowl in the refrigerator to chill.

In a small bowl, combine the superfine sugar and tangerine zest, stirring until well blended. Let stand for 30 minutes to allow the sugar to pick up the citrus flavor of the zest.

Fill the bottom pan of a double boiler or medium saucepan about ¼ full of water. Over medium-high heat, bring the water to a gentle boil.

In the top pan of a double boiler or a medium metal bowl, lightly beat the whole eggs and egg yolks. Gradually whisk in the sugar and zest until well blended. Stir in the tangerine juice. Add the butter pieces.

Place the pan or bowl over the pan of boiling water. Make sure the top pan sits well above the water so the curd will be cooked by the steam only, not the boiling water. Reduce the heat to keep the water from boiling too vigorously.

Slowly heat the mixture, stirring constantly with a flexible spatula or a spoon. Stir gently or the curd will be filled with tiny air bubbles. Scrape the bottom of the pan frequently to prevent scorching or curdling. Cook the mixture until it reaches a temperature between 168F and 170F (76C and 77C), about 5 to 7 minutes.

Remove the top pan or bowl from the double boiler and place it on a dish towel. Continue to stir the mixture until the curd thickens and coats the back of a metal spoon, about 5 minutes.

Remove the chilled bowl from the refrigerator. Place a fine-meshed sieve over the bowl. Slowly pour the curd through the sieve and into the chilled bowl to strain the zest and any small lumps from the curd. Gently stir the curd to remove any air bubbles.

Ladle the curd into hot jars, leaving ¼-inch headspace. Using a plastic knife, remove any trapped air bubbles. Wipe the jar rims and threads with a clean, damp cloth. Cover with hot lids and apply screw rings. Process 4-ounce jars and half-pint jars for 10 minutes at 11 pounds of pressure in a dial-gauge pressure canner or at 10 pounds pressure in a weighted-gauge pressure canner.

Fruit

CANNING FRUIT

If you are fortunate to have prolific fruit trees growing in your yard or have access to quantities of fresh, tree-ripened fruit, canning is an excellent way to preserve the flavor and texture of the harvest for enjoyment throughout the year. The wonderful flavor of the fruit can be preserved to enjoy during the late fall, winter and early spring when most fresh produce is out-of-season and imported fruit is very expensive.

What a delight to open a perfect jar of sunny peaches on a cold, winter morning. Or serve them over ice cream for a simple and elegant dessert any time of the year. The flavor of home-canned fruit is far superior to any canned fruit you can buy in the store. Canning fruit is a relatively simple process; all you really need is some perfectly ripe fruit and a little time. With a few simple tech-

niques, you can prepare beautifully canned fruit the first time and every time.

Flavorings, extracts and liqueurs may be added to canned fruit to create special flavor combinations. Two or more fruits can be mixed to create pleasing and eye-catching color presentations. Nuts, such as almonds, may lend their flavor to such fruits as apricots, peaches or pears.

Special Equipment

There are a few special utensils and tools that make canning fruit easier and more efficient. While they are not absolutely essential to the job, fruit prepared with the proper tools has a cleaner, more uniform appearance. Here are a few suggested items that you may want to add to your collection, if you do not already have them.

Apple corer
Apple peeler

Cherry pitter

Colander or strainer

Collapsible wire mesh basket (for blanching fruit to remove their skins)

Fruit and vegetable peeler

Melon baller

Pear corer

Pitting spoon or thin-bowled tableware tablespoon (for pitting peaches and mangoes or removing the seeds from papayas)

Small paring knife or fruit knife

Selecting Fruit

The weight and quantities of fruit given in the recipes are the approximate amounts that will be needed to fill the size and number of jars indicated. The actual jar yields will depend on the size, shape, texture and weight of the fruit; how the fruit is prepared and which type of pack you use to fill the jars.

Use only top-quality, firm, perfectly ripe fruit, free of any bruises or blemishes. Underripe and overripe fruit or fruit that is spoiled or damaged in any way does not preserve well and yields an inferior product. Fresh fruit is highly perishable and should be used as close to harvest as possible or as soon as it reaches peak ripeness. Keep a close eye on the harvested fruit, and when it is ready, can it immediately.

Preparing Fruit

When preparing fruit for canning, rinse only enough fruit for one batch at a time. Once the fruit has been rinsed, it will deteriorate quite rapidly and needs to be canned and processed immediately. Determine how many jars will fit in your water bath canner, allowing at least 1 inch of space between the jars for proper heating and safe canning. This will give you the maximum number of jars of fruit that you should prepare and

process in one batch. The recipes for fruit may be doubled, as long as you have room in your water bath canner to safely hold all of the filled jars. Otherwise, prepare and process the jars in smaller batches.

Rinse the fruit thoroughly in a sink or bowl full of cool, clean water. If any of the fruit floats to the surface of the water, set it aside, as it may be underripe or a worm or other small creature may have taken up residence inside. Do not use a brush or cloth to scrub the fruit, as ripe fruit can easily be bruised or damaged. Immediately drain the fruit on several layers of paper towels. Do not allow fruit to stand in water or remain wet, as its quality will quickly deteriorate.

Depending upon the variety or specific type of fruit to be canned, it may be preserved whole, halved or sliced. When canning unpeeled whole fruit, such as grapes or sweet cherries, prick the blossom end of the fruit 2 or 3 times with the tip of a sterilized needle. This will help reduce the number of split skins, a common occurrence when canning fruit whole, and will prevent the fruit from bursting during water bath processing. The high temperature of the water bath will inevitably cause some of the skins on whole fruit to split, but pricking the fruit will keep the splits small. Most judges accept that some split skins are to be expected in home-canned grapes and a few other fruits, and they will not deduct points for minor splits. Jars with fruit containing large splits or fruit that has burst during processing, indicate poor canning technique, and the judges will deduct points for these preventable imperfections.

Peeling Fruit

Most fruit should be peeled before canning, even when the fruit is to be canned whole. Some exceptions to this rule are cherries and grapes, which are canned with their skins still intact.

Apricot halves hold their shape better when canned with their skins on, but they may also be peeled. For entries that will be exhibited at a fair, it is recommended that the skins be left on apricot halves for a neater and more uniform appearance in the jar.

To peel fruit that will not easily slip out of their skins, such as pears, carefully remove the peel using a small paring knife, being careful not to remove too much of the flesh and to maintain the natural shape of the fruit.

PEELING PEACHES AND APRICOTS: Fruits such as peaches and apricots are easily peeled and maintain their natural shape when the boiling water method is used to slip off their skins. Place the fruit, in small batches of 5 to 10, depending on the size of the fruit, into a collapsible wire mesh basket and lower it into a large pan of gently boiling water. Or you can use a large slotted spoon to lower the fruit, a few pieces at a time, into the gently boiling water. Do not crowd the pan with fruit or the water temperature will drop too low to loosen the skins. Let the fruit remain in the water for 30 to 45 seconds, depending on the size of the fruit. Remove the fruit from the water and immediately plunge it into a large bowl of ice water to stop the cooking process. Let the fruit cool in the ice water for at least 1 minute. Remove the fruit from the water and drain it well in a strainer. Using your hands or a small paring knife, carefully slip the loose skins from the fruit. If the skin remains tightly attached to a piece of fruit, repeat the above process to loosen the skin. If the skin still remains firmly attached, the fruit is probably immature, underripe or blemished and should be discarded.

Treating Fruit to Prevent Browning

The delicate flesh of light-colored fruits, such as apples, peaches, pears and apricots, has a tendency to oxidize and turn brown with exposure to air. While not a health risk, oxidized fruit will quickly lose both its flavor and texture. Careful handling of the fruit is needed to prevent this unsightly and unappetizing occurrence. Fair judges will make a serious deduction in the score of any entry that shows even the slightest signs of oxidation.

To prevent light-colored fruits from darkening after peeling, soak the fruit in an antioxidant solution before canning. This process will also help the fruit maintain its color after canning and during storage in the jars. There are good commercial antioxidant products available in most grocery stores and are usually found alongside the other canning supplies. They contain primarily ascorbic acid crystals, which you may also purchase in bulk from health food stores.

Before peeling the fruit, prepare a bowl of antioxidant solution according to the recipe or the manufacturer's instructions. As you peel each piece of fruit, gently drop it into the solution. Make sure that the fruit is completely covered, or turn the fruit frequently to treat all sides. Do not leave the fruit in the solution for more than 20 minutes, or it may absorb too much of the solution and develop a sour taste. Rinse the fruit thoroughly under cool running water and drain it well before adding the fruit to a hot syrup or packing it into the jars.

Syrups for Canning

Canning fruit in a sugar syrup helps the fruit to retain both its shape and firmness as well as preserving the color. The flavor of fruits that are either low in sugar or high in acid is greatly improved by canning them in a sugar syrup.

While most of the recipes in this chapter call for preserving fruits in a light or medium syrup, there are other options that will also work well. Fruit may be canned in heavy syrup or a very light syrup to suit your taste. Depending on how you

Sugar Syrups

TYPE OF SYRUP	SUGAR	WATER	YIELD (APPROX.)
Extra light	1 cup	1 quart	4½ cups
Light	2 cups	1 quart	5 cups
Medium	3 cups	1 quart	5½ cups
Heavy	4 cups	1 quart	6 cups
Extra heavy	5 cups	1 quart	6½ cups

plan to use it, fruit may also be canned in sweetened or unsweetened natural fruit juices or even plain water.

Fruit is more likely to float in the jar when it is canned in a heavy syrup. The higher sugar content makes the syrup heavier than the fruit, causing the lighter fruit to rise to the surface. This is especially common when the fruit is packed raw. Use a light or medium syrup to reduce the chance of floating fruit. If you want to use a heavy syrup, be sure to can fruit using the hot pack method.

Fruit may be preserved in a syrup ranging from extra light to extra heavy. To adjust the syrup strength, refer to the chart above. It takes between ½ to 1¼ cups of syrup per quart jar, depending on the size and shape of the fruit and the air spaces between the fruit pieces.

Preparing Syrups

To prepare the syrup, combine the sugar and water in a large saucepan over medium heat, stirring constantly until the sugar is completely dissolved. Crystals can form in the cooled syrup if it is brought to a boil before all of the sugar is completely dissolved. After the sugar is completely dissolved, bring the syrup to a boil and boil it for 5 minutes to slightly reduce the syrup. Lower the heat and keep the syrup hot until it is needed. Cover the pan to prevent evaporation and re-crystallization of the sugar.

Substituting Corn Syrup for Sugar in Syrups

TYPE OF SYRUP	SUGAR	CORN SYRUP	WATER	YIELD (APPROX.)
Light	1 cup	⅔ cup	1 quart	5 cups
Medium	1½ cups	1 cup	1 quart	5½ cups

Substituting Honey for Sugar in Syrups

TYPE OF SYRUP	SUGAR	HONEY	WATER	YIELD (APPROX.)
Light	⅔ cup	⅔ cup	1 quart	5 cups
Medium	1 cup	1 cup	1 quart	5½ cups

Using Corn Syrup or Honey

When making syrups, corn syrup or honey may be substituted for part of the sugar. Be aware that the use of corn syrup or honey can have a significant impact on the flavor of the finished preserves. Corn syrup contains vanilla extract, and honeys can vary widely in flavor, from mild to very strong. When using honey, select a very mild variety with a flavor that will complement the flavor of the specific fruit.

To accommodate personal tastes or dietary needs, fruit may be packed in plain water, without added sugar. Fruit may also be canned in homemade or commercially prepared sweetened or unsweetened fruit juices. White grape juice is an excellent choice for canning most fruits. Be aware that fruit canned without sugar tends to be softer in texture, and the natural color can fade rapidly. Fruit canned without added sugar, especially when packed raw, is more apt to float in the jar after processing. When fruit is canned with water or unsweetened fruit juice, it must be packed using the hot pack method.

Never use saccharin, aspartame or any other artificial sweeteners when canning fruit. They can lose their sweetening ability and become quite bitter when heated to the high temperatures needed for safe canning and processing. It is better to can the fruit without sugar and add any sweeteners just before serving.

Hot Pack Versus Raw Pack

A common problem when canning fruit, whether whole or cut into pieces, is that the fruit tends to float to the top of the jar after processing, leaving the bottom part of the jar void of fruit and filled only with syrup. This is caused by using fruit that is underripe, by packing the fruit in too heavy of a syrup or by air that remains trapped inside the cells of the fruit. The pieces of fruit in the top of the jar that are not covered by the syrup may oxidize and turn brown. While the fruit is perfectly safe to eat, it is not very attractive. To reduce the chances of floating fruit, only can fruit that is fully ripe.

Hot Pack Method

Heating the fruit in a syrup before packing it into the jars will replace much of the air inside the fruit tissues with liquid and help reduce the chance of the fruit floating to the top of the jar. This is referred to as the hot pack method of canning. When the fruit is heated, it is also more pliable and more fruit can usually be packed into the jar. A tighter pack also means less chance of floating fruit. The hot pack method is strongly recommended to help prevent floating fruit. For fruit that is to be canned without added sugar, the hot pack method must be used to ensure an attractive and safe canned product.

To can fruit using the hot pack method: Heat the prepared fruit in syrup, juice or water according to the recipe instructions. Pack the hot fruit snugly into hot jars, leaving ½-inch headspace. (The canning jars should be hot to prevent them from cracking when filled with the hot fruit or boiling syrup.) Cover the fruit completely with the boiling syrup, juice or water, maintaining the same ½-inch headspace. Wipe the jar rims and threads, apply the hot lids and screw rings and process the jars in a hot water bath for the amount of time specified in the recipe.

Raw Pack Method

The raw pack method is when unheated fruit is packed into the jars, then covered with a boiling syrup. This method is used for delicate fruits, such as berries, that would not maintain their shape and texture if first cooked in a syrup. Fruit packed using the raw pack method has a greater tendency to float in the jars because it contains more air and also cannot be packed as snugly into the jar.

To can fruit using the raw pack method: Tightly pack the prepared fruit into hot jars, leaving ½-inch headspace. (Cold jars may crack from the drastic temperature change when filled with boiling syrup or when placed into the hot water bath for processing.) Be careful not to crush the fruit. Cover the fruit completely with boiling syrup, maintaining the same ½-inch headspace. Wipe the jar rims and threads, apply the hot lids and screw rings and process the jars in a hot water bath for the amount of time specified in the recipe.

Jars

Packing Jars with Fruit

Ladle about ½ cup of the syrup into the bottom of a hot jar. Pack the fruit snugly into the jar without crushing. Fruit that has been cut in halves or quarters presents a more attractive appearance in the jar when the center or cut side of the fruit is placed down. Do not leave any large gaps between the pieces of fruit. If necessary, tap the jar gently on a dish towel to settle the contents and release any trapped air bubbles.

When jar is about half full, use a plastic knife or bubble freer to release any trapped air bubbles in the bottom part of the jar. Hold the jar up, without tipping it, and look at the bottom of the jar from underneath. Air bubbles often become trapped under the bottom piece of fruit, especially when canning something like peach or pear halves. Be sure to release these air bubbles before completing the filling of the jar, as it is almost impossible to remove them from a full jar without damaging the fruit.

Pack the jar with fruit, leaving a full ½-inch headspace in the top of the jar. Ladle the syrup into the jar, maintaining the ½-inch headspace. Release all air bubbles from the jar and, if necessary, add additional syrup to bring the headspace back up to ½ inch. With a clean, warm, damp cloth, wipe the jar rims and threads clean of any spilled syrup and apply the hot lids and screw rings.

If you plan to enter your canned fruit into competition at a fair, be sure to select jars that are full and do not contain floating fruit. There should not be a space at the bottom of the jar that contains only liquid and no fruit. Floating fruit indicates poor technique and results in major deductions from fair judges. In canned fruit competitions, improper headspace and floating fruit are the most common point reductions made by the judges.

Processing Jars

All jars of canned fruit must be processed in a hot water bath for safety. To prevent the fruit from becoming soft and to reduce the number of split skins in jars of whole fruit, process the jars in a simmering water bath at a temperature of 190F to 200F (88c to 93c). Processing fruit at a full rolling boil will often result in a soft, mushy, overprocessed product. The lower temperature will safely seal the jars and help the fruit keep its natural shape, texture and flavor. Use an instant read thermometer and check the water temperature periodically to maintain the proper heat.

Immediately remove the jars from the water bath after the processing time is complete. If the jars are left in the water bath longer, the fruit will overprocess, become soft and the color and flavor will fade. Remove the jars from the water bath using a jar lifter and place at least 2 inches apart on a rack or kitchen towel. Allow the jars to cool, undisturbed, for 12 to 24 hours before checking the seals. Should a jar fail to seal properly, do not reprocess it, as the fruit will lose its texture. Instead, store the jar in the refrigerator and use the contents within 2 weeks.

If the syrup level in the jar is low after processing, do not open the jar to add more syrup. Opening the jar will break the seal, making it necessary to reprocess the fruit, and reprocessing will cause the fruit to become mushy and lose its flavor. Store the jars as normal and use any jars with low syrup levels first. Fruit that is not covered by the syrup may darken from oxidation. While they may not be as pretty and flavorful as the rest, the oxidized pieces of fruit are still safe to eat. They may simply be removed when the jar is opened or eaten right along with the rest of the fruit.

Applesauce

Select slightly tart varieties of apples that are ripe and unblemished. Granny Smith, Jonathon, McIntosh, Rome Beauty and Gravenstein all make excellent applesauce.

MAKES ABOUT 4 PINT JARS OR 2 QUART JARS

7 pounds apples
2 cups apple juice or water
1½ to 2 cups sugar
2 tablespoons strained fresh lemon juice

Rinse the apples in cool water and drain well. Core and chop the apples.

In an 8-quart pan, combine the apple juice or water and 1 cup of the sugar.

Over medium-low heat, stirring constantly, heat the mixture until the sugar is completely dissolved. Add the apples.

Over medium-high heat, bring the fruit mixture to a boil. Reduce the heat, cover and boil gently until the apples are soft, about 15 to 20 minutes. Remove the pan from the heat.

Press the apples and juice through a food mill or fine-meshed sieve. Discard the skins. Return the apple pulp to the pan. Stir in the remaining sugar to taste and add the lemon juice.

Over medium-low heat, stirring constantly, heat the mixture until the sugar is completely dissolved. Increase the heat to medium and bring the mixture to a boil. Reduce the heat and simmer, stirring frequently, until the sauce thickens, about 10 to 20 minutes. Remove the pan from the heat.

Ladle the sauce into hot jars, filling the jars about ⅓ full. Using a plastic spoon, press out any trapped air bubbles. Fill the jars ⅔ full and press out any trapped air bubbles. Fill the jars, leaving ½-inch headspace. Using a plastic knife or bubble freer, remove any remaining trapped air bubbles. Wipe the jar rims and threads with a clean, damp cloth. Cover with hot lids and apply screw rings. Process both pint jars and quart jars in a 200F (93C) water bath for 20 minutes.

Chunky Family-Style Applesauce

This is a great sauce for people who prefer a sauce with small chunks of apples rather than a smooth sauce.

MAKES ABOUT 4 PINT JARS OR 2 QUART JARS

7 pounds unblemished firm apples
2 cups apple juice or water
1½ to 2 cups sugar
2 tablespoons strained fresh lemon juice

🌱 Rinse the apples in cool water and drain well. Core, peel and chop the apples.

In an 8-quart pan, combine the apple juice or water and 1 cup of the sugar.

Over medium-low heat, stirring constantly, heat the mixture until the sugar is completely dissolved. Add the apples.

Over medium-high heat, bring the fruit mixture to a boil. Reduce the heat, cover and boil gently until the apples are soft and translucent, about 20 minutes. Stir occasionally to prevent sticking. Remove the pan from the heat.

Using a vegetable masher or the back of a large spoon, gently crush the apples to the desired texture. Stir in the remaining sugar to taste and add the lemon juice.

Over medium-low heat, stirring constantly, heat the mixture until the sugar is completely dissolved. Increase the heat to medium and bring the mixture to a boil. Reduce the heat and simmer, stirring frequently, until the sauce thickens, about 10 minutes. Remove the pan from the heat.

Ladle the sauce into hot jars, filling the jars about ⅓ full. Using a plastic spoon, press out any trapped air bubbles. Fill the jars ⅔ full and press out any trapped air bubbles. Fill the jars, leaving ½-inch headspace. Using a plastic knife or bubble freer, remove any remaining trapped air bubbles. Wipe the jar rims and threads with a clean, damp cloth. Cover with hot lids and apply screw rings. Process both pint jars and quart jars in a 200F (93C) water bath for 20 minutes.

Rich and Spicy Applesauce

The flavor of this sauce is reminiscent of fresh-baked apple pie.

MAKES ABOUT 4 PINT JARS OR 2 QUART JARS

7 pounds apples
2 cups apple juice or water
1 cup granulated sugar
¾ cup firmly packed light brown sugar
2 tablespoons strained fresh lemon juice
1 teaspoon ground cinnamon
½ teaspoon grated nutmeg

🌱 Rinse the apples in cool water and drain well. Core and chop the apples.

In an 8-quart pan, combine the apple juice or water and the granulated sugar.

Over medium-low heat, stirring constantly, heat the mixture until the sugar is completely dissolved. Add the apples.

Over medium-high heat, bring the fruit mixture to a boil. Reduce the heat, cover and boil gently until the apples are soft, about 15 to 20 minutes. Remove the pan from the heat.

Press the apples and juice through a food mill or fine-meshed sieve. Discard the skins. Return the apple pulp to the pan. Stir in the brown sugar, lemon juice, cinnamon and nutmeg.

Over medium-low heat, stirring constantly, heat the mixture until the sugar is completely dissolved. Increase the heat to medium and bring the mixture to a boil. Reduce the heat and simmer, stirring frequently, until the sauce thickens, about 10 to 20 minutes. Remove the pan from the heat.

Ladle the sauce into hot jars, filling the jars about ⅓ full. Using a plastic spoon, press out any trapped air bubbles. Fill the jars ⅔ full and press out any trapped air bubbles. Fill the jars, leaving ½-inch headspace. Using a plastic knife or bubble freer, remove any remaining trapped air bubbles. Wipe the jar rims and threads with a clean, damp cloth. Cover with hot lids and apply screw rings. Process both pint jars and quart jars in a 200F (93C) water bath for 20 minutes.

Apple-Apricot Sauce

The apples and apricots make a wonderful pairing of flavors in this sauce variation.

MAKES ABOUT 3 PINT JARS

4 cups cored, peeled and chopped tart
    apples, such as Granny Smith
2 cups water

4 cups pitted, peeled and chopped ripe
    apricots
1½ cups sugar
2 tablespoons strained fresh lemon juice

In a 4-quart pan, combine the apples and water.

Over medium-high heat, bring the fruit mixture to a boil. Reduce the heat, cover and boil gently for 15 minutes. Stir occasionally to prevent sticking. Add the apricots and cook for 5 minutes more. Remove the pan from the heat.

Press the fruit mixture through a food mill or fine-meshed sieve. Discard any tough fibers. Rinse the pan. Return the fruit pulp to the pan. Stir in the sugar and lemon juice.

Over medium-low heat, stirring constantly, heat the mixture until the sugar is completely dissolved. Increase the heat to medium and bring the mixture to a boil. Reduce the heat and simmer, stirring frequently, until the sauce thickens, about 10 to 15 minutes. Remove the pan from the heat.

Ladle the sauce into hot jars, filling the jars about ⅓ full. Using a plastic spoon, press out any trapped air bubbles. Fill the jars ⅔ full and press out any trapped air bubbles. Fill the jars, leaving ½-inch headspace. Using a plastic knife or bubble freer, remove any remaining trapped air bubbles. Wipe the jar rims and threads with a clean, damp cloth. Cover with hot lids and apply screw rings. Process both pint jars and quart jars in a 200F (93C) water bath for 20 minutes.

Cranberry Applesauce

A delightful variation on the traditional sauce, it combines the flavor of apples with the tang of cranberries.

MAKES ABOUT 3 PINT JARS

4 cups sorted and stemmed fresh
  cranberries
4 cups cored and finely chopped tart apples,
  such as Granny Smith
2 cups water
2 cups sugar

In a 4-quart pan, combine the cranberries, apples and water.

Over medium-high heat, bring the fruit mixture to a boil. Reduce the heat, cover and boil gently until the cranberries have popped their skins and the apples are soft, about 15 minutes. Remove the pan from the heat.

Press the fruit mixture through a food mill or fine-meshed sieve. Discard the skins and seeds. Rinse the pan. Return the fruit pulp to the pan. Stir in the sugar.

Over medium-low heat, stirring constantly, heat the mixture until the sugar is completely dissolved. Increase the heat to medium and bring the mixture to a boil. Reduce the heat and simmer, stirring frequently, until the sauce thickens, about 10 to 15 minutes. Remove the pan from the heat.

Ladle the sauce into hot jars, filling the jars about 1/3 full. Using a plastic spoon, press out any trapped air bubbles. Fill the jars 2/3 full and press out any trapped air bubbles. Fill the jars, leaving 1/2-inch headspace. Using a plastic knife or bubble freer, remove any remaining trapped air bubbles. Wipe the jar rims and threads with a clean, damp cloth. Cover with hot lids and apply screw rings. Process both pint jars and quart jars in a 200F (93C) water bath for 20 minutes.

Apricots

Open a jar of these golden, sun-drenched gems to serve with breakfast or brunch on a cold winter morning. They are a multiple blue ribbon winner.

Tree-ripened apricots may also be canned whole. Prick the skins several times with a sterilized needle to help keep the skins from bursting during processing. If the apricots were harvested before they were fully ripe, or if store-bought fruit is used, the pits must be removed before canning to prevent spoilage.

MAKES ABOUT 4 PINT JARS OR 2 QUART JARS

5 pounds unblemished firm, ripe
  apricots
4 cups water
1½ cups sugar
8 cups cold water
2 tablespoons antioxidant crystals or
  ascorbic acid crystals

Rinse the apricots in cool water and drain well.

In a 4-quart pan, combine the 4 cups water and sugar. Over medium-low heat, stirring constantly, heat until the sugar is completely dissolved. Increase the heat to medium-high and bring the mixture to a boil. Boil for 5 minutes. Reduce the heat to low, cover and keep the syrup hot until needed.

In a large bowl, combine the 8 cups cold water and the antioxidant crystals. Stir until the crystals are completely dissolved.

Cut each apricot in half, remove the pit and drop the fruit into the antioxidant solution to prevent browning. Do not allow the fruit to remain in the solution for longer than 20 minutes. Remove the apricot halves from the solution and rinse under cool water. Drain well.

Add the apricots to the syrup. Over medium-low heat, stirring occasionally, gently heat the apricots for 3 to 4 minutes. Remove the pan from the heat.

Ladle ¼ cup of the hot syrup into each hot jar. Pack the apricots, cut side down, into the jars, leaving ½-inch headspace.

Place a sieve over a medium saucepan and line the sieve with 3 or 4 layers of clean, damp cheesecloth. Strain the syrup through the cheesecloth. Over medium-high heat, quickly bring the syrup to a boil. Remove the pan from the heat.

Ladle the hot syrup into the jars, covering the apricots and leaving ½-inch headspace. Using a bubble freer or a plastic knife, remove any trapped air bubbles. Hold the jar up and check from the bottom for any air bubbles trapped under the fruit. If necessary, add more syrup to maintain the headspace. Wipe the jar rims and threads with a clean, damp cloth. Cover with hot lids and apply screw rings. Process pint jars in a 190 to 200F (88 to 93C) water bath for 20 minutes, quart jars for 25 minutes.

Variations

Brandied Apricots: Add 1 cup of brandy to the cooked syrup before adding the apricots. Heat, pack and seal the apricots as instructed.

Raw Pack Method: Apricots may also be canned using the raw pack method; however, the chances of the fruit floating in the jars after processing is greatly increased.

Prepare the apricots as described, but do not heat them in the syrup. Pour ½ cup hot syrup into each hot jar, then pack the apricots, cut side down, into the jars, leaving ½-inch headspace. Pack the apricots snugly into hot jars, but do not crush or bruise the fruit. Ladle the hot syrup into the jars, covering the apricots and leaving ½-inch headspace. Remove any trapped air bubbles. Wipe the rims and apply the hot lids and screw rings. Process pint jars in a 190 to 200F (88 to 93C) water bath for 25 minutes, quart jars for 30 minutes.

Berries

Blackberries, blueberries, boysenberries, loganberries and olallieberries all work well in this recipe. Select berries that are of uniform size, and avoid berries that are very large or rather small for their type.

MAKES ABOUT 4 PINT JARS OR 2 QUART JARS

2½ to 3 quarts unblemished firm, ripe
   berries
4 cups water
1 cup sugar

Gently rinse the berries in cool water and drain well on several layers of paper towels.

In a 4-quart pan, combine the water and sugar. Over medium-low heat, stirring constantly, heat until the sugar is completely dissolved. Increase the heat to medium-high and bring the mixture to a boil. Boil for 5 minutes. Reduce the heat to low, cover and keep the syrup hot until needed.

Pack the berries into hot jars, leaving ½-inch headspace. Gently shake the jars a few times during packing to settle the berries and achieve a snug pack.

Ladle the hot syrup into the jars, covering the berries and leaving ½-inch headspace. Using a bubble freer or a plastic knife, remove any trapped air bubbles. Hold the jar up and check from the bottom for any air bubbles trapped under the fruit. If necessary, add more syrup to maintain the headspace. Wipe the jar rims and threads with a clean, damp cloth. Cover with hot lids and apply screw rings. Process pint jars in a 190 to 200F (88 to 93C) water bath for 15 minutes, quart jars for 20 minutes.

Sweet Cherries

Cherries may be canned with or without the pits. Remove the pits easily using a handheld cherry pitter, available in many grocery and cooking supply stores. To pit large quantities of cherries, I use a Westmark Kirschomat cherry pitter. Made in Germany, this self-feeding pitter makes quick work of pitting several pounds of cherries. It can usually be found in larger cooking stores.

Cherries may also be canned using the raw pack method. To raw pack cherries, pack the prepared fruit directly into the jars, without cooking the cherries in the hot syrup. Process raw pack pint and quart jars for 25 minutes.

MAKES ABOUT 4 PINT JARS OR 2 QUART JARS

5 pounds unblemished firm, ripe sweet cherries
4 cups water
1½ cups sugar

Rinse the cherries in cool water and drain well.

In a 4-quart pan, combine the water and sugar. Over medium-low heat, stirring constantly, heat until the sugar is completely dissolved. Increase the heat to medium-high and bring the mixture to a boil. Boil for 5 minutes. Reduce the heat to low, cover and keep the syrup hot until needed.

Pit the cherries, if desired. If cherries are canned whole without pitting, prick the blossom end of the fruit 2 to 3 times with a large sterilized needle to reduce the chances of the skins splitting during processing.

Add the cherries to the syrup. Over medium-low heat, stirring occasionally, gently heat the cherries for 2 minutes. Remove the pan from the heat.

Pack the cherries into hot jars, leaving ½-inch headspace. Gently shake the jars a few times during packing to settle the cherries and attain a snug pack.

Place a sieve over a medium saucepan and line the sieve with 3 or 4 layers of clean, damp cheesecloth. Strain the syrup through the cheesecloth. Over medium-high heat, quickly bring the syrup to a boil. Remove the pan from the heat.

Ladle the hot syrup into the jars, covering the cherries and leaving ½-inch headspace. Using a bubble freer or a plastic knife, remove any trapped air bubbles. Hold the jar up and check from the bottom for any air bubbles trapped under the fruit. If necessary, add more syrup to maintain the headspace. Wipe the jar rims and threads with a clean, damp cloth. Cover with hot lids and apply screw rings. Process pint jars in a 190 to 200F (88 to 93C) water bath for 20 minutes, quart jars for 25 minutes.

Variation

Sour Cherries: When canning sour cherries, increase the sugar to 2 cups. The pits should always be removed from sour cherries before canning.

Maraschino Cherries

The flavor of home-canned Maraschino cherries is far superior to the bland, overly sweet type found in stores.

MAKES ABOUT 5 HALF-PINT JARS

2½ pounds unblemished firm, ripe Royal
    Anne cherries or sour red cherries
8 cups cold water
2 tablespoons antioxidant crystals or
    ascorbic acid crystals
1½ cups water
3 cups sugar
2 tablespoons red food coloring
1 tablespoon pure almond extract

Rinse the cherries in cool water and drain well. Remove the pits.

In a large bowl, combine the 8 cups cold water and the antioxidant crystals. Stir until the crystals are completely dissolved. Add the cherries to the solution. Do not allow the fruit to remain in the solution for longer than 20 minutes. Remove the cherries from the solution and rinse under cool water. Drain well.

In a 4-quart pan, combine the 1½ cups water and sugar. Over medium-low heat, stirring constantly, heat until the sugar is completely dissolved. Increase the heat to medium-high and bring the mixture to a boil. Stir in the food coloring. Add the cherries. Reduce the heat and simmer gently for 5 minutes. Remove the pan from the heat and cool completely. Cover and let the cherries stand in the syrup for 24 hours.

Over medium heat, bring the cherries and syrup just to a boil. Remove the pan from the heat. Stir in the almond extract.

Pack the hot cherries into hot jars, leaving ½-inch headspace. Gently shake the jars a few times during packing to settle the cherries and attain a snug pack.

Place a sieve over a medium saucepan and line the sieve with 3 or 4 layers of clean, damp cheesecloth. Strain the syrup through the cheesecloth. Over medium-high heat, quickly bring the syrup to a boil. Remove the pan from the heat.

Ladle the hot syrup into the jars, covering the cherries and leaving ½-inch headspace. Using a bubble freer or a plastic knife, remove any trapped air bubbles. Hold the jar up and check from the bottom for any air bubbles trapped under the fruit. If necessary, add more syrup to maintain the headspace. Wipe the jar rims and threads with a clean, damp cloth. Cover with hot lids and apply screw rings. Process half-pint jars in a 190 to 200F (88 to 93C) water bath for 15 minutes.

Grapes

Red Flame grapes work best for canning, but any seedless variety of crisp grape may be canned using this recipe. The grapes must be crisp, or they will become soft during processing.

MAKES ABOUT 4 PINT JARS OR 2 QUART JARS

8 to 9 cups stemmed, unblemished, crisp, ripe Red Flame grapes

4 cups water

1½ cups sugar

☙ Rinse the grapes in cool water and drain well.

In a 4-quart pan, combine the water and sugar. Over medium-low heat, stirring constantly, heat until the sugar is completely dissolved. Increase the heat to medium-high and bring the mixture to a boil. Boil for 5 minutes. Reduce the heat to low, cover and keep the syrup hot until needed.

Prick the ends of the grapes 2 to 3 times with a large sterilized needle to reduce the chances of the skins splitting during processing.

Pack the grapes into hot jars, leaving ½-inch headspace. Gently shake the jars a few times during packing to settle the grapes and attain a snug pack.

Ladle the hot syrup into the jars, covering the grapes and leaving ½-inch headspace. Using a bubble freer or a plastic knife, remove any trapped air bubbles. Hold the jar up and check from the bottom for any air bubbles trapped under the fruit. If necessary, add more syrup to maintain the headspace. Wipe the jar rims and threads with a clean, damp cloth. Cover with hot lids and apply screw rings. Process pint jars in a 190 to 200F (88 to 93C) water bath for 20 minutes, quart jars for 25 minutes.

Grapefruit Sections

Can the grapefruit immediately after segmenting to prevent the fruit from turning dark or bitter from exposure to the air. White, pink or red grapefruit may be used, however the pink and red colors will fade somewhat during processing, and they may not hold their shape as well as white grapefruit.

MAKES ABOUT 4 PINT JARS OR 2 QUART JARS

5 to 6 pounds firm, ripe grapefruit

4 cups water

1¾ cups sugar

☙ Rinse the grapefruit in cool water, using a soft vegetable brush to remove any dirt. Rinse the fruit again and drain well.

In a 4-quart pan, combine the water and sugar. Over medium-low heat, stirring constantly, heat until the sugar is completely dissolved. Increase the heat to medium-high and bring the mixture to a boil. Boil for 5 minutes. Reduce the heat to low, cover and keep the syrup hot until needed.

Using a sharp fruit knife or paring knife, peel the grapefruit, removing all of the outer white pith. Separate the grapefruit segments from the white membrane, being careful not to break or damage the pieces. Discard the membrane. Remove any seeds from the segments and discard the seeds.

Pack the grapefruit segments into hot jars, leaving ½-inch headspace. Gently shake the jars a few times during packing to settle the grapefruit and attain a snug pack.

Ladle the hot syrup into the jars, covering the grapefruit and leaving ½-inch headspace. Using a bubble freer or a plastic knife, remove any trapped air bubbles. Hold the jar up and check from the bottom for any air bubbles trapped under the fruit. If necessary, add more syrup to maintain the headspace. Wipe the jar rims and threads with a clean, damp cloth. Cover with hot lids and apply screw rings. Process both pint jars and quart jars in a 190 to 200F (88 to 93C) water bath for 20 minutes.

Brandied Kumquats

These golden gems make a delightful addition to a Sunday brunch or an afternoon tea. Try serving them over ice cream for a simple and elegant dessert that is sure to impress your guests.

MAKES ABOUT 4 PINT JARS OR 2 QUART JARS

2½ pounds unblemished, firm kumquats
2½ cups water
1 cup sugar
1 vanilla bean, split lengthwise
2 cups brandy

Rinse the kumquats in cool water, using a soft vegetable brush to gently remove any dirt. Be careful not to scrape or damage the outer peel. Rinse the fruit again and drain well.

Fill an 8-quart pan about half full of water. Over medium-high heat, bring the water to a simmer. Using a mesh basket or slotted spoon, carefully lower part of the kumquats into the water for 30 seconds. Remove the kumquats from the pan and immediately plunge them into a large bowl of ice water for 1 to 2 minutes. Transfer the fruit to a strainer. Drain well and cool. Repeat with the remaining kumquats in 2 or 3 more batches.

Prick the blossom end of the kumquats 4 to 5 times with a large sterilized needle to allow the fruit to absorb the syrup and reduce the chances of the skins splitting during processing.

In a 4-quart pan, combine the water and sugar. Over medium-low heat, stirring constantly, heat until the sugar is completely dissolved. Add the vanilla bean. Increase the heat to medium-high and bring the mixture to a boil. Reduce the heat and simmer for 10 minutes.

Add the kumquats to the pan and simmer gently for 5 minutes. Remove the pan from the heat. Remove the vanilla bean from the pan.

Using a slotted spoon, pack the kumquats into hot jars, leaving ½-inch headspace. Gently shake the jars a few times during packing to settle the kumquats and attain a snug pack.

Place a sieve over a medium saucepan and line the sieve with 3 or 4 layers of clean, damp cheesecloth. Strain the syrup through the cheesecloth. Over medium-high heat, quickly bring the syrup to a boil. Remove the pan from the heat. Stir the brandy into the syrup.

Ladle the hot syrup into the jars, covering the kumquats and leaving ½-inch headspace. Using a bubble freer or a plastic knife, remove any trapped air bubbles. Hold the jar up and check from the bottom for any air bubbles trapped under the fruit. If necessary, add more syrup to maintain the headspace. Wipe the jar rims and threads with a clean, damp cloth. Cover with hot lids and apply screw rings. Process pint jars in a 190 to 200F (88 to 93C) water bath for 20 minutes, quart jars for 25 minutes.

Mandarin Oranges

If you or someone you know has a Mandarin orange tree, the fruit may be canned for later use. Tangerines may also be used in this recipe.

MAKES ABOUT 4 HALF-PINT JARS OR 2 PINT JARS

2½ to 3 pounds firm, ripe Mandarin
    oranges
2 cups water
¾ cup sugar

Rinse the Mandarin oranges in cool water, using a soft vegetable brush to remove any dirt. Rinse the fruit again and drain well.

In a 4-quart pan, combine the water and sugar. Over medium-low heat, stirring constantly, heat until the sugar is completely dissolved. Increase the heat to medium-high and bring the mixture to a boil. Boil for 5 minutes. Reduce the heat to low, cover and keep the syrup hot until needed.

Peel the oranges by hand, removing all of the outer white pith. Using a sharp fruit knife or paring knife, cut a slit in the white membrane surrounding each segment. Remove the white membrane from the orange segments, being careful not to break or damage the pieces. Discard the membrane. Remove any seeds from the segments and discard the seeds.

Pack the orange segments into hot jars, leaving ½-inch headspace. Gently shake the jars a few times during packing to settle the oranges and attain a snug pack.

Ladle the hot syrup into the jars, covering the orange segments and leaving ½-inch headspace. Using a bubble freer or a plastic knife, remove any trapped air bubbles. Hold the jar up and check from the bottom for any air bubbles trapped under the fruit. If necessary, add more syrup to maintain the headspace. Wipe the jar rims and threads with a clean, damp cloth. Cover with hot lids and apply screw rings. Process half-pint jars in a 190 to 200F (88 to 93C) water bath for 15 minutes, pint jars for 20 minutes.

Mangoes and Pineapple

Mangoes and pineapples make a wonderful tropical canned fruit combination. By alternating the fruits in the jar, they have an attractive appearance and presentation.

MAKES ABOUT 4 PINT JARS

4 cups water
2 cups sugar
3 to 4 pounds ripe pineapples
5 to 6 large firm, ripe mangoes

In a 4-quart pan, combine the 4 cups water and sugar. Over medium-low heat, stirring constantly, heat until the sugar is completely dissolved. Increase the heat to medium-high and bring the mixture to a boil. Boil for 5 minutes. Reduce the heat to low, cover and keep the syrup hot until needed.

Using a sharp knife, peel the pineapples. Remove the "eyes" and cores. Cut the pineapples into ¾-inch spears, 4 inches in length.

Add the pineapple to the syrup. Over medium heat, stirring occasionally, gently simmer the pineapple until tender, about 5 to 7 minutes. Remove the pan from the heat. Using a slotted spoon, remove the pineapple from the syrup and drain.

Using a sharp paring knife, cut through the skin and flesh on the side of the mango until the knife hits the pit. Continue cutting around the mango until you have made a circular cut all the way around the fruit. Holding the mango in the palm of your hand and using a thin-bowled tablespoon, slide the spoon into the cut from the end of the mango. Gently slide the spoon up and over the pit, slowly sliding the spoon back and forth to the sides, until the mango half is separated from the pit. Slide the spoon under the pit and remove the pit from the other half of the mango.

Carefully remove the outer peel from the mango and cut the fruit lengthwise into ¾-inch slices.

Lay the hot pint jars on their sides. Pack the mango slices and pineapple spears snugly into the jars, alternating the fruits around the sides of the jars and filling in the centers, leaving ½-inch headspace. Stand the jars upright. If the headspace at the top of the jar is significantly larger than ½-inch, cut small triangles of pineapple and arrange them in a star or circular pattern on top of the fruit in the jar. Be sure to leave ½-inch headspace.

Place a sieve over a medium saucepan and line the sieve with 3 or 4 layers of clean, damp cheesecloth. Strain the syrup through the cheesecloth. Over medium-high heat, quickly bring the syrup to a boil. Remove the pan from the heat.

Ladle the hot syrup into the jars, covering the fruit and leaving ½-inch headspace. Using a bubble freer or a plastic knife, remove any trapped air bubbles. Hold the jar up and check from the bottom for any air bubbles trapped under the fruit. If necessary, add more syrup to maintain the headspace. Wipe the jar rims and threads with a clean,

damp cloth. Cover with hot lids and apply screw rings. Process pint jars in a 190 to 200F (88 to 93C) water bath for 20 minutes.

Nectarines

Select nectarines with golden or yellow flesh. White nectarines are excellent for eating fresh, but they tend to fall apart or lose their flavor when heated and do not make a good canned product.

MAKES ABOUT 4 PINT JARS OR 2 QUART JARS

5 to 6 pounds unblemished firm, ripe nectarines
4 cups water
2 cups sugar
8 cups cold water
2 tablespoons antioxidant crystals or ascorbic acid crystals

Rinse the nectarines in cool water and drain well.

In a 4-quart pan, combine the 4 cups water and sugar. Over medium-low heat, stirring constantly, heat until the sugar is completely dissolved. Increase the heat to medium-high and bring the mixture to a boil. Boil for 5 minutes. Reduce the heat to low, cover and keep the syrup hot until needed.

In a large bowl, combine the 8 cups cold water and the antioxidant crystals. Stir until the crystals are completely dissolved.

Fill an 8-quart pan about half full of water. Over medium-high heat, bring the water to a simmer. Using a mesh basket or slotted spoon, carefully lower the nectarines, a few at a time, into the water for 45 to 60 seconds. Remove the nectarines from the pan and immediately plunge them into a large bowl of ice water for 1 to 2 minutes. Transfer the fruit to a strainer. Drain well and cool. Repeat with the remaining nectarines.

Using a sharp paring knife, carefully slip the skins from the nectarines. Cut each nectarine in half and remove the pit. Using a thin-bowled tableware spoon or a pitting spoon, carefully remove the red fibers from the center of the nectarines. Cut the nectarines into slices. Drop the fruit into the antioxidant solution to prevent browning. Do not allow the fruit to remain in the solution for longer than 20 minutes. Remove the nectarine slices from the solution and rinse under cool water. Drain well.

Add the nectarines to the syrup. Over medium-low heat, stirring occasionally, gently heat the nectarines for 2 to 3 minutes. Remove the pan from the heat.

Ladle ¼ cup of the hot syrup into each hot jar. Pack the nectarine slices into the jars, leaving ½-inch headspace.

Place a sieve over a medium saucepan and line the sieve with 3 or 4 layers of clean, damp cheesecloth. Strain the syrup through the cheesecloth. Over medium-high heat, quickly bring the syrup to a boil. Remove the pan from the heat.

Ladle the hot syrup into the jars, covering the nectarines and leaving ½-inch headspace. Using a bubble freer or a plastic knife, remove any trapped air bubbles. Hold the jar up and check from the bottom for any air bubbles trapped under the fruit. If necessary, add more syrup to maintain the headspace. Wipe the jar rims and threads with a clean, damp cloth. Cover with hot

lids and apply screw rings. Process pint jars in a 190 to 200F (88 to 93C) water bath for 20 minutes, quart jars for 25 minutes.

Peaches

Peaches may be canned as halves or slices. Freestone peaches are recommended over clingstone varieties for canning. Clingstone peaches are easily bruised or damaged while trying to remove the pit.

MAKES ABOUT 4 PINT JARS OR 2 QUART JARS

> 5 to 6 pounds unblemished firm, ripe
>   peaches
> 4 cups water
> 1½ cups sugar
> 8 cups cold water
> 2 tablespoons antioxidant crystals or
>   ascorbic acid crystals

Rinse the peaches in cool water and drain well.

In a 4-quart pan, combine the 4 cups water and sugar. Over medium-low heat, stirring constantly, heat until the sugar is completely dissolved. Increase the heat to medium-high and bring the mixture to a boil. Boil for 5 minutes. Reduce the heat to low, cover and keep the syrup hot until needed.

In a large bowl, combine the 8 cups cold water and the antioxidant crystals. Stir until the crystals are completely dissolved.

To peel the peaches: Fill an 8-quart pan about half full of water. Over medium-high heat, bring the water to a simmer. Using a mesh basket or slotted spoon, carefully lower the peaches, a few at a time, into the water for 30 seconds. Remove the peaches from the pan and immediately plunge them into a large bowl of ice water for 1 to 2 minutes. Transfer the fruit to a strainer. Drain well and cool. Repeat with the remaining peaches.

Using a sharp paring knife, carefully slip the skins from the peaches. Cut each peach in half and remove the pit. Using a thin-bowled tableware spoon or a pitting spoon, carefully remove the red fibers from the center of the peaches. Drop the fruit into the antioxidant solution to prevent browning. Do not allow the fruit to remain in the solution for longer than 20 minutes. Remove the peach halves from the solution and rinse under cool water. Drain well.

Add the peaches to the syrup. Over medium-low heat, stirring occasionally, gently heat the peaches for 3 to 4 minutes. Remove the pan from the heat.

Ladle ¼ cup of the hot syrup into each hot jar. Pack the peaches, cut side down, into the jars, leaving ½-inch headspace.

Place a sieve over a medium saucepan and line the sieve with 3 or 4 layers of clean, damp cheesecloth. Strain the syrup through the cheesecloth. Over medium-high heat, quickly bring the syrup to a boil. Remove the pan from the heat.

Ladle the hot syrup into the jars, covering the peaches and leaving ½-inch headspace. Using a bubble freer or a plastic knife, remove any trapped air bubbles. Hold the jar up and check from the bottom for any air bubbles trapped under the fruit. If necessary, add more syrup to maintain the headspace. Wipe the jar rims and threads with a clean, damp cloth. Cover with hot lids and apply screw rings. Process pint jars in a 190 to 200F (88 to 93C) water bath for 20 minutes, quart jars for 25 minutes.

Tropical Peaches

These peaches are easy to make and have a great tropical flavor. Use any tropical juice blend that you like, just be sure that it is unsweetened.

MAKES ABOUT 4 PINT JARS OR 2 QUART JARS

5 to 6 pounds unblemished firm, ripe peaches
3½ to 4 cups unsweetened papaya and passion fruit juice blend or other tropical fruit juice blend
1 cup water
1½ cups sugar
8 cups cold water
2 tablespoons antioxidant crystals or ascorbic acid crystals

Rinse the peaches in cool water and drain well.

Place a sieve over a bowl or pan and line it with a paper coffee filter. Pour the papaya and passion fruit juice blend into the sieve and strain it through the filter. Measure 3 cups of juice.

In a 4-quart pan, combine the juice, 1 cup water and sugar. Over medium-low heat, stirring constantly, heat until the sugar is completely dissolved. Increase the heat to medium-high and bring the mixture to a boil. Boil for 2 minutes.

Reduce the heat to low, cover and keep the syrup hot until needed.

In a large bowl, combine the 8 cups cold water and the antioxidant crystals. Stir until the crystals are completely dissolved.

Peel and pit the peaches as instructed on pages 199–200. Cut the peaches into slices. Drop the fruit into the antioxidant solution to prevent browning. Do not allow the fruit to remain in the solution for longer than 20 minutes. Remove the peach slices from the solution and rinse under cool water. Drain well.

Add the peaches to the syrup. Over medium-low heat, stirring occasionally, gently heat the peaches for 3 to 4 minutes. Remove the pan from the heat.

Ladle ¼ cup of the hot syrup into each hot jar. Pack the peaches into the jars, leaving ½-inch headspace.

Place a sieve over a medium saucepan and line the sieve with 3 or 4 layers of clean, damp cheesecloth. Strain the syrup through the cheesecloth. Over medium-high heat, quickly bring the syrup to a boil. Remove the pan from the heat.

Ladle the hot syrup into the jars, covering the peaches and leaving ½-inch headspace. Using a bubble freer or a plastic knife, remove any trapped air bubbles. Hold the jar up and check from the bottom for any air bubbles trapped under the fruit. If necessary, add more syrup to maintain the headspace. Wipe the jar rims and threads with a clean, damp cloth. Cover with hot lids and apply screw rings. Process pint jars in a 190 to 200F (88 to 93C) water bath for 20 minutes, quart jars for 25 minutes.

Pears

I like to use Bartlett pears because they have an excellent flavor and hold their shape well during processing, but any variety of flavorful, firm pears may be used. Prepare pears one at a time and immediately place them into the antioxidant solution to prevent browning. Because pears can quickly and easily turn brown during handling, a jar of perfect pears shows off the skill and expertise of the home canner. I have earned blue ribbons for both hot pack and raw pack pears, but I prefer the texture and appearance of the hot pack pears. This recipe has earned multiple blue ribbons, a Best of Division award and the first-place Alltrista Premium Food Preservation Award.

MAKES ABOUT 4 PINT JARS OR 2 QUART JARS

5 to 6 pounds unblemished firm, ripe
   Bartlett pears
4 cups water
2 cups sugar
8 cups cold water
2 tablespoons antioxidant crystals or
   ascorbic acid crystals

Rinse the pears in cool water and drain well.

In a 4-quart pan, combine the 4 cups water and sugar. Over medium-low heat, stirring constantly, heat until the sugar is completely dissolved. Increase the heat to medium-high and bring the mixture to a boil. Boil for 5 minutes. Reduce the heat to low, cover and keep the syrup hot until needed.

In a large bowl, combine the 8 cups cold water and the antioxidant crystals. Stir until the crystals are completely dissolved.

Using a sharp paring knife, peel the pears one at a time. Cut each pear in half or into quarters.

Using a pear corer or a melon baller, remove the center core and stem from each pear piece. Drop the fruit into the antioxidant solution to prevent browning. Do not allow the fruit to remain in the solution for longer than 20 minutes. Remove the pears from the solution and rinse under cool water. Drain well.

Add the pears to the syrup. Over medium-low heat, stirring occasionally, gently heat the pears for 2 minutes. Remove the pan from the heat.

Ladle ¼ cup of the hot syrup into each hot jar. Pack the pears, cut side down, into the jars, leaving ½-inch headspace.

Place a sieve over a medium saucepan and line the sieve with 3 or 4 layers of clean, damp cheesecloth. Strain the syrup through the cheesecloth. Over medium-high heat, quickly bring the syrup to a boil. Remove the pan from the heat.

Ladle the hot syrup into the jars, covering the pears and leaving ½-inch headspace. Using a bubble freer or a plastic knife, remove any trapped air bubbles. Hold the jar up and check from the bottom for any air bubbles trapped under the fruit. If necessary, add more syrup to maintain the headspace. Wipe the jar rims and threads with a clean, damp cloth. Cover with hot lids and apply screw rings. Process pint jars in a 190 to 200F (88 to 93C) water bath for 20 minutes, quart jars for 25 minutes.

Amaretto Pears

These almond-flavored pears can make any day a special occasion. They also make wonderful pear tarts.

MAKES ABOUT 6 PINT JARS OR 3 QUART JARS

7½ to 8 pounds small, unblemished, firm, ripe Bartlett pears
5 cups water
2 cups sugar
8 cups cold water
2 tablespoons antioxidant crystals or ascorbic acid crystals
½ cup amaretto or 1 tablespoon pure almond extract

Rinse the pears in cool water and drain well.

In a 4-quart pan, combine the 5 cups water and sugar. Over medium-low heat, stirring constantly, heat until the sugar is completely dissolved. Increase the heat to medium-high and bring the mixture to a boil. Boil for 5 minutes. Reduce the heat to low, cover and keep the syrup hot until needed.

In a large bowl, combine the 8 cups cold water and the antioxidant crystals. Stir until the crystals are completely dissolved.

Using a sharp paring knife, peel the pears one at a time. Cut each pear into quarters. Using a pear corer or a melon baller, remove the center core and stem from each pear piece. Drop the fruit into the antioxidant solution to prevent browning. Do not allow the fruit to remain in the solution for longer than 20 minutes. Remove the pears from the solution and rinse under cool water. Drain well.

Add the pears to the syrup. Over medium-low heat, stirring occasionally, gently heat the pears for 2 minutes. Remove the pan from the heat. Stir in the amaretto.

Ladle ¼ cup of the hot syrup into each hot jar. Pack the pears, cut side down, into the jars, leaving ½-inch headspace.

Place a sieve over a medium saucepan and line the sieve with 3 or 4 layers of clean, damp cheesecloth. Strain the syrup through the cheesecloth. Over medium-high heat, quickly bring the syrup to a boil. Remove the pan from the heat.

Ladle the hot syrup into the jars, covering the pears and leaving ½-inch headspace. Using a bubble freer or a plastic knife, remove any trapped air bubbles. Hold the jar up and check from the bottom for any air bubbles trapped under the fruit. If necessary, add more syrup to maintain the headspace. Wipe the jar rims and threads with a clean, damp cloth. Cover with hot lids and apply screw rings. Process pint jars in a 190 to 200F (88 to 93C) water bath for 20 minutes, quart jars for 25 minutes.

Variation

Amaretto Peaches: Use small, firm ripe freestone peaches in place of the pears. Use a thin-bowled tableware spoon to remove the red fibers from the center of the peaches before dropping the fruit into the antioxidant solution.

Drunken Pears

These are very special pears with a marvelous flavor and beautiful pink color.

MAKES ABOUT 4 PINT JARS OR 2 QUART JARS

> **4 to 6 pounds small, unblemished, firm, ripe Bartlett pears**
> **2 cups red wine**
> **2 cups sherry**
> **2 cups sugar**
> **1 vanilla bean, split lengthwise**
> **8 cups cold water**
> **2 tablespoons antioxidant crystals or ascorbic acid crystals**

Rinse the pears in cool water and drain well.

In a 4-quart pan, combine the wine, sherry, sugar and vanilla bean. Over medium-low heat, stirring constantly, heat until the sugar is completely dissolved. Increase the heat to medium and bring the mixture to a simmer. Simmer gently for 5 minutes. Reduce the heat to low, cover and keep the syrup hot until needed.

In a large bowl, combine the 8 cups cold water and the antioxidant crystals. Stir until the crystals are completely dissolved.

Using a sharp paring knife, peel the pears one at a time. Cut each pear in half or into quarters. Using a pear corer or a melon baller, remove the center core and stem from each pear piece. Drop the fruit into the antioxidant solution to prevent browning. Do not allow the fruit to remain in the solution for longer than 20 minutes. Remove the pears from the solution and rinse under cool water. Drain well.

Add the pears to the syrup. Over medium-low heat, stirring occasionally, gently heat the pears for 2 minutes. Remove the pan from the heat. Remove the vanilla bean.

Ladle ¼ cup of the hot syrup into each hot jar. Pack the pears, cut side down, into the jars, leaving ½-inch headspace.

Place a sieve over a medium saucepan and line the sieve with 3 or 4 layers of clean, damp cheesecloth. Strain the syrup through the cheesecloth. Over medium-high heat, quickly bring the syrup to a boil. Remove the pan from the heat.

Ladle the hot syrup into the jars, covering the pears and leaving ½-inch headspace. Using a bubble freer or a plastic knife, remove any trapped air bubbles. Hold the jar up and check from the bottom for any air bubbles trapped under the fruit. If necessary, add more syrup to maintain the headspace. Wipe the jar rims and threads with a clean, damp cloth. Cover with hot lids and apply screw rings. Process pint jars in a 190 to 200F (88 to 93C) water bath for 20 minutes, quart jars for 25 minutes.

Pineapple

When choosing pineapples, smaller is better. During the first year of growth, a pineapple plant only produces one large pineapple. While these large pineapples are impressive in size and yield more usable fruit, they are not very sweet or flavorful. During the next 3 to 4 years of growth, the plant will produce a crop of several smaller pineapples instead of the 1 large fruit. These smaller pineapples have much more flavor and are substantially sweeter than the large fruit produced in the first year.

If canning pineapple rings, be sure to use wide-mouth quart jars to make packing the jars easier.

MAKES ABOUT 4 PINT JARS OR 2 QUART JARS

4 cups water
2 cups sugar
6 to 8 pounds ripe pineapple

In a 4-quart pan, combine the water and sugar. Over medium-low heat, stirring constantly, heat until the sugar is completely dissolved. Increase the heat to medium-high and bring the mixture to a boil. Boil for 5 minutes. Reduce the heat to low, cover and keep the syrup hot until needed.

Using a sharp knife, peel the pineapples. Remove the "eyes" and cores. Slice the pineapples into ½-inch rings or cut the fruit into ¾-inch-wide spears, 4 inches in length, or into 1-inch chunks.

Add the pineapple to the syrup. Over medium heat, stirring occasionally, gently simmer the pineapple until tender, about 5 to 7 minutes. Remove the pan from the heat.

Ladle ¼ cup of the hot syrup into each hot jar. Stack pineapple rings in a wide-mouth quart jar, leaving ½-inch headspace. Stand spears on end or spoon chunks into pint or quart jars, leaving ½-inch headspace.

Place a sieve over a medium saucepan and line the sieve with 3 or 4 layers of clean, damp cheesecloth. Strain the syrup through the cheesecloth. Over medium-high heat, quickly bring the syrup to a boil. Remove the pan from the heat.

Ladle the hot syrup into the jars, covering the pineapple and leaving ½-inch headspace. Using a bubble freer or a plastic knife, remove any trapped air bubbles. Hold the jar up and check from the bottom for any air bubbles trapped under the fruit. If necessary, add more syrup to maintain the headspace. Wipe the jar rims and threads with a clean, damp cloth. Cover with hot lids and apply screw rings. Process pint jars in a 190 to 200F (88 to 93C) water bath for 20 minutes, quart jars for 25 minutes.

Plums

Freestone varieties of plums may also be canned as halves. Cut the plums in half and remove the pits. Leave the skins on and prepare, pack and process the fruit by either the hot pack or raw pack method.

MAKES ABOUT 4 PINT JARS OR 2 QUART JARS

5 pounds unblemished firm, ripe plums
4 cups water
1½ cups sugar

 Rinse the plums in cool water and drain well.

In a 4-quart pan, combine the water and sugar. Over medium-low heat, stirring constantly, heat until the sugar is completely dissolved. Increase the heat to medium-high and bring the mixture to a boil. Boil for 5 minutes. Reduce the heat to low, cover and keep the syrup hot until needed.

Prick the blossom end of the plums 2 to 3 times with a large sterilized needle to reduce the chances of the skins splitting during processing.

Add the plums to the syrup. Over medium-low heat, stirring occasionally, gently heat the plums for 2 minutes. Remove the pan from the heat.

Pack the plums into hot jars, leaving ½-inch headspace. Gently shake the jars a few times during packing to settle the plums and attain a snug pack.

Place a sieve over a medium saucepan and line the sieve with 3 or 4 layers of clean, damp cheesecloth. Strain the syrup through the cheesecloth. Over medium-high heat, quickly bring the syrup to a boil. Remove the pan from the heat.

Ladle the hot syrup into the jars, covering the plums and leaving ½-inch headspace. Using a bubble freer or a plastic knife, remove any trapped air bubbles. Hold the jar up and check from the bottom for any air bubbles trapped under the fruit. If necessary, add more syrup to maintain the headspace. Wipe the jar rims and threads with a clean, damp cloth. Cover with hot lids and apply screw rings. Process pint jars in a 190 to 200F (88 to 93C) water bath for 20 minutes, quart jars for 25 minutes.

Variation
Raw Pack Method: To can plums using the raw pack method, prepare the syrup as described above. Remove the skins from the plums. Pack the plums snugly into hot jars, being careful not to crush or bruise the fruit, leaving ½-inch headspace. Ladle the hot syrup into the jars, covering the plums and leaving ½-inch headspace. Remove any trapped air bubbles. Wipe the rims and apply the hot lids and screw rings. Process pint jars in a 190 to 200F (88 to 93C) water bath for 25 minutes, quart jars for 30 minutes.

Sherried Strawberries

Strawberries preserved with sherry hold their shape and texture well and develop a special flavor.

MAKES ABOUT 4 PINT JARS

2⅔ cups sugar

2 cups sherry

4 quarts small firm whole strawberries

In a 4-quart pan, combine the sugar and sherry. Over medium-low heat, stirring constantly, heat until the sugar is completely dissolved. Increase the heat to medium and bring the mixture to just below simmering. Small bubbles will dance on the bottom of the pan. Remove the pan from the heat and let cool.

Gently rinse the strawberries in cool water and drain well. Using a tomato corer or a sharp paring knife, remove the stems. Discard any hollow berries.

Add the strawberries to the syrup. Over medium-low heat, bring the mixture just to a gently simmer. Remove the pan from the heat. Let cool for 20 minutes.

Stir the strawberries gently. Cover the pan and let the strawberries stand in the syrup for 8 to 12 hours to allow the strawberries to absorb some of the syrup and plump and to prevent the fruit from floating in the jars after processing.

Pack the strawberries into hot jars, leaving ½-inch headspace. Gently shake the jars a few times during packing to settle the strawberries and attain a snug pack.

Place a sieve over a medium saucepan and line the sieve with 3 or 4 layers of clean, damp cheesecloth. Strain the syrup through the cheesecloth. Over medium heat, quickly heat the syrup to 190F (88C). Remove the pan from the heat.

Ladle the hot syrup into the jars, covering the strawberries and leaving ½-inch headspace. Using a bubble freer or a plastic knife, remove any trapped air bubbles. Hold the jar up and check from the bottom for any air bubbles trapped under the fruit. If necessary, add more syrup to maintain the headspace. Wipe the jar rims and threads with a clean, damp cloth. Cover with hot lids and apply screw rings. Process pint jars in a 190 to 200F (88 to 93C) water bath for 15 minutes.

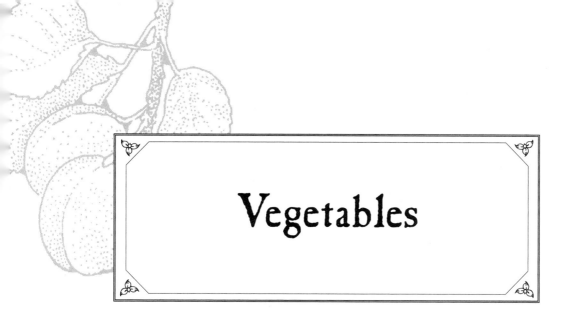

Vegetables

CANNING VEGETABLES

Canning vegetables is a wonderful way to preserve the fresh flavors from summer's bountiful gardens. Open a jar of tender, crisp corn or flavorful young green beans in the middle of winter, and your efforts will be more than repaid. A piping-hot bowl of hearty home-canned soup will quickly chase away winter's chill.

Fresh vegetables can deteriorate quickly. It is important to can vegetables on the same day that they are harvested and as close to harvest time as possible. If necessary, root vegetables, such as onions, carrots and potatoes can be stored for a short period of time before canning. Green beans, other bean varieties, peas, tomatoes, asparagus, summer squash and other tender crops are very fragile and should be preserved within a few hours of harvest.

Corn is perhaps the most fragile and perishable vegetable, because its natural sugars begin turning to starch the moment it is picked. Therefore, corn should be canned immediately after harvest to preserve its tenderness and natural sweetness. Have everything set up and ready to begin canning, then go out to the garden and harvest the corn. If you will be using corn purchased from a roadside field stand, check with the seller to be sure the corn was harvested that same day. Buy the corn early in the morning while it is still fresh and can it as soon as you get home.

Salt

Salt is added to vegetables to help them retain their crisp texture and to enhance their natural flavor. If you prefer, vegetables may be canned without adding salt. The omission of the salt will result in only minimal changes in color and a slightly softer finished preserve.

Selecting Vegetables

For best results, vegetables should be canned within a few hours of harvest. Vegetables grown in the home garden and those purchased from farmers' markets or local produce markets are strongly recommended for use in home canning. These vegetables can usually be obtained within hours of harvest and are loaded with flavor. When purchasing vegetables from farmers' markets or produce markets, be sure to ask when the produce was harvested and verify that it has not been sprayed with any pesticides.

Grocery store produce is frequently harvested days, even weeks before being delivered to the store. This storage and shipping time can seriously affect the quality and freshness of these vegetables. To prevent insect damage while growing, the produce is commonly treated with pesticides. Many of the vegetables found in supermarkets have also been coated with a nontoxic vegetable wax to enhance the appearance of the produce and to retard the growth of mold during shipping. This wax can cause serious problems during canning. It is very difficult to remove the wax without vigorous scrubbing, which can damage the delicate skin, reducing the quality of the produce and promoting the chance of spoilage. The wax can also inhibit the absorption of liquids, trapping air inside the vegetables, causing pieces to float in the jar after processing. Because most vegetables are preserved without peeling, supermarket produce should be avoided for canning.

Select fresh, crisp, tender, young vegetables that are firm and not wilted. Avoid vegetables that are very large or overmature. These will contain more water and larger seeds, making them poor choices for home canning. They will also have larger cell structures, which may contain more air, increasing the chances that the vegetables will float in the jars.

Select tomatoes that are fresh, ripe and firm. Bruised, damaged or overripe tomatoes can contain bacteria or other contaminants, and frequently have reduced acid levels that can lead to spoilage. When canning homegrown tomatoes, do not use any harvested from dried or frost-killed vines. The acidity of these tomatoes will be too low to ensure safe water bath processing.

The quantities of vegetables listed in the recipes are the approximate amounts needed to fill the size and number of jars indicated and should be used as a guide. You may find that you need slightly more or less than the amount listed. The actual quantity can vary depending on the size of the vegetables, how they are prepared and the type of pack you use to fill the jars.

Preparing Vegetables

Wash the vegetables just before use and prepare only enough vegetables for one batch at a time. Gently scrub the vegetables with a very soft brush to remove any dirt, being careful not to scratch the peels or bruise the vegetables. Rinse the vegetables 2 to 3 times in clean, cool water, changing the water between each rinsing. Drain the vegetables well on paper towels and dry them completely. Excess water can have a negative impact on the preservation of some vegetables, such as cream-style corn, that are not blanched before being packed into the jars.

Blanching Vegetables to Preserve Color

Vegetables are blanched, or cooked briefly, before being packed into the jars to help maintain their natural color and to remove excess air from the vegetables, allowing for a tighter pack. Blanching also reduces the chances of the vegetables floating in the jars after processing. When blanching or cooking vegetables at altitudes above 5,000 feet, add 1 minute to the heating time given in the recipe.

Avoid blanching or cooking vegetables in water that is at a full rolling boil. Cooking the vegetables at too high of a temperature before filling the jars may cause light-colored vegetables to turn brown during processing in the pressure canner. Instead of boiling water, blanch vegetables in gently simmering water. A small amount of strained lemon juice or baking soda added to the water before blanching will help the vegetables maintain their bright color during canning and processing. This is especially helpful with green vegetables that tend to fade quickly when heated.

Hot Pack Versus Raw Pack

A common problem when canning vegetables is that the vegetables tend to float to the top of the jar after processing. This is often caused by air trapped inside the cells of the vegetables. The vegetables at the top of the jar that are not covered by liquid may oxidize and turn brown. While these vegetables may not be very attractive, they are perfectly safe to eat.

Hot Pack Method

Briefly cooking the vegetables before packing them into the jars will replace much of the air inside the vegetables with liquid and help reduce the chance of the vegetables floating to the top of the jar. This is referred to as the hot pack method of canning. When the vegetables are heated, they become more pliable and more vegetables can usually be packed into the jars. A tighter pack also means there is less chance of the vegetables floating. The hot pack method is strongly recommended for most vegetables to help prevent floating vegetables and to create preserved foods with excellent quality.

To can vegetables using the hot pack method: Heat the prepared vegetables in simmering water according to the recipe instructions. Pack the hot vegetables into the hot jars, leaving 1-inch head-

space. (The canning jars should be hot to prevent them from cracking when filled with the hot vegetables or boiling water.) Cover the vegetables completely with the hot cooking water, maintaining the same 1-inch headspace. Wipe the jar rims and threads, apply the hot lids and screw rings and process the jars in a pressure canner for the amount of time and at the pressure specified in the recipe.

Raw Pack Method

The raw pack method is when unheated vegetables are packed directly into the jars, then covered with boiling water. This method may be used for delicate vegetables, such as summer squash, that would not maintain their shape and texture if cooked first. Vegetables packed using the raw pack method have a greater tendency to float in the jars because they contain more air and cannot be packed as tightly into the jar.

To can vegetables using the raw pack method: Tightly pack the prepared vegetables into hot jars, leaving a full 1-inch headspace. (The canning jars should be hot to prevent them from cracking when filled with boiling water.) Cover the vegetables completely with boiling water, maintaining the same 1-inch headspace. Wipe the jar rims and threads, apply the hot lids and screw rings, and process the jars in a pressure canner for the amount of time and at the pressure specified in the recipe.

Packing Jars

Pack the vegetables into the jars without crushing. Do not leave any large gaps between the pieces of vegetables. Fill the jar, leaving a 1-inch headspace in the top of the jar. Do not pack the vegetables into the jars too tightly. There needs to be enough room for the liquid to circulate around the vegetables. Otherwise, some of the liquid may be forced out of the jars during the high tempera-

High-Altitude Adjustments

ALTITUDE	DIAL-GAUGE PRESSURE CANNER	WEIGHTED-GAUGE PRESSURE CANNER
1 to 1,000 feet	11 pounds	10 pounds
1,001 to 2,000 feet	11 pounds	15 pounds
2,001 to 4,000 feet	12 pounds	15 pounds
4,001 to 6,000 feet	13 pounds	15 pounds
6,001 to 8,000 feet	14 pounds	15 pounds
8,001 to 10,000 feet	15 pounds	15 pounds

tures reached in the pressure canner. When the liquid is forced out of the jar during processing, it will increase the amount of headspace in the jar and may leave some vegetables at the top of the jar uncovered. Ladle the canning liquid into the jar, maintaining the 1-inch headspace. Using a bubble freer or plastic knife, release any air bubbles trapped in the jar. If necessary, add additional vegetables or liquid to bring the headspace back up to 1 inch. With a clean, damp cloth, wipe the jar rims and threads clean of any spilled liquid and apply the hot lids and screw rings.

When packing jars for fair exhibition, use either a decorative pack or an attractive, uniform pack. Vegetables for family use may be packed with a more casual appearance. Because of the serious risk of contamination in jars of vegetables that have not been correctly processed in a pressure canner, most fairs do not judge vegetables on their taste but rather on their appearance in the jar. Some judges will open the jars and inspect the contents, judging the vegetables on their texture and aroma as well as their appearance. Check the fair handbook for the specific vegetable judging criteria for your fair. If the jars are to be entered into a fair competition where they will be judged on their appearance only, a decorative pack is recommended, unless the individual fair specifies

"no fancy packs" or gives other restrictions on the presentation of the preserved food.

If you plan to enter your canned vegetables into competition at a fair, be sure to select jars that are full and do not contain floating vegetables. There should not be a space at the bottom of the jar that just contains liquid and no vegetables. Jars containing floating vegetables will receive low marks from the judges.

Processing Vegetables

With the exception of some tomato products that have an acid content high enough to allow for safe processing in a water bath, all home-canned vegetables must be processed in a pressure canner to ensure safety. For safe pressure canning methods, follow the procedures described in Canning Basics (page 24) or follow the manufacturer's instructions packaged with the canner. Use the processing times and pressures listed in each recipe for your type of canner. Never reduce the processing time or the vegetables may be unsafe to eat. Remember to adjust the processing pressure for vegetables canned at altitudes above 1,000 feet.

Processing the jars in a pressure canner for too long or at a pressure that is too high may cause light-colored vegetables to darken and turn brown during the processing. Pay careful attention to the pressure gauge on the canner and use a timer to accurately keep track of the processing time.

If the liquid level in the jar is low after processing, do not open the jar to add more liquid. Opening the jar will break the seal, making it necessary to reprocess the vegetables. Reprocessing will cause the vegetables to become mushy and lose their flavor. Store the jars as normal and use the jars with low liquid levels first. The vegetables in the top of the jar that are not covered by liquid may oxidize and darken during storage. While they may not be as pretty as the rest, these oxidized vegetables are still fine for eating. Depending on your preference, they may be removed when the jar is open or eaten right along with the other vegetables.

Home-Canned Soups

Home-canned soups are packed with flavor and the freshest ingredients. They contain no preservatives and have a much better texture and taste than commercially prepared canned soups. The fragrant aroma of a hot bowl of home-canned soup is a welcome and comforting pleasure on a cold, blustery day.

Judges look for flavorful soups with good texture for the type, whether it be a smooth puree or a vegetable soup with pieces chopped in even sizes. For a vegetable soup, the pieces should not be too chunky, nor should they be very small unless you are also adding rice or other grains. The judge should not have to chew a mouthful of only one or two large pieces, or hunt around trying to figure out which vegetables are in the soup. As with other preserved foods, cream soups made with dairy products are usually prohibited in preserved foods competitions.

A Few Words About Safety

With the exception of meats, fish and poultry, there is a greater risk of food poisoning from canned vegetables than from any other type of home-canned foods. Care must be used during all steps of preparation, and the jars of vegetables must be processed in a pressure canner for the amount of time and at the pressure specified in the recipe. Be sure to adjust the pressure if you live at an altitude above 1,000 feet (see box, page 210). Storing jars in a warm location can make the contents of the jars expand, causing the lids to bulge and the seals to fail. Always store canned foods in a cool, dry, dark location.

Carefully inspect all jars of vegetables both before and after opening the jars. If the liquid is murky, the seal is weak or broken, the lid is bulging or you smell an off or unpleasant odor when you open the jar, *do not taste* the contents. Boil both the jar and the contents, then dispose of them so that no animal or human will come into contact with the contaminated food.

Properly prepared, processed and stored home-canned vegetables should be perfectly safe to eat without any additional cooking. The vegetables can simply be warmed and served, retaining more of their fresh flavor and texture. However, because of the low acid levels of vegetables, there is a serious risk for bacterial contamination in foods that were not cleaned, handled or stored properly. Failure to correctly process the vegetables in a pressure canner for the necessary amount of time at the specified pressure can also lead to contamination and bacteria growth. The USDA recommends boiling all home-canned vegetables, except for tomatoes, for 10 minutes before tasting or using the preserved food. If you are at an altitude of more than 1,000 feet above sea level, add an additional 1 minute of boiling time for each 1,000 feet of elevation.

Asparagus

Select firm, tender, tight-tipped asparagus spears that are about the size of a pencil or slightly larger. Spears that are too small may overcook during processing and become mushy. Large spears of asparagus are too mature and are likely to be tough and woody.

MAKES ABOUT 6 PINT JARS OR 3 QUART JARS

6 to 8 pounds ¼-inch-diameter fresh, tender
    asparagus spears
2 tablespoons strained fresh lemon juice
1 tablespoon salt

Gently rinse the asparagus 2 to 3 times in cool water to remove any sand or dirt. Drain well. Cut the spears 3¾ inches long for pint jars and 5¾ inches long for quart jars.

Fill a 4-quart pan about half full of water. Over medium-high heat, bring the water to a simmer. Stir in the lemon juice.

Place a handful of asparagus spears into the water and blanch for 1 minute. Remove the asparagus spears from the pan and immediately plunge them into a large bowl or pan of ice water for 2 minutes to stop the cooking process. Remove the asparagus from the ice water and drain well. Repeat with additional handfuls of asparagus until all of the spears have been blanched. Set aside.

Place a sieve over a medium saucepan and line the sieve with 3 or 4 layers of clean, damp cheesecloth. Strain the hot cooking liquid through the cheesecloth. Over medium-high heat, quickly bring the liquid to a boil. Remove the pan from the heat.

Add ½ teaspoon salt to each hot pint jar or 1 teaspoon salt to each hot quart jar. Lay the jars on their sides. Gently pack the asparagus into the jars, with the tips pointed up. Stand the jars upright.

Ladle the hot cooking liquid into the jars, covering the asparagus spears and leaving 1-inch headspace. Using a bubble freer or plastic knife, remove any trapped air bubbles. If necessary, add more liquid to maintain 1-inch headspace. Wipe the jar rims and threads with a clean, damp cloth. Cover with hot lids and apply screw rings.

Process pint jars for 30 minutes, quart jars for 40 minutes, at 11 pounds of pressure in a dial-gauge pressure canner or at 10 pounds pressure in a weighted-gauge pressure canner.

Variation

Hot Pack Method: To can asparagus using the hot pack method, cut the asparagus spears into 1½-inch pieces. Blanch the cut asparagus in simmering water for 2 minutes. Do not chill the asparagus in ice water. Add ½ teaspoon salt to each hot pint jar or 1 teaspoon salt to each hot quart jar. Pack the hot asparagus pieces into the jars, leaving 1-inch headspace. Cover with the strained hot canning liquid, leaving 1-inch headspace and proceed as directed above.

Baked Beans

This rich, old-fashioned recipe contains salt pork or bacon, which may be omitted if you prefer. Because the salt pork or bacon has been cured, it poses far less of a contamination risk than raw meat. The beans and salt pork may be safely processed in a pressure canner.

MAKES ABOUT 6 PINT JARS OR 3 QUART JARS

6 cups small white beans
1½ teaspoons salt
1½ cups firmly packed dark brown sugar
⅔ cup molasses
¼ cup light corn syrup
1 teaspoon dry mustard
⅓ pound salt pork or thick sliced bacon, cut into 1-inch pieces

Rinse the beans thoroughly in cool water and drain well.

Place the beans in a 6- to 8-quart pan and add 3 quarts water. Cover the pan and let the beans soak for 12 hours or overnight.

Drain the beans and return them to the pan. Add 3 quarts of water and the salt.

Over medium heat, bring the mixture to a boil. Reduce the heat and simmer, stirring occasionally for 1 hour. Remove the pan from the heat. Drain the beans, reserving 2 cups of the cooking liquid.

In a large bowl or pan, combine the brown sugar, molasses, corn syrup and mustard. Stir in the reserved cooking liquid. Add the salt pork or bacon. Add the beans and stir until evenly combined. Pour the mixture into a 4- to 6-quart greased bean pot or deep casserole or baking pan. Cover with a lid or foil.

Bake the beans at 250F (120C) for 6 to 8 hours. Stir occasionally to prevent sticking. If needed, add more water to keep the beans from drying out. Remove the pan from the oven.

Ladle the hot beans into hot jars, leaving 1-inch headspace. Using a bubble freer or plastic knife, remove any trapped air bubbles. If necessary, add more beans to maintain 1-inch headspace. Wipe the jar rims and threads with a clean, damp cloth. Cover with hot lids and apply screw rings.

Process pint jars for 80 minutes, quart jars for 95 minutes, at 11 pounds of pressure in a dial-gauge pressure canner or at 10 pounds pressure in a weighted-gauge pressure canner.

Beets

Small beets may be left whole or sliced. Use a crinkle-cut slicer for a more attractive presentation in the jar and on your plate.

MAKES ABOUT 6 PINT JARS OR 3 QUART JARS

6 pounds 1- to 1½-inch-diameter baby beets (80 to 90 small beets)
1 tablespoon salt
Boiling water

Cut off the beet greens, leaving 1 inch of the stem. Rinse the beets in cold water and scrub well with a soft brush to remove dirt. Trim the taproot to ½ inch long.

Fill an 8-quart pan about half full of water. Over medium-high heat, bring the water to a boil. Cook the beets, in 4 batches, for 10 to 15 minutes, depending on the size. Using a slotted spoon, remove the beets from the water and plunge them into a bowl of ice water for 1 minute to stop the cooking process and loosen the skins. Peel the beets, trimming off the stems and taproots. If desired, cut the beets into ¼-inch-thick slices. Discard the water.

Add ½ teaspoon salt to each hot pint jar or 1 teaspoon salt to each hot quart jar. Pack the beets into the jars, leaving 1-inch headspace. Ladle boiling water into the jars, covering the beets and leaving 1-inch headspace. Using a bubble freer or plastic knife, remove any trapped air bubbles. If necessary, add more water to maintain 1-inch headspace. Wipe the jar rims and threads with a clean, damp cloth. Cover with hot lids and apply screw rings.

Process pint jars for 30 minutes, quart jars for 35 minutes, at 11 pounds of pressure in a dial-gauge pressure canner or at 10 pounds pressure in a weighted-gauge pressure canner.

Carrots

Can whole carrots while they are still young and tender. Large carrots can become woody and should be sliced or chopped before canning. Select long, straight, uniform-sized carrots, about ¾ inch in diameter.

MAKES ABOUT 6 PINT JARS OR 3 QUART JARS

8 pounds carrots
1 tablespoon salt

Rinse the carrots in cold water and scrub well with a soft brush to remove dirt. Trim off the stems and taproots. Peel the carrots and rinse again. Cut the carrots into ¼-inch-thick slices.

Fill an 8-quart pan about half full of water. Over medium-high heat, bring the water to a boil. Carefully add the carrots to the boiling water. Bring the water back to a boil. Reduce the heat

and simmer, uncovered, for 4 to 5 minutes. Remove the pan from the heat.

Add ½ teaspoon salt to each hot pint jar or 1 teaspoon salt to each hot quart jar. Using a slotted spoon, drain the carrots and pack the hot carrots into the jars, leaving 1-inch headspace.

Place a sieve over a medium saucepan and line the sieve with 3 or 4 layers of clean, damp cheesecloth. Strain the hot cooking liquid through the cheesecloth. Over medium-high heat, quickly bring the liquid to a boil. Remove the pan from the heat.

Ladle the hot canning liquid into the jars, covering the carrots and leaving 1-inch headspace. Using a bubble freer or plastic knife, remove any trapped air bubbles. If necessary, add more liquid to maintain 1-inch headspace. Wipe the jar rims and threads with a clean, damp cloth. Cover with hot lids and apply screw rings.

Process pint jars for 25 minutes, quart jars for 30 minutes, at 11 pounds of pressure in a dial-gauge pressure canner or at 10 pounds pressure in a weighted-gauge pressure canner.

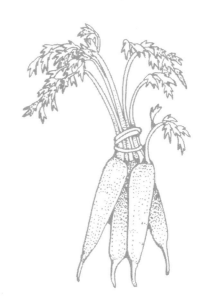

Sugar-Glazed Carrots

Packaged baby carrots are perfect for this recipe. Choose carrots that are about ½ inch in diameter. Large carrots may also be used.

MAKES ABOUT 6 PINT JARS OR 3 QUART JARS

6 to 7 pounds baby carrots

3 cups water

2 cups firmly packed light brown sugar

3 tablespoons frozen orange juice
    concentrate, thawed

 Rinse the carrots in cold water and drain well.

If using large carrots, scrub well with a soft brush to remove dirt, rinse and drain well. Trim off the stems and taproots. Peel the carrots and rinse again. Cut the carrots into 2-inch-long pieces.

In a medium saucepan, combine the water and brown sugar. Over medium-low heat, stirring constantly, heat the mixture until the sugar is completely dissolved. Increase the heat to medium and bring the mixture to a simmer. Simmer for 3 minutes. Add the orange juice concentrate and stir until thoroughly combined. Reduce the heat, cover and keep the syrup hot until needed.

Fill an 8-quart pan about half full of water. Over medium-high heat, bring the water to a boil. Carefully add the carrots to the boiling water. Bring the water back to a boil. Reduce the heat and simmer, uncovered, for 4 to 5 minutes. Remove the pan from the heat.

Using a slotted spoon, drain the carrots and pack the hot carrots into the jars, leaving 1-inch headspace.

Ladle the hot syrup into the jars, covering the carrots and leaving 1-inch headspace. Using a bubble freer or plastic knife, remove any trapped air bubbles. If necessary, add more syrup to maintain 1-inch headspace. Wipe the jar rims and threads with a clean, damp cloth. Cover with hot lids and ply screw rings.

Process both pint jars and quart jars for 30 minutes at 11 pounds of pressure in a dial-gauge pressure canner or at 10 pounds pressure in a weighted-gauge pressure canner.

Whole-Kernel Sweet Corn

Preserve corn as quickly after harvesting as possible. As soon as the ears are picked, the sugar in the kernels will immediately begin turning into starch and the corn will start to lose its sweetness.

A sharp knife or a corn cutter may be used to remove the whole kernels from the cob. A corn cutter has a long, tubular handle with a circular blade in the center. The cutter is positioned over the end of the ear of corn and, when turned, the sharp teeth on the blade cut the kernels from the cob.

MAKES ABOUT 6 PINT JARS OR 3 QUART JARS

15 pounds fresh ears yellow corn (about 25
    ears)

6 cups water

1½ teaspoons salt

 Husk the ears of corn and remove the silk. Use a very soft brush to gently remove any silk trapped between the kernels. Rinse the corn under cool running water and drain well.

With a sharp knife, cut off the tip and stalk ends of each ear of corn. Stand an ear of corn on end and, using a sharp knife or corn cutter, cut off kernels, being careful not to cut into the cob. Leave any small or undeveloped kernels on the cob. Do not scrape the remaining parts of the kernels from the cob, as this will cause the canning liquid to be cloudy.

In an 8-quart pan, combine the cut corn, water and salt. Over medium heat, stirring frequently, bring the corn to a boil. Reduce the heat and simmer for 2 minutes. Remove the pan from the heat.

With a slotted spoon, drain the corn and pack the hot corn into hot jars, leaving 1-inch headspace.

Place a sieve over a medium saucepan and line the sieve with 3 or 4 layers of clean, damp cheesecloth. Strain the hot cooking liquid through the cheesecloth. Over medium-high heat, quickly bring the liquid to a boil. Remove the pan from the heat.

Ladle the hot cooking liquid into the jars, covering the corn and leaving 1-inch headspace. Using a bubble freer or plastic knife, remove any trapped air bubbles. If necessary, add more liquid to maintain 1-inch headspace. Wipe the jar rims and threads with a clean, damp cloth. Cover with hot lids and apply screw rings.

Process pint jars for 55 minutes, quart jars for 85 minutes, at 11 pounds of pressure in a dial-gauge pressure canner or at 10 pounds pressure in a weighted-gauge pressure canner.

Golden Cream-Style Corn

The use of white corn is not recommended for making cream-style corn because it does not maintain its shape well when processed and tends to become mushy when reheated for serving.

Because of the denseness of cream-style corn, it is difficult for the heat in the canner to fully penetrate the contents of quart-sized jars; therefore, cream-style corn should only be canned in pint jars to ensure safe processing. Cream-style corn must be packed into the jars hot for proper heat penetration.

MAKES ABOUT 6 PINT JARS

22 to 25 medium fresh ears yellow corn

❦ Husk the ears of corn and remove the silk. Use a very soft brush to gently remove any silk trapped between the kernels. Rinse the corn under cool running water and drain well.

With a sharp knife, cut off the tip and stalk ends of each ear of corn. Stand an ear of corn on end and carefully slide a sharp knife down the cob from the top, cutting off the kernels at about ⅔ of their depth. Using a table knife, scrape the cobs to remove the remaining pulp and milk, being careful not to scrape off any of the fibrous cob material. Combine the pulp and milk with the cut corn.

Measure the corn mixture, then pour it into an 8-quart pan. To every pint of corn mixture, add 1 cup water. Over medium heat, stirring frequently, bring the corn to a boil. Remove the pan from the heat.

Ladle the hot corn into hot pint jars, leaving 1-inch headspace. Using a bubble freer or plastic knife, remove any trapped air bubbles. If necessary, add more corn to maintain 1-inch headspace.

Wipe the jar rims and threads with a clean, damp cloth. Cover with hot lids and apply screw rings.

Process pint jars for 85 minutes at 11 pounds of pressure in a dial-gauge pressure canner or at 10 pounds pressure in a weighted-gauge pressure canner.

Garden Green Beans

Green beans are one of the easiest and most popular vegetables to can. They are also an abundantly productive crop to grow in a home garden. Good-quality beans can also be obtained from many farmers' markets. For best results, can green beans as soon after picking as possible and always on the same day they are harvested.

The small amount of lemon juice called for in the recipe will help the beans maintain more of their natural color during the blanching process. Be sure to strain the lemon juice through three or four layers of clean, damp cheesecloth before measuring.

MAKES ABOUT 6 PINT JARS OR 3 QUART JARS

6½ pounds young, tender green beans
2 tablespoons strained fresh lemon juice
1 tablespoon salt

Sort the green beans and discard any that are blemished, too mature or immature. Gently wash the beans 3 or 4 times in a sink or extra-large bowl filled with clean, cold water. Lift the beans out of the rinse water, leaving the dirt or soil particles undisturbed on the bottom of the sink or bowl. Change the water after each rinsing. Spread the beans on paper towels to drain.

Fill an 8-quart pan about half full of water. Over medium-high heat, bring the water to a boil.

Using a sharp knife, trim the blossom and stem ends from the beans. Slice the beans into uniform pieces about 1½ inches long. Cutting the beans on a slight diagonal makes for an attractive canned product.

Carefully add the green beans to the boiling water. Stir in the lemon juice. Bring the water back to a simmer. Reduce the heat and simmer, uncovered, for 5 minutes. Remove the pan from the heat.

With a slotted spoon, drain the green beans and pack the hot beans into hot jars, leaving 1-inch headspace.

Place a sieve over a medium saucepan and line the sieve with 3 or 4 layers of clean, damp cheesecloth. Strain the hot cooking liquid through the cheesecloth. Over medium-high heat, quickly bring the liquid to a boil. Remove the pan from the heat.

Add ½ teaspoon salt to each hot pint jar or 1 teaspoon salt to each hot quart jar. Ladle the hot cooking liquid into the jars, covering the beans and leaving 1-inch headspace. Using a bubble freer or plastic knife, remove any trapped air bubbles. If necessary, add more liquid to maintain 1-inch headspace. Wipe the jar rims and threads with a clean, damp cloth. Cover with hot lids and apply screw rings.

Process pint jars for 20 minutes, quart jars for 25 minutes, at 11 pounds of pressure in a dial-gauge pressure canner or at 10 pounds pressure in a weighted-gauge pressure canner.

Variations

Whole Green Beans: Green beans may also be canned whole, using wide-mouth jars. Wash the beans and trim the stem ends. Cut beans 3¾ inches long for pint jars and 5¾ inches long for quart jars. Cook the beans as directed above. Pack the beans one at a time into the jar, placing the cut stem end down. Cover with the hot canning liquid or boiling water, leaving 1-inch headspace and proceed as directed above.

This is a particularly good way to pack green beans if you plan to enter them in a fair competition.

Thyme Green Beans: My aunt Jeanie Lee taught me that "it takes thyme to cook green beans," and I love to can beans using this variation. The fresh thyme gives a special flavor to the beans, earning them high praise from the judges such as "Great job. These beans are a pleasure to judge!" The judges honored this entry with the Best of Division award for the most outstanding vegetable exhibit.

Tie a few sprigs of thoroughly rinsed fresh thyme in a piece of cheesecloth and add it to the blanching water for 2 to 3 minutes as the water heats. Remove the thyme before adding the green beans.

Dilled Green Beans: Place 2 sprigs of fresh dill in each jar of green beans before sealing.

English Peas

For the best flavor and texture, can only young, tender peas that are about ¼ inch in diameter. Large or overmature peas may be tough and lacking in flavor.

MAKES ABOUT 6 PINT JARS OR 3 QUART JARS

8 pounds English (green) peas or other
    small, flavorful pea variety
2 tablespoons strained fresh lemon juice
1 tablespoon salt

Rinse the pea pods in cool water and drain. Remove the peas from the shells. Rinse the shelled peas in cool water and drain well.

Fill an 8-quart pan about half full of water. Over medium-high heat, bring the water to a boil. Stir in the lemon juice.

Carefully add the peas to the boiling water. Blanch the peas for 1 minute. Remove the pan from the heat.

Add ½ teaspoon salt to each hot pint jar or 1 teaspoon salt to each hot quart jar. Using a slotted spoon, drain the peas and pack the hot peas into hot jars, leaving 1-inch headspace.

Place a sieve over a medium saucepan and line the sieve with 3 or 4 layers of clean, damp cheesecloth. Strain the hot cooking liquid through the cheesecloth. Over medium-high heat, quickly bring the liquid to a boil. Remove the pan from the heat.

Ladle the hot cooking liquid into the jars, covering the peas and leaving 1-inch headspace. Using a bubble freer or plastic knife, remove any trapped air bubbles. If necessary, add more liquid to maintain 1-inch headspace. Wipe the jar rims and threads with a clean, damp cloth. Cover with hot lids and apply screw rings.

Process both pint jars and quart jars for 40 minutes at 11 pounds of pressure in a dial-gauge pressure canner or at 10 pounds pressure in a weighted-gauge pressure canner.

Lima Beans

Select young, tender lima beans, ½ inch to ¾ inch in length.

MAKES ABOUT 6 PINT JARS OR 3 QUART JARS

8 pounds lima beans
2 tablespoons strained fresh lemon juice
1 tablespoon salt

❦ Rinse the lima bean pods in cool water and drain. Remove the beans from the shells. Rinse the shelled beans in cool water and drain well.

Fill an 8-quart pan about half full of water. Over medium-high heat, bring the water to a boil. Stir in the lemon juice.

Carefully add the lima beans to the boiling water. Blanch the lima beans for 2 to 3 minutes, depending on the size of the beans. Remove the pan from the heat.

Add ½ teaspoon salt to each hot pint jar or 1 teaspoon salt to each hot quart jar. Using a slotted spoon, drain the lima beans and pack the hot beans into hot jars, leaving 1-inch headspace.

Place a sieve over a medium saucepan and line the sieve with 3 or 4 layers of clean, damp cheesecloth. Strain the hot cooking liquid through the cheesecloth. Over medium-high heat, quickly bring the liquid to a boil. Remove the pan from the heat.

Ladle the hot cooking liquid into the jars, covering the lima beans and leaving 1-inch headspace. Using a bubble freer or plastic knife, remove any trapped air bubbles. If necessary, add more liquid to maintain 1-inch headspace. Wipe the jar rims and threads with a clean, damp cloth. Cover with hot lids and apply screw rings.

Process pint jars for 40 minutes, quart jars for 50 minutes, at 11 pounds of pressure in a dial-gauge pressure canner or at 10 pounds pressure in a weighted-gauge pressure canner.

Pumpkin

If you have access to sweet, flavorful pie pumpkins, this is a great way to preserve their tender flesh for use in pies and soups throughout the year. Be sure to use the small, sweet pumpkins that are grown specifically for making pies and using in cooking. Jack-o'-lantern pumpkins have a very bland flavor and are too watery to be canned or used for baking pies.

MAKES ABOUT 6 PINT JARS OR 3 QUART JARS

12 to 14 pounds sugar pumpkins or other varieties of pumpkins for pies

❦ With a vegetable knife or pumpkin carving knife, remove the stems from the pumpkins. Cut the pumpkins in half. Remove the seeds and scrape out the fibrous material. Cut the pumpkins into 1- to 2-inch-wide strips.

Place the prepared pumpkin strips into an 8-quart pan. Add just enough water to cover the pumpkin completely.

Over medium-high heat, bring the water to a boil. Reduce the heat and boil gently until the flesh is tender and soft when pierced with a fork, about 30 to 40 minutes. Remove the pan from the heat. Drain the pumpkin and cover loosely with a piece of foil to prevent the pumpkin from drying out. Let the pumpkin stand until cool enough to handle.

Scrape the flesh from the rind and press it through a food mill or a fine-meshed sieve. Discard any stringy fibers. Return the pulp to the pan.

Over medium-low heat, stirring constantly to prevent sticking or scorching, heat the pulp until hot. Remove the pan from the heat.

Ladle the hot pumpkin into hot jars, leaving 1-inch headspace. Using a bubble freer or plastic knife, remove any trapped air bubbles. If necessary, add more pumpkin to maintain 1-inch headspace. Wipe the jar rims and threads with a clean, damp cloth. Cover with hot lids and apply screw rings.

Process pint jars for 85 minutes, quart jars for 115 minutes, at 11 pounds of pressure in a dial-gauge pressure canner or at 10 pounds pressure in a weighted-gauge pressure canner.

Rhubarb

Rhubarb makes a wonderful appetizer course and a refreshing alternative to soup on a hot summer day. The key to preserving rhubarb is to allow the sugar to permeate the cells of the stalks and then to boil it very briefly before packing it into the jars. Overcooking the rhubarb will cause it to turn mushy.

MAKES ABOUT 6 PINT JARS OR 3 QUART JARS

6 pounds fresh tender cherry rhubarb or
  other variety
2¼ cups sugar
¼ cup water

Rinse the rhubarb in cool water, being careful to remove any dirt or sand. Drain well. Remove the leaves and any woody portions of the stalks. Slice the rhubarb into 1-inch-long pieces. Measure 12 cups rhubarb.

In an 8-quart pan, combine the rhubarb, sugar and water. Stir gently until the rhubarb is coated with the sugar. Cover and let stand 5 to 6 hours.

Over medium-low heat, stirring constantly, heat the rhubarb until the sugar is completely dissolved. Increase the heat to medium and bring the rhubarb to a gentle boil, stirring constantly. Boil the rhubarb for 20 seconds. Immediately remove the pan from the heat.

Using a slotted spoon, pack the hot rhubarb into hot jars, leaving ½-inch headspace.

Place a sieve over a medium saucepan and line the sieve with 3 or 4 layers of clean, damp cheesecloth. Strain the hot syrup through the cheesecloth. Over medium-high heat, quickly bring the syrup to a boil. Remove the pan from the heat.

Ladle the hot syrup into the jars, covering the rhubarb and leaving ½-inch headspace. Using a bubble freer or plastic knife, remove any trapped air bubbles. If necessary, add more syrup to maintain ½-inch headspace. Wipe the jar rims and threads with a clean, damp cloth. Cover with hot lids and apply screw rings. Process both pint and quart jars in a 190 to 200F (88 to 93C) water bath for 15 minutes.

Sweet Potatoes

These potatoes are far superior to the commercially canned yams found in grocery stores. Be careful not to overcook the sweet potatoes or they will become too soft and not hold their shape in the jars.

MAKES ABOUT 6 PINT JARS OR 3 QUART JARS

10 pounds 1- to 1½-inch-diameter
    unblemished firm sweet potatoes
6 cups water
2 cups sugar

Using a soft vegetable brush, gently scrub the sweet potatoes to remove any dirt. Rinse the potatoes under cool running water and drain well.

Place the sweet potatoes in an 8- to 10-quart saucepan and add enough water to cover the potatoes.

Over medium-high heat, bring the water to a boil. Reduce the heat, cover and boil gently just until the skins will slip off easily, about 15 to 20 minutes. Remove the pan from the heat. Drain the potatoes and let cool for 5 to 10 minutes.

In a medium saucepan, combine the water and sugar. Over medium-low heat, stirring constantly, heat the mixture until the sugar is completely dissolved. Increase the heat to medium and bring the mixture to a boil. Boil for 5 minutes. Reduce the heat, cover and keep the syrup hot until needed.

Cut off the ends of the sweet potatoes and peel. Slice the potatoes into 1½-inch-long pieces. Pack the hot potatoes into hot jars, leaving 1-inch headspace.

Ladle the hot syrup into the jars, covering the sweet potatoes and leaving 1-inch headspace.

Using a bubble freer or plastic knife, remove any trapped air bubbles. If necessary, add more syrup to maintain 1-inch headspace. Wipe the jar rims and threads with a clean, damp cloth. Cover with hot lids and apply screw rings.

Process pint jars for 65 minutes, quart jars for 90 minutes, at 11 pounds of pressure in a dial-gauge pressure canner or at 10 pounds pressure in a weighted-gauge pressure canner.

Whole Tomatoes, Raw Packed

While botanically classified as a fruit, tomatoes are usually considered a vegetable. Because tomatoes contain a fairly high acid level, they can be processed in a water bath canner. Tomato recipes include bottled lemon juice to ensure that the correct level of acidity is maintained to permit safe processing. Do not omit or reduce the amount of bottled lemon juice called for in any tomato recipe. Tomatoes may also be halved or quartered before packing them into the jars.

While most fair handbooks list tomatoes as vegetables, ½-inch headspace is usually required as part of the judging criteria. However, be sure to check the handbook for your fair for the specific headspace requirements for canned tomatoes, as some fairs require 1-inch headspace.

MAKES ABOUT 8 PINT JARS OR 4 QUART JARS

15 to 16 pounds firm, ripe medium
tomatoes
½ cup bottled lemon juice
Boiling water

Remove any stems from the tomatoes. Gently rinse the tomatoes in cool water and drain.

To peel the tomatoes: Fill an 8-quart pan about half full of water. Over medium-high heat, bring the water to a simmer. Using a mesh basket or slotted spoon, carefully lower the tomatoes, a few at a time, into the water for 30 seconds. Remove the tomatoes from the pan and immediately plunge them into a large bowl of ice water for 1 to 2 minutes. Transfer the tomatoes to a strainer. Drain well and cool. Repeat with the remaining tomatoes. Discard the water. Using a sharp paring knife, carefully slip the skins from the tomatoes. Using a tomato huller, carefully remove the white hulls, or cores, from the tomatoes.

Pack the tomatoes into hot jars, leaving 1/2-inch headspace. Be careful not to crush or bruise the tomatoes. Add 1 tablespoon bottled lemon juice to each pint jar or 2 tablespoons bottled lemon juice to each quart jar.

Ladle boiling water into the jars, covering the tomatoes and leaving 1/2-inch headspace. Using a bubble freer or plastic knife, remove any trapped air bubbles. If necessary, add more water to maintain 1/2-inch headspace. Wipe the jar rims and threads with a clean, damp cloth. Cover with hot lids and apply screw rings. Process pint jars in a 212F (100C) water bath for 40 minutes, quart jars for 45 minutes.

Whole Tomatoes, Hot Packed

Plum tomatoes, such as Romas, work very well in this recipe because they maintain their shape when heated. Hot packed tomatoes are less likely to float in the jars after processing than raw packed tomatoes.

MAKES ABOUT 8 PINT JARS OR 4 QUART JARS

15 to 16 pounds firm, ripe medium plum tomatoes
1/2 cup bottled lemon juice

Remove any stems from the tomatoes. Gently rinse the tomatoes in cool water and drain.

Peel the tomatoes following the instructions at left.

Place the tomatoes in an 8-quart pan and add enough water to completely cover the tomatoes.

Over medium heat, bring the water to a boil. Reduce the heat and simmer gently for 2 minutes. Remove the pan from the heat.

Using a slotted spoon, pack the hot tomatoes into hot jars, leaving 1/2-inch headspace. Be careful not to crush or bruise the tomatoes. Add 1 tablespoon bottled lemon juice to each pint jar or 2 tablespoons bottled lemon juice to each quart jar.

Place a sieve over a medium saucepan and line the sieve with 3 or 4 layers of clean, damp cheesecloth. Strain the hot cooking liquid through the cheesecloth. Over medium-high heat, quickly bring the liquid to a boil. Remove the pan from the heat.

Ladle the hot cooking liquid into the jars, covering the tomatoes and leaving 1/2-inch headspace. Using a bubble freer or plastic knife, remove any trapped air bubbles. If necessary, add more liquid to maintain ½-inch headspace. Wipe the jar rims and threads with a clean, damp cloth. Cover with hot lids and apply screw rings. Process pint jars in a 212F (100C) water bath for 40 minutes, quart jars for 45 minutes.

½-inch headspace. Wipe the jar rims and threads with a clean, damp cloth. Cover with hot lids and apply screw rings. Process both pint jars and quart jars in a 212F (100C) water bath for 85 minutes.

Stew Vegetables

Preparing homemade stews, soups and pot pies is quick and easy when you have jars of vegetables ready and waiting to be added to cooked meat, chicken or turkey. If using canned vegetable broth, omit the salt from the ingredients list. This recipe can be doubled.

MAKES ABOUT 6 PINT JARS OR 3 QUART JARS

10 cups vegetable broth or water
6 cups peeled sliced carrots
4 cups 1-inch-long sliced green beans
3 cups shelled green peas
3 cups peeled cubed potatoes or parsnips
2 cups sliced celery
1½ cups coarsely chopped onions
¼ cup minced fresh Italian parsley
1 teaspoon freshly ground black pepper
1 teaspoon salt

Whole Tomatoes, Packed in Their Juice

This is the best recipe to use for preserving juicy tomatoes.

MAKES ABOUT 6 PINT JARS OR 3 QUART JARS

10 pounds ripe medium tomatoes
6 tablespoons bottled lemon juice
1 tablespoon sugar (optional)
1½ teaspoons salt

Remove any stems from the tomatoes. Gently rinse the tomatoes in cool water and drain.

Peel the tomatoes following the instructions on page 222.

Pack the tomatoes into hot jars, pressing gently to fill in the spaces and release the juice from tomatoes, leaving ½-inch headspace. Add 1 tablespoon bottled lemon juice and ½ teaspoon sugar and ¼ teaspoon salt to each pint jar. Add 2 tablespoons bottled lemon juice and 1 teaspoon sugar and ½ teaspoon salt to each quart jar.

Using a bubble freer or plastic knife, remove any trapped air bubbles. If necessary, squeeze a few tomatoes and add enough juice to maintain

In an 8-quart pan, combine all of the ingredients.

Over medium-high heat, bring the mixture to a boil. Reduce the heat and simmer for 5 minutes. Remove the pan from the heat.

Using a slotted spoon, ladle the hot vegetables into hot jars, leaving 1-inch headspace. Ladle the hot broth into the jars, covering the vegetables and leaving 1-inch headspace. Using a bubble freer or plastic knife, remove any trapped air bubbles. If necessary, add more broth to maintain 1-inch headspace. Wipe the jar rims and threads with a clean, damp cloth. Cover with hot lids and apply screw rings.

Process both pint jars and quart jars for 40 minutes at 11 pounds of pressure in a dial-gauge pressure canner or at 10 pounds pressure in a weighted-gauge pressure canner.

Bean Soup

This hearty soup is perfect for a brisk fall evening. If you like, add some diced ham to the pan as you heat the soup before serving, then serve bowls of the piping-hot soup along with some hot crusty French bread or a rich, dark brown bread.

MAKES ABOUT 10 PINT JARS OR 5 QUART JARS

½ cup dried kidney beans
½ cup dried navy beans
½ cup dried black beans
½ cup dried pinto beans
½ cup dried small white beans
¼ cup dried small lima beans
¼ cup dried garbanzo beans (chickpeas)
¼ cup dried split peas
¼ cup dried lentils
4 quarts water
2 cups sliced peeled carrots
1½ cups sliced celery
1 cup chopped onions
2 garlic cloves, minced
¼ teaspoon freshly ground black pepper
¼ teaspoon salt

 In a large sieve or a colander with very small holes, combine the beans, split peas and lentils. Rinse well under cool running water and drain.

Transfer the beans to an 8-quart pan. Add the water to the pan. Over medium heat, stirring frequently, bring the mixture to a boil. Reduce the heat and boil gently for 1 hour.

Add the carrots, celery, onions, garlic, pepper and salt to the pan. Continue to boil gently until the beans and vegetables are tender, about 30 minutes. Stir occasionally to prevent sticking. If the soup becomes too thick, add more water as needed. Remove the pan from the heat.

Ladle the hot soup into hot jars, leaving 1-inch headspace. Using a bubble freer or plastic knife, remove any trapped air bubbles. If necessary, add more soup to maintain 1-inch headspace. Wipe the jar rims and threads with a clean, damp cloth. Cover with hot lids and apply screw rings.

Process pint jars for 75 minutes, quart jars for 90 minutes, at 11 pounds of pressure in a dial-gauge pressure canner or at 10 pounds pressure in a weighted-gauge pressure canner.

Split-Pea Soup

If you prefer a smooth soup, all of the cooked split peas may be pressed through a food mill or fine-meshed sieve. The use of a blender or food processor to puree the peas is not recommended, as the puree will be full of tiny trapped air bubbles that will cause the soup to foam. These air bubbles may not dissipate during cooking and may give the finished soup a cloudy appearance.

MAKES ABOUT 6 PINT JARS OR 3 QUART JARS

2 (16-ounce) packages dried split peas
2½ quarts water
1½ cups sliced peeled carrots, preferably ½ inch diameter
1 cup chopped onions
¼ teaspoon freshly ground black pepper
¼ teaspoon salt

❧ Place split peas in a large sieve or a colander with very small holes. Rinse the split peas well under cool running water and drain.

Transfer the split peas to an 8-quart pan. Add the water to the pan. Over medium heat, stirring frequently, bring the mixture to a boil. Reduce the heat and boil gently until the peas are tender, about 1 hour. Remove the pan from the heat.

Press half of the split peas through a food mill or fine-meshed sieve. Return the pea pulp to the pan.

Add the carrots, onions, pepper and salt to the pan. Over medium heat, bring the mixture to a boil. Reduce the heat and simmer for 30 minutes. Stir frequently to prevent sticking. If the soup becomes too thick, add more water as needed. Remove the pan from the heat.

Ladle the hot soup into hot jars, leaving 1-inch headspace. Using a bubble freer or plastic knife, remove any trapped air bubbles. If necessary, add more soup to maintain 1-inch headspace. Wipe the jar rims and threads with a clean, damp cloth. Cover with hot lids and apply screw rings.

Process pint jars for 75 minutes, quart jars for 90 minutes, at 11 pounds of pressure in a dial-gauge pressure canner or at 10 pounds pressure in a weighted-gauge pressure canner.

Vegetable Soup

This soup is very attractive in the jars and has a wonderful fresh flavor. For a spicier soup, you may also add some coarsely chopped red, green or yellow bell peppers to the pan or even a couple of finely minced jalapeño chile peppers for even more zing. If you use canned vegetable broth, omit the salt from the ingredients list.

MAKES ABOUT 6 PINT JARS OR 3 QUART JARS

3 cups vegetable broth or water
3 cups peeled, cored and chopped plum tomatoes
2 cups cubed peeled potatoes or parsnips
2 cups sliced peeled carrots
1½ cups whole-kernel corn
2 cups sliced celery
1 cup 1-inch-long sliced green beans
¾ cup coarsely chopped onions
2 tablespoons minced fresh Italian parsley
1 teaspoon minced fresh thyme leaves
1 large clove garlic, peeled and minced
½ teaspoon freshly ground black pepper
½ teaspoon salt

❧ In an 8-quart pan, combine all of the ingredients.

Over medium-high heat, bring the mixture to a boil. Reduce the heat and simmer for 5 minutes. Remove the pan from the heat.

Ladle the hot soup into hot jars, leaving 1-inch headspace. Using a bubble freer or plastic knife, remove any trapped air bubbles. If necessary, add more soup to maintain 1-inch headspace. Wipe the jar rims and threads with a clean, damp cloth. Cover with hot lids and apply screw rings.

Process pint jars for 60 minutes, quart jars for 75 minutes, at 11 pounds of pressure in a dial-gauge pressure canner or at 10 pounds pressure in a weighted-gauge pressure canner.

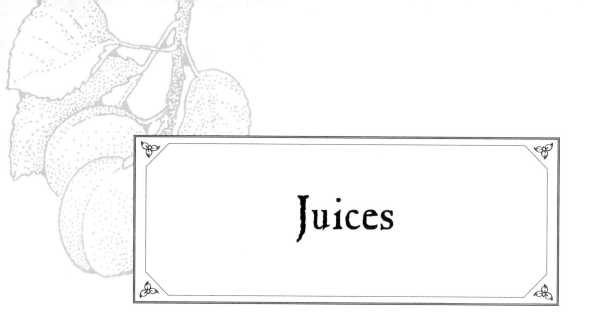

Juices

CANNING JUICES

An excellent way to preserve an abundant crop of apricots, apples, peaches, tomatoes or just about any other type of fruit is to turn them into juice. Home-canned fruit and vegetable juices, made from a prolific orchard tree or garden crop growing in your yard or that of a friend or a neighbor, are less expensive and far superior in flavor to any store-bought canned or bottled juices. And a juice made from a frozen concentrate cannot even come close to the flavor and texture of a juice that you make and can yourself with homegrown fresh produce.

Fruit juices may be blended to create unique and pleasing flavor combinations. The best blends contain at least one or more acid juices, such as citrus, pineapple or cranberry, which give the juice character and enhance the flavor of the other juice or juices. The flavor combinations you can create are endless—apricot orange, cranberry apple, orange papaya, apricot pineapple or any other special blend that appeals to you. The flavors will develop better if they are combined before canning rather than blending the juices just before serving.

Because the acid content of tomatoes can vary substantially, it is necessary to add acid to all tomato products to ensure safe canning. Bottled lemon juice, not fresh juice, must be used when canning tomato products because the bottled lemon juice has a consistent acid level, which will prevent bacteria growth. Fresh lemon juice is added to some light-colored juices to help preserve their color during storage. Jars of juices should be stored in a cool, dry location, ideally with temperatures below 65 degrees. The color and flavor can fade rapidly when juices are stored at higher temperatures.

While juices may be canned with or without

sugar, the addition of a small amount of sugar greatly enhances the natural flavor of high-acid and low-sugar fruits and also helps to preserve the color of the juice. Unless the fruit used is naturally very sweet, when preparing a juice that will be entered at a fair, it is advisable to sweeten the juice with a little sugar. For the most part, judges tend to prefer juices that have been sweetened over those that do not contain sugar.

If you prefer an unsweetened juice, any juice may be canned without sugar. However, the juice should not be kept very long, as the color and flavor will deteriorate quicker than in a juice that contains added sugar. If the juice is stored at temperatures above 65 degrees, the deterioration rate of an unsweetened juice will increase rapidly.

Sugar substitutes should not be used to sweeten a juice before canning, as the artificial sweeteners frequently lose their ability to sweeten and may turn bitter during processing. The extended heating time in the water bath can cause the sugar substitutes to undergo a chemical change that results in this bitter taste. To use sugar substitutes, can the juice without sugar and then sweeten it just before serving. Do not use honey or corn syrup to sweeten fruit juices, as they can substantially alter the natural flavor of the fruit, giving the juice an unpleasant taste.

Selecting Fruit

A high-quality, flavorful juice can best be obtained by using fresh picked, tree-ripened or vine-ripened fruits and vegetables. As with other preserved foods, select sound, fully ripe fruits and vegetables that are free from damage or any signs of spoilage or bruising. Small surface blemishes may be cut out without affecting the quality of the finished juice.

Plum tomatoes are firmer than salad tomatoes and make a fuller-bodied juice with a good, strong flavor. Do not try cooking a thin tomato or veg-etable juice for longer than instructed in the recipe in an attempt to evaporate off some of the water and thicken the juice. This will only succeed in producing an inferior juice with a dark color and an overcooked flavor.

Preparing Fruit

Sort the fruit and gently rinse it 2 to 3 times in clean, cool water, changing the water after each rinsing. Drain the produce well.

Slip the skins from fruits such as apricots, peaches and tomatoes by placing small quantities of whole fruit into gently simmering water for 30 to 40 seconds. Remove the fruit from the hot water and quickly plunge them into a bowl of ice water for 1 minute to stop the cooking process. Transfer the fruit to a strainer or colander and drain it well. Using your hands or a small paring knife, gently slip the loosened skins from the fruit. Remove the pits or cores from the fruit.

Large fruits such as apples, peaches, apricots and pineapple should be peeled, cored or pitted and then sliced or chopped into small pieces. Gently crush small fruits such as grapes and berries to release their precious juice. Tomatoes should be peeled and chopped just before preparing the juice. To neutralize the enzymes responsible for changes in texture and consistency, tomatoes should be heated as soon as possible after being cut.

Extracting and Preparing Juice

It is easier to extract the juice from some types of fruits if the fruit is heated first. Apricots, peaches, grapes and berries produce larger quantities of a more flavorful juice when they are heated before extracting their juice.

To release the juice from firmer fruits such as apples, apricots or peaches, the prepared fruit is combined in a large pan with water, slowly brought to a simmer and cooked until soft. The soft pulp is then strained and filtered to make it clear or pressed through a food mill or fine sieve to give the juice a smooth texture. Sugar and lemon juice are added and the juice is heated just to simmering, 190F (88C), then ladled into hot jars, sealed and processed in a water bath.

When preparing tomato juices, the best texture is achieved by cooking the tomatoes until they are soft before extracting the juice. The juice extracted from cooked tomatoes will be smoother and thicker, with a rich tomato flavor. Raw tomatoes will produce a thin, watery juice with a milder flavor.

When extracting citrus juices, be careful not to squeeze the peel or the white pith under the peel. Natural oils from the citrus peel and the white pith can give the juice a bitter flavor and affect the color of the juice. Citrus juices have a better taste when the juice is extracted using a hand juicer rather than an electric juicer, which can also process a small part of the very bitter white pith or extract some of the oils from the peel. Citrus juices should be heated and sealed in jars immediately after extraction. Exposure to the air can cause chemical changes that may make the juice turn bitter.

Apricot, peach, tomato and vegetable juices have a thicker texture and are rich with smooth fruit pulp. This texture is taken into consideration during judging. Citrus and pineapple juices contain a moderate amount of pulp, while most other juices are strained or filtered to remove the pulp and make them clear. While any juice may be left unfiltered for family use, remember that for fair competitions, judges prefer juices such as apple and grape to be clear, without any residual pulp.

Juices may be canned without straining or filtering, depending on the type of juice and your personal preference. Some juices such as an apricot nectar or tomato juice are characteristically thick, containing lots of pureed pulp. Citrus juices should be strained to remove excess pulp and seeds, while juices such as apple or grape should be filtered to make them clear. For a smoother-textured juice, strain through 2 or 3 layers of damp cheesecloth. For a clear juice, after straining through cheesecloth, filter the juice through a sieve lined with a paper coffee filter.

Care should be taken when heating fruit juices before canning, as they can develop an unpleasant cooked flavor if heated to a temperature that is too high or if the juice is heated at a moderate temperature for too long. To maintain the fresh flavor and natural color of the fruit, use an instant read thermometer and watch the temperature and time carefully. Do not allow the juice to boil, unless specifically instructed to in the recipe. Many juices, such as citrus and grape, should not be boiled, as they can develop a bitter flavor when heated to too high of a temperature.

In thick juices, the pulp is heavier than the juice and the juice and pulp will separate during storage. This is perfectly normal and does not affect the quality or flavor of the juice. Even with a filtered juice, a small amount of sediment will settle in the bottom of the jar. Before serving or exhibiting at a fair, shake the jar gently to blend the juice and pulp.

Apple Juice

Select firm, ripe, sound apples that are free of bruises. Try Jonathon, McIntosh or Gravenstein apples or a blend of two or more apple varieties for an equally delicious juice. This juice has won multiple blue ribbons.

MAKES ABOUT 4 PINT JARS OR 2 QUART JARS

9 pounds Granny Smith apples
2½ cups water
½ cup sugar (optional)

Rinse apples in cool water and drain well. Peel, core and chop the apples.

In an 8-quart pan, combine the apples and water. Over medium heat, bring the mixture to a boil. Reduce the heat, cover and simmer for 25 minutes, or until the apples are very soft, stirring occasionally to prevent sticking. Remove the pan from the heat.

Place a fine-meshed sieve over a pan or bowl. Ladle the apple pulp and juice into the sieve to separate the pulp from the juice. Discard the pulp. Rinse the sieve and line it with 4 layers of clean, damp cheesecloth. Strain the juice through the cheesecloth 3 times, rinsing the cheesecloth between each straining.

Measure the juice and pour it into a 4-quart pan. If desired, add ¼ cup sugar for each quart of juice to achieve desired sweetness. Over medium-low heat, stirring constantly until the sugar is completely dissolved, heat the juice to 190F (88C). Do not allow the juice to boil. Remove the pan from the heat.

Ladle the hot juice into hot jars, leaving ½-inch headspace. Wipe the jar rims and threads with a clean, damp cloth. Cover with hot lids and apply screw rings. Process both pint and quart jars in a 200F (93C) water bath for 15 minutes.

Apricot Nectar

Ambrosia! The gorgeous color and full flavor of this juice are amazing. This juice has not only won multiple first-place awards, but also several Best of Division and other special awards.

MAKES ABOUT 4 PINT JARS OR 2 QUART JARS

4 cups pitted, peeled and sliced ripe apricots
(40 to 50 apricots, depending on size)
4 cups water
2 cups sugar
2 tablespoons strained fresh lemon juice

In an 8-quart pan, combine the apricots and water. Over medium heat, bring the mixture to a boil. Reduce the heat, cover and simmer for 10 to 15 minutes, or just until the fruit is tender. Remove the pan from the heat. Skim off the foam.

Press the apricots and liquid through a food mill or fine-meshed sieve. Discard the stringy pulp. Rinse the pan and return the apricot juice to the pan. Stir in the sugar. Over medium heat, stirring constantly, heat the juice until the sugar is completely dissolved. Add more water if the juice is too thick. Add the lemon juice. Remove the pan from the heat.

Ladle the hot juice into hot jars, leaving ½-inch headspace. Wipe the jar rims and threads with a clean, damp cloth. Cover with hot lids and apply screw rings. Process both pint and quart jars in a 200F (93C) water bath for 15 minutes.

Apricot-Pineapple Juice

A favorite combination of flavors creates this marvelous juice blend, which has earned first-place and Best of Show awards.

MAKES ABOUT 4 PINT JARS OR 2 QUART JARS

3 cups pitted, peeled and sliced ripe apricots
(30 to 35 apricots, depending on size)
3⅔ cups water
1 medium pineapple, peeled, cored and
finely chopped or ground
2 tablespoons strained fresh lemon juice
1½ cups sugar

In an 8-quart stainless steel pan, combine the apricots and water. Over medium heat, bring the mixture to a boil. Reduce the heat, cover and simmer for 10 minutes. Add the pineapple to the pan and simmer for 5 minutes more, stirring occasionally to prevent sticking. Remove the pan from the heat and skim off any foam. Cover the pan and let stand for 30 minutes.

Place a fine-meshed sieve over a pan or bowl. Ladle the fruit pulp and juice into the sieve to separate the pulp from the juice. Using the back of a spoon, press the apricots through the sieve. Discard any remaining pineapple pulp and the stringy apricot fibers. Rinse the pan and return the juice to the pan.

Add the lemon juice to the juice in the pan. Stir in the sugar. Over medium heat, stirring constantly, heat the juice until the sugar is completely dissolved. If the juice is too thick, add more water. Heat the juice to 190F (88C). Remove the pan from the heat.

Ladle the hot juice into hot jars, leaving ½-inch headspace. Wipe the jar rims and threads with a clean, damp cloth. Cover with hot lids and apply screw rings. Process both pint and quart jars in a 200F (93C) water bath for 15 minutes.

Boysenberry Juice

This is a marvelous juice with an intense berry flavor that is well worth the effort. It is also excellent made with blackberries. Substitute red raspberries and add 1 tablespoon of fresh lemon juice to make a wonderful raspberry juice.

MAKES ABOUT 4 PINT JARS OR 2 QUART JARS

6 quarts fresh or frozen ripe
boysenberries
1 cup water
⅔ cup sugar

Rinse the fresh berries in cool water and drain well. If using frozen berries, defrost the berries but do not rinse them. Using a vegetable masher, gently crush the berries to release the juice.

In an 8-quart stainless steel pan, combine the boysenberries and water. Over medium-low heat, bring the mixture to 180F (82C) and heat the berries for 10 minutes. Do not allow the berry mixture to boil. Remove the pan from the heat, cover and let stand for 20 minutes.

Place a fine-meshed sieve over a pan or bowl. Ladle the boysenberry pulp and juice into the sieve to separate the pulp from the juice. Discard the pulp and seeds. Rinse the sieve and line it with 4 layers of clean, damp cheesecloth. Strain the juice through the cheesecloth 3 times, rinsing the cheesecloth between each straining. Cover and refrigerate the juice overnight.

Ladle or pour the juice into another container, being careful not to disturb or pick up any of the sediment from the bottom of the original container. Place a fine-meshed sieve over a pan or bowl. Line the sieve with 4 layers of clean, damp cheesecloth. Strain the juice through the cheesecloth. For a clearer juice, line the sieve with 2 layered paper coffee filters and strain the juice through the filters.

Pour the juice into a 4-quart pan. Stir in the sugar. Over medium-low heat, stirring constantly until the sugar is completely dissolved, heat the juice to 190F (88C). Remove the pan from the heat.

Ladle the hot juice into hot jars, leaving ½-inch headspace. Wipe the jar rims and threads with a clean, damp cloth. Cover with hot lids and apply screw rings. Process both pint and quart jars in a 200F (93C) water bath for 15 minutes.

Cranberry Juice

This tangy juice tastes far better than anything that comes out of a commercial bottle. If you prefer a sweeter juice, increase the amount of sugar. This juice has earned multiple blue ribbons.

MAKES ABOUT 4 PINT JARS OR 2 QUART JARS

2¼ pounds fresh or frozen cranberries
  (about 3 [12-ounce] bags)
7 cups water
1⅓ cups sugar

Remove any stems from the cranberries. Rinse the berries in cool water and drain well.

In an 8-quart stainless steel pan, combine the cranberries and water. Over medium-high heat, bring to a boil. Reduce the heat and boil gently for 15 minutes or until all of the berries have popped their skins and turned soft. Remove the pan from the heat, cover and let stand for 1 hour.

Place a fine-meshed sieve over a pan or bowl. Ladle the cranberry pulp and juice into the sieve to separate the pulp from the juice. Discard the pulp and seeds. Rinse the sieve and line it with 4 layers of clean, damp cheesecloth. Strain the juice through the cheesecloth 3 times, rinsing the cheesecloth between each straining. Cover and refrigerate the juice overnight.

Ladle or pour the juice into another container, being careful not to disturb or pick up any of the sediment from the bottom of the original container. Place a fine-meshed sieve over a pan or bowl. Line the sieve with 4 layers of clean, damp cheesecloth. Strain the juice through the cheesecloth. For a clearer juice, line the sieve with 2 layered paper coffee filters and strain the juice through the filters.

Pour the juice into a 4-quart pan. Stir in the sugar. Over medium-low heat, stirring constantly until the sugar is completely dissolved, heat the juice to 190F (88C). Remove the pan from the heat.

Ladle the hot juice into hot jars, leaving ½-inch headspace. Wipe the jar rims and threads with a clean, damp cloth. Cover with hot lids and apply screw rings. Process both pint and quart jars in a 200F (93C) water bath for 20 minutes.

Cranberry, Apple and Grape Juice

This fruity juice blend can be easily prepared using bottled juices.

MAKES ABOUT 4 PINT JARS OR 2 QUART JARS

4 cups white grape juice
3 cups filtered apple juice
2 cups filtered cranberry juice
¾ to 1 cup sugar

 In an 8-quart pan, combine the grape, apple and cranberry juices. Add sugar to taste to achieve desired sweetness.

Over medium-low heat, stirring constantly until the sugar is completely dissolved, heat the juice to 190F (88C). Do not allow the juice to boil. Remove the pan from the heat.

Ladle the hot juice into hot jars, leaving ½-inch headspace. Wipe the jar rims and threads with a clean, damp cloth. Cover with hot lids and apply screw rings. Process both pint and quart jars in a 200F (93C) water bath for 15 minutes.

Concord Grape Juice

Concord grapes make a robust, intensely flavorful juice, and this recipe has earned both first-place and Best of Division awards. The judges' remarks included, "Thank you for your excellent product! Very fresh and fragrant." If you prefer a mild or white grape juice, try Red Flame or Thompson

Seedless grapes. These two varieties are sweeter than Concords, so be sure to adjust the quantity of sugar used in the recipe.

MAKES ABOUT 4 PINT JARS OR 2 QUART JARS

6 pounds ripe Concord grapes
Water
½ to 1 cup sugar (optional)

Remove the grapes from the stems and rinse the grapes thoroughly. Drain well.

In a large, flat-bottomed bowl or pan, using a vegetable masher or large spoon, partially crush the grapes in small batches. Measure the grape pulp and place it in an 8-quart pan. Add ¼ cup water per quart of pulp. Over medium-low heat, heat the grape pulp to 190F (88C). Cook gently for 5 to 7 minutes, stirring occasionally. Do not allow the pulp to boil or overcook, as the juice will lose its flavor. Remove the pan from the heat.

Place a fine-meshed sieve over a pan or bowl. Ladle the grape pulp and juice into the sieve to separate the pulp from the juice. Discard the pulp. Rinse the sieve and line it with 4 layers of clean, damp cheesecloth. Strain the juice through the cheesecloth 3 times, rinsing the cheesecloth between each straining. Cover and refrigerate the juice overnight.

Ladle or pour the juice into another container, being careful not to disturb or pick up any of the sediment from the bottom of the original container. Place a fine-meshed sieve over a pan or bowl. Line the sieve with 4 layers of clean, damp cheesecloth. Strain the juice through the cheesecloth. For a clearer juice, line the sieve with 2 layered paper coffee filters and strain the juice through the filters.

Measure the juice and pour it into a 4-quart pan. If desired, add ¼ to ½ cup sugar for each quart of juice to achieve desired sweetness. Over medium-low heat, stirring constantly until the sugar is completely dissolved, heat the juice to 190F (88C). Do not allow the juice to boil. Remove the pan from the heat.

Ladle the hot juice into hot jars, leaving ½-inch headspace. Wipe the jar rims and threads with a clean, damp cloth. Cover with hot lids and apply screw rings. Process both pint and quart jars in a 200F (93C) water bath for 15 minutes.

Easy Grape Juice

This quick-to-prepare recipe makes a very nice juice, although not quite as intense in flavor as the Concord Grape Juice. Store the jars in a cool, dark location for 2 to 3 months before using to allow the full flavor of the juice to develop. The liquid in the jars will attain a deep color when the juice is ready.

MAKES ABOUT 4 QUART JARS

6 cups stemmed, ripe Concord grapes
3 quarts water
2 cups sugar

Rinse the grapes thoroughly and drain well.

In a 4-quart pan, combine the water and sugar. Over medium-low heat, stirring constantly, heat until the sugar is completely dissolved. Increase the heat to medium-high and bring the mixture to a boil. Reduce the heat and boil the syrup for 5 minutes. Keep hot until needed.

Place 1½ cups grapes in each hot quart jar. Ladle syrup into jars, leaving ½-inch headspace.

Using a plastic knife or bubble freer, remove any air bubbles. If necessary, add more syrup to maintain ½-inch headspace. Wipe the jar rims and threads with a clean, damp cloth. Cover with hot lids and apply screw rings. Process both pint and quart jars in a 200F (93C) water bath for 20 minutes.

Grapefruit Juice

Citrus fruits should be juiced by hand, rather than using an electric juicer, to prevent any of the white pith or the peel from being squeezed along with the juice. The pith and peel can give the juice an unpleasant, bitter flavor. While white grapefruit usually make the best flavored juice, pink or red grapefruit may also be used. The juice is best when used within 6 months of canning. It is a multiple blue ribbon winner.

MAKES ABOUT 4 PINT JARS OR 2 QUART JARS

8 to 10 medium to large white grapefruit
1½ to 2½ cups sugar

Scrub the grapefruit with a vegetable brush to remove any dirt. Rinse well in cool water and drain.

Extract the juice from the grapefruit using a hand juicer. Strain the juice through a fine-meshed sieve to remove excess pulp and small seeds.

Pour the juice into an 8-quart stainless steel pan. Add sugar to the juice, depending on the sweetness of the grapefruit, to achieve the desired taste. Over medium-low heat, stirring constantly until the sugar is completely dissolved, heat the juice to 190F (88C). Do not allow the juice to boil, as it may turn bitter. Remove the pan from the heat.

Ladle the hot juice into hot jars, leaving ½-inch headspace. Wipe the jar rims and threads with a clean, damp cloth. Cover with hot lids and apply screw rings. Process both pint and quart jars in a 200F (93C) water bath for 15 minutes.

Orange Juice

For the best flavor, select sweet, fully ripe fruit with deep orange flesh. Squeeze citrus fruits just before canning to prevent them from turning bitter from exposure to the air. The flavor of the juice is best when used within 6 months of canning. This juice has won multiple first-place awards.

MAKES ABOUT 4 PINT JARS OR 2 QUART JARS

25 to 35 medium to large Valencia oranges
½ to 1 cup sugar

 Scrub the oranges with a vegetable brush to remove any dirt. Rinse well in cool water and drain.

Extract the juice from the oranges using a hand juicer. Strain the juice through a fine-meshed sieve to remove excess pulp and small seeds.

Pour the juice into an 8-quart stainless steel pan. Add sugar to the juice, depending on the sweetness of the oranges, to achieve the desired taste. Over medium-low heat, stirring constantly

until the sugar is completely dissolved, heat the juice to 190F (88C). Do not allow the juice to boil, as it may turn bitter. Remove the pan from the heat.

Ladle the hot juice into hot jars, leaving ½-inch headspace. Wipe the jar rims and threads with a clean, damp cloth. Cover with hot lids and apply screw rings. Process both pint and quart jars in a 200F (93C) water bath for 15 minutes.

Orange-Apricot Juice

A delightful combination of flavors, oranges and apricots bring out the best of each fruit.

MAKES ABOUT 4 PINT JARS OR 2 QUART JARS

10 medium to large Valencia oranges
2 cups pitted, peeled and sliced ripe apricots
   (20 to 25 apricots, depending on size)
2 cups water
1 tablespoon strained fresh lemon juice
1⅓ cups sugar

 Scrub the oranges with a vegetable brush to remove any dirt. Rinse well in cool water and drain.

In a 4-quart pan, combine the apricots and water. Over medium heat, bring the mixture to a boil. Reduce the heat, cover and simmer for 10 minutes, or just until the fruit is tender. Remove the pan from the heat. Skim off the foam.

Press the apricots and liquid through a food mill or fine-meshed sieve. Discard the stringy pulp. Rinse the pan and return the apricot juice to the pan.

Extract the juice from the oranges using a hand juicer. Strain the juice through a fine-meshed sieve to remove excess pulp and small seeds.

Add the orange juice and lemon juice to the apricot juice in the pan. Stir in the sugar. Over medium heat, stirring constantly, heat the juice until the sugar is completely dissolved. If the juice is too thick, add more orange juice or water. Heat the juice to 190F (88C). Do not allow the juice to boil, as it may turn bitter. Remove the pan from the heat.

Ladle the hot juice into hot jars, leaving ½-inch headspace. Wipe the jar rims and threads with a clean, damp cloth. Cover with hot lids and apply screw rings. Process both pint and quart jars in a 200F (93C) water bath for 15 minutes.

Orange-Papaya Juice

This tropical juice blend is sure to brighten any morning.

MAKES ABOUT 4 PINT JARS OR 2 QUART JARS

10 medium to large Valencia oranges
6 ripe papayas
2 cups water
1 cup sugar

 Scrub the oranges with a vegetable brush to remove any dirt. Rinse well in cool water and drain.

Rinse and dry the papayas. Cut the papayas in half and use a spoon to remove the seeds. With a sharp knife, cut a multiple cross-hatch pattern all the way through the papaya flesh; do not cut through the skin. Holding the outer edges of the papaya half with your fingers, use your thumbs to push against the center of the skin to gently turn the papaya inside out. Slice the papaya from the peel in chunks.

In a 4-quart pan, combine the papayas and water. Over medium heat, bring the mixture to a boil. Reduce the heat, cover and simmer for 5 to 10 minutes, or just until the fruit is tender. Remove the pan from the heat. Skim off any foam.

Press the papayas and liquid through a food mill or fine-meshed sieve. Discard any stringy pulp. Rinse and dry the pan and return the papaya juice to the pan.

Extract the juice from the oranges using a hand juicer. Strain the juice through a fine-meshed sieve to remove excess pulp and small seeds.

Add the orange juice to the papaya juice in the pan. Stir in the sugar. Over medium heat, stirring constantly, heat the juice until the sugar is completely dissolved. If the juice is too thick, add more orange juice or water. Heat the juice to 190F (88C). Do not allow the juice to boil, as it may turn bitter. Remove the pan from the heat.

Ladle the hot juice into hot jars, leaving ½-inch headspace. Wipe the jar rims and threads with a clean, damp cloth. Cover with hot lids and apply screw rings. Process both pint and quart jars in a 200F (93C) water bath for 15 minutes.

Peach Juice

This delicately flavored juice makes a wonderful accompaniment to scones or biscuits for a light breakfast or morning snack. This juice is the winner of multiple first-place awards.

MAKES ABOUT 4 PINT JARS OR 2 QUART JARS

5 cups pitted, peeled and chopped
    unblemished, ripe peaches (about 4½
    pounds)
4 cups water
2 tablespoons strained fresh lemon juice
¾ cup sugar

❧ In an 8-quart pan, combine the peaches and water. Over medium heat, bring the mixture to a boil. Reduce the heat, cover and simmer for 10 minutes, or just until the fruit is tender. Remove the pan from the heat. Skim off any foam.

Press the peaches and liquid through a food mill or fine-meshed sieve. Discard the stringy pulp. Rinse the pan and return the peach juice to the pan. Add the lemon juice and stir in the sugar. Over medium heat, stirring constantly, heat the juice until the sugar is completely dissolved. Add more water if the juice is too thick. Remove the pan from the heat.

Ladle the hot juice into hot jars, leaving ½-inch headspace. Wipe the jar rims and threads with a clean, damp cloth. Cover with hot lids and apply screw rings. Process both pint and quart jars in a 200F (93C) water bath for 15 minutes.

Pineapple Juice

Pineapple makes a flavorful, refreshing juice to serve with breakfast or at any time of the day.

MAKES ABOUT 4 PINT JARS OR 2 QUART JARS

2 large or 3 medium pineapples
2 cups water
2 tablespoons strained fresh lemon juice
⅔ to ¾ cup sugar

❧ Peel, core and coarsely chop the pineapples, removing the "eyes" and woody core. Finely chop or grind the pineapple.

In an 8-quart stainless steel pan, combine the pineapple and water. Over medium heat, bring the mixture to a boil. Reduce the heat and simmer for 5 minutes, stirring occasionally to prevent sticking. Remove the pan from the heat, cover and let stand for 1 hour.

Place a fine-meshed sieve over a pan or bowl. Ladle the pineapple pulp and juice into the sieve to separate the pulp from the juice. Discard the pulp. Rinse the sieve and line it with 4 layers of clean, damp cheesecloth. Strain the juice through the cheesecloth 3 times, rinsing the cheesecloth between each straining.

Pour the juice into an 8-quart stainless steel pan. Stir in the lemon juice. Add sugar to the juice to achieve the desired sweetness. Over medium-low heat, stirring constantly until the sugar is completely dissolved, heat the juice to 190F (88C). Remove the pan from the heat.

Ladle the hot juice into hot jars, leaving ½-inch headspace. Wipe the jar rims and threads with a clean, damp cloth. Cover with hot lids and apply screw rings. Process both pint and quart jars in a 200F (93C) water bath for 20 minutes.

Tomato Juice

This full-flavored tomato juice is a great way to use up those extra tomatoes. Plum tomatoes are recommended for making juice because they will make a thicker juice. Firmer varieties of salad-type tomatoes may be used to make a juice with a slightly thinner consistency. This juice has won first-place awards across the country.

MAKES ABOUT 4 PINT JARS OR 2 QUART JARS

7 to 8 pounds fully ripe plum tomatoes
⅛ teaspoon salt
¼ cup bottled lemon juice

Gently rinse the tomatoes in cool water and drain well. Remove the cores and cut the tomatoes into quarters.

Place about half of the tomatoes in an 8-quart stainless steel pan. Using a vegetable masher, crush the tomatoes to release some of the juice so the tomatoes will not stick to the bottom of the pan while cooking. Add the remaining tomatoes to the pan.

Over medium heat, bring the tomatoes to a boil. Reduce the heat, cover and simmer gently until the tomatoes are very soft, about 15 to 20 minutes. Remove the pan from the heat.

Press the tomatoes through a food mill or fine-meshed sieve to separate the juice from the seeds and skins. Discard the seeds and skins. Rinse the pan and return the juice to the pan.

Over medium-low heat, bring the juice to 190F (88C) and heat for 5 minutes. Do not allow the juice to boil. Stir in the salt. Remove the pan from the heat.

To each hot pint jar, add 1 tablespoon bottled lemon juice. To each hot quart jar, add 2 table-spoons bottled lemon juice. Ladle the hot juice into the jars, leaving ½-inch headspace. Wipe the jar rims and threads with a clean, damp cloth. Cover with hot lids and apply screw rings. Process pint jars for 40 minutes in a 200F (93C) water bath, quart jars for 45 minutes.

Spicy Tomato-Basil Juice

This spicy tomato juice, rich with the flavor of basil, is a great way to start the day.

MAKES ABOUT 4 PINT JARS OR 2 QUART JARS

7 to 8 pounds fully ripe plum tomatoes
5 large fresh basil leaves
1 teaspoon Tabasco or other hot pepper sauce
⅛ teaspoon salt
¼ cup bottled lemon juice

Gently rinse the tomatoes in cool water and drain well. Remove the cores and cut the tomatoes into quarters.

Place about half of the tomatoes in an 8-quart stainless steel pan. Using a vegetable masher, crush the tomatoes to release some of the juice so the tomatoes will not stick to the bottom of the pan while cooking. Add the remaining tomatoes to the pan.

Over medium heat, bring the tomatoes to a boil. Reduce the heat, cover and simmer gently until the tomatoes are very soft, about 15 to 20 minutes. Remove the pan from the heat.

Press the tomatoes through a food mill or fine-meshed sieve to separate the juice from the seeds and skins. Discard the seeds and skins. Rinse the pan and return the juice to the pan.

Add the basil leaves and the hot pepper sauce to the pan. Over medium-low heat, bring the juice to 190F (88C) and heat for 5 minutes, stirring frequently to blend the flavors. Do not allow the juice to boil. Stir in the salt. Remove the pan from the heat and remove the basil leaves.

To each hot pint jar, add 1 tablespoon bottled lemon juice. To each hot quart jar, add 2 tablespoons bottled lemon juice. Ladle the hot juice into the jars, leaving 1/2-inch headspace. Wipe the jar rims and threads with a clean, damp cloth. Cover with hot lids and apply screw rings. Process pint jars for 40 minutes in a 200F (93C) water bath, quart jars for 45 minutes.

Vegetable Juice

A blending of great flavors makes this juice special.
MAKES ABOUT 6 PINT JARS OR 3 QUART JARS

14 pounds fully ripe plum tomatoes, peeled, cored and quartered
2 large carrots, peeled and diced
2 large stalks celery, chopped

1 small green bell pepper, seeded and chopped
1 small red onion, chopped
1/4 cup chopped fresh Italian parsley
1/2 teaspoon salt
3/4 teaspoon hot pepper sauce (optional)
6 tablespoons bottled lemon juice

In a 10-quart stainless steel pan, combine the tomatoes, carrots, celery, bell pepper, onion and parsley. Over medium heat, bring the mixture to a boil. Reduce the heat and simmer gently until the vegetables are very soft, about 30 minutes. Remove the pan from the heat.

Press the vegetables through a food mill or fine-meshed sieve to separate the juice from the seeds and skins. Discard the seeds and skins. Rinse the pan and return the juice to the pan.

Add the salt and hot pepper sauce, if desired, to the pan. Over medium-low heat, bring the juice to 190F (88C) and heat for 5 minutes, stirring frequently to blend the flavors. Do not allow the juice to boil. Remove the pan from the heat.

To each hot pint jar, add 1 tablespoon bottled lemon juice. To each hot quart jar, add 2 tablespoons bottled lemon juice. Ladle the hot juice into the jars, leaving 1/2-inch headspace. Wipe the jar rims and threads with a clean, damp cloth. Cover with hot lids and apply screw rings. Process pint jars for 40 minutes in a 200F (93C) water bath, quart jars for 45 minutes.

Sauces

CANNING SAUCES

When you open your pantry and find a variety of tasty homemade sauces waiting on the shelf, preparing quick and easy, flavorful dinners is a breeze. A spaghetti dinner made with homemade sauce is ready in just the time it takes to cook the pasta. Add a salad and some crusty bread and you are ready to eat. Or cook up a few chicken breasts and spoon on some zesty Basil Marinara Sauce or fragrant Tropical Sauce for a special treat. Backyard barbecued ribs coated with rich Barbecue Sauce or fragrant Hawaiian Barbecue Sauce rival or surpass those found in the best rib joints.

Because of the increased risks of serious contamination and the necessary precautions that must be taken when canning meat, none of the sauce recipes in this book contain meat, poultry or seafood. If the meat is not completely cooked to the point of well done, bacteria can remain that could lead to serious contamination. This intense cooking can dry out the meat and leave it with little flavor. It is much better to cook the meat fresh and add it to the sauce just before serving. That way you know that your food will be safe and it will have better flavor, too.

If you decide to can a sauce from another cookbook or other source and the recipe contains meat, be sure that the meat is thoroughly cooked before adding it to the sauce and that the instructions for processing the jars in a pressure canner comply with the USDA time and pressure recommendations for meat sauces. Sauces containing meat must be processed for a longer period of time than sauces that do not contain meat. Any preserved food containing meat, poultry or seafood must be properly processed in a pressure canner to kill any potentially deadly bacteria. It is not safe to can meat sauces by the water bath method because the temperatures reached in the water bath are not sufficient to kill the bacteria.

Selecting Ingredients

Use fully ripe fruits and vegetables that do not show any signs of spoilage. The best-flavored sauces will be obtained when the produce used is at the peak of ripeness.

When making tomato sauces, Italian plum tomatoes, such as Romas, are recommended because they are a firm, well-flavored variety and contain less water than most salad-type tomatoes. Other varieties of tomatoes may be used with reasonable success, but they will require a substantial amount of additional cooking time for the sauce to reduce to a thick consistency, and the finished sauce will have a cooked flavor rather than the fresh flavor of the vegetables.

Bell Peppers

Sweet peppers are commonly known as bell peppers because of their shape. They are available in a variety of colors, ranging from green to yellow to orange to red. For the most part, the different colored sweet peppers can be used interchangeably to provide color and visual interest to a recipe, especially for a sauce where the peppers are to be chopped and not pureed. The red bell peppers have a more fully developed, sweeter flavor, while the green peppers are usually crisper and slightly tangier.

Chile Peppers

Each hot chile pepper variety has its own distinct characteristics. Some have more flavor, which can range from mild to fiery hot, while others are known more for their heat than their flavor. Here are some basic characteristics of the most commonly available chile peppers.

ANAHEIM: Mild, very flavorful and spicy, long shape, green color

ANCHO: Mild to moderate heat, very flavorful, long shape, green color

BANANA: Very mild, flavorful, long shape, yellow-green color

CALIFORNIA: Another name for the Anaheim pepper

 SCOVILLE SCALE FOR CHILES

The Scoville Scale measures the heat intensity of chile peppers in units; the higher the number of units, the hotter the chile peppers. The scale ranges from 0 to 500,000 units. The intensity of a particular type of pepper can vary depending on the growing conditions, weather and maturity of the pepper at the time of harvest. The following list gives the Scoville Scale heat intensities for some of the most commonly used chile and sweet peppers. These numbers will help you in selecting peppers for use in home canning and in gauging the fire factor of your finished preserves.

Caribbean or Scotch Bonnet: 300,000 to
  500,000 units
Habanero: 300,000 units
Cayenne: 30,000 to 50,000 units
Serrano: 5,000 to 25,000 units
Jalapeño: 2,500 to 5,000 units
Anaheim: 900 to 3,500 units
Hungarian Wax: 100 to 250 units
Paprika: 0 to 100 units
Sweet Banana: 0 units
Pimiento: 0 units
Bell Peppers: 0 units

CARIBBEAN: Hottest of the hot, small and wrinkled, bright red

CAYENNE: Very hot, more heat than flavor, small and thin shape, green to bright red in color

CHERRY: Medium hot, flavorful, small, round shape, red color

COLORADO: Mild heat, very flavorful, long shape, green color

HABANERO: Extremely hot, flavorful, small, round shape, green to orange in color

HUNGARIAN WAX: Ranges from mild to moderately hot, very flavorful, medium-long shape, light green to yellow in color

JALAPEÑO: Hot, flavorful and pungent, small, dark green to red in color

POBLANO: Mild to moderate, flavorful, long and heart-shaped, dark green color; known as the ancho when dried

SERRANO: Hot to very hot, flavorful, very small, dark-green color

Safe Handling of Chile Peppers

The oils that give chile peppers their flavor and heat can also cause chemical burns and other skin irritations. Whenever handling, seeding or chopping chile peppers, especially the hotter ones, always wear rubber or latex gloves to protect your hands. If you do not have any rubber or latex gloves, coating your hands with vegetable oil may provide a protective shield from the raw pepper oil, but it will not protect as well as the gloves.

After seeding and cutting the peppers, and before removing the gloves, wash all of the knives, cutting boards and other utensils used to prepare peppers. Use hot water and soap to thoroughly clean the items, then wash and dry the gloves well before removing them. These steps will greatly reduce the chances of your skin becoming irritated and will keep the hot pepper flavors from being transferred to other foods.

If you suffer burns on your skin, wash the affected area with soap and water, then soak the burns in a dish of milk or cover them with a milk compress. Be sure to use whole milk, as the higher fat content reduces the inflammation better. For mouth burns, drinking a glass of whole milk will coat your mouth and tongue and neutralize the pepper oils. If your skin is particularly sensitive, you may need to use an antihistamine cream to soothe the burns.

When working with hot peppers, be sure to keep your hands away from your face, especially your eyes and mouth. The oils can cause serious burns to the delicate tissues of these sensitive areas. If you accidentally get hot pepper oil in your eyes, immediately remove the gloves and wash your hands with soap and water. Repeatedly flush the affected eye or eyes with cool clean water. If the burning continues, seek medical attention immediately. A glass of milk will help reduce the burning sensation in your mouth after eating hot salsa.

Preparing Tomatoes

Some recipes may call for removing the skins from tomatoes before they are cooked. Place several tomatoes in a collapsible wire mesh basket and lower them into a pan of gently boiling water for 30 to 45 seconds. Then plunge the tomatoes into a bowl or pan of ice water for 1 minute to stop the cooking process. Drain the tomatoes and slip the skins off using your hands or a small paring knife.

Tomatoes that will be pressed through a food mill or sieve to remove their seeds should first be cooked until they are soft. Not only will they be easier to sieve, but the resulting puree will be thicker than that produced by raw tomatoes. A puree made from raw tomatoes can be as liquid as canned tomato juice and makes a very thin sauce.

Other Ingredients

Acids: Never omit or reduce the amount of vinegar, lemon juice or lime juice called for in a recipe. These ingredients are required to raise the acid level high enough to allow for safe processing in a water bath. Sauces with a low acid level must be processed in a pressure canner. The processing times listed in the recipes are not interchangeable for the different methods of processing.

A small amount of sugar or baking soda may be added to a tomato-based sauce to help reduce the acidic flavor. This tart taste comes from using tomatoes that are either underripe or have a poorly developed flavor. Ripe tomatoes yield a sauce with a rich, full-bodied flavor and aroma. For the best-flavored sauces, always use fruits and vegetables that are fully ripe.

Seasonings: Spices and seasonings are added to sauces to enhance the flavor. They may be increased, decreased, varied or even omitted to suit your personal taste and that of your family. Garlic should be added early in the cooking process for a sweet mellow, garlic flavor. For a stronger, sharper garlic taste, add the garlic near the end of the cooking time.

Some of the sauce recipes call for the use of fresh ginger, also known as gingerroot, which can be found in the produce section of most markets. Gingerroot is sold in large pieces called hands or smaller pieces called fingers, so named because of their shape and appearance. Select firm ginger hands or fingers that have smooth skin. Ginger with dry, cracked or wrinkled skin has been stored too long and is past its prime. Old ginger will have lost much of its pungent flavor, turned woody and will be difficult to grate.

Peel the gingerroot carefully with a vegetable peeler. Attempting to peel gingerroot with a paring knife can be very dangerous and is not recommended, as the knife can easily slip against the tough skin of the root, resulting in cut fingers. Scrape the peeled root against the fine holes of a vegetable or cheese grater. Discard the fibrous material that forms on the top of the grater and use only the smooth ginger that passes through the holes of the grater. If you do not have a grater, the peeled ginger may be finely minced using a sharp knife.

Special Techniques
Sauce Texture and Consistency

The texture of a sauce is very important, especially when being judged at a fair. The fruit or vegetable ingredients used in a sauce should be cut into pieces that are uniform in size. This uniformity is important to give the sauce its smoothness of texture and mouth appeal. When pieces are the same size, it creates a balanced flavor and keeps one flavor from dominating over the taste of the other ingredients and standing out above the rest in a mouthful of sauce. When making sauces, smaller pieces produce a more pleasing texture and consistency than the large chunks you might use when making a salsa.

Hot chile peppers should always be cut into fine pieces. Otherwise, a large piece of fiery pepper can easily overwhelm the rest of the flavors, and the burning fire of the peppers will be the only thing you or the fair judge will be able to taste. A sauce that is overpowered by one flavor will not receive high marks from a judge. For a balanced taste, the hot peppers need to be well distributed throughout the sauce. They should enhance the flavor of the sauce, not hide it.

To receive high marks from the judges, the texture and consistency of a sauce should be smooth and appropriate for its particular type. A sauce should smoothly pour from a spoon without being too thin and dripping or being too thick and dropping off in chunks. The flavors should be well-balanced and delight the taste buds, while the sauce should be smooth on the palate, without any hint of graininess.

Reducing Sauces

Many of the sauce recipes in this chapter require simmering the sauce for a period of time to reduce the volume of the liquid in the mixture and thicken the sauce. The amount of time actually needed to thicken a sauce varies with each batch and depends on the amount of water contained in the fruits and vegetables used. Depending on this water content, a sauce may thicken in less time than indicated in the recipe, or it may take a substantially longer amount of time. You will have to use your judgment as to when the sauce is thick enough to suit your taste or if it needs to be cooked and thickened longer.

Attaining the right consistency for a sauce requires some patience and paying careful attention to the pan. To preserve its flavor, the sauce should be cooked at a simmer rather than a full boil and must be stirred frequently to prevent it from sticking and scorching. As the sauce starts to thicken, it needs to be watched closer and stirred more often. If the sauce on the bottom of the pan scorches, it can affect the flavor of the entire batch, ruining the sauce.

If you notice that a sauce is starting to scorch, remove the pan from the heat. Pour the sauce off into another pan or heatproof bowl. Do not scrape the bottom of the pan. Any sauce that does not easily pour out of the pan is probably stuck to the bottom and burned. Taste the sauce, being careful not to burn your tongue. If the sauce has a scorched flavor, there is no hope for recovery, and the mixture should be discarded. If the sauce has a good flavor and does not taste burned, you are probably okay and can continue cooking the sauce. Wash the pan and return the sauce to it. Resume cooking, watch the sauce more carefully and stir it constantly as it thickens.

Filling Jars

When filling the jars, watch out for air bubbles that easily become trapped in thicker sauces. Aerobic bacteria can grow in large trapped air bubbles, making the sauce unsafe to eat. Air pockets trapped inside the jar can also affect the tightness of the seal and the headspace and allow oxidation to occur during storage. If you plan to enter your sauces at a fair, air bubbles can result in serious score deductions from the judges. No matter how tasty the sauce is, trapped air bubbles will prevent you from taking home a blue ribbon.

After ladling the sauce into the jars, remove any trapped air bubbles. To settle the contents and release any large hidden air bubbles, gently tap the jars on a counter or table lined with a soft kitchen towel. Slide a plastic knife down between the sauce and the sides of the jar to remove air bubbles and gently cut through the sauce in the middle of the jar just as you would to remove air bubbles from an angel food cake batter. After removing the air bubbles, you may need to add a little more sauce to raise the headspace back up to the proper level.

Most fairs require a ½-inch headspace for all sauces. The judging criteria for a fair is often based on recommendations from the local Cooperative Extension Service, which may vary slightly from USDA recommendations. Be sure to read the fair's competitive handbook for any listed headspace requirements before you begin canning. The headspace given for all recipes in this chapter is ½-inch, which is the required headspace for sauce entries at most fairs. For home use, a minimum ¼-inch headspace is usually sufficient for smooth sauces, such as ketchup, tomato sauce or a marinara. For chunky sauces, such as chili, salsa or spaghetti, a ½-inch headspace should always be used.

When wiping the rims of the jars before applying the hot lids, be sure to wipe the inside of the jar so the headspace area is clear. Many fair judges mark off points if the headspace inside the jar is not clean. This cloudiness from sloshed sauce is often seen as a sign of poor technique or incorrect handling of the jars after canning. It may also indicate to the judge that the jars were inverted after filling rather than having been properly processed in a water bath or pressure canner. Always keep jars upright after filling, during storage and when transporting them to a fair competition.

Barbecue Sauce

A perfect pairing for ribs, steaks and other cuts of beef, this sauce has won first-place awards at fairs across the country.

MAKES ABOUT 4 PINT JARS

4 quarts peeled, cored and chopped ripe
    plum tomatoes (about 24 large)
2 cups chopped onions (about 2 medium)
1½ cups seeded deribbed and chopped red
    bell peppers (about 2 large)
1 cup chopped celery (about 2 stalks)

2 hot, red chile peppers, seeded and finely
    chopped
3 cloves garlic, minced
8 whole black peppercorns
1¼ cups firmly packed dark brown sugar
1 cup red wine vinegar
½ cup dark corn syrup
2 teaspoons kosher salt or pickling salt
2 teaspoons paprika
2 teaspoons dry mustard
1 teaspoon Tabasco or other hot pepper
    sauce
⅛ teaspoon cayenne pepper

In an 8-quart stainless steel pan, combine the tomatoes, onions, bell peppers, celery, chile peppers and garlic.

Over medium heat, bring the mixture to a boil, stirring frequently to prevent sticking. Reduce the heat and simmer until the vegetables are soft, about 30 minutes, stirring frequently to prevent sticking. Remove the pan from the heat.

Press the mixture through a food mill or fine sieve. Return the sauce to the pan. Simmer, stirring occasionally, until the mixture is reduced by half, about 45 to 50 minutes.

Tie the peppercorns in a spice bag or a piece of cheesecloth. Add the spice bag to the pan. Add the brown sugar, wine vinegar, corn syrup, salt, paprika, mustard, hot pepper sauce and cayenne pepper to the tomato mixture, stirring well after each addition. Simmer gently for 1½ hours, or until the mixture is the consistency of ketchup. As the sauce thickens, stir frequently to prevent sticking. Remove the pan from the heat and remove the spice bag.

Ladle the sauce into hot jars, leaving ½-inch headspace. Using a plastic knife, remove any trapped air bubbles. Wipe the jar rims and threads with a clean, damp cloth. Cover with hot lids and apply screw rings. Process pint jars in a 212F (100C) water bath for 20 minutes.

Easy Barbecue Sauce

This barbecue sauce is easy to make and has a wonderful flavor.

MAKES ABOUT 5 PINT JARS

4 (12-ounce) cans tomato paste
2 (15-ounce) cans tomato sauce
2 cups red wine vinegar
2 tablespoons olive oil
½ cup finely chopped onion
3 cloves garlic, minced or crushed
1 (10-ounce) can sweet red peppers, drained
2 cups firmly packed dark brown sugar
¾ cup light corn syrup
2 teaspoons dry mustard
1 teaspoon kosher salt or pickling salt
1 teaspoon Tabasco or other hot pepper sauce (optional)
½ teaspoon Liquid Smoke (optional)
¼ teaspoon finely ground black pepper
¼ teaspoon cayenne pepper

In an 8-quart stainless steel pan, combine the tomato paste, tomato sauce and wine vinegar.

Over medium-low heat, bring the mixture to a simmer, stirring frequently to prevent sticking. Simmer gently for 10 minutes, stirring frequently to prevent sticking.

Meanwhile, in a small skillet over medium-low heat, heat the oil. Add the onion and sauté, stir-

ring frequently to prevent browning, just until tender, about 5 minutes. Add the garlic and red peppers to the pan and sauté for another 3 minutes, stirring frequently to prevent browning. Remove the pan from the heat.

Press the onion mixture through a food mill or fine sieve. Add to the tomato sauce mixture and stir until well combined. Add the brown sugar, corn syrup, mustard, salt, hot pepper sauce, Liquid Smoke, black pepper and cayenne pepper, stirring well after each addition.

Simmer gently until the mixture is the consistency of ketchup, about 30 minutes. As the sauce thickens, stir frequently to prevent sticking. Remove the pan from the heat.

Ladle the sauce into hot jars, leaving ½-inch headspace. Using a plastic knife, remove any trapped air bubbles. Wipe the jar rims and threads with a clean, damp cloth. Cover with hot lids and apply screw rings. Process pint jars in a 212F (100C) water bath for 20 minutes.

Hawaiian Barbecue Sauce

A family favorite, this marvelous sauce gives barbecued baby-back pork ribs an incredible flavor. It is also wonderful brushed on beef, chicken and shrimp. Cornstarch may be used in place of the Clearjel powder; however, the sauce may separate slightly during storage. The separation can easily be repaired by simply heating the sauce before using.

A multiple blue ribbon winner, this barbecue sauce has also been awarded the first-place All-

trista Premium Food Preservation Award for all pickles, relishes and sauces entered at the Los Angeles County Fair.

MAKES 6 TO 7 PINT JARS

4½ cups soy sauce, preferably low or
reduced sodium
3 cups cooking sherry
3 cups water
3 tablespoons rice wine vinegar
1½ cups firmly packed light brown sugar
¾ cup Instant Clearjel powder
1½ teaspoons Chinese five-spice powder
1½ cups orange blossom or other mild
honey
4 tablespoons minced garlic
1 tablespoon peeled and minced or grated
fresh ginger

In a large bowl or pan, combine the soy sauce, sherry, water and rice wine vinegar. Set aside.

In a 6- to 8-quart stainless steel pan, combine the brown sugar, Clearjel and five-spice powder until thoroughly blended. Add the soy sauce mixture to the pan all at once. Using a spoon, stir gently to thoroughly blend the liquid ingredients into the dry ingredients. Do not use a whisk, as it will cause the sauce to be full of air bubbles. Stir in the honey, garlic and ginger.

Over low heat, stirring gently, gradually heat the mixture until it is warm, the Clearjel is completely dissolved and the mixture turns translucent and thickens, about 2 to 5 minutes. Do not allow the sauce to boil or it will be full of air bubbles. Remove the pan from the heat.

Ladle the sauce into hot jars, leaving ½-inch headspace. Using a plastic knife, remove any trapped air bubbles. Wipe the jar rims and threads with a clean, damp cloth. Cover with hot lids and apply screw rings. Process pint jars in a 200F (93C) water bath for 15 minutes.

Chili Pepper Sauce

Colorful and zesty, this sauce makes a great condiment for hamburgers, meat loaf and chicken.

MAKES ABOUT 6 PINT JARS

4 quarts peeled, cored and chopped
ripe plum tomatoes
2 cups chopped onions (about 2 medium)
1 red bell pepper, seeded, deribbed and
chopped
1 green bell pepper, seeded, deribbed
and chopped
1 yellow bell pepper, seeded, deribbed
and chopped
1 orange bell pepper, seeded, deribbed
and chopped
2 jalapeño chile peppers, seeded and
minced
1 cup sugar
4 teaspoons kosher salt or pickling salt
2½ cups white vinegar
1 teaspoon whole allspice
1 teaspoon whole celery seed
1 teaspoon whole mustard seed

In an 8- to 10-quart stainless steel pan, combine the tomatoes, onions, bell peppers, jalapeño peppers, sugar and salt.

Over medium heat, bring the mixture to a boil, stirring frequently to prevent sticking. Reduce the heat and simmer 45 minutes, stirring frequently to prevent sticking.

Stir in the vinegar. Tie the allspice, celery seed and mustard seed in a spice bag or a piece of fine-meshed cheesecloth. Add the spice bag to the pan. Simmer until the sauce thickens and reaches the desired consistency, about 45 to 60 minutes. As the sauce thickens, stir frequently to prevent sticking. Remove the pan from the heat and remove the spice bag.

Ladle the sauce into hot jars, leaving ½-inch headspace. Using a plastic knife, remove any trapped air bubbles. Wipe the jar rims and threads with a clean, damp cloth. Cover with hot lids and apply screw rings. Process pint jars in a 212F (100C) water bath for 15 minutes.

Cranberry Ketchup

Cranberry ketchup is the perfect condiment to use on turkey sandwiches and other poultry dishes. The spices may be increased or omitted, depending on your personal taste. Do not use soft or badly bruised cranberries, as they can give the ketchup an unpleasant flavor. If using frozen cranberries, sort and measure them before rinsing, as the berries will defrost and start to turn soft when rinsed.

MAKES ABOUT 4 HALF-PINT JARS OR 2 PINT JARS

4 cups sorted and rinsed fresh or frozen
    cranberries (about 2 [12-ounce] bags)
1¼ cups red wine vinegar
1¼ cups water
2 cups firmly packed light brown sugar

⅛ teaspoon ground cinnamon
⅛ teaspoon ground allspice
⅛ teaspoon grated nutmeg

In a 4-quart stainless steel pan, combine the cranberries, red wine vinegar and water.

Over medium heat, bring the mixture to a boil. Reduce the heat and simmer until all cranberries are soft and have popped, about 20 minutes. Stir frequently to prevent sticking. Remove the pan from the heat. Skim off any foam.

Press the cranberry mixture through a food mill or fine-meshed sieve. Discard the skins and seeds. Return the cranberry pulp to the pan.

Stir in the brown sugar and the spices. Over medium heat, bring the mixture to a boil. Reduce the heat and simmer, stirring frequently, until the ketchup thickens, about 10 minutes. Remove the pan from the heat.

Ladle the ketchup into hot jars, leaving ½-inch headspace. Using a plastic knife, remove any trapped air bubbles. Wipe the jar rims and threads with a clean, damp cloth. Cover with hot lids and apply screw rings. Process half-pint jars in a 212F (100C) water bath for 10 minutes, pint jars for 15 minutes.

Tomato Ketchup

Rich and flavorful, homemade ketchup beats anything you can buy in a grocery store.

MAKES ABOUT 6 HALF-PINT JARS OR 3 PINT JARS

1½ teaspoons celery seed

1 teaspoon mustard seed

1 teaspoon whole allspice

½ teaspoon black peppercorns

4 quarts peeled, cored and chopped ripe
   plum tomatoes

1 cup chopped onions

¾ cup seeded and chopped red bell peppers

1 cup cider vinegar

⅔ cup sugar

2 teaspoons kosher salt or pickling salt

2 teaspoons paprika

Tie the celery seed, mustard seed, allspice and peppercorns in a spice bag or a piece of fine-meshed cheesecloth.

In an 8-quart stainless steel pan, combine the tomatoes, onions, peppers and the spice bag. Over low heat, heat and stir the mixture until the juice is released from the tomatoes. Increase the heat to medium and bring to a boil. Cook the mixture, stirring frequently, until the vegetables are soft, about 20 minutes. Remove the pan from the heat and remove the spice bag.

Place a sieve over a heatproof bowl or pan. Ladle the vegetables into the sieve and drain off the liquid. Discard the liquid or save it for soup stock. Press the pulp through a food mill or a fine-meshed sieve to remove the seeds.

Return the pulp to the pan and stir in the vinegar, sugar, salt and paprika. Over medium heat, bring the mixture to a simmer, stirring frequently to prevent sticking. Reduce the heat and simmer for about 15 to 20 minutes, or until the ketchup reaches the desired consistency, stirring frequently.

To test the consistency of the ketchup, place a small spoonful on a plate. If the ketchup mounds up and does not spread, it is done. If a ring of liquid forms around the outside edge, the ketchup needs to be cooked a few minutes longer.

Ladle the ketchup into hot jars, leaving ½-inch headspace. Using a plastic knife, remove any trapped air bubbles. Wipe the jar rims and threads with a clean, damp cloth. Cover with hot lids and apply screw rings. Process half-pint jars in a 212F (100C) water bath for 15 minutes, pint jars for 20 minutes.

Easy Ketchup

This sauce is quick to prepare and will please ketchup fans of all ages.

MAKES ABOUT 9 HALF-PINT JARS OR 4 PINT JARS

3 (12-ounce) cans tomato paste

1 (15-ounce) can tomato sauce

1½ cups red wine vinegar

¾ cup firmly packed light brown sugar

½ cup corn syrup

¼ cup bottled lemon juice

1½ teaspoons dry mustard

½ teaspoon kosher salt or pickling salt

¼ teaspoon garlic powder

¼ teaspoon onion powder

In an 8-quart stainless steel pan, combine tomato paste, tomato sauce and wine vinegar. Stir until smooth and thoroughly blended. Add brown sugar, corn syrup, lemon juice, mustard, salt, garlic powder and onion powder, stirring well after each addition.

Over medium heat, bring the mixture to a boil. Reduce the heat and simmer gently for 5 minutes, stirring frequently to prevent sticking. Remove the pan from the heat.

Ladle the ketchup into hot jars, leaving ½-inch headspace. Using a plastic knife, remove any trapped air bubbles. Wipe the jar rims and threads with a clean, damp cloth. Cover with hot lids and apply screw rings. Process half-pint jars in a 212F (100C) water bath for 15 minutes, pint jars for 20 minutes.

Prepared Horseradish

When my father, Lee Amendt, was a young boy growing up in Iowa, his family used to make horseradish to sell to the local butcher shops. It was the job of my dad and his older brother, Gilbert, to take turns going down into the basement to grind the large quantities of the pungent root. When one of them would come up with tears streaming down his cheeks, the other would go down and quickly grind as much horseradish as he could before being overcome by tears.

Horseradish that is grated by hand has a far more uniform texture than horseradish prepared in a blender or food processor. If you do decide to grind the horseradish in a blender or food processor, cut the peeled roots into small pieces and process them in small batches with some of the

vinegar in the recipe to keep it from binding the cutting blades. Be careful to turn your face away as you remove the lid from the container, as horseradish fumes are very intense.

MAKES ABOUT 4 HALF-PINTS

1 cup plus 2 tablespoons white vinegar
1 teaspoon kosher salt or pickling salt
1 teaspoon sugar
1 teaspoon antioxidant crystals or ascorbic acid crystals
3 cups lightly packed peeled and finely grated horseradish (2½ to 3 pounds horseradish root)

In a medium glass or stainless steel bowl or pan, combine the vinegar, salt, sugar and antioxidant crystals. Stir until the salt, sugar and antioxidant crystals are completely dissolved. Stir in the horseradish.

Ladle the horseradish into hot jars, leaving ½-inch headspace. Using a plastic knife, remove any trapped air bubbles. If necessary, add more horseradish to maintain ½-inch headspace. Wipe the jar rims and threads with a clean, damp cloth. Cover with hot lids and apply screw rings. Process half-pint jars in a 212F (100C) water bath for 15 minutes.

Asian Marinade

The combination of citrus and soy sauce gives this marinade a special zing that goes great with chicken or pork. This recipe can easily be doubled.

MAKES ABOUT 4 HALF-PINT JARS OR 2 PINT JARS

1⅓ cups soy sauce, preferably low or
    reduced sodium
1 cup water
6 tablespoons frozen orange juice
    concentrate, thawed
⅓ cup firmly packed light brown sugar
3 tablespoons strained fresh lemon juice
3 tablespoons minced or finely grated fresh
    orange zest
3 tablespoons minced or finely grated fresh
    lemon zest
6 garlic cloves, minced
1 tablespoon peeled and minced or grated
    fresh ginger

In a 2-quart stainless steel saucepan, combine all of the ingredients.

Over medium-low heat, stirring constantly, heat the marinade until the sugar is completely dissolved. Increase the heat to medium and heat the marinade until it comes to just below a simmer. Do not allow the marinade to boil. Remove the pan from the heat.

Ladle the hot marinade into hot jars, leaving ½-inch headspace. Wipe the jar rims and threads with a clean, damp cloth. Cover with hot lids and apply screw rings. Process half-pint and pint jars in a 212F (100C) water bath for 10 minutes.

Wine Marinade

This marinade is excellent for lamb, pork or beef. The acid, in the form of wine vinegar, helps to tenderize the meat. A well-washed sprig of fresh herb may be added to each jar just before filling.

MAKES ABOUT 4 HALF-PINT JARS OR 2 PINT JARS

3 cups red wine
2 cups red wine vinegar
2 tablespoons minced shallots
4 garlic cloves, minced
2 teaspoons peeled and minced or grated
    fresh ginger
⅛ teaspoon salt
1 medium onion, peeled and quartered
8 whole black peppercorns
3 to 4 sprigs each of fresh thyme, rosemary
    and Italian parsley

In a 3-quart stainless steel saucepan, combine the wine, wine vinegar, shallots, garlic, ginger and salt. Tie the onion, peppercorns and fresh herbs in a spice bag or a piece of fine-meshed cheesecloth. Add the spice bag to the pan.

Over medium heat, bring the marinade to a simmer. Reduce the heat and simmer gently for 10 minutes. Remove the pan from the heat and remove the spice bag.

Ladle the hot marinade into hot jars, leaving ½-inch headspace. Wipe the jar rims and threads with a clean, damp cloth. Cover with hot lids and apply screw rings. Process half-pint and pint jars in a 212F (100C) water bath for 10 minutes.

Basil Marinara Sauce

Rich with fresh basil and red wine, this classic sauce is perfect for pasta, ravioli, tortelloni and lasagna.

MAKES ABOUT 5 PINT JARS

1 tablespoon olive oil or vegetable oil
¾ cup chopped onion
6 cloves garlic, minced
15 pounds plum tomatoes, peeled, cored and chopped
1 cup red wine
¼ cup chopped fresh sweet basil
1 tablespoon chopped fresh oregano
2 teaspoons sugar
1¼ teaspoons kosher salt or pickling salt
⅛ teaspoon freshly ground black pepper
⅓ cup bottled lemon juice

In an 8-quart stainless steel pan over medium-low heat, heat the olive oil. Add the onion and sauté until tender, about 10 minutes, stirring frequently to prevent browning. Add the garlic and sauté 3 minutes. Stir in the tomatoes. Increase the heat to medium and bring the mixture to a boil. Reduce the heat and simmer for 20 minutes, or until the tomatoes are soft. Remove the pan from the heat.

Press the tomato mixture through a food mill or fine sieve. Discard the seeds. Return the pulp to the pan. Stir in the wine, basil, oregano, sugar, salt and pepper.

Over medium heat, cook the sauce, stirring frequently, until it reduces by about half, or to the desired consistency. This may take 30 to 60 minutes, depending on the liquid content of the tomatoes. Stir frequently to prevent sticking or scorching. Remove the pan from the heat and stir in the lemon juice.

Ladle the sauce into hot jars, leaving ½-inch headspace. Using a plastic knife, remove any trapped air bubbles. Wipe the jar rims and threads with a clean, damp cloth. Cover with hot lids and apply screw rings. Process pint jars in a 212F (100C) water bath for 35 minutes.

Pizza Sauce

Try using a homemade pizza sauce the next time you prepare a pizza for your family. You will be amazed at the fresh flavor; it is far superior to any commercially canned pizza sauce. This recipe can easily be doubled.

MAKES ABOUT 4 HALF-PINT JARS OR 2 PINT JARS

1 tablespoon olive oil or vegetable oil
½ cup chopped onion
2 cloves garlic, crushed or finely chopped
2½ cups drained canned tomatoes
1 (12-ounce) can tomato paste
1 tablespoon sugar
1 tablespoon finely chopped fresh oregano or ½ teaspoon dried oregano, crushed
1 teaspoon kosher salt or pickling salt
⅛ teaspoon freshly ground black pepper

In a 3-quart stainless steel pan over medium heat, heat the olive oil. Add the onion. Reduce the heat and sauté until translucent, about 15 minutes, stirring frequently to prevent browning. Add the garlic and sauté 3 minutes.

Add the tomatoes, tomato paste, sugar, oregano, salt and pepper to the pan. Stir well to combine. Cover and simmer for 30 minutes, or until thick, stirring occasionally to prevent sticking. Remove the pan from the heat.

Process the sauce in a blender, in small batches, until smooth. Return the sauce to the pan. Over medium heat, bring the sauce to a simmer. Remove the pan from the heat.

Ladle the sauce into hot jars, leaving ½-inch headspace. Using a plastic knife, remove any trapped air bubbles. Wipe the jar rims and threads with a clean, damp cloth. Cover with hot lids and apply screw rings. Process half-pint jars for 20 minutes, pint jars for 25 minutes in a pressure canner at 11 pounds of pressure in a dial-gauge pressure canner or at 10 pounds pressure in a weighted-gauge pressure canner.

Sweet and Sour Plum Sauce

When the Santa Rosa plum tree in my background is loaded with ripe fruit, I make jars of this special sauce for use throughout the year. Flavorful and tangy, this Asian-style sweet and sour sauce makes a wonderful dipping sauce for shrimp, chicken and pork. Full-flavored varieties of red or purple plums work best for this recipe. Yellow plums are usually milder, and their flavor tends to get lost amid the other ingredients.

MAKES ABOUT 4 PINT JARS

8 cups pitted, peeled and chopped ripe plums (about 4½ pounds)
1½ cups firmly packed light brown sugar
1 cup granulated sugar
1 cup rice wine vinegar or cider vinegar
½ cup minced red onion (about 1 small)
1 teaspoon dry mustard
1 teaspoon kosher salt or pickling salt
1 teaspoon peeled and grated or minced fresh ginger
1 cup superfine sugar
⅓ cup Instant Clearjel powder

In an 8-quart stainless steel pan, combine the plums, brown sugar, granulated sugar and vinegar. Stir in the onion, mustard, salt and ginger.

Over medium heat, bring the mixture to a boil, stirring constantly. Reduce the heat and simmer until the sauce thickens, about 30 minutes, stirring frequently to prevent sticking and scorching. Remove the pan from the heat. Skim off any foam.

Press the mixture through a food mill or fine-meshed sieve. Discard the pulp. Rinse the pan and return the sieved mixture to the pan.

In a small bowl, thoroughly combine the superfine sugar and the Clearjel.

Over low heat, heat the sauce until warm. Gradually sprinkle the Clearjel mixture over the surface of the sauce in a thin layer, stirring frequently and breaking up any clumps that form. It will take about 3 minutes to gradually stir in all of the Clearjel mixture. Stir gently to avoid trapping air bubbles in the sauce. Continue to stir until the Clearjel mixture is completely incorporated into the sauce and no lumps remain. Remove the pan from the heat.

Ladle the sauce into hot jars, leaving ½-inch headspace. Using a plastic knife, remove any trapped air bubbles. Wipe the jar rims and threads with a clean, damp cloth. Cover with hot lids and apply screw rings. Process pint jars in a 200F (93C) water bath for 20 minutes.

Hot Pepper Sauce

Use this spicy condiment anytime you want to liven up the flavor of food. Use sparingly though, as this sauce is fiery and a little goes a long way. When working with chile peppers, be sure to wear rubber gloves to protect your hands from burns.

MAKES ABOUT 8 (4-OUNCE) JARS OR
4 HALF-PINT JARS

2 quarts peeled, cored and chopped ripe
    plum tomatoes
2 cups peeled, seeded and chopped hot red
    chile peppers (about 32)
1 large onion, peeled and chopped
6 large cloves garlic, crushed or chopped
2 cups distilled white vinegar
1 tablespoon whole black peppercorns
½ cup sugar
2 teaspoons kosher salt or pickling salt

In an 8-quart stainless steel pan, combine the tomatoes, chile peppers, onion, garlic and vinegar. Tie the peppercorns in a spice bag or a piece of cheesecloth. Add the spice bag to the pan.

Over low heat, stirring constantly, heat the mixture until the juice is released from the tomatoes. Increase the heat to medium and bring the mixture to a boil. Cook, stirring frequently, until the vegetables are soft, about 20 minutes. Remove the pan from the heat and remove the spice bag.

Press the tomato mixture through a food mill or fine sieve. Discard the seeds. Return the pulp to the pan. Stir in the sugar and salt.

Over medium heat, bring the mixture to a simmer and cook the sauce until it begins to thicken, about 15 minutes, stirring frequently to prevent sticking. Remove the pan from the heat.

Ladle the sauce into hot jars, leaving ½-inch headspace. Wipe the jar rims and threads with a clean, damp cloth. Cover with hot lids and apply screw rings. Process half-pint jars in a 212F (100C) water bath for 15 minutes, 4-ounce jars for 10 minutes.

Mexican Garden Salsa

Be sure to use plum tomatoes, such as Romas, to make this salsa. Salad-type tomatoes contain too much juice and will make a very thin, watery salsa. Wear rubber gloves when working with chile peppers to protect your skin from burns.

MAKES ABOUT 12 HALF-PINT JARS OR 6 PINT JARS

12 cups cored and chopped plum tomatoes
3 cups chopped onions
3 cups seeded and chopped Anaheim,
    Colorado or poblano chile peppers
1¾ cups seeded and chopped jalapeño chile
    peppers (about 40)
½ cup white wine vinegar
½ cup strained fresh lime juice
2 tablespoons kosher salt or pickling salt

In an 8-quart stainless steel pan, combine all of the ingredients.

Over medium-low heat, bring the mixture to a simmer and simmer gently for 10 minutes, stirring frequently to prevent sticking.

Ladle the salsa into hot jars, leaving ½-inch headspace. Using a plastic knife, remove any trapped air bubbles. If necessary, add more salsa to maintain ½-inch headspace. Wipe the jar rims and threads with a clean, damp cloth. Cover with hot lids and apply screw rings. Process both half-pint and pint jars in a 212F (100C) water bath for 15 minutes.

Spaghetti Sauce

A jar or two of this flavor-packed sauce makes for a quick and easy dinner. If you like, add some browned ground beef or turkey to the sauce before serving.

Because of the increased risks of contamination when canning any food containing meat, it is better to cook the meat and add it to the sauce just before serving. If you do decide to add meat to the sauce before canning, be sure to cook the meat thoroughly and add it along with the other ingredients prior to reducing the sauce. For a sauce containing meat, the headspace must be increased to 1 inch and the processing time must also be increased to 60 minutes.

MAKES ABOUT 4 PINT JARS

15 pounds ripe plum tomatoes, cored and quartered or chopped

2 tablespoons olive oil or vegetable oil
1 cup chopped onions
4 cloves garlic, minced
1 cup sliced fresh mushrooms
1 cup red wine
¼ cup chopped fresh Italian parsley
2 tablespoons chopped fresh oregano
1 tablespoon chopped fresh sweet basil
½ teaspoon salt
¼ teaspoon freshly ground black pepper

In an 8- to 10-quart stainless steel pan over medium heat, bring the tomatoes to a boil, stirring frequently. Reduce the heat and simmer, uncovered, until the tomatoes are soft, about 20 minutes, stirring frequently to prevent sticking. Remove the pan from the heat.

Press the tomatoes through a food mill or fine sieve. Discard the seeds and skins. Set the pulp aside. Rinse and dry the pan.

Over medium heat, heat the olive oil in the pan. Add the onions. Reduce the heat and sauté until almost tender but not browned, about 10 minutes, stirring occasionally. Add the garlic and mushrooms. Sauté gently until the mushrooms release their liquid and it evaporates, stirring frequently to prevent browning.

Add the tomato pulp to the pan. Stir in the wine, parsley, oregano, basil, salt and pepper. Over medium heat, bring the mixture to boil. Reduce the heat and simmer until the sauce is reduced by about half, or to the desired consistency. This may take between 1½ to 2 hours, depending on the liquid content of the tomatoes. Stir frequently as the sauce thickens to prevent sticking or scorching. Remove the pan from the heat.

Ladle the sauce into hot jars, leaving ½-inch headspace. Using a plastic knife, remove any trapped air bubbles. If necessary, add more sauce to maintain ½-inch headspace. Wipe the jar rims and threads with a clean, damp cloth. Cover with hot lids and apply screw rings. Process pint jars for 30 minutes at 11 pounds of pressure in a dial-gauge pressure canner or at 10 pounds pressure in a weighted-gauge pressure canner.

Easy Spaghetti Sauce

If you do not have a garden overflowing with ripe tomatoes, you can still make and can your own spaghetti sauce. This sauce is also great to make during the winter months when ripe, flavorful tomatoes are hard to find.

MAKES ABOUT 4 PINT JARS

2 tablespoons olive oil or vegetable oil

1 cup chopped onions

3 cloves garlic, minced

1 cup sliced fresh mushrooms

3 (8-ounce) cans tomato sauce

3 (6-ounce) cans tomato paste

1 (29-ounce) can whole tomatoes, chopped

1 cup red wine

2 teaspoons dried oregano, crushed

1 teaspoon dried basil, crushed

½ teaspoon dried Italian seasoning, crushed

½ teaspoon salt

¼ teaspoon freshly ground black pepper

In a 4-quart stainless steel pan over medium heat, heat the olive oil. Add the onions. Reduce the heat and sauté until almost tender but not browned, about 10 minutes, stirring occasionally. Add the garlic and mushrooms. Sauté gently until the mushrooms release their liquid and it evaporates, stirring frequently to prevent browning.

Stir in the tomato sauce and tomato paste. Add the whole tomatoes, wine, oregano, basil, Italian seasoning, salt and pepper. Over medium heat, bring the mixture to boil. Reduce the heat and simmer 1 hour. As the sauce thickens, stir frequently to prevent sticking or scorching. Remove the pan from the heat.

Ladle the sauce into hot jars, leaving ½-inch headspace. Using a plastic knife, remove any trapped air bubbles. If necessary, add more sauce to maintain ½-inch headspace. Wipe the jar rims and threads with a clean, damp cloth. Cover with hot lids and apply screw rings. Process pint jars for 30 minutes at 11 pounds of pressure in a dial-gauge pressure canner or at 10 pounds pressure in a weighted-gauge pressure canner.

Tomato Sauce

This basic sauce is a great way to use up excess tomatoes from the garden and makes a wonderful base for soups and stews. If you want to create a sauce with more zest, add some minced garlic and freshly ground black pepper to the tomato puree before reducing.

MAKES ABOUT 8 PINT JARS OR 4 QUART JARS

25 pounds plum tomatoes, cored and quartered

2 teaspoons kosher salt or pickling salt

½ cup bottled lemon juice

In an 8- to 10-quart stainless steel pan over medium heat, bring the tomatoes to a boil, stirring frequently to prevent sticking. Reduce the heat and simmer for 20 minutes, or until the tomatoes are soft, stirring frequently to prevent sticking. Remove the pan from the heat.

Press the tomatoes through a food mill or fine sieve. Discard the seeds and skins. Return the pulp to the pan. Stir in the salt.

Over medium heat, cook the pulp, stirring frequently, until it reduces by about half, or to the desired consistency. This may take 45 to 90 minutes, depending on the liquid content of the tomatoes. Stir frequently to prevent sticking or scorching. Remove the pan from the heat and stir in the lemon juice.

Ladle the sauce into hot jars, leaving ½-inch headspace. Using a plastic knife, remove any trapped air bubbles. Wipe the jar rims and threads with a clean, damp cloth. Cover with hot lids and apply screw rings. Process pint jars in a 212F (100C) water bath for 35 minutes, quart jars for 40 minutes.

Tropical Sauce

This sauce came about through an inspiration from my friend and fellow canner, Sandra Manning. I had made every apricot and plum jam, jelly and preserve I could think of and still had boxes of ripe fruit sitting on my kitchen table, with more fruit still on the trees. When Sandra suggested adding mango and pineapple, this recipe was born. The combination appealed to the fair judges, too. This exotic sauce has won several blue ribbons, a Best of Class award and the first-place Alltrista Premium Food Preservation Award for all pickles, relishes and sauces entered at the Los Angeles County Fair.

Do not puree the fruit. The sauce should contain small pieces of each fruit variety. This sauce is especially good served warm over grilled chicken or shrimp.

MAKES ABOUT 6 PINT JARS

5 cups pitted, peeled and crushed ripe apricots (about 4½ pounds)
¼ cup strained fresh lemon juice
2 cups pitted, peeled and crushed ripe Santa Rosa or other red plums (about 2½ pounds)
2 cups pitted, peeled and crushed ripe mangoes (about 4 medium mangoes)
1 (20-ounce) can crushed pineapple packed in juice
2¾ cups sugar
1 cup mango-passion fruit juice cocktail or water

In an 8-quart stainless steel pan, combine the apricots and lemon juice, stirring just until the apricots are well coated. Add the plums, mangoes, pineapple with its juice, sugar and juice cocktail, stirring gently after each addition.

Over medium heat, bring the fruit mixture to a simmer, stirring frequently. Reduce the heat and simmer, stirring gently, for 5 minutes. Remove the pan from the heat. Skim off any foam.

Ladle the sauce into hot jars, leaving ½-inch headspace. Using a plastic knife, remove any trapped air bubbles. If necessary, add more sauce to maintain ½-inch headspace. Wipe the jar rims and threads with a clean, damp cloth. Cover with hot lids and apply screw rings. Process pint jars in a 200F (93C) water bath for 20 minutes.

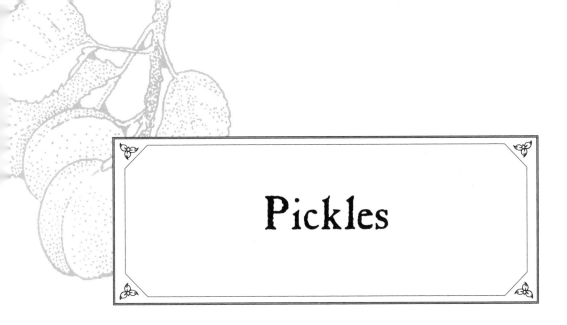

Pickles

Pickling is the method of preserving foods in a vinegar or salt solution. The vegetables to be pickled are sometimes soaked in a salt brine to release excess liquid before pickling. There are three basic types of pickles: fresh packed and quick process pickles, both of which are considered a quick-method type of pickle because they can be prepared fairly easily, brined or fermented pickles, which require careful attention for several weeks, and relishes.

FRESH PACKED PICKLES: The raw vegetables are simply packed into jars and then covered with a vinegar solution or salt brine. Fresh packed pickles take a long time for their flavors to blend and develop. There is also a greater chance that the pickles will float in the jar because of the air that remains trapped in the cells of the vegetables.

QUICK PROCESS PICKLES: The vegetables are usually soaked in a salt brine for a few hours, then cooked for a short period of time in a vinegar syrup before being packed into the jars. The short brining permits excess water to be removed from the vegetables, while the cooking allows air in the vegetable cells to escape and be replaced with the vinegar syrup.

BRINED OR FERMENTED PICKLES: These are created by soaking the prepared vegetables in a salt brine for 3 to 6 weeks, sometimes longer, before packing them into jars. For some recipes, the brined pickles are heated in a vinegar syrup before packing, while others are packed into the jars and then covered with the hot syrup or a salt solution. Brining is a traditional, though complicated, method of making pickles that helps prevent the vegetables from shriveling and imparts a distinctive flavor to the pickles.

RELISHES: These condiments are made by cooking chopped vegetables in a vinegar syrup before packing them into the hot jars. They are usually served alongside meats or on hamburgers, hot dogs and sandwiches.

In this book, I primarily cover the quick method of making pickles, where the vegetables are usually soaked in a salt brine for a short period of time and then either packed raw and covered with a boiling vinegar syrup, or they are partially cooked and then packed into the jars with the syrup. These are the easiest and most common types of pickles to make, and excellent results can be achieved with these pickles by canners of all skill levels.

Brined fermented pickles, where cucumbers or other vegetables are placed in a large crock then covered with a salt brine and allowed to ferment for several weeks, can be difficult to master, especially for the beginning pickler. They require careful attention to prevent spoilage. The brine must be changed every day or so, the scum that forms must be skimmed from the surface and the vegetables must be kept weighted down so that they are held below the surface of the brine throughout the fermenting process. If these steps are not carefully and rigorously followed, bacteria can grow on the vegetables and the pickles can quickly become contaminated and unsafe to eat. When canned and water bath processed for storage, many fermented pickles will lose some of their crispness and flavor, causing them to become soft and bland.

If you do want to try your hand at making fermented pickles, I suggest contacting your local Cooperative Extension Service office or the USDA. They can provide you with tested recipes and safe canning instructions for making a variety of fermented pickles. Avoid any recipes you may find in old or new cookbooks that do not require either the fermented pickles be processed in a water bath canner or the finished pickles to be stored in the refrigerator. Pickles that are improperly sealed or stored can develop bacteria and present a major health risk.

Canning Pickles

Blue ribbon pickles do not happen by chance. They require reliable modern methods and use of the best quality ingredients available. Paying careful attention to detail and using the correct processing techniques will lead to first-rate pickles. Although pickles made from cucumbers are the most common variety, pickles can be made from a wide range of vegetables and fruit. Some are highly spiced, while others are mild, allowing the natural flavors of the produce to come through.

Of the many varieties of pickles made by home canners and those produced commercially, one thing is common: They all have a high acid content, usually from the vinegar solution in which they are canned. This solution can be flavored with spices and herbs or sweetened with sugar. The correct proportions of vinegar, sugar and salt must be maintained at all times or the finished pickles will be soft, soggy and lacking in flavor. If the salt or acid levels are lowered, unfriendly organisms may grow, making the pickles unsafe to eat.

Many old recipes call for the use of alum or lime to crisp the pickles. These ingredients may be hard to find and require special handling to achieve the desired results without negatively affecting the flavor of the pickled foods. By using fresh vegetables, following modern pickling methods and processing the pickles at lower temperatures, the use of these additives is no longer necessary or recommended.

Special Equipment

Canning pickles does not really require any special equipment, but there are a few rules to follow when choosing pans, bowls and utensils. Use only glass, stainless steel or stoneware bowls and stainless steel pans for making pickles. Aluminum, brass, copper, zinc or iron pans and utensils can react with the high acid levels of the vinegar, damaging the finish on the equipment and affecting the flavor, color and quality of the pickles. Acids or salts that come in contact with galvanized pans and utensils may produce a toxic reaction, poisoning the pickles.

Selecting Vegetables

Use perishable vegetables as soon after harvest as possible. Vegetables can deteriorate quickly and old vegetables may result in soft, mushy pickles with little flavor. When purchasing vegetables at a farmers' market, be sure to examine the produce well and ask when it was harvested. When comparison shopping, remember that the better the price, the older the vegetables are likely to be.

Weather, especially rainstorms, can have a definite effect on homegrown produce. Rain can cause vegetables such as cucumbers and squash to become waterlogged. The excess water absorbed into the cells of these vegetables is hard to remove and would cause the pickles to have a soft texture and bland taste. Wait at least 2 days after a heavy rain before harvesting vegetables for making pickles.

Select firm, fresh, unblemished vegetables of uniform size for your pickles A jar of cucumber pickles or dilled beans looks funny when filled with half large, fat vegetables and half small, skinny vegetables. Uniformity is one of the major criteria fair judges use to determine the quality of a jar of pickles, and this standard should be followed even for pickles that will be made for home use or given away as gifts.

Only use the short, pickling varieties of cucumbers for making pickles and relishes. Pickling cucumbers will make crisper, crunchier pickles than the common table varieties of salad or slicing cucumbers. Long, slicing cucumbers contain too much water and have seeds that are too large to make good pickles. Pickling cucumbers have small seeds, contain less water and may be harvested at almost any size, depending on the type of pickle to be canned. Many slicing cucumbers available at grocery stores and produce markets have been treated with a nontoxic vegetable wax to make them shine and keep them fresh longer. This wax is virtually impossible to scrub off without damaging the cucumbers, and it will not allow the brine or vinegar syrup to penetrate through the cucumber's skin. The result is limp, watery pickles with little or no flavor.

Whenever possible, use cucumbers that you, your friend or a neighbor have grown. After harvesting, cucumbers to be used for making pickles have a very short window of freshness. Pickles should always be made from cucumbers that have been harvested within the last 24 hours. This canning rule also applies to zucchini and any other squash varieties to be used for pickling. Have you ever eaten a homemade pickle, either made by yourself or someone else, that had a hollow center? The reason is that the cucumbers used to make those pickles were more than a day or two old. Cucumbers and squash will begin to develop hollow centers when you let them stand for 24 hours or more after harvest before beginning the pickling process.

Cucumbers that have developed hollow centers should not be used for making whole pickles or pickle slices. The hollow centers of whole cucumbers can trap air that will cause the pickles to float in the jars and may harbor bacteria that can cause the pickles to spoil. Hollow pickles also tend to lose their crispness and turn soft during storage.

Pickle slices with hollow centers will not hold their shape well and will often become soft or mushy. In fair competitions, whole and sliced cucumber pickles with hollow centers will receive significantly reduced scores from the fair judges.

Be wary of store-bought cucumbers and those you purchase from a farmers' market, produce market or roadside stand. Unless you have a good relationship with the grower and can trust his or her word that the cucumbers were harvested that very morning, it may be best to pass, no matter how good the price. It can be very difficult to tell the difference between a just-harvested cucumber and one that was picked two days ago. If the stem is still attached, check to see if it shows any sign of wilting. Fresh cucumbers will be firm to the touch and will not give when pressed firmly.

Selecting Vinegar

The most common vinegars used for canning homemade pickles are distilled white vinegar and cider vinegar. While these vinegars are both excellent for pickling, they can be very strong in flavor. Some recipes may call for the less stringent flavor of a wine vinegar or even a rice vinegar to keep the acid taste from overpowering the desired flavor of the vegetables in the finished pickles. Cider vinegar or red wine vinegar can cause pickles to darken during storage. For light-colored vegetables, it is best to select one of the white vinegar types.

While the spices and seasonings in pickle recipes can be adjusted to suit your personal taste, do not change the proportions of vegetables, vinegar and water. The proper ratio of these ingredients must be maintained to ensure the safety of the finished product. For every pint jar of quick method pickles produced, the syrup should contain at least ¼ cup of vinegar with an acidity level of 5 to 6 percent. A lower vinegar ratio, or the use of a vinegar with a lower acidity level, may permit the growth of harmful bacteria in the jars of pickles. Never decrease the amount of vinegar in the recipe or the pickles may not be safe to eat. To make a pickle recipe less sour, increase the amount of sugar in the syrup.

Always measure the vinegar carefully. Reducing the amount of vinegar can result in soft, mushy pickles, while too much vinegar will cause the pickles to shrivel. Avoid boiling the vinegar solution at high temperatures or for a longer time than instructed in the recipe. High temperatures and extended heating can reduce the acetic acid level of vinegar. Acetic acid is important to keep the pickles from turning soft and to ensure the safe canning of pickled foods.

Homemade vinegars have an unknown acid content and should never be used to make pickles. The acid content of a homemade vinegar can be substantially lower than the acid level that is necessary to safely can pickles. Always use a commercially produced vinegar with a known acid strength of 5 to 6 percent for canning pickles.

Importance of the Water

Water is used in pickling for several purposes—to rinse the vegetables to remove any dirt or sand, to a make brine for soaking the vegetables when combined with salt, and to add to the vinegar and sugar to dilute the syrup solution so that it is not too strong nor too sour. While tap water is perfectly fine for rinsing the vegetables before canning, it contains minerals, such as iron and lime, which can have a negative effect on the quality of pickles. These minerals can cause the pickles to change color and darken or even turn black during storage and can cause the pickling liquid to become cloudy and darken as well. Excessive amounts of these minerals can also cause pickles to become soft and limp in the jars during storage.

The solution to these problems is to use bottled distilled water for canning pickles. Distilled water has been filtered to remove the minerals, making it an excellent option for pickling. Even in areas with soft water, it is still advisable to use distilled water. Vegetables may be washed in tap water to remove dirt and also rinsed well after brining to remove the excess salt, but they should not be allowed to soak in tap water for any length of time, and tap water should not be used for making pickling syrups or brines. To prevent the pickles from darkening and turning soft, always use distilled water for brines and pickling liquids.

Salt, Herbs, Spices and Sugar

Salt is an essential ingredient in making pickles. It is used for seasoning, preserving and in brining to draw out the excess juices from vegetables. Salt adds both flavor and crispness to pickles. Because table salt contains additives to prevent the salt from caking, it should not be used for canning pickles. These additives will cause the brines and pickling syrups to become cloudy. Many table salts also contain iodine, which can cause pickles to darken or even turn black after canning.

Pickling salt, often called canning salt, should be used to make pickles. Kosher salt is also an excellent choice, inexpensive and readily available in grocery stores. Sea salt may also be used, but it is more expensive and may be cost prohibitive for use in pickling where large quantities of salt are needed.

Always measure the salt used for brining carefully. A brine that is too salty will often cause cucumbers to shrivel. If too little salt is added to the brine, the vegetables will not release enough water and the pickles will tend to be soft. They will also absorb less of the vinegar syrup and seasonings during storage, resulting in pickles with an uneven flavor blend or pickles that will take a long time to develop their full flavor.

Fresh herbs impart a wonderful flavor to pickles, and many recipes in this section call for the use of fresh herbs. Dill, thyme, tarragon, basil and even garlic all impart a delicious flavor to pickled foods. The quantities of herbs added to the vegetables may be adjusted to produce a strong taste or just a hint of the herb flavor. Dried herbs are frequently used to season pickling liquids before canning and may be added to jars to deepen the flavor as the pickles develop.

Spices, ranging from sweet to peppery and mild to hot, are used to give pickles a more complex flavor. Their quantity and mix can be adjusted to suit personal tastes and to achieve the desired final flavor. When adding spices to pickling liquids, always use whole spices rather than ground spices. The ground spices can cause the pickling liquid to darken and appear cloudy, thus obscuring the shape and overall appearance of the pickles. Whole spices are often tied in a spice bag that can later be easily removed from the vinegar solution before canning the pickles. For a stronger flavor, spices and herbs can be placed directly in the bottom of the jars. Spices used for pickling should be recently purchased and have a strong, distinct, fresh aroma when the jar or package is opened.

Store-bought pickling spice is a blend of a variety of spices and herbs. Because each tablespoon of mixed pickling spice will contain a slightly different blend of these herbs and spices, I prefer to measure the spices individually to attain a more uniform flavor from one batch of pickles to the next. Also, not every pickle recipe benefits from the flavors of all of the spices found in a pre-made blend. A more subtle or bolder flavor of one particular seasoning or another may be desired. This is difficult to accomplish with a generic mixture of spices and herbs.

The following dried herbs and spices are commonly found in most commercial mixed pickling spice. Purchase the whole spices separately and create your own personal pickling blend. Or you can measure the spices individually as needed for each recipe.

Spices in Pickling Mixes
Allspice berries
Bay leaves
Black peppercorns
Celery seeds
Coriander seeds
Dill seeds
Ginger
Mustard seeds
Whole cinnamon sticks
Whole cloves

Others Spices in Some Pickling Mixes
Cardamom pods
Red pepper flakes
White peppercorns

Sugar helps keep pickles firm, but too much sugar in the vinegar syrup can cause the pickles to shrivel. Only granulated white sugar should be used for making pickling syrups. Honey and corn syrup, when combined with the vinegar and spices, can impart unpleasant flavors and are not recommended for use in pickled foods. Avoid brown sugar, as it will make the pickling liquid very dark in color. Sugar is also used to cut the tart flavor of the vinegar and mellow the flavor of the pickling syrup. If you find your pickles are too sour for your taste, increase the amount of sugar in the recipe the next time you make them. Never decrease the amount of vinegar or dilute it with more water, as this will change the acid content of the pickles and will lead to spoilage.

Preparing Vegetables
Rinse all of the vegetables under cool running water. A soft brush may be used to remove dirt and sand, but be careful not to bruise, scrape or otherwise damage the vegetables. Rinse cucumbers well, especially around the stems, to remove all signs of dirt. Residual dirt on cucumbers can contain bacteria that can cause a surface scum to form in pickle jars. Any jar of pickles containing scum should be considered to be contaminated and should not be eaten. Sort the vegetables according to size and can like-sized produce in the same jar.

Cut a 1/16-inch slice from the blossom end of each cucumber. This is an important step and should not be omitted. The blossom end contains bacteria that may grow and contaminate the pickles and also enzymes that can create scum and soften the pickles during fermentation and storage. The vegetables may be kept whole or sliced, depending on the type of pickle to be prepared. For sliced pickles, cut the vegetables into slices of uniform thickness. When making pickle spears or chunky pickles, cut the vegetables into wedges or pieces that are the same size and length. Very large cucumbers should be cut in half or quarters after brining to make it easier to pack them into the jars and to allow for sufficient heat penetration and safe water bath processing.

When making relishes, the vegetables should be chopped into small, uniform pieces for a nice appearance and an even distribution of all the flavors. If you have hollow cucumbers, this is the way to use them. When chopped into small pieces, it does not matter whether the cucumbers used had hollow centers or not.

Brining Vegetables
Some pickle varieties are brined before being cooked in a vinegar syrup or before being packed raw into jars. This simply means that they are soaked in a salt water solution for a few hours or overnight to draw the excess liquid out of the vegetables. By removing this excess water, the vegetables will remain crisper and they can absorb

more of the vinegar syrup in which they will be cooked and packed. When the vegetables absorb more of the syrup, the pickles will develop a stronger and fuller flavor.

During the brining process, the vegetables need to be completely submerged in the salt water brine. Place the vegetables in a large bowl and cover them with the brine. Fill a water-tight, gallon-size, zip-closure food storage bag with water and seal it tight. Place the water-filled bag on top of the vegetables to submerge them below the level of the brine. The brine should cover all the vegetables. Remove any air bubbles trapped under the bag. A plate weighted down by jars or other heavy objects may also be used to keep the vegetables covered by the brine, but this method often crushes or bruises the vegetables and is not recommended.

Because cucumbers will release a significant quantity of liquid during the brining process, use a bowl that is larger than the size required to hold the vegetables, brine and water-filled bag. If there is only a small amount of room left in the bowl after adding the bag, you may want to place the bowl on a tray, large plate or in a roasting pan to catch any overflowing water. Keep an eye on the water level in the bowl and lower it if necessary to keep it from overflowing.

Packing Jars

Pack the pickles into the jars according to their type, preparation and presentation appearance. Always leave a full ½-inch headspace in each jar. Fill the jars with the hot vinegar syrup, maintaining ½-inch headspace and making sure the syrup covers the pickles. Use a bubble freer or plastic knife to remove any air bubbles trapped in the jar. If necessary, add additional syrup to maintain proper headspace. After wiping the rims and threads clean of any spilled syrup, seal the jars and process all pickles in a hot water bath for the time indicated in the recipe.

Water Bath Processing for Pickles

The high temperature of a boiling water bath, even for a short period of time, can rob pickles of their crispness and color, causing them to become limp and soft. To prevent this, all pickles should be processed for a longer period of time in a 180F (82C) to 185F (85C) water bath to pasteurize the contents of the jars. This method is called low-temperature pasteurization and it allows the pickles to remain crisp and retain their natural color, while still making them safe for storage.

Bring the water bath temperature up to 185F (85C), add the sealed jars and start timing the water bath as soon as the last jar of pickles is lowered into the water. Be sure to keep an eye on the water temperature and use an instant read thermometer for accurate measurement. Do not let the temperature fall below 180F (82C) or rise above 190F (88C). At too low of a temperature, the contents of the jars may not reach the proper internal temperature to be pasteurized and the jars may fail to seal. A temperature that is too high will fade the colors of the vegetables and make soft, limp pickles.

Refrigerator storage is not a good substitute for water bath processing. Surface yeast and mold growth are common types of spoilage that occur during refrigeration of pickles that have not been heat processed. Pickles showing any kind of spoilage should not be eaten and should be discarded.

Storing Pickles

Store the jars of pickles in a cool, dark, dry location. If pickles are kept in an area that is warm or if they are exposed to light, the color and flavor of the vegetables can quickly fade and deteriorate. Pickles stored in a location that is too warm will also tend to turn soft.

Wait at least a month before opening most types of pickles or relishes to allow the flavors to fully develop. Whole cucumber pickles may take between 4 and 6 months for the vinegar syrup to penetrate to the center of the cucumbers, for the seasonings to blend and be absorbed evenly into the pickles and for the vinegar flavor to mellow.

Never use a jar of pickles that shows any kind of spoilage. If the liquid in the jar is murky and cloudy or if the liquid effervesces and bubbles rise to the top of the jar, do not eat the pickles. These are indications of spoilage, yeast formation or bacterial contamination. Slimy pickles or those that give off an unusual or unpleasant odor should be disposed of without tasting. Boil both the jar and its contents, then carefully dispose of the contents so that no human or animal will accidentally eat them.

Dilled Asparagus

Pickled asparagus has become a popular favorite to add to relish trays and serve at parties and is available in upscale gourmet and specialty food stores. When asparagus is plentiful, create your own elegant pickles using this simple and delicious recipe.

MAKES ABOUT 4 PINT JARS

4 pounds fresh tender ¼-inch-diameter
    asparagus spears
2½ cups white wine vinegar
2½ cups distilled water
2 teaspoons pickling salt or kosher salt
4 cloves garlic, peeled
4 sprigs fresh dill
12 whole black peppercorns

Gently rinse the asparagus 2 to 3 times in cool, clear water to remove any sand or dirt. Drain well. Cut the spears into 4-inch-long pieces.

Fill a 4-quart pan about half full of water. Over medium-high heat, bring the water to a simmer. Place a handful of asparagus spears into the water and blanch for 1 minute. Remove the asparagus spears from the pan and immediately plunge them into a large bowl or pan of ice water for 2 minutes to stop the cooking process. Remove the asparagus from the ice water and drain well. Repeat with additional handfuls of asparagus until all of the spears have been blanched. Set aside.

In a 2- to 3-quart stainless steel pan, combine the wine vinegar, distilled water and salt. Stir well to combine. Over medium heat, bring the mixture to a boil. Reduce the heat and keep hot until needed.

Lay hot pint jars on their sides. Place 1 garlic clove along the inside bottom edge of each jar. Arrange 1 sprig of dill, stem end down, against the inside of each jar next to the garlic clove. Add 3 peppercorns to each jar. Pack the asparagus snugly into the jars with the tips pointed up. Stand the jars upright.

Ladle the hot liquid into the jars, covering the asparagus and leaving ½-inch headspace. Using a bubble freer or plastic knife, remove any air bubbles. If necessary, add more liquid to maintain the headspace. Wipe the jar rims and threads with a clean, damp cloth. Cover with hot lids and apply screw rings. Process pint jars in a 180 to 185F (82 to 85C) water bath for 30 minutes.

Baby Beet Pickles

Beets are an easy crop to grow in a home garden, and freshly harvested beets make the best pickles. The young, tender greens can be cooked like spinach or used raw in salads. These beet pickles make a wonderful addition to a green salad or a special treat on a relish tray. The sweet, spicy flavor of the pickled beets is enhanced and brightened by the addition of the raspberry vinegar.

For pickling, only use commercially produced vinegars, never homemade. Vinegar must have a minimum acidity level of 5 percent for safe pickle canning. The acidity level of homemade vinegars cannot be guaranteed.

MAKES ABOUT 6 PINT JARS OR 3 QUART JARS

6 pounds 1- to 1½-inch-diameter baby beets
    (80 to 90 small beets)
3 cups raspberry vinegar
1½ cups distilled white vinegar
2 cups sugar
⅔ cup distilled water
2 teaspoons whole allspice
1½ teaspoons pickling salt or kosher salt
½ cinnamon stick

Cut off the beet greens, leaving 1 inch of the stem. Rinse the beets in cold water and scrub well with a soft brush to remove dirt. Trim the taproot to ½ inch long.

In an 8-quart pan, cook the beets in boiling water, in 4 batches, for 8 to 10 minutes, depending on the size of the beets. Remove the beets from the water and drain. Plunge the beets into a bowl of ice water for 1 minute to stop the cooking process and loosen the skins. Peel the beets, trimming off the stems and taproots.

In an 8-quart stainless steel pan combine the raspberry vinegar, white vinegar, sugar, distilled water, allspice, salt and cinnamon stick. Over medium-low heat, gradually heat the mixture, stirring constantly, until the sugar is completely dissolved. Increase the heat to medium-high and bring the syrup to a boil. Add the peeled beets and simmer for 5 minutes.

Using a slotted spoon, pack the beets into hot jars, leaving ½-inch headspace. Line a sieve with 2 to 3 layers of fine-meshed cheesecloth. Strain the pickling syrup through the sieve. Ladle the hot syrup into the jars, covering the beets and maintaining the ½-inch headspace. Using a bubble freer or plastic knife, remove any air bubbles. If necessary, add more syrup to maintain the headspace. Wipe the jar rims and threads with a clean, damp cloth. Cover with hot lids and apply screw rings. Process both pint and quart jars in a 180 to 185F (82 to 85C) water bath for 30 minutes.

Bread and Butter Pickles

A pickle classic, bread and butter pickles may be served alongside a variety of foods or piled high on hamburgers and sandwiches. This recipe is a variation on one given to me by my aunt, Rosa Lollar.

MAKES ABOUT 6 PINT JARS OR 3 QUART JARS

15 to 18 1- to 1½-inch-diameter firm fresh
    pickling cucumbers
2 to 3 medium onions
½ cup pickling salt or kosher salt
2 to 3 quarts distilled water, chilled
3 cups sugar
2 cups distilled white vinegar
2 cups cider vinegar
2 teaspoons mustard seeds
1 teaspoon celery seeds
1 teaspoon ground turmeric

Using a soft vegetable brush, gently scrub the cucumbers, being careful not to scratch the peel. Rinse the cucumbers 2 to 3 times in cool water, changing the water after each rinsing. Drain well. Cut the cucumbers into ¼-inch slices, discarding the blossom and stem ends. Measure 2 quarts sliced cucumbers.

Peel the onions and cut into ¼-inch slices. Cut the slices into quarters. Measure 1 quart onion slices.

In a large bowl, layer the cucumber and onion slices, sprinkling salt between each layer. Add enough of the cold distilled water to completely cover the vegetables. Let stand for 2 hours.

Drain the salt water from the vegetables. Rinse the vegetables thoroughly with cold water to remove all of the salt. Drain well.

In an 8-quart stainless steel pan, combine the sugar, white vinegar, cider vinegar, mustard seeds, celery seeds and turmeric. Over medium-low heat, gradually heat the mixture, stirring constantly, until the sugar is completely dissolved. Increase the heat to medium-high and bring the syrup to a boil. Add the drained vegetables to the syrup and heat for 3 minutes. Remove the pan from the heat.

Ladle the hot vegetables into hot jars, leaving ½-inch headspace. Ladle the syrup into the jars, covering the vegetables and maintaining the ½-inch headspace. Using a bubble freer or plastic knife, remove any air bubbles. If necessary, add more syrup to maintain the headspace. Wipe the jar rims and threads with a clean, damp cloth. Cover with hot lids and apply screw rings. Process both pint and quart jars in a 180 to 185F (82 to 85C) water bath for 30 minutes.

Carrot Pickles

Tasty carrot pickles make a pleasant change from traditional cucumber pickles. Commercial peeled "baby" carrots, which are actually made from small pieces of large carrots, make very nice, easy pickles using this recipe also. If you prefer, you can make carrot pickle chips by cutting large, peeled carrots into ¼-inch-thick slices.

MAKES ABOUT 4 PINT JARS

2½ pounds 4-inch baby carrots, trimmed
    and peeled,
2½ cups white wine vinegar
2½ cups distilled water
½ cup sugar
2 teaspoons pickling salt or kosher salt

4 cloves garlic, peeled (optional)

4 fresh dill sprigs

12 whole black peppercorns

In a 6- to 8-quart pan over medium-high heat, cook the carrots in simmering water for 5 minutes. Remove the carrots from the pan and drain. Immediately plunge the carrots into a large bowl or pan of ice water for 3 minutes to stop the cooking process. Remove from the water and drain well. Set aside.

In a 2- to 3-quart stainless steel pan, combine the wine vinegar, distilled water, sugar and salt. Over medium-low heat, gradually heat the mixture, stirring constantly, until the sugar is completely dissolved. Increase the heat to medium-high and bring the syrup to a boil. Reduce the heat and keep the syrup hot until needed.

Lay hot pint jars on their sides. Place 1 garlic clove along the inside bottom edge of each jar. Arrange 1 dill sprig, stem end down, against the inside of each jar next to the garlic clove. Add 3 peppercorns to each jar. Pack the carrots snugly into the jars, with the stem end at the top of the jar. Stand the jars upright.

Ladle the hot syrup into the jars, covering the carrots and leaving 1/2-inch headspace. Using a bubble freer or plastic knife, remove any air bubbles. If necessary, add more syrup to maintain the headspace. Wipe the jar rims and threads with a clean, damp cloth. Cover with hot lids and apply screw rings. Process pint jars in a 180 to 185F (82 85C) water bath for 30 minutes.

Cauliflower and Onion Pickles

Trim the cauliflower well, removing the woody stalk. The cauliflower heads may be broken by hand or cut into florets.

MAKES ABOUT 6 PINT JARS OR 3 QUART JARS

3 quarts 1-inch cauliflower florets

2 cups peeled pearl onions

1/4 cup pickling salt or kosher salt

4 cups ice cubes

3 cups white wine vinegar

1 cup distilled water

1 1/2 cups sugar

1 tablespoon mustard seeds

1 teaspoon turmeric

In a large bowl, layer the cauliflower and onions, sprinkling salt between each layer. Gently stir until well combined. Spread the ice cubes over top of the vegetables. Let stand for 3 to 4 hours.

Drain the water from the vegetables. Rinse the vegetables thoroughly with cold water to remove as much of the salt as possible. Drain well.

In an 8-quart stainless steel pan, combine the wine vinegar, distilled water, sugar, mustard seeds and turmeric. Over medium-low heat, gradually heat the mixture, stirring constantly, until the sugar is completely dissolved. Increase the heat to medium-high and bring the syrup to a boil. Add the drained vegetables to the syrup and simmer for 5 minutes. Remove the pan from the heat.

Ladle the vegetables into hot jars, leaving 1/2-inch headspace. Ladle the syrup into the jars, covering the vegetables and maintaining 1/2-inch headspace. Using a bubble freer or plastic knife, remove any air bubbles. If necessary, add more syrup to maintain the headspace. Wipe the jar rims and threads with a clean, damp cloth. Cover with hot lids and apply screw rings. Process both pint and quart jars in a 180 to 185F (82 to 85C) water bath for 30 minutes.

Crunchy Dill Pickles

Select cucumbers that are about 1 inch in diameter, and make pickles within 24 hours of harvesting. If using fat cucumbers, slice them in half lengthwise after brining and rinsing.

MAKES ABOUT 6 PINT JARS OR 3 QUART JARS

7 pounds 4-inch-long firm fresh pickling
    cucumbers (about 30)
3 quarts distilled water
½ cup pickling salt or kosher salt
3 cups distilled white vinegar
¾ cup sugar
2 teaspoons dill seeds
1 teaspoon mustard seeds
1 teaspoon celery seeds
1 teaspoon coriander seeds
1 teaspoon whole black peppercorns
18 sprigs fresh dill

Using a soft vegetable brush, gently scrub the cucumbers to remove all dirt or sand, being careful not to scratch the peel. Rinse the cucumbers 2 to 3 times in cool water, changing the water after each rinsing. Drain well. Using a sharp paring knife, remove an ⅛-inch slice from the blossom end of each cucumber. Place the cucumbers in a large container or crock.

In a 4-quart pan over medium heat, heat the distilled water until warm. Add the salt and stir until completely dissolved. Remove the pan from the heat. Pour the brine over the cucumbers. Use a gallon-size water-filled zipper storage bag or a plate to weigh down the cucumbers. Be sure the cucumbers are completely submerged in the brine and that no air pockets are trapped under the weight. Let the cucumbers soak for 24 hours.

Drain the cucumbers and rinse well. Rinse the container or crock to remove any salt. Return the cucumbers to the container and cover the cucumbers with cold water. Let soak for 20 minutes. Drain the cucumbers again and rinse well. Return the cucumbers to the container again and set aside.

In an 8-quart stainless steel pan, combine the vinegar and sugar. Over medium-low heat, gradually heat the mixture, stirring constantly, until the sugar is completely dissolved. Tie the dill seeds, mustard seeds, celery seeds, coriander seeds and peppercorns in a spice bag or a piece of fine-meshed cheesecloth. Add the spice bag to the syrup. Increase the heat to medium-high and bring the syrup to a boil. Boil the syrup for 5 minutes. Remove the pan from the heat and remove the spice bag.

Pour the boiling hot syrup over the cucumbers. Allow the syrup to cool, then place the water-filled storage bag or plate over the cucumbers. Be sure the cucumbers are completely submerged in the syrup and that no air pockets are trapped under the weight. Let the cucumbers soak for 24 hours.

Drain the cucumbers, reserving the syrup. Pack the cucumbers into hot pint or quart jars, leaving ½-inch headspace. Add 3 sprigs of fresh dill to each pint jar, or 6 sprigs of dill to each quart jar.

In a stainless steel pan, heat the syrup to a full boil. Ladle the syrup into the jars, covering the cucumbers and maintaining the ½-inch headspace. Using a bubble freer or plastic knife, remove any air bubbles. If necessary, add more syrup to maintain the headspace. Wipe the jar rims and threads with a clean, damp cloth. Cover with hot lids and apply screw rings. Process both pint and quart jars in a 180 to 185F (82 to 85C) water bath for 30 minutes.

Dilled Green Beans

To create an attractive appearance and for ease in packing the jars, select straight beans that are 5 to 6 inches in length. For a stronger dill flavor, use 2 sprigs of dill per jar. Yellow wax beans may be substituted for the green beans, or use a combination of both and alternate the colors for an eye-catching presentation.

To pack dilled beans family style, cut the beans into 1- to 1½-inch pieces and ladle the beans into the jars, leaving ½-inch headspace.

MAKES ABOUT 4 PINT JARS

2½ pounds straight, young, tender green beans
2½ cups distilled water
1½ cups white wine vinegar
1 cup distilled white vinegar
2 tablespoons pickling salt or kosher salt
4 garlic cloves, peeled
4 (3-inch) sprigs fresh dill
12 whole black peppercorns

Gently rinse the beans 3 to 4 times in cool, clear water to remove any sand or dirt. Change the water between each rinsing. Drain well.

Cut off the stem end of the beans and trim the blossom end, cutting just below the base of the "tail." Measure the beans to 4 inches in length and cut off the excess on the stem end.

Place the beans in an 8-quart pan and cover them with boiling water. Over medium-high heat, bring the water to a boil. Reduce the heat and simmer for 3 minutes. Remove the pan from the heat and drain. Immediately plunge the beans into a large bowl or pan of ice water for 2 minutes to stop the cooking process. Remove the beans from the ice water and drain well. Set aside.

In a 2- to 3-quart stainless steel pan, combine the distilled water, wine vinegar, white vinegar and salt. Stir well to combine. Over medium heat, bring the mixture to a boil. Reduce the heat and keep hot until needed.

Lay hot pint jars on their sides. Place 1 garlic clove along the inside bottom edge of each jar. Arrange 1 sprig of dill, stem end down, against the inside of each jar next to the garlic clove. Add 3 peppercorns to each jar. Pack the beans snugly into the jars, with the stem ends at the bottom of the jar. Stand the jars upright.

Ladle the hot liquid into the jars, covering the beans and leaving ½-inch headspace. Using a bubble freer or plastic knife, remove any air bubbles. If necessary, add more liquid to maintain the headspace. Wipe the jar rims and threads with a clean, damp cloth. Cover with hot lids and apply screw rings. Process pint jars in a 180 to 185F (82 to 85C) water bath for 30 minutes.

Variation

Thyme Beans: Substitute 8 sprigs of thyme for the dill sprigs. Pack 2 sprigs of thyme into each jar. For a stronger thyme flavor, pack 3 sprigs of thyme in each jar.

Kosher Dill Pickles

Garlic gives kosher pickles their distinctive flavor and special zing.

MAKES ABOUT 6 PINT JARS OR 3 QUART JARS

7 pounds 4-inch-long firm fresh pickling cucumbers (about 30)

3 quarts distilled water

½ cup pickling salt or kosher salt

3 cups distilled white vinegar

¾ cup sugar

4 cloves garlic, peeled and sliced or quartered

2 teaspoons dill seeds

1 teaspoon mustard seeds

1 teaspoon celery seeds

1 teaspoon coriander seeds

1 teaspoon whole black peppercorns

18 sprigs fresh dill

6 cloves garlic, peeled

Using a soft vegetable brush, gently scrub the cucumbers to remove all dirt or sand, being careful not to scratch the peel. Rinse the cucumbers 2 to 3 times in cool water, changing the water after each rinsing. Drain well. Using a sharp par-ing knife, remove an ⅛-inch slice from the blossom end of each cucumber. Place the cucumbers in a large container or crock.

In a 4-quart pan over medium heat, heat the distilled water until warm. Add the salt and stir until completely dissolved. Remove the pan from the heat. Pour the brine over the cucumbers. Use a gallon-size water-filled zipper storage bag or a plate to weigh down the cucumbers. Be sure the cucumbers are completely submerged in the brine and that no air pockets are trapped under the weight. Let the cucumbers soak for 24 hours.

Drain the cucumbers and rinse well. Rinse the container or crock to remove any salt. Return the cucumbers to the container and cover the cucumbers with cold water. Let soak for 20 minutes. Drain the cucumbers again and rinse well. Return the cucumbers to the container again and set aside.

In an 8-quart stainless steel pan, combine the vinegar and sugar. Over medium-low heat, gradually heat the mixture, stirring constantly, until the sugar is completely dissolved. Tie the sliced garlic, dill seeds, mustard seeds, celery seeds, coriander seeds and peppercorns in a spice bag or a piece of fine-meshed cheesecloth. Add the spice bag to the syrup. Increase the heat to medium-high and bring the syrup to a boil. Boil the syrup for 5 minutes. Remove the pan from the heat and remove the spice bag.

Pour the boiling hot syrup over the cucumbers. Allow the syrup to cool, then place the water-filled storage bag or plate over the cucumbers. Be sure the cucumbers are completely submerged in the syrup and that no air pockets are trapped under the weight. Let the cucumbers soak for 24 hours.

Drain the cucumbers, reserving the syrup. Pack the cucumbers into hot pint or quart jars, leaving ½-inch headspace. Add 3 sprigs of fresh dill and 1 clove of garlic to each pint jar, or 6 sprigs of dill and 2 cloves of garlic to each quart jar.

In a stainless steel pan, heat the syrup to a full boil. Ladle the syrup into the jars, covering the cucumbers and maintaining the ½-inch headspace. Using a bubble freer or plastic knife, remove any air bubbles. If necessary, add more syrup to maintain the headspace. Wipe the jar rims and threads with a clean, damp cloth. Cover with hot lids and apply screw rings. Process both pint and quart jars in a 180 to 185F (82 to 85C) water bath for 30 minutes.

Cocktail Onions

Perfect for a relish tray, these onion gems disappear in a hurry.

MAKES ABOUT 4 PINT JARS

2 quarts peeled pearl onions
½ cup pickling salt or kosher salt
6 cups distilled water
5 cups white wine vinegar
1 cup sugar
1 tablespoon peeled and grated fresh
    horseradish or 1½ tablespoons prepared
    horseradish
1 tablespoon mustard seeds
1 tablespoon whole black peppercorns

In a large bowl, layer the onions and the salt. Gently stir until well combined. Add the distilled water. Use a gallon-size water-filled zipper stor-

age bag or a plate to weigh down the onions. Be sure the onions are completely submerged in the brine, adding additional distilled water if necessary, and that no air pockets are trapped under the weight. Let stand for 12 to 14 hours.

Drain the salt water from the onions. Rinse the onions thoroughly with cold water to remove as much of the salt as possible. Drain well.

In a 6- to 8-quart stainless steel pan, combine the wine vinegar, sugar, horseradish, mustard seeds and peppercorns. Over medium-low heat, gradually heat the mixture, stirring constantly, until the sugar is completely dissolved. Increase the heat to medium-high and bring the syrup to a boil. Reduce the heat and simmer the syrup for 5 minutes. Add the drained onions to the syrup and heat for 2 minutes. Remove the pan from the heat.

Pack the hot onions into hot jars, leaving ½-inch headspace. Ladle the hot syrup into the jars, covering the onions and maintaining the ½-inch headspace. Using a bubble freer or plastic knife, remove any air bubbles. If necessary, add more syrup to maintain the headspace. Wipe the jar rims and threads with a clean, damp cloth. Cover with hot lids and apply screw rings. Process pint jars in a 180 to 185F (82 to 85C) water bath for 30 minutes.

Red Onions in Wine Vinegar

These onions are quick to prepare and make a salad special and are great on hamburgers and roast beef sandwiches.

MAKES ABOUT 4 PINT JARS

2½ pounds small red onions, peeled and cut crosswise into ¼-inch slices
4½ cups white wine vinegar
½ cup sugar
1 teaspoon whole black peppercorns

❧ Separate onion slices into rings.

In a 6- to 8-quart stainless steel pan, combine the wine vinegar, sugar and peppercorns. Over medium-low heat, gradually heat the mixture, stirring constantly, until the sugar is completely dissolved. Increase the heat to medium-high and bring the syrup to a boil. Reduce the heat and simmer the syrup for 5 minutes. Add the onion slices to the syrup and heat for 5 minutes. Remove the pan from the heat.

Pack the hot onion slices into hot jars, leaving ½-inch headspace. Ladle the hot syrup into the jars, covering the onions and maintaining the ½-inch headspace. Using a bubble freer or plastic knife, remove any air bubbles. If necessary, add more syrup to maintain the headspace. Wipe the jar rims and threads with a clean, damp cloth. Cover with hot lids and apply screw rings. Process pint jars in a 180 to 185F (82 to 85C) water bath for 30 minutes.

Pickled Hot Peppers

While jalapeño peppers are the most common hot chile pepper used for pickling, any variety of small pepper works well. Watch out for habanero and serrano peppers; they are good, but pure fire! Cascabella peppers are popular on the West Coast and are an excellent choice for pickling. Choose small chile peppers in a variety of colors for a beautiful preserve.

Always wear rubber gloves when handling hot chile peppers to avoid chemical burns from the pepper oils. The small slits made in the peppers allow air to escape and the vinegar mixture to be absorbed, enhancing the flavor and reducing the possibility of the peppers floating in the jars.

MAKES ABOUT 4 PINT JARS

2¼ pounds jalapeño chile peppers or small mixed chile peppers
2 cups distilled white vinegar
1 cup white wine vinegar
2 cups distilled water
4 cloves garlic, chopped
1 teaspoon salt

❧ Rinse the jalapeño peppers in cool water and drain well. Trim the stems to ¼ inch long. Using a sharp paring knife, make 2 small, ½- to 1-inch slits in each pepper, one on either side of the pepper. Be careful not to cut the peppers in half.

In a 2- to 3-quart stainless steel pan, combine the white vinegar, wine vinegar, distilled water, garlic and salt. Over medium-high heat, bring the mixture to a boil. Reduce the heat and simmer the mixture for 5 minutes. Remove the pan from the heat.

Line a sieve with 2 layers of fine-meshed cheesecloth. Strain the hot vinegar mixture through the cheesecloth. Discard the garlic. Return the mixture to the pan and keep hot until needed.

Pack the chile peppers into hot jars, leaving ½-inch headspace. Ladle the hot liquid into the jars, covering the peppers and maintaining the ½-inch headspace. Using a bubble freer or plastic knife, remove any air bubbles. If necessary, add more liquid to maintain the headspace. Wipe the jar rims and threads with a clean, damp cloth. Cover with hot lids and apply screw rings. Process pint jars in a 180 to 185F (82 to 85C) water bath for 30 minutes.

Sweet Pickles

Sweet pickle fans will be in heaven with these little gems. They are perfect for snacks, relish trays and eating straight from the jar.

These pickles take several steps and a few days to prepare but are worth the effort. The gradual increase of the sugar level in the syrup will prevent the pickles from shriveling and floating in the jars.

MAKES 6 TO 7 PINT JARS

4 quarts 2- to 2½-inch-long firm fresh
    pickling cucumbers (about 4 to 5 pounds)
3 quarts distilled water
½ cup pickling salt or kosher salt
2½ cups cider vinegar, divided use
2½ cups distilled white vinegar, divided use
6½ cups sugar, divided use
3 teaspoons mustard seeds
2 teaspoons celery seeds
½ teaspoon coriander seeds

½ teaspoon dill seeds
12 whole black peppercorns

Using a soft vegetable brush, gently scrub the cucumbers to remove all dirt or sand, being careful not to scratch the peel. Rinse the cucumbers 2 to 3 times in cool water, changing the water after each rinsing. Drain well. Using a sharp paring knife, remove an ⅛-inch slice from the blossom end of each cucumber. Place the cucumbers in a large container or crock.

In a 4-quart pan over medium heat, heat the distilled water until warm. Add the salt and stir until completely dissolved. Remove the pan from the heat. Pour the brine over the cucumbers. Use a gallon-size water-filled zipper storage bag or a plate to weigh down the cucumbers. Be sure the cucumbers are completely submerged in the brine and that no air pockets are trapped under the weight. Let the cucumbers soak for 24 hours.

Drain the cucumbers and rinse well. Rinse the container or crock to remove any salt. Return the cucumbers to the container and cover the cucumbers with cold water. Let soak for 20 minutes. Drain the cucumbers again and rinse well. Prick each cucumber 3 to 4 times with a fork. Return the cucumbers to the container again and set aside.

In a 3-quart stainless steel pan, combine 1½ cups of the cider vinegar, 1½ cups of the white vinegar and 3 cups of the sugar. Over medium-low heat, gradually heat the mixture, stirring constantly, until the sugar is completely dissolved. Increase the heat to medium-high and bring the syrup to a boil. Remove the pan from the heat.

Pour the boiling hot syrup over the cucumbers. Allow the syrup to cool, then place the water-filled storage bag or plate over the cucumbers. Be sure the cucumbers are completely submerged in the syrup and that no air pockets are trapped under the weight. Let the cucumbers soak for 6 to 8 hours.

Drain the cucumbers, reserving the syrup. Line a sieve with 2 pieces of fine-meshed cheese-cloth. Strain the syrup through the cheesecloth. Pour syrup into the stainless steel pan. Add the remaining 1 cup cider vinegar, remaining 1 cup white vinegar and 2½ cups of the sugar. Over medium-low heat, gradually heat the mixture, stirring constantly, until the sugar is completely dissolved. Increase the heat to medium-high and bring the syrup to a boil. Remove the pan from the heat.

Pour the boiling hot syrup over the cucumbers. Allow the syrup to cool, then place the water-filled storage bag or plate over the cucumbers. Be sure the cucumbers are completely submerged in the syrup and that no air pockets are trapped under the weight. Let the cucumbers soak for 6 to 8 hours.

Drain the cucumbers, reserving the syrup. Line a sieve with 2 pieces of fine-meshed cheese-cloth. Strain the syrup through the cheesecloth. Pour syrup into the stainless steel pan. Add the remaining 1 cup sugar. Over medium-low heat, gradually heat the syrup, stirring constantly, until the sugar is completely dissolved. Tie the mustard seeds, celery seeds, coriander seeds, dill seeds and peppercorns in a spice bag or a piece of fine-meshed cheesecloth. Add the spice bag to the syrup. Increase the heat to medium-high and bring the syrup to a boil. Remove the pan from the heat.

Pour the boiling hot syrup over the cucumbers. Allow the syrup to cool, then place the water-filled storage bag or plate over the cucumbers. Be sure the cucumbers are completely submerged in

the syrup and that no air pockets are trapped under the weight. Let the cucumbers soak for 6 to 8 hours.

Remove the spice bag from the syrup. Drain the cucumbers, reserving the syrup. Pack the cucumbers into hot pint jars, leaving ½-inch headspace.

In a stainless steel pan, heat the syrup to a full boil. Ladle the syrup into the jars, covering the cucumbers and maintaining the ½-inch head-space. Using a bubble freer or plastic knife, remove any air bubbles. If necessary, add more syrup to maintain the headspace. Wipe the jar rims and threads with a clean, damp cloth. Cover with hot lids and apply screw rings. Process pint jars in a 180 to 185F (82 to 85C) water bath for 30 minutes.

Sweet Pickle Slices

Here is a quick sweet pickle recipe that is easy to prepare.

MAKES ABOUT 6 PINT JARS OR
3 QUART JARS

5 pounds 4-inch-long firm fresh pickling
    cucumbers
⅓ cup pickling salt or kosher salt
2 to 3 quarts distilled water, chilled
7 cups cider vinegar
5 cups sugar
2 tablespoons mustard seeds
1½ teaspoons celery seeds

Using a soft vegetable brush, gently scrub the cucumbers to remove all dirt or sand, being careful not to scratch the peel. Rinse the cucumbers 2 to 3 times in cool water, changing the water after each rinsing. Drain well. Using a sharp paring knife, remove an ⅛-inch slice from both the blossom end and the stem end of each cucumber. Cut the cucumbers into ¼-inch slices.

In a large bowl, layer the cucumber slices and the salt. Add enough of the cold distilled water to completely cover the cucumbers. Let stand for 4 hours.

Drain the salt water from the cucumber slices. Rinse the cucumbers thoroughly with cold water to remove all of the salt. Drain well.

In an 8-quart stainless steel pan, combine the cider vinegar, sugar, mustard seeds and celery seeds. Over medium-low heat, gradually heat the mixture, stirring constantly, until the sugar is completely dissolved. Increase the heat to medium-high and bring the syrup to a boil. Add the drained cucumber slices to the syrup and heat for 2 minutes. Remove the pan from the heat.

Ladle the hot cucumbers into hot jars, leaving ½-inch headspace. Ladle the syrup into the jars, covering the cucumbers and maintaining the ½-inch headspace. Using a bubble freer or plastic knife, remove any air bubbles. If necessary, add more syrup to maintain the headspace. Wipe the jar rims and threads with a clean, damp cloth. Cover with hot lids and apply screw rings. Process both pint and quart jars in a 180 to 185F (82 to 85C) water bath for 30 minutes.

Zucchini Pickles

Pickle zucchini within 24 hours of harvest to prevent soft or hollow pickles. The addition of the bright bell peppers creates colorful jars of preserves, but they may be omitted if you prefer a straight zucchini pickle.

MAKES ABOUT 6 PINT JARS OR
3 QUART JARS

4 pounds 1-inch-diameter firm, fresh
　　unblemished zucchini
2 medium onions
1 medium red bell pepper
1 medium yellow bell pepper
½ cup pickling salt or kosher salt
2 to 3 quarts distilled water, chilled
2⅔ cups sugar
2 cups distilled white vinegar
2 cups cider vinegar
2 teaspoons mustard seeds
1 teaspoon celery seeds
1 teaspoon turmeric

With a soft vegetable brush, gently scrub the zucchini, being careful not to scratch the peel. Rinse the zucchini 2 to 3 times in cool water, changing the water after each rinsing. Drain well. Cut the zucchini into ¼-inch slices, discarding the blossom and stem ends.

Peel the onions and cut into ¼-inch-thick slices. Cut the slices into quarters. Core the bell peppers and remove the seeds and pithy ribs. Cut the peppers into ¼-inch-wide slices, then cut the slices into quarters.

In a large bowl, layer the zucchini, onion and pepper slices, sprinkling salt between each layer. Add enough of the cold distilled water to completely cover the vegetables. Let stand for 2 hours.

Drain the salt water from the vegetables. Rinse the vegetables thoroughly with cold water to remove all of the salt. Drain well.

In an 8-quart stainless steel pan, combine the sugar, white vinegar, cider vinegar, mustard seeds, celery seeds and turmeric. Over medium-low heat, gradually heat the mixture, stirring constantly, until the sugar is completely dissolved. Increase the heat to medium-high and bring the syrup to a boil. Add the drained vegetables to the syrup and heat for 3 minutes. Remove the pan from the heat.

Ladle the hot vegetables into hot jars, leaving ½-inch headspace. Ladle the syrup into the jars, covering the vegetables and maintaining the ½-inch headspace. Using a bubble freer or plastic knife, remove any air bubbles. If necessary, add more syrup to maintain the headspace. Wipe the jar rims and threads with a clean, damp cloth. Cover with hot lids and apply screw rings. Process both pint and quart jars in a 180 to 185F (82 to 85C) water bath for 30 minutes.

German Red Cabbage

Red cabbage is a traditional side dish served in German and Danish homes. Although the flavor is not quite the same, if you prefer white cabbage, it may be substituted for the red with a good white wine vinegar used in place of the red wine vinegar. The cabbage will develop its flavor and be ready to eat after about a month.

MAKES ABOUT 4 PINT JARS OR 2 QUART JARS

5 pounds red cabbage
¼ cup pickling salt or kosher salt
3 cups red wine vinegar
¾ cup sugar
2 tablespoons mustard seeds
2 teaspoons whole black peppercorns
1 teaspoon whole allspice

Remove the outer leaves from the cabbage, trim the stem and remove the core. Shred or slice the cabbage into ⅛-inch-thick strips.

In a large bowl, layer the cabbage and the salt, sprinkling the salt evenly over the cabbage. Cover the bowl with plastic wrap and let stand in a cool, dry place for 18 to 24 hours.

Drain the liquid from the cabbage. Spread the cabbage out on several layers of paper towels. Allow the cabbage to drain for 4 to 6 hours. Change the paper towels if they become soggy.

In a 2-quart stainless steel pan, combine the vinegar and sugar. Over medium-low heat, gradually heat the mixture, stirring constantly, until the sugar is completely dissolved. Tie the mustard seeds, peppercorns and allspice in a spice bag or a piece of fine-meshed cheesecloth. Add the spice bag to the syrup. Increase the heat to medium-high and bring the syrup to a boil. Boil the syrup for 5 minutes. Remove the pan from the heat.

Pack the drained cabbage into hot jars, leaving ½-inch headspace. Remove the spice bag from the syrup. Ladle the syrup into the jars, covering the cabbage and maintaining the ½-inch headspace. Using a bubble freer or plastic knife, remove any air bubbles. If necessary, add more syrup to maintain the headspace. Wipe the jar rims and threads with a clean, damp cloth. Cover with hot lids and apply screw rings. Process both pint and quart jars in a 180 to 185F (82 to 85C) water bath for 30 minutes.

Sweet Cucumber Relish

An excellent relish for hot dogs, the flavor blend in this recipe is neither too sweet nor too spicy.

MAKES ABOUT 4 PINT JARS

6 cups finely chopped pickling cucumbers
2 cups finely chopped onions
3 tablespoons pickling salt or kosher salt
2 to 3 quarts distilled water, chilled
3 cups sugar
2 cups cider vinegar
1½ teaspoons mustard seeds
1½ teaspoons celery seeds

In a large bowl, layer the cucumber and onion, sprinkling salt between each layer. Add enough of the cold distilled water to completely cover the vegetables. Let stand for 2 hours.

Drain the vegetables thoroughly. Press out the excess liquid.

In a 6- to 8-quart stainless steel pan, combine the sugar, vinegar, mustard seeds and celery seeds. Over medium-low heat, gradually heat the mixture, stirring constantly, until the sugar is completely dissolved. Increase the heat to medium-high and bring the syrup to a boil. Add the drained vegetables to the syrup, reduce the heat to medium and simmer for 10 minutes, stirring frequently. Remove the pan from the heat.

Ladle the hot relish into hot jars, leaving ½-inch headspace. Using a bubble freer or plastic knife, remove any air bubbles. If necessary, add more relish to maintain the headspace. Wipe the jar rims and threads with a clean, damp cloth. Cover with hot lids and apply screw rings. Process pint jars in a 212F (100C) water bath for 15 minutes.

Onion Relish

A nice change from cucumber relishes, this condiment gives a unique zest to hot dogs, hamburgers, sandwiches and meats.

MAKES ABOUT 4 PINT JARS

8 cups finely chopped sweet onions
1 tablespoon pickling salt or kosher salt
1¾ cups white wine vinegar
1 cup sugar
1 tablespoon minced fresh tarragon or ¾ teaspoon crushed dried tarragon
2 garlic cloves, crushed or minced

In a large bowl, layer the onions and salt. Gently stir until well combined. Let stand for 4 hours.

Drain the onions thoroughly. Press out the excess liquid.

In a 6- to 8-quart stainless steel pan, combine the vinegar, sugar, tarragon and garlic. Over medium-low heat, gradually heat the mixture, stirring constantly, until the sugar is completely dissolved. Increase the heat to medium-high and bring the syrup to a boil. Add the drained onions to the syrup, reduce the heat to medium and simmer for 10 minutes, stirring frequently. Remove the pan from the heat.

Ladle the hot relish into hot jars, leaving ½-inch headspace. Using a bubble freer or plastic knife, remove any air bubbles. If necessary, add more relish to maintain the headspace. Wipe the jar rims and threads with a clean, damp cloth. Cover with hot lids and apply screw rings. Process pint jars in a 212F (100C) water bath for 15 minutes.

Pepper Relish

I like to use a variety of bell peppers to create a colorful relish, but you can use all red or green bell peppers if you prefer. This relish is good served with meat or on sandwiches or spooned on crackers spread with cream cheese. For a tangier relish, use distilled white vinegar instead of the cider vinegar.

MAKES ABOUT 4 PINT JARS

6 large red bell peppers
3 large green bell peppers
3 large yellow or orange bell peppers
2 medium onions, finely chopped
2 cups cider vinegar
1¼ cups sugar
1 tablespoon pickling salt or kosher salt

Rinse the bell peppers well in cool water and drain. Cut the peppers in half and remove the stems, seeds, white membranes and ribs. Finely chop the peppers.

In a large pan or heatproof bowl, combine the peppers and onions. Add just enough boiling water to cover the vegetables. Let stand for 10 minutes. Drain the vegetables well in a large sieve. Return the vegetables to the pan or bowl and cover again with boiling water. Let stand for 5 minutes. Drain the vegetables again. Allow the vegetables to drain in the sieve for 1 hour.

In a 6- to 8-quart stainless steel pan, combine the vinegar, sugar and salt. Over medium-low heat, gradually heat the mixture, stirring constantly, until the sugar is completely dissolved. Increase the heat to medium-high and bring the syrup to a boil. Add the drained peppers and onions to the syrup, reduce the heat to medium and simmer for 15 minutes, stirring frequently to prevent sticking and scorching. Remove the pan from the heat.

Ladle the hot relish into hot jars, leaving ½-inch headspace. Using a bubble freer or plastic knife, remove any air bubbles. If necessary, add more relish to maintain the headspace. Wipe the jar rims and threads with a clean, damp cloth. Cover with hot lids and apply screw rings. Process pint jars in a 212F (100C) water bath for 15 minutes.

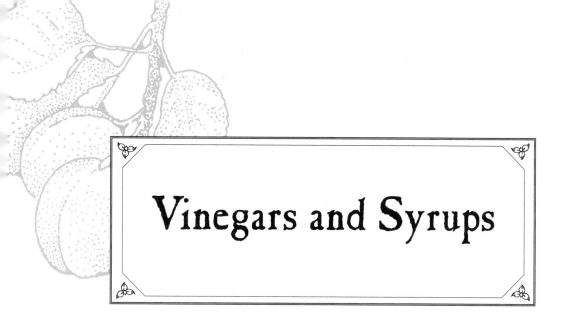

Vinegars and Syrups

Making homemade vinegars has started to gain enormous popularity in the past few years. The wonderful spark these flavored vinegars can add to favorite and specialty dishes is delightful. They can liven up seafood, meats, soups, stews, even fruit and desserts. Add a dash or two of a flavored vinegar to sauces for an extra special zing. Salad dressings made with flavored vinegars are terrific and the variety can be endless. Flavored vinegars are great for marinating meats and chicken, drizzling over vegetables or fish or deglazing a pan when making sauces.

The fancy vinegars found in gourmet and specialty shops command high prices that often keep them out of reach of the average cook. But making your own exotic flavors is really quite simple, easy and inexpensive. By making specialty vinegars at home, you can balance the flavors to meet your personal tastes and individual needs. Create family favorites and exciting new taste combinations. Ranging in flavor from delicate to intense, the use of these vinegars is limited only by your imagination.

The art and idea of making homemade syrups in a variety of flavors is just really starting to catch on in this country. Nothing you can buy in the store can compare to the fresh, fruity sweetness of a homemade syrup. These versatile concoctions can be used for almost everything from turning pancakes, waffles or French toast into something extra special, to adding a zing to your favorite beverage or sparkling water, incorporating them into a special dessert recipe or as a topping for ice cream to create exquisite sundaes.

Displayed in specialty bottles or wrapped with a festive ribbon, vinegars and syrups make welcome gifts. Attach a card with a favorite salad recipe to a lively bottle of vinegar or package a sparkling jar of syrup with a bag of homemade pancake or waffle mix to create a special hostess gift or welcome present for any occasion.

CANNING VINEGARS

Making homemade flavored vinegars is a relatively simple process. Because of the high acid content present in vinegar, which prevents the growth of harmful bacteria, it is not necessary to water bath process homemade vinegars.

Vinegars can be flavored with a wide variety of herbs, spices, flowers, fruit, even vegetables. Flavoring ingredients can be used alone or combined together to create exciting and exotic blends. Different types of base vinegars may be paired with the flavoring ingredients and can be used to create strong or mildly flavored vinegars. The flavor combinations are limited only by your imagination.

Homemade vinegar should never be used for canning pickles or for any other form of food preservation. The acid content of homemade vinegars is usually substantially lower than that of commercially produced vinegars. While this lower acidity is great for cooking, it is not safe for use in other areas of home canning where acid levels must be strictly maintained to ensure food safety. Homemade vinegars can also cause the liquid in jars of home canned pickles to turn cloudy.

Selecting Vinegar Bottles

Decorative, long-necked glass vinegar bottles and cruets can be purchased at import and specialty housewares stores. These may be sealed with tight-fitting corks, screw caps or snug, plastic-lined glass stoppers. Unlike with other types of homemade preserves that must be water bath processed, recycled commercial glass bottles may be used for holding vinegars. Save attractive, clear glass bottles from bottled water, beverages, salad dressings, oils, vinegars, even small wine bottles. Remove the labels and any residual glue that may remain on the outside of the bottles.

Clear bottles are recommended for canning and storing your homemade vinegars because they do not distort the color of the vinegar. Smooth-surfaced bottles without heavy decoration are best. Highly decorated bottles can hide the pretty contents inside. Corks and screw caps should be new, although screw caps may be reused if thoroughly washed and carefully rinsed.

Choosing a Base Vinegar

Many different types of commercial vinegars make excellent bases for homemade flavored vinegars. You can use one type of vinegar alone or blend two or three to achieve your desired effect. Have some fun experimenting and finding the combinations of vinegars and flavorings that you and your family like best.

Always choose a high-quality commercial vinegar with an acidity level of 5 to 6 percent. Never use a homemade vinegar as the base for a flavored vinegar. The acidity level of homemade vinegars is unknown and may be too low for safe preparation and preservation without contamination. While homemade vinegars are perfectly safe to eat and use in cooking, they are not strong enough to use as a preservative in other areas of home canning.

Suggested Vinegar Combinations

Here are some vinegars and their suggested flavor pairings to help get you started.

Chinese Rice Vinegar:

This mild, sweet vinegar is the perfect base for a homemade fruit vinegar. Try fruit vinegars on salads, fresh fruit or in dessert sauces for an added zing.

Red Wine Vinegar:

Stronger in flavor than white wine vinegar, it blends well with herbs, especially rosemary, garlic, onions and black pepper. Flavored red wine vinegars makes an excellent addition to soups, stews, meats and salad dressings.

Sherry Vinegar:

Stronger and less sweet than rice vinegar, sherry vinegar has a slightly nutty flavor. Herb vinegars, such as tarragon or thyme, made with a sherry vinegar base complement chicken dishes as well as tomato or cream soups and sauces.

White Wine Vinegar:

An excellent choice for fruit and mild herb vinegars, its delicate flavor will not overpower the fruit. Flavored white wine vinegar is perfect for salads, sauces and seafood dishes.

Balsamic Vinegar:

A traditional Italian vinegar, balsamic vinegar is dark and earthy. It is great for use with red meats or in stews but is too intense for use in making homemade flavored vinegars. Its strong flavor masks the taste of even the most pungent flavorings, such as rosemary, and garlic.

The following types of vinegars are not recommended as bases for flavored vinegars.

Cider Vinegar:

Although made from apples, the flavor of cider vinegar is too strong and masks the flavors of the other ingredients.

Distilled White Vinegar:

White vinegar is the most common of all of the vinegar types. While it is perfect for making pickles, it is far too intense and overpowering to use as a base for homemade flavored vinegars.

Herbs and Seasonings

The flavors of homemade vinegars can be anywhere from mild to strong depending on how long the fruit, herbs, spices or other seasonings are left in the vinegar to steep before straining and bottling the vinegar. The strength of the flavor is a matter of personal choice. Fair judges like clear, intensely flavored vinegars that pack a strong taste of the fruit or herbs without being overpowered by the vinegar. Sample the vinegar periodically as it steeps. When it achieves the intensity of flavor that you desire, remove the seasonings and filter, bottle and seal the vinegar.

To attain the fullest flavor, herbs should be used as soon after harvesting or purchasing as possible. If you have an herb garden, harvest the herbs early in the day when they contain the most moisture and are at their best. Herbs that are about ready to flower have the most intense flavor. This is the ideal time to use them for making vinegars and other homemade preserves. Dried herbs should not be used to make flavored vinegars. Their flavorful oils have been dried during processing and will not yield as satisfactory a flavor. Dried herbs will also produce a cloudy vinegar filled with fine sediment.

As with herbs, fruit should be used as close to harvest time as possible. If additional ripening is necessary, keep a close eye on the fruit and make the vinegar as soon as the fruit reaches full ripeness. Fruit used to make flavored vinegars should be fully ripe, fresh and free of bruising or any other signs of spoilage. Unsweetened frozen berries, raspberries, blueberries, blackberries and boysenberries produce very flavorful vinegars. Most other frozen fruits are packed and frozen slightly underripe and are not recommended for vinegar-making, as they will yield a vinegar with a very mild, sometimes indistinguishable flavor.

Making Herb Vinegars

Carefully rinse the fresh herbs several times in cool, clean water, being sure to remove all dirt, sand and grit. Gently pat the herbs dry between several layers of paper towels. Carefully remove the leaves from the stems. Discard the stems, as they can give the vinegar a bitter taste. Measure the quantity of herbs indicated in the recipe. Chop large or straight leaves, such as basil, tarragon or rosemary, or crush small leaves, such as thyme, to release their flavorful oils. Place the herbs in a large, clean glass jar, 1 to 2 quarts in size. A glass fruit juice jar or a mayonnaise jar both work well for this purpose. While a wide-mouthed jar makes it easier to add the herbs, a jar with a narrower opening may be used with a little more patience.

Heat the vinegar in a stainless steel pan until hot but still below simmering. Do not permit the vinegar to boil. Pour the hot vinegar over the herbs in the jar. To prevent corrosion of a metal lid or screw ring, cover the jar with plastic wrap before screwing on the lid or ring. Set the jar in a cool, dark place and let the mixture steep. Gently shake or swirl the jar every few days to blend the flavors.

Start tasting the vinegar after about 2 weeks. If you would like the vinegar to have a stronger flavor, wait another week and sample the vinegar again. Most herb vinegars will take from 2 to 6 weeks to develop their full flavor, depending on the intensity of the variety of herbs used and when they were harvested.

Making Fruit Vinegars

Rinse the fresh fruit in clear, cool water. Drain and gently pat dry with paper towels. Frozen berries should not be rinsed before using. Defrost the berries and lightly crush them, retaining all of the juice. Peel and pit fruit that contains large seeds, then chop it into small pieces and lightly crush. Measure the fruit and any juice and place it in a clean glass jar, 1 to 2 quarts in size.

Heat the vinegar in a stainless steel pan until hot but still below simmering. Do not permit the vinegar to boil. Pour the hot vinegar over the fruit in the jar. To prevent corrosion of a metal lid or screw ring, cover the jar with plastic wrap before screwing on the lid or ring. Set the jar in a cool, dark place and let the mixture steep. Gently shake or swirl the jar every few days to blend the flavors.

Start tasting the vinegar after about 2 weeks. If you would like a vinegar with a stronger flavor, wait another week and sample the vinegar again. Most fruit vinegars will take from 2 to 4 weeks to develop their full flavor, depending on the type and ripeness of the fruit used.

Filtering the Vinegar and Filling the Jars

When the vinegar has reached the desired strength, remove the herb leaves or fruit pulp by pouring the mixture through a sieve. Then line the sieve with 3 layers of clean, damp cheesecloth and strain the vinegar again. To clarify the liquid, strain the vinegar through a sieve lined with 2 layered paper coffee filters. Pour the vinegar into a clean container, cover and let the vinegar stand overnight to allow any sediment to settle to the bottom of the container. Slowly pour the vinegar again through a sieve lined with 2 layered coffee filters, being careful not to disturb any of the sediment on the bottom of the container.

The bottles in which the vinegar will be canned should always be washed in hot, soapy water and thoroughly rinsed in hot water to remove all soap residue. The clean bottles should be filled with boiling water and allowed to stand for 10 minutes. Just before bottling the vinegar, empty out the water and turn the bottles upside down to drain.

Using a funnel, pour the vinegar into the prepared bottles. Depending on the type of closure you are using, allow about ½ inch of headspace between the vinegar and the top of the bottle or between the vinegar and the bottom of the cork. Seal each bottle with a new cork or screw cap.

For an eye-catching decorative touch, add a few small sprigs of fresh herbs, pieces of fruit or other seasonings to the bottles before filling them with the vinegar. Always use fresh, clean herbs or fruit for this purpose. Do not use the chopped or crushed flavoring pieces that were used in steeping the vinegar, as they will have lost both their flavor and their fresh, attractive appearance.

Garlic cloves added to bottles of vinegar as an accent should be peeled and whole, without any blemishes, cuts or dings. Cut edges on garlic can react with the vinegar and oxidize, turning bright blue or pink after only a short time in the bottles. While this color change is not harmful, it may be viewed as unattractive and raise an eyebrow or two by the recipient if given as a gift. Oxidized garlic is also seen as a sign of poor technique and may cause reduced scores from some fair judges. To prevent the occurrence of oxidation, peel perfect cloves of garlic by hand. Do not use a knife, as it may accidentally nick the garlic, and do not cut off the bottom of the clove.

Storing Vinegars

As with other preserved foods, store your finished vinegars in a cool, dark location. While it may be tempting to keep an array of decorative flavored vinegars displayed in your kitchen window where they will catch the light and be on view for all visitors to see, light and heat are the worst enemies of vinegars, or any other preserves for that matter. They will rob your creations of flavor and color, undoing all of your careful and creative efforts. It is better to keep the vinegars stored away in the dark and bring them out only for use. If you want to show them off for your friends, bring the bottles out before your guests arrive, then quickly store them away again as soon as they leave.

CANNING SYRUPS

Homemade syrup served over hot pancakes, waffles or French toast is a great way to start off the day. It also makes a welcome surprise and delightful taste-treat for special visitors. Be careful though, as some thoughtless guests may not fully appreciate your efforts, use excessive amounts of your special creations and leave puddles of unused syrup on their plates. Others may enjoy it so much that they forget their manners and clean you out of syrup.

Syrups can also be used as flavorings in homemade milk shakes or added to sparkling water for a refreshing beverage. They can be spooned over ice cream, cottage cheese and yogurt or drizzled on cheesecakes, pound cakes, fresh fruit or just about anything else you can think of.

Preparing Ingredients

There are two basic methods used to extract the juice from the fruit when making homemade syrups. Some types of fruit will need to be combined with sugar and allowed to stand for several hours or overnight to release their juice. Others will require a process that is basically the same as that used for extracting juice to make jelly, where the fruit is first crushed and then heated to release the juice. Instructions for the specific method of fruit preparation are given in each recipe.

After the juice has been extracted from the fruit, it should be strained through a sieve to remove any seeds and excess pulp. For a clearer syrup, the juice should be strained through a sieve lined with three layers of clean, damp cheesecloth to remove the fine pulp. For very clear syrup, after straining the juice through the cheese-cloth, filter it though a sieve lined with a paper coffee filter.

Filtering the juice is recommended if you are planning to enter your syrup in a fair competition, as judges usually give higher scores to clear syrups. Syrups thick with fruit pulp are great for family use, but judges prefer clear syrups for their smooth texture. Apricot syrup, with its fine pulp, is an exception to this rule. As with jelly-making, a clear syrup demonstrates a higher skill level of the home canner and shows that more care was taken to preparing the syrup.

Making Syrups

In order for a syrup to thicken properly and not be too thin, it should contain equal parts of juice and sugar. This may sound like a lot of sugar, but it is actually a substantially lower ratio of sugar to fruit than that contained in most of the commercial syrups you buy in the store. Sugar helps to thicken the juices during cooking and also works as a natural preservative.

You may reduce the amount of sugar called for in the recipe if you don't mind a thin syrup that runs all over your plate. Cooking the juice and smaller quantity of sugar for a longer period of time to reduce the juice and thicken the syrup is not recommended, as the syrup will develop an off flavor from overcooking. Any syrup that you plan to enter at a fair should be made with the full amount of sugar, or points will be knocked off for the syrup being too thin.

Heat the juice and the sugar over low heat until the sugar is completely dissolved. Only after the sugar is completely dissolved should the mixture be brought to a boil. Crystallization is a common occurrence in syrups when the juice and sugar are brought to a boil before the sugar has been completely dissolved. Any sign of sugar crystals in a syrup will cause a dramatic reduction in the points given by a fair judge.

Do not cook a syrup for longer than the amount of time indicated in the recipe or you run the risk of creating a thin jelly rather than a thick syrup. While trying to reduce the liquid by cooking it longer, some of the pectin in the fruit may start to set. The quantity of sugar may prevent the syrup from completely turning into jelly, but you could easily end up with a lumpy syrup. Also, syrups that are cooked too long tend to develop an unpleasant and overcooked flavor.

Basil Vinegar

The flavor of this vinegar makes it a wonderful addition to tomato soups, pasta sauces, chicken and salads.

MAKES ABOUT 4 (8-OUNCE) BOTTLES OR
2 (16-OUNCE) BOTTLES

1¼ cups lightly packed fresh basil leaves
1 garlic clove, sliced (optional)
4 cups white wine vinegar

Rinse the basil leaves 2 to 3 times in cool, clean water to remove any dirt or sand. Change the water between each rinsing. Gently pat the herbs dry between several layers of paper towels. Chop the basil leaves to release their flavorful oils.

Place the chopped basil leaves and the garlic, if desired, in a 1½- to 2-quart clean glass jar.

In a medium stainless steel saucepan over low heat, heat the vinegar until hot but still below simmering. Do not allow the vinegar to boil. Remove the pan from the heat.

Pour the hot vinegar over the basil in the jar. Swirl the jar to gently mix the ingredients, then set aside to cool. When the mixture is cool, cover the jar opening with 2 layers of plastic wrap, then screw on the jar lid or a screw ring. Place the jar in a paper bag and set it in a cool, dry, dark location and let the mixture steep for 2 weeks. Gently shake or swirl the jar every few days to blend the flavors.

Start tasting the vinegar after about 2 weeks. If you would like a vinegar with a stronger flavor, wait another week and sample the vinegar again. The vinegar will take from 2 to 4 weeks to develop its full flavor.

When the vinegar has reached the desired strength, place a fine-meshed sieve over a bowl or pan and strain the vinegar. Discard the herbs. Rinse the sieve and line it with 3 layers of clean, damp cheesecloth. Strain the vinegar through the cheesecloth. Line the sieve with a paper coffee filter and strain the vinegar again. Pour the vinegar into a clean container, cover and let stand overnight to allow any sediment to settle to the bottom of the container.

Line the sieve with 2 layered paper coffee filters. Slowly pour the vinegar through the sieve, being careful not to disturb any sediment on the bottom of the container.

Wash decorative vinegar bottles in hot, soapy water and rinse well. Fill the bottles with boiling water and allow them to stand for 10 minutes. Just before bottling the vinegar, empty the water out of the bottles and turn them upside down to drain.

Using a funnel, pour the filtered vinegar into the bottles, leaving about ½-inch headspace between the vinegar and the top of the bottle, if using a screw cap, or if using a cork, between the vinegar and the bottom of the cork. Seal each bottle with a new cork or screw cap.

Blackberry Vinegar

This fruity vinegar makes an extra special gift.
MAKES ABOUT 4 (8-OUNCE) BOTTLES OR
2 (16-OUNCE) BOTTLES

4 cups fresh or frozen blackberries, crushed
4 cups rice vinegar

Place the crushed blackberries in a 1½- to 2-quart clean glass jar.

In a medium stainless steel saucepan over low heat, heat the vinegar until hot but still below simmering. Do not allow the vinegar to boil. Remove the pan from the heat.

Pour the hot vinegar over the fruit in the jar. Swirl the jar to gently mix the ingredients, then set aside to cool. When the mixture is cool, cover the jar opening with 2 layers of plastic wrap, then screw on the jar lid or a screw ring. Place the jar in a paper bag and set it in a cool, dry, dark location and let the mixture steep for 2 weeks. Gently shake or swirl the jar every few days to blend the flavors.

Start tasting the vinegar after about 2 weeks. If you would like a vinegar with a stronger flavor, wait another week and sample the vinegar again. The vinegar will take from 2 to 4 weeks to develop its full flavor, depending on the ripeness of the fruit used.

When the vinegar has reached the desired strength, place a fine-meshed sieve over a bowl or pan and strain the vinegar. Discard the seeds and pulp. Rinse the sieve and line it with 3 layers of clean, damp cheesecloth. Strain the vinegar through the cheesecloth. Line the sieve with a paper coffee filter and strain the vinegar again. Pour the vinegar into a clean container, cover and let stand overnight to allow any sediment to settle to the bottom of the container.

Line the sieve with 2 layered paper coffee filters. Slowly pour the vinegar through the sieve, being careful not to disturb any sediment on the bottom of the container.

Wash decorative vinegar bottles in hot, soapy water and rinse well. Fill the bottles with boiling water and allow them to stand for 10 minutes. Just before bottling the vinegar, empty the water out of the bottles and turn them upside down to drain.

Using a funnel, pour the filtered vinegar into the bottles, leaving about ½-inch headspace between the vinegar and the top of the bottle, if using a screw cap, or if using a cork, between the vinegar and the bottom of the cork. Seal each bottle with a new cork or screw cap.

Blueberry Vinegar

This is a pleasant vinegar with a strong berry flavor.
MAKES ABOUT 4 (8-OUNCE) BOTTLES OR
2 (16-OUNCE) BOTTLES

3 cups fresh or frozen blueberries, crushed
4 cups rice vinegar

Place the crushed blueberries in a 1½- to 2-quart clean glass jar.

In a medium stainless steel saucepan over low heat, heat the vinegar until hot but still below simmering. Do not allow the vinegar to boil. Remove the pan from the heat.

Pour the hot vinegar over the fruit in the jar. Swirl the jar to gently mix the ingredients, then set aside to cool. When the mixture is cool, cover the jar opening with 2 layers of plastic wrap, then screw on the jar lid or a screw ring. Place the jar in a paper bag and set it in a cool, dry, dark location and let the mixture steep for 2 weeks. Gently shake or swirl the jar every few days to blend the flavors.

Start tasting the vinegar after about 2 weeks. If you would like a vinegar with a stronger flavor, wait another week and sample the vinegar again. The vinegar will take from 2 to 4 weeks to develop its full flavor, depending on the ripeness of the fruit used.

When the vinegar has reached the desired strength, place a fine-meshed sieve over a bowl or pan and strain the vinegar. Discard the seeds and pulp. Rinse the sieve and line it with 3 layers of clean, damp cheesecloth. Strain the vinegar through the cheesecloth. Line the sieve with a paper coffee filter and strain the vinegar again. Pour the vinegar into a clean container, cover and let stand overnight to allow any sediment to settle to the bottom of the container.

Line the sieve with 2 layered paper coffee filters. Slowly pour the vinegar through the sieve, being careful not to disturb any sediment on the bottom of the container.

Wash decorative vinegar bottles in hot, soapy water and rinse well. Fill the bottles with boiling water and allow them to stand for 10 minutes. Just before bottling the vinegar, empty the water out of the bottles and turn them upside down to drain.

Using a funnel, pour the filtered vinegar into the bottles, leaving about ½-inch headspace between the vinegar and the top of the bottle, if using a screw cap, or if using a cork, between the vinegar and the bottom of the cork. Seal each bottle with a new cork or screw cap.

Cranberry Vinegar

The tangy cranberry flavor of this vinegar gives a special zing to fruit dishes, salads and even desserts.

**MAKES ABOUT 4 (8-OUNCE) BOTTLES OR
2 (16-OUNCE) BOTTLES**

**3 cups cranberries, coarsely chopped
4 cups rice vinegar**

Place the chopped cranberries in a 1½- to 2-quart clean glass jar.

In a medium stainless steel saucepan over low heat, heat the vinegar until hot but still below simmering. Do not allow the vinegar to boil. Remove the pan from the heat.

Pour the hot vinegar over the fruit in the jar. Swirl the jar to gently mix the ingredients, then set aside to cool. When the mixture is cool, cover the jar opening with 2 layers of plastic wrap, then screw on the jar lid or a screw ring. Place the jar in a paper bag and set it in a cool, dry, dark location and let the mixture steep for 2 weeks. Gently shake or swirl the jar every few days to blend the flavors.

Start tasting the vinegar after about 2 weeks. If you would like a vinegar with a stronger flavor, wait another week and sample the vinegar again. The vinegar will take from 2 to 4 weeks to develop its full flavor, depending on the ripeness of the fruit used.

When the vinegar has reached the desired strength, place a fine-meshed sieve over a bowl or pan and strain the vinegar. Discard the seeds and pulp. Rinse the sieve and line it with 3 layers of clean, damp cheesecloth. Strain the vinegar through the cheesecloth. Line the sieve with a paper coffee filter and strain the vinegar again. Pour the vinegar into a clean container, cover and let stand overnight to allow any sediment to settle to the bottom of the container.

Line the sieve with 2 layered paper coffee filters. Slowly pour the vinegar through the sieve, being careful not to disturb any sediment on the bottom of the container.

Wash decorative vinegar bottles in hot, soapy water and rinse well. Fill the bottles with boiling water and allow them to stand for 10 minutes. Just before bottling the vinegar, empty the water out of the bottles and turn them upside down to drain.

Using a funnel, pour the filtered vinegar into the bottles, leaving about ½-inch headspace between the vinegar and the top of the bottle, if using a screw cap, or if using a cork, between the vinegar and the bottom of the cork. Seal each bottle with a new cork or screw cap.

Garlic Vinegar

The wonderful flavor of garlic makes this vinegar a great addition to meats, sauces and stews. For variety, and depending on your intended use, this recipe may also be made using all white wine vinegar or all red wine vinegar.

MAKES ABOUT 4 (8-OUNCE) BOTTLES OR
2 (16-OUNCE) BOTTLES

2 large heads of garlic (about 35 cloves)
2 cups white wine vinegar
2 cups red wine vinegar

Clean and peel the garlic cloves. Slice or coarsely chop the garlic.

Place the garlic in a 1½- to 2-quart clean glass jar.

In a medium stainless steel saucepan over low heat, heat the wine vinegars until hot but still below simmering. Do not allow the vinegar to boil. Remove the pan from the heat.

Pour the hot vinegar over the garlic in the jar. Swirl the jar to gently mix the ingredients, then set aside to cool. When the mixture is cool, cover the jar opening with 2 layers of plastic wrap, then screw on the jar lid or a screw ring. Place the jar in a paper bag and set it in a cool, dry, dark location and let the mixture steep for 2 weeks. Gently shake or swirl the jar every few days to blend the flavors.

Start tasting the vinegar after about 2 weeks. If you would like a vinegar with a stronger flavor, wait another week and sample the vinegar again. The vinegar will take from 2 to 4 weeks to develop its full flavor.

When the vinegar has reached the desired strength, place a fine-meshed sieve over a bowl or pan and strain the vinegar. Discard the pulp. Rinse the sieve and line it with 3 layers of clean, damp cheesecloth. Strain the vinegar through the cheesecloth. Line the sieve with a paper coffee filter and strain the vinegar again. Pour the vinegar into a clean container, cover and let stand overnight to allow any sediment to settle to the bottom of the container.

Line the sieve with 2 layered paper coffee filters. Slowly pour the vinegar through the sieve, being careful not to disturb any sediment on the bottom of the container.

Wash decorative vinegar bottles in hot, soapy water and rinse well. Fill the bottles with boiling water and allow them to stand for 10 minutes. Just before bottling the vinegar, empty the water out of the bottles and turn them upside down to drain.

Using a funnel, pour the filtered vinegar into the bottles, leaving about ½-inch headspace between the vinegar and the top of the bottle, if using a screw cap, or if using a cork, between the vinegar and the bottom of the cork. Seal each bottle with a new cork or screw cap.

Asian Ginger Vinegar

This vinegar is perfect for adding flavor to Asian dishes, steamed vegetables, fresh fruit and rice.

MAKES ABOUT 4 (8-OUNCE) BOTTLES OR
2 (16-OUNCE) BOTTLES

2 cups peeled and thinly sliced fresh ginger
Zest of 1 lemon
4 cups rice vinegar

Place the sliced ginger and lemon zest in a 1½- to 2-quart clean glass jar.

In a medium stainless steel saucepan over low heat, heat the vinegar until hot but still below simmering. Do not allow the vinegar to boil. Remove the pan from the heat.

Pour the hot vinegar over the ginger and lemon zest in the jar. Swirl the jar to gently mix the ingredients, then set aside to cool. When the mixture is cool, cover the jar opening with 2 layers of plastic wrap, then screw on the jar lid or a screw ring. Place the jar in a paper bag and set it in a cool, dry, dark location and let the mixture steep for 2 weeks. Gently shake or swirl the jar every few days to blend the flavors.

Start tasting the vinegar after about 2 weeks. If you would like a vinegar with a stronger flavor, wait another week and sample the vinegar again. The vinegar will take from 2 to 4 weeks to develop its full flavor.

When the vinegar has reached the desired strength, place a fine-meshed sieve over a bowl or pan and strain the vinegar. Discard the pulp. Rinse the sieve and line it with 3 layers of clean, damp cheesecloth. Strain the vinegar through the cheesecloth. Line the sieve with a paper coffee filter and strain the vinegar again. Pour the vinegar into a clean container, cover and let stand overnight to allow any sediment to settle to the bottom of the container.

Line the sieve with 2 layered paper coffee filters. Slowly pour the vinegar through the sieve, being careful not to disturb any sediment on the bottom of the container.

Wash decorative vinegar bottles in hot, soapy water and rinse well. Fill the bottles with boiling water and allow them to stand for 10 minutes. Just before bottling the vinegar, empty the water out of the bottles and turn them upside down to drain.

Using a funnel, pour the filtered vinegar into the bottles, leaving about ½-inch headspace between the vinegar and the top of the bottle, if using a screw cap, or if using a cork, between the vinegar and the bottom of the cork. Seal each bottle with a new cork or screw cap.

Mango Vinegar

This special vinegar lends a tropical flare to everyday dishes.

MAKES ABOUT 4 (8-OUNCE) BOTTLES OR
2 (16-OUNCE) BOTTLES

**2 large ripe mangoes, pitted, peeled and
    chopped**
4 cups rice vinegar

Place the chopped mangoes in a 1½- to 2-quart clean glass jar.

In a medium stainless steel saucepan over low heat, heat the vinegar until hot but still below simmering. Do not allow the vinegar to boil. Remove the pan from the heat.

Pour the hot vinegar over the fruit in the jar. Swirl the jar to gently mix the ingredients, then set aside to cool. When the mixture is cool, cover the jar opening with 2 layers of plastic wrap, then screw on the jar lid or a screw ring. Place the jar in a paper bag and set it in a cool, dry, dark location and let the mixture steep for 2 weeks. Gently

shake or swirl the jar every few days to blend the flavors.

Start tasting the vinegar after about 2 weeks. If you would like a vinegar with a stronger flavor, wait another week and sample the vinegar again. The vinegar will take from 2 to 4 weeks to develop its full flavor, depending on the ripeness of the fruit used.

When the vinegar has reached the desired strength, place a fine-meshed sieve over a bowl or pan and strain the vinegar. Discard the pulp. Rinse the sieve and line it with 3 layers of clean, damp cheesecloth. Strain the vinegar through the cheesecloth. Line the sieve with a paper coffee filter and strain the vinegar again. Pour the vinegar into a clean container, cover and let stand overnight to allow any sediment to settle to the bottom of the container.

Line the sieve with 2 paper coffee filters. Slowly pour the vinegar through the sieve, being careful not to disturb any sediment on the bottom of the container.

Wash decorative vinegar bottles in hot, soapy water and rinse well. Fill the bottles with boiling water and allow them to stand for 10 minutes. Just before bottling the vinegar, empty the water out of the bottles and turn them upside down to drain.

Using a funnel, pour the filtered vinegar into the bottles, leaving about ½-inch headspace between the vinegar and the top of the bottle, if using a screw cap, or if using a cork, between the vinegar and the bottom of the cork. Seal each bottle with a new cork or screw cap.

Mint Vinegar

Add a touch of this vinegar to marinades for lamb and beef, or add a dash to iced tea for a refreshing beverage.

MAKES ABOUT 4 (8-OUNCE) BOTTLES OR
2 (16-OUNCE) BOTTLES

1½ cups lightly packed fresh spearmint or
    lemon mint leaves
Zest of 2 lemons
4 cups white wine vinegar
⅓ cup sugar

Rinse the mint leaves 2 to 3 times in cool, clean water to remove any dirt or sand. Change the water between each rinsing. Gently pat the herbs dry between several layers of paper towels. Chop the mint leaves to release their flavorful oils.

Place the chopped mint leaves and the lemon zest in a 1½- to 2-quart clean glass jar.

In a medium stainless steel saucepan over low heat, heat the vinegar and the sugar until hot but still below simmering, stirring constantly until the sugar is completely dissolved. Do not allow the vinegar to boil. Remove the pan from the heat.

Pour the hot vinegar over the herbs in the jar. Swirl the jar to gently mix the ingredients, then set aside to cool. When the mixture is cool, cover the jar opening with 2 layers of plastic wrap, then screw on the jar lid or a screw ring. Place the jar in a paper bag and set it in a cool, dry, dark location and let the mixture steep for 2 weeks. Gently shake or swirl the jar every few days to blend the flavors.

Start tasting the vinegar after about 2 weeks. If you would like a vinegar with a stronger flavor, wait another week and sample the vinegar again. The vinegar will take from 2 to 4 weeks to develop its full flavor.

When the vinegar has reached the desired strength, place a fine-meshed sieve over a bowl or pan and strain the vinegar. Discard the herbs. Rinse the sieve and line it with 3 layers of clean, damp cheesecloth. Strain the vinegar through the cheesecloth. Line the sieve with a paper coffee filter and strain the vinegar again. Pour the vinegar into a clean container, cover and let stand overnight to allow any sediment to settle to the bottom of the container.

Line the sieve with 2 layered paper coffee filters. Slowly pour the vinegar through the sieve, being careful not to disturb any sediment on the bottom of the container.

Wash decorative vinegar bottles in hot, soapy water and rinse well. Fill the bottles with boiling water and allow them to stand for 10 minutes. Just before bottling the vinegar, empty the water out of the bottles and turn them upside down to drain.

Using a funnel, pour the filtered vinegar into the bottles, leaving about ½-inch headspace between the vinegar and the top of the bottle, if using a screw cap, or if using a cork, between the vinegar and the bottom of the cork. Seal each bottle with a new cork or screw cap.

Nasturtium Vinegar

This peppery and colorful floral vinegar is delight-ful in salad dressings and sprinkled on vegetables. A mixture of yellow, orange and red nasturtium blossoms will create a vinegar with a beautiful color.

MAKES ABOUT 4 (8-OUNCE) BOTTLES OR
2 (16-OUNCE) BOTTLES

4 cups lightly packed fresh nasturtium
 blossoms
½ cup small fresh nasturtium leaves
4 cups rice vinegar

Gently rinse the nasturtium blossoms and leaves 2 to 3 times in cool, clean water to remove any dirt or sand. Change the water between each rinsing. Gently pat the blossoms and leaves dry between several layers of paper towels. Chop the blossoms and leaves to release their flavorful oils.

Place the chopped nasturtium blossoms and leaves in a 1½- to 2-quart clean glass jar.

In a medium stainless steel saucepan over low heat, heat the vinegar until hot but still below simmering. Do not allow the vinegar to boil. Remove the pan from the heat.

Pour the hot vinegar over the blossoms and leaves in the jar. Swirl the jar to gently mix the ingredients, then set aside to cool. When the mixture is cool, cover the jar opening with 2 layers of plastic wrap, then screw on the jar lid or a screw ring. Place the jar in a paper bag and set it in a cool, dry, dark location and let the mixture steep for 2 weeks. Gently shake or swirl the jar every few days to blend the flavors.

Start tasting the vinegar after about 2 weeks. If you would like a vinegar with a stronger flavor, wait another week and sample the vinegar again. The vinegar will take from 2 to 4 weeks to develop its full flavor.

When the vinegar has reached the desired strength, place a fine-meshed sieve over a bowl or pan and strain the vinegar. Discard the blossoms and leaves. Rinse the sieve and line it with 3 layers of clean, damp cheesecloth. Strain the vinegar through the cheesecloth. Line the sieve with a paper coffee filter and strain the vinegar again. Pour the vinegar into a clean container, cover and let stand overnight to allow any sediment to settle to the bottom of the container.

Line the sieve with 2 layered paper coffee fil-ters. Slowly pour the vinegar through the sieve, being careful not to disturb any sediment on the bottom of the container.

Wash decorative vinegar bottles in hot, soapy water and rinse well. Fill the bottles with boiling water and allow them to stand for 10 minutes. Just before bottling the vinegar, empty the water out of the bottles and turn them upside down to drain.

Using a funnel, pour the filtered vinegar into the bottles, leaving about ½-inch headspace between the vinegar and the top of the bottle, if using a screw cap, or if using a cork, between the vinegar and the bottom of the cork. Seal each bot-tle with a new cork or screw cap.

Raspberry Vinegar

Raspberry Vinegar is exquisite sprinkled on fresh fruit and in salad dressings. Try it over mixed baby greens, by itself or blended with a light oil.

MAKES ABOUT 4 (8-OUNCE) BOTTLES OR
2 (16-OUNCE) BOTTLES

4 cups fresh or frozen raspberries, crushed
4 cups rice vinegar

Place the crushed raspberries in a 1½- to 2-quart clean glass jar.

In a medium stainless steel saucepan over low heat, heat the vinegar until hot but still below simmering. Do not allow the vinegar to boil. Remove the pan from the heat.

Pour the hot vinegar over the fruit in the jar. Swirl the jar to gently mix the ingredients, then set aside to cool. When the mixture is cool, cover the jar opening with 2 layers of plastic wrap, then screw on the jar lid or a screw ring. Place the jar in a paper bag and set it in a cool, dry, dark location and let the mixture steep for 2 weeks. Gently shake or swirl the jar every few days to blend the flavors.

Start tasting the vinegar after about 2 weeks. If you would like a vinegar with a stronger flavor, wait another week and sample the vinegar again. The vinegar will take from 2 to 4 weeks to develop its full flavor, depending on the ripeness of the fruit used.

When the vinegar has reached the desired strength, place a fine-meshed sieve over a bowl or pan and strain the vinegar. Discard the seeds and pulp. Rinse the sieve and line it with 3 layers of clean, damp cheesecloth. Strain the vinegar through the cheesecloth. Line the sieve with a paper coffee filter and strain the vinegar again.

Pour the vinegar into a clean container, cover and let stand overnight to allow any sediment to settle to the bottom of the container.

Line the sieve with 2 paper coffee filters. Slowly pour the vinegar through the sieve, being careful not to disturb any sediment on the bottom of the container.

Wash decorative vinegar bottles in hot, soapy water and rinse well. Fill the bottles with boiling water and allow them to stand for 10 minutes. Just before bottling the vinegar, empty the water out of the bottles and turn them upside down to drain.

Using a funnel, pour the filtered vinegar into the bottles, leaving about ½-inch headspace between the vinegar and the top of the bottle, if using a screw cap, or if using a cork, between the vinegar and the bottom of the cork. Seal each bottle with a new cork or screw cap.

Rosemary Vinegar

This vinegar is a nice complement to pork roasts, chops and stews. Use young, tender leaves and sprigs without woody stems to make this special vinegar.

MAKES ABOUT 4 (8-OUNCE) BOTTLES OR
2 (16-OUNCE) BOTTLES

2 cups lightly packed fresh rosemary leaves
4 cups red wine vinegar

Rinse the rosemary leaves 2 to 3 times in cool, clean water to remove any dirt or sand. Change the water between each rinsing. Gently pat the herbs dry between several layers of paper towels. Chop the rosemary leaves to release their flavorful oils.

Place the chopped rosemary leaves in a 1½- to 2-quart clean glass jar.

In a medium stainless steel saucepan over low heat, heat the vinegar until hot but still below simmering. Do not allow the vinegar to boil. Remove the pan from the heat.

Pour the hot vinegar over the herbs in the jar. Swirl the jar to gently mix the ingredients, then set aside to cool. When the mixture is cool, cover the jar opening with 2 layers of plastic wrap, then screw on the jar lid or a screw ring. Place the jar in a paper bag and set it in a cool, dry, dark location and let the mixture steep for 2 weeks. Gently shake or swirl the jar every few days to blend the flavors.

Start tasting the vinegar after about 2 weeks. If you would like a vinegar with a stronger flavor, wait another week and sample the vinegar again. The vinegar will take from 2 to 4 weeks to develop its full flavor.

When the vinegar has reached the desired strength, place a fine-meshed sieve over a bowl or pan and strain the vinegar. Discard the herbs. Rinse the sieve and line it with 3 layers of clean, damp cheesecloth. Strain the vinegar through the cheesecloth. Line the sieve with a paper coffee filter and strain the vinegar again. Pour the vinegar into a clean container, cover and let stand overnight to allow any sediment to settle to the bottom of the container.

Line the sieve with 2 layered paper coffee filters. Slowly pour the vinegar through the sieve, being careful not to disturb any sediment on the bottom of the container.

Wash decorative vinegar bottles in hot, soapy water and rinse well. Fill the bottles with boiling

water and allow them to stand for 10 minutes. Just before bottling the vinegar, empty the water out of the bottles and turn them upside down to drain.

Using a funnel, pour the filtered vinegar into the bottles, leaving about ½-inch headspace between the vinegar and the top of the bottle, if using a screw cap, or if using a cork, between the vinegar and the bottom of the cork. Seal each bottle with a new cork or screw cap.

Tarragon Vinegar

Tarragon Vinegar is a perfect pairing with chicken or game hens and is also an excellent choice for salad dressings.

MAKES ABOUT 4 (8-OUNCE) BOTTLES OR
2 (16-OUNCE) BOTTLES

1½ cups lightly packed fresh tarragon leaves
4 cups white wine vinegar

Rinse the tarragon leaves 2 to 3 times in cool, clean water to remove any dirt or sand. Change the water between each rinsing. Gently pat the herbs dry between several layers of paper towels. Chop the tarragon leaves to release their flavorful oils.

Place the chopped tarragon leaves in a 1½- to 2-quart clean glass jar.

In a medium stainless steel saucepan over low heat, heat the vinegar until hot but still below simmering. Do not allow the vinegar to boil. Remove the pan from the heat.

Pour the hot vinegar over the herbs in the jar. Swirl the jar to gently mix the ingredients, then set aside to cool. When the mixture is cool, cover the jar opening with 2 layers of plastic wrap, then screw on the jar lid or a screw ring. Place the jar in a paper bag and set it in a cool, dry, dark location and let the mixture steep for 2 weeks. Gently shake or swirl the jar every few days to blend the flavors.

Start tasting the vinegar after about 2 weeks. If you would like a vinegar with a stronger flavor, wait another week and sample the vinegar again. The vinegar will take from 2 to 4 weeks to develop its full flavor.

When the vinegar has reached the desired strength, place a fine-meshed sieve over a bowl or pan and strain the vinegar. Discard the herbs. Rinse the sieve and line it with 3 layers of clean, damp cheesecloth. Strain the vinegar through the cheesecloth. Line the sieve with a paper coffee filter and strain the vinegar again. Pour the vinegar into a clean container, cover and let stand overnight to allow any sediment to settle to the bottom of the container.

Line the sieve with 2 layered paper coffee filters. Slowly pour the vinegar through the sieve, being careful not to disturb any sediment on the bottom of the container.

Wash decorative vinegar bottles in hot, soapy water and rinse well. Fill the bottles with boiling water and allow them to stand for 10 minutes. Just before bottling the vinegar, empty the water out of the bottles and turn them upside down to drain.

Using a funnel, pour the filtered vinegar into the bottles, leaving about 1/2-inch headspace between the vinegar and the top of the bottle, if using a screw cap, or if using a cork, between the vinegar and the bottom of the cork. Seal each bottle with a new cork or screw cap.

Thyme Vinegar

Green beans and other vegetables sprinkled with this vinegar come alive with flavor.

MAKES ABOUT 4 (8-OUNCE) BOTTLES OR 2 (16-OUNCE) BOTTLES

2 cups fresh English thyme or lemon thyme leaves

Zest of 1 lemon

4 cups rice vinegar or white wine vinegar

Rinse the thyme leaves 2 to 3 times in cool, clean water to remove any dirt or sand. Change the water between each rinsing. Gently pat the herbs dry between several layers of paper towels. Crush or chop the thyme leaves to release their flavorful oils.

Place the crushed or chopped thyme leaves and the lemon zest in a 1 1/2- to 2-quart clean glass jar.

In a medium stainless steel saucepan over low heat, heat the vinegar until hot but still below simmering. Do not allow the vinegar to boil. Remove the pan from the heat.

Pour the hot vinegar over the herbs in the jar. Swirl the jar to gently mix the ingredients, then set aside to cool. When the mixture is cool, cover the jar opening with 2 layers of plastic wrap, then screw on the jar lid or a screw ring. Place the jar in a paper bag and set it in a cool, dry, dark location and let the mixture steep for 2 weeks. Gently shake or swirl the jar every few days to blend the flavors.

Start tasting the vinegar after about 2 weeks. If you would like a vinegar with a stronger flavor, wait another week and sample the vinegar again. The vinegar will take from 2 to 4 weeks to develop its full flavor.

When the vinegar has reached the desired strength, place a fine-meshed sieve over a bowl or pan and strain the vinegar. Discard the herbs. Rinse the sieve and line it with 3 layers of clean, damp cheesecloth. Strain the vinegar through the cheesecloth. Line the sieve with a paper coffee filter and strain the vinegar again. Pour the vinegar into a clean container, cover and let stand overnight to allow any sediment to settle to the bottom of the container.

Line the sieve with 2 layered paper coffee filters. Slowly pour the vinegar through the sieve, being careful not to disturb any sediment on the bottom of the container.

Wash decorative vinegar bottles in hot, soapy water and rinse well. Fill the bottles with boiling water and allow them to stand for 10 minutes. Just before bottling the vinegar, empty the water out of the bottles and turn them upside down to drain.

Using a funnel, pour the filtered vinegar into the bottles, leaving about ½-inch headspace between the vinegar and the top of the bottle, if using a screw cap, or if using a cork, between the vinegar and the bottom of the cork. Seal each bottle with a new cork or screw cap.

Apricot Syrup

A golden orange syrup, it has a rich apricot flavor.
MAKES ABOUT 4 HALF-PINT JARS OR 2 PINT JARS

4 cups chopped apricots
3 cups sugar
2 tablespoons strained fresh lemon juice

In a 4-quart pan, combine the apricots and sugar. Cover and let stand 2 to 3 hours.

Over medium-low heat, heat the apricot mixture, stirring constantly, until the sugar is completely dissolved. Increase the heat to medium-high and bring the mixture to a boil. Reduce the heat, cover and simmer gently for 10 minutes. Remove the pan from the heat. Remove the cover and skim off any foam. Let cool for 10 minutes.

Place a fine-meshed sieve over a bowl or pan. Ladle the apricot mixture into the sieve and strain the syrup from the pulp. Discard the pulp. Rinse the sieve and line it with 3 layers of clean, damp cheesecloth. Strain the syrup through the cheesecloth.

In a medium saucepan, combine the syrup and lemon juice. Over medium-high heat, bring the syrup to a boil. Reduce the heat and simmer the syrup for 10 minutes. Remove the pan from the heat. Skim off any foam.

Ladle the hot syrup into hot jars, leaving ¼-inch headspace. Wipe the jar rims and threads with a clean, damp cloth. Cover with hot lids and apply screw rings. Process half-pint jars in a 200F (93C) water bath for 10 minutes, pint jars for 15 minutes.

Blueberry Syrup

An easy syrup to make, this is wonderful served over buttermilk or blueberry pancakes. Frozen blueberries will release a larger quantity of juice and yield a more flavorful syrup than fresh blueberries.

MAKES ABOUT 6 HALF-PINT JARS OR 3 PINT JARS

Blueberry Juice
3 quarts frozen blueberries (3 to 4 [16-ounce] bags), crushed
1½ cups sugar

Syrup Ingredients
4 cups blueberry juice
1¾ cups sugar
2 teaspoons filtered fresh lemon juice

To extract the juice: In a 4-quart pan, combine the crushed blueberries and sugar. Cover and let stand overnight.

Over medium-low heat, stirring constantly, heat the blueberry mixture until the sugar is completely dissolved. Remove the pan from the heat. Let cool for 5 minutes.

Place a fine-meshed sieve over a bowl or pan. Ladle the blueberry mixture into the sieve and strain the juice from the pulp. Discard the pulp and seeds. Rinse the sieve thoroughly and line it with 3 to 4 layers of clean, damp cheesecloth. Strain the juice through the cheesecloth. Line the sieve with a paper coffee filter and strain the juice again. Measure 4 cups of juice.

To make the syrup: In a medium saucepan, combine the blueberry juice, sugar and lemon juice. Over medium-low heat, stirring constantly, heat until the sugar is completely dissolved. Increase the heat to medium-high and bring the syrup to a boil. Reduce the heat and simmer the syrup for 20 minutes. Remove the pan from the heat. Skim off any foam.

Ladle the hot syrup into hot jars, leaving ¼-inch headspace. Wipe the jar rims and threads with a clean, damp cloth. Cover with hot lids and apply screw rings. Process half-pint jars in a 200F (93C) water bath for 10 minutes, pint jars for 15 minutes.

Boysenberry Syrup

A very berry syrup with an intense flavor, it is also great when made with olallieberries, loganberries or blackberries. Frozen berries work very well for making syrup. You will need about 3 to 4 (16-ounce) bags of frozen berries to yield 4 cups of juice.

MAKES ABOUT 6 HALF-PINT JARS OR 3 PINT JARS

Boysenberry Juice
3 quarts fresh or frozen boysenberries, crushed

Syrup Ingredients
4 cups boysenberry juice
3½ cups sugar

To extract the juice: In an 8-quart pan over medium heat, stirring frequently, bring the crushed boysenberries to a simmer. Reduce the heat, cover and simmer gently for 5 minutes. Remove the pan from the heat. Remove the cover and skim off any foam. Let cool for 15 minutes.

Place a fine-meshed sieve over a bowl or pan. Ladle the boysenberries into the sieve and strain the juice from the pulp. Discard the pulp and seeds. Rinse the sieve thoroughly and line it with 3 to 4 layers of clean, damp cheesecloth. Strain the juice through the cheesecloth. Line the sieve with a paper coffee filter and strain the juice again. Measure 4 cups of juice.

To make the syrup: In a medium saucepan, combine the boysenberry juice and sugar. Over medium-low heat, stirring constantly, heat until the sugar is completely dissolved. Increase the heat to medium-high and bring the syrup to a boil. Reduce the heat and simmer the syrup for 20 minutes. Remove the pan from the heat. Skim off any foam.

Ladle the hot syrup into hot jars, leaving ¼-inch headspace. Wipe the jar rims and threads with a clean, damp cloth. Cover with hot lids and apply screw rings. Process half-pint jars in a 200F (93C) water bath for 10 minutes, pint jars for 15 minutes.

Cherry Syrup

This syrup has an exquisite cherry flavor that is excellent served over pancakes or waffles and also makes fabulous cherry milk shakes.

MAKES ABOUT 6 HALF-PINT JARS OR 3 PINT JARS

Cherry Juice
4½ pounds sweet cherries, pitted and
   chopped
½ cup water

Syrup Ingredients
4 cups cherry juice
2 cups sugar
2 tablespoons filtered fresh lemon juice
1 cup light corn syrup

To extract the juice: In an 8-quart pan, combine the cherries and water. Over medium-high heat, bring the mixture to a boil. Reduce the heat, cover and simmer gently for 10 minutes. Remove the pan from the heat. Remove the cover and skim off any foam. Let cool for 15 minutes.

Place a fine-meshed sieve over a bowl or pan. Ladle the cherries into the sieve and strain the juice from the pulp. Discard the pulp. Rinse the sieve thoroughly and line it with 3 to 4 layers of clean, damp cheesecloth. Strain the juice through the cheesecloth. Line the sieve with a paper coffee filter and strain the juice again. Measure 4 cups of juice.

To make the syrup: In a medium saucepan, combine the cherry juice, sugar and lemon juice. Over medium-low heat, stirring constantly, heat until the sugar is completely dissolved. Increase the heat to medium-high and bring the syrup to a boil. Reduce the heat and simmer the syrup for 10 minutes. Stir in the corn syrup and simmer the syrup for 10 minutes more. Remove the pan from the heat. Skim off any foam.

Ladle the hot syrup into hot jars, leaving ¼-inch headspace. Wipe the jar rims and threads with a clean, damp cloth. Cover with hot lids and apply screw rings. Process half-pint jars in a 200F (93C) water bath for 10 minutes, pint jars for 15 minutes.

Grenadine Syrup

The flavor of homemade grenadine syrup is far superior to any that you can buy in a store. Grenadine is great over ice cream or drizzled on pancakes for a special treat. Add a tablespoon or two to a glass of sparkling water or champagne for a refreshing beverage. Grenadine is also the essential ingredient for making classic Shirley Temple cocktails (see below).

A word of caution: Be careful when handling pomegranates, as the juice will stain both clothing and skin. Wearing an apron and rubber or latex gloves is definitely recommended.

MAKES ABOUT 4 HALF-PINT JARS OR 2 PINT JARS

6 to 7 large pomegranates
2¾ cups sugar
1 tablespoon filtered fresh lemon juice

With a sharp knife, score the pomegranates into quarters, cutting just through the outside skin and being careful not to damage the seeds. Submerge the pomegranates in a large bowl or basin filled with water. Break the fruit apart along the score lines.

Using your fingers, gently remove seeds from the white pith, being careful not to break the seeds. The white pith will rise to the surface of the water, while the seeds will sink to the bottom of the bowl or basin. Skim the pith from the top of the water. Be sure to remove all of the white pith from the seeds, as it is very bitter and will give the syrup a bad flavor. Carefully transfer the seeds to a colander. Gently rinse the seeds and drain well.

Measure 5 cups of pomegranate seeds. In a flat-bottomed bowl or pan, using a vegetable masher or the back of a large spoon, gently crush the seeds to release their juice. Take care not to crush the hard centers of the seeds. These are very bitter and, if crushed, will ruin the flavor of the syrup.

In a large bowl, combine the crushed seeds and juice with the sugar. Cover the bowl and let stand overnight.

Stir the seeds to dissolve any remaining sugar. Let sit for 2 hours. Stir again.

Place a fine-meshed sieve over a bowl or pan and strain the syrup. Discard the seeds. Line the sieve with 3 layers of fine-meshed clean, damp cheesecloth. Strain the syrup through the cheesecloth. Line the sieve with a paper coffee filter and strain the juice again.

In a medium saucepan, combine the syrup and the lemon juice. Over medium-high heat, bring the syrup to a boil. Reduce the heat and simmer the syrup for 10 minutes. Remove the pan from the heat.

Ladle the hot syrup into hot jars, leaving ¼-inch headspace. Wipe the jar rims and threads with a clean, damp cloth. Cover with hot lids and apply screw rings. Process half-pint jars in a 200F (93C) water bath for 10 minutes, pint jars for 15 minutes.

Shirley Temple
6 ounces ginger ale
1 tablespoon Grenadine Syrup

Combine the ginger ale and grenadine until well blended. Pour over ice and top with a maraschino cherry.

Plum Syrup

Santa Rosa plums produce a syrup with an intense plum taste. If you do not have access to Santa Rosa plums, any other flavorful, juicy variety of plum may be used instead.

MAKES ABOUT 6 HALF-PINT JARS OR 3 PINT JARS

Plum Juice
6 pounds Santa Rosa plums, pitted, peeled
    and crushed or finely chopped
1 cup water

Syrup Ingredients
4 cups Santa Rosa plum juice
5 cups sugar

To extract the juice: In an 8-quart pan, combine the plums and water. Over medium-high heat, bring the mixture to a boil. Reduce the heat, cover and simmer gently for 10 minutes. Remove the pan from the heat. Remove the cover and skim off any foam. Let cool for 15 minutes.

Place a fine-meshed sieve over a bowl or pan. Ladle the plums into the sieve and strain the juice from the pulp. Discard the pulp. Rinse the sieve thoroughly and line it with 3 to 4 layers of clean, damp cheesecloth. Strain the juice through the cheesecloth. Line the sieve with a paper coffee filter and strain the juice again. Measure 4 cups of juice.

To make the syrup: In a medium saucepan, combine the juice and sugar. Over medium-low heat, stirring constantly, heat until the sugar is completely dissolved. Increase the heat to medium-high and bring the syrup to a boil. Reduce the heat and simmer the syrup for 15 minutes. Remove the pan from the heat. Skim off any foam.

Ladle the hot syrup into hot jars, leaving ¼-inch headspace. Wipe the jar rims and threads with a clean, damp cloth. Cover with hot lids and apply screw rings. Process half-pint jars in a 200F (93C) water bath for 10 minutes, pint jars for 15 minutes.

Raspberry Syrup

The vibrant color and exquisite flavor of this syrup will make any breakfast or dessert a special treat. Frozen raspberries work very well for making syrup. You will need about 4 (16-ounce) bags of frozen berries to yield 4 cups of juice. If you live in an area of the country where black raspberries are plentiful, use them in place of the red raspberries.

MAKES ABOUT 6 HALF-PINT JARS OR 3 PINT JARS

Raspberry Juice
3½ quarts fresh or frozen red raspberries,
    crushed

Syrup Ingredients
4 cups raspberry juice
4 cups sugar
¼ cup filtered fresh lemon juice

To extract the juice: In an 8-quart pan over medium heat, stirring frequently, bring the crushed raspberries to a simmer. Reduce the heat, cover and simmer gently for 5 minutes. Remove the pan from the heat. Remove the cover and skim off any foam. Let cool for 15 minutes.

Place a fine-meshed sieve over a bowl or pan. Ladle the raspberries into the sieve and strain the juice from the pulp. Discard the pulp and seeds. Rinse the sieve thoroughly and line it with 3 to 4 layers of clean, damp cheesecloth. Strain the juice through the cheesecloth. Line the sieve with a paper coffee filter and strain the juice again. Measure 4 cups of juice.

To make the syrup: In a medium saucepan, combine the raspberry juice, sugar and lemon juice. Over medium-low heat, stirring constantly, heat until the sugar is completely dissolved. Increase the heat to medium-high and bring the syrup to a boil. Reduce the heat and simmer the syrup for 15 minutes. Remove the pan from the heat. Skim off any foam.

Ladle the hot syrup into hot jars, leaving ¼-inch headspace. Wipe the jar rims and threads with a clean, damp cloth. Cover with hot lids and apply screw rings. Process half-pint jars in a 200F (93C) water bath for 10 minutes, pint jars for 15 minutes.

Strawberry Syrup

The bright, refreshing flavor of this syrup makes excellent strawberry milk shakes.

MAKES ABOUT 6 HALF-PINT JARS OR 3 PINT JARS

Strawberry Juice
3 quarts ripe strawberries
1 cup water

Syrup Ingredients
4 cups strawberry juice

4 cups sugar
¼ cup filtered fresh lemon juice

To extract the juice: Gently rinse the strawberries in cool water and drain. Remove the stems and cut the berries into quarters. In a flat-bottomed bowl or pan, use a vegetable masher or large spoon to crush the strawberries one batch at a time.

In an 8-quart pan, combine the strawberries and water. Over medium-high heat, bring the mixture to a boil. Reduce the heat, cover and simmer gently for 10 minutes. Remove the pan from the heat. Remove the cover and skim off any foam. Let cool for 15 minutes.

Place a fine-meshed sieve over a bowl or pan. Ladle the strawberries into the sieve and strain the juice from the pulp. Discard the pulp. Rinse the sieve thoroughly and line it with 3 to 4 layers of clean, damp cheesecloth. Strain the juice through the cheesecloth. Line the sieve with a paper coffee filter and strain the juice again. Measure 4 cups of juice.

To make the syrup: In a medium saucepan, combine the strawberry juice, sugar and lemon juice. Over medium-low heat, stirring constantly, heat until the sugar is completely dissolved. Increase the heat to medium-high and bring the syrup to a boil. Reduce the heat and simmer the syrup for 15 minutes. Remove the pan from the heat. Skim off any foam.

Ladle the hot syrup into hot jars, leaving ¼-inch headspace. Wipe the jar rims and threads with a clean, damp cloth. Cover with hot lids and apply screw rings. Process half-pint jars in a 200F (93C) water bath for 10 minutes, pint jars for 15 minutes.

Specialty Preserves

As the popularity of canning specialty preserves at home has risen substantially in the past few years, state and county fairs around the country are responding by creating new entry divisions and classes of competition for these unique preserved foods. Mostly consisting of preserved foods used for desserts, specialty preserves may also be any form of home-canned product that does not fall into the regular or standard classifications commonly thought of for preserved foods.

Specialty preserves are fun and flavorful items to have available on your pantry shelves. A selection of jars of different flavored pie fillings makes preparing fresh, home-baked pies fast and easy. Ice-cream toppings, in a variety of flavor choices, provide the perfect excuse to have an ice-cream sundae party. Exotic after-dinner cordials are a wonderful ending to a gourmet meal or a relaxing evening by the fire.

CANNING SPECIALTY PRESERVES

The techniques used for making specialty preserves are the same as for making other types of preserved foods. To create outstanding specialty preserves that will shine above anything you can buy in the store, follow the recipes closely, use top-quality ingredients and pay attention to the fine details.

Pie Fillings

When making pie fillings, there are two important ingredients that you will want to locate and have on hand: Instant Clearjel powder (see page 15) and superfine sugar. Instant Clearjel is a very fine type of cornstarch. This special thickener will prevent your pie fillings from separating the way regular cornstarch, flour and tapioca can when they are exposed to the extended heating of water bath processing. Instant Clearjel is relatively inexpensive and, though hard to find in stores, it is readily available by mail order. Check the Mail-Order Source (see page 337) for more information.

Instant Clearjel does not need to be boiled in order for it to thicken the liquid to which it is added, nor does it have a strong starchy flavor. With regular cornstarch, flour and tapioca, the mixture must be boiled in order for it to thicken. Flour and cornstarch must also be cooked to eliminate their starchy taste. The extended boiling that is necessary to thicken pie fillings made with these other starches can trap a large number of air bubbles in the filling. These air bubbles are extremely difficult to remove and can result in a reduced score if you enter your pie filling into a fair competition.

When working with Instant Clearjel, I always use superfine sugar rather than regular granulated sugar. Superfine sugar is ground into finer granules than regular sugar. It blends better with the Instant Clearjel, evenly distributing the starch throughout the pie filling. This even distribution of the thickener is an important element in achieving a smooth pie filling that is free of starch lumps. To create very smooth pie fillings, I strongly recommend that you use superfine sugar, which can be found in supermarkets. If you cannot find superfine sugar, regular granulated sugar may be substituted. The texture of granulated sugar may be made finer by briefly processing it in a blender or food processor. Regular granulated sugar may also be used as is. Whisk it together well with the Instant Clearjel for about 1 minute until thoroughly and evenly blended.

To receive the best scores and highest awards in a preserved foods competition, your pie fillings must be packed with plump, flavorful fruit. The filling should be smooth and free from lumps or any grittiness or graininess from undissolved sugar. Air bubbles should be carefully removed from the filled jars to prevent a deduction of points that could prevent the entry from winning a ribbon.

Ice-Cream Toppings and Sauces

Because of the increased risk of contamination and spoilage when home canning foods with a dairy base, fairs do not accept preserved foods entries containing milk or cream. Ice-cream topping recipes containing cream tend to curdle or separate during water bath processing and have a very short shelf life. Toppings prepared with cream must be stored in the refrigerator for up to 2 weeks to maintain their texture, flavor and freshness. The ice-cream topping recipes in this book do not contain cream, can be safely preserved by home-canning methods and are acceptable for entry into fair competitions.

Some ice-cream sauces, such as a hot fudge sauce, are best when heated before serving. In the jar, these sauces may appear quite thick and rather stiff. This is normal and is to be expected, otherwise the sauce would be very thin when heated and spooned over ice cream. For a fair competition, if you enter an ice-cream topping that is designed to be heated before being served, label the jar of topping as a hot sauce and indicate this on the entry form as well. When properly identified as a sauce that is to be served heated, the judges will evaluate the topping entry based on that criteria.

Chocolate, butterscotch, hot fudge or similar sauces will become gritty if the sugar in the topping is not completely dissolved during the cooking process. Use superfine sugar to ensure that the sugar dissolves quickly and completely. These sauces need to be ladled into the jars and sealed quickly, as exposure to the air can cause sugar crystals to form in the topping, giving it a grainy texture. This graininess will result in the sauce receiving a serious reduction in its competitive score and placing. To earn top scores and ribbons, these toppings should also have a smooth, rich feel in the mouth. For home use, heating a grainy sauce before serving it will reduce or eliminate the sugar crystals. The crystals may re-form as the topping cools.

To avoid scorching the topping during cooking, many sauces should be prepared in the top of a double boiler set over hot but not boiling water. This will protect fragile ingredients, like chocolate and other flavored chips, from overcooking, sticking to the bottom of the pan or developing a burned taste. By using a double boiler, the sauce will also have a smoother, silkier texture, earning higher scores from the fair judges.

When ladling smooth ice-cream sauces into the jars, small air bubbles may become trapped in the jars, especially at the bottom. These air bubbles must be removed, or the fair judge will deduct points and the entry may be knocked out of the running for awards or its placement may be lowered. To remove trapped air bubbles, slide a plastic knife down the inside of the jar to make a path for the bubbles to escape. Be careful not to leave any new air bubbles in the jar as you slowly remove the knife.

Fruit toppings should be prepared and cooked quickly to maintain the shape and texture of the fruit. These toppings are usually served at room temperature but may also be heated briefly for hot sundaes. The sauce may be thick or thin, depending on the type of topping. Fruit toppings should be loaded with fruit and flavor to win awards.

Nut sauces have a better and fuller flavor when the nuts are toasted before making the topping. Toasting the nuts releases and dries their natural oils, intensifying their flavor and keeping them from turning mushy or rancid during storage. Nuts may be toasted in the oven or in a sauté pan on the stove or cooktop (see page 157). Butter is frequently added to the nuts during toasting to give them a richer flavor.

Cordials

Homemade cordials have become quite popular in recent years. They are easy to prepare but will take several weeks for the flavors to fully develop. Cordials may be served as an apéritif before dinner, but because of their sweetness, they are usually best served at the end of the meal or after dessert.

Select a good-quality liquor or wine as the base for your flavored cordial. Cream should not be used in making cordials, because there is a significant chance of spoilage occurring in cordials made with cream. The alcohol in the cordial may not preserve the cream and may, in fact, actually cause it to curdle. Homemade cream cordials are prohibited from fair competitions and entries containing cream, or any other dairy product, will be disqualified. If you enjoy cream cordials, add the cream just before serving the liqueur.

Cordials need to steep in a cool, dry, dark place away from both heat and light. Do not steep the cordial in the refrigerator, as the temperature will be too cold to allow the fruit and other ingredients to release their full flavors. Place the jar in a brown paper bag and fold over the top of the bag before placing the cordial in a pantry, cabinet or closet to steep. Depending on the type of cordial, it should be set aside for 3 to 6 weeks to allow the flavors to become infused into the liqueur.

When the cordial has finished steeping, it will need to be strained through a sieve lined with cheesecloth then through a paper coffee filter to make it clear. The filtered cordial may be packaged in decorative bottles and sealed with either screw caps or clamp closures. Leave about ½-inch headspace between the cordial and the bottom of the cap or other closure. Store the bottles in a cool, dark location. The flavor of the cordial will continue to mellow after bottling. While cordials will keep indefinitely, they should be used within 3 to 4 months, after which time the flavors will gradually begin to fade.

When scoring cordials, the judges look for the color, clarity and intense flavor of the cordial. Mild cordials do not score as well as those with a strong flavor; however, if the flavor is overpowering or the cordial is too sweet, it may also lose points with the judges. While there is no specific headspace requirement for cordials, about ½-inch headspace or slightly less is generally considered an appropriate amount. The bottle should be clean and attractive, and the screw cap or clamp closure should be new and seal the container tightly.

Apple Pie Filling

With a few jars of this wonderful preserve on your shelf, you will be ready to bake a homemade apple pie or crisp anytime. Apple pie in a jar! What could be better?

For best flavor and texture, use a firm apple that will hold its shape when cooked. Jonathon, Rome Beauty, McIntosh and Granny Smith are all excellent choices.

**MAKES ABOUT 8 PINT JARS OR
4 QUART JARS**

3 quarts cold water
3 tablespoons antioxidant crystals or
    ascorbic acid crystals
4 quarts peeled and sliced tart apples
    (½-inch-thick slices)
3⅔ cups superfine sugar
1 cup Instant Clearjel powder
2 teaspoons ground cinnamon
½ teaspoon ground nutmeg
5 cups warm apple juice
½ cup strained fresh lemon juice
2 tablespoons unsalted butter

In a large bowl or pan, combine the cold water and antioxidant crystals. Stir until the crystals are completely dissolved.

As you cut the apples, place them into the antioxidant solution to prevent browning. Do not allow the apples to soak in the solution for longer than 20 minutes or they may absorb too much of the solution and turn sour. Rinse the apples thoroughly under cool running water and drain well.

Fill an 8-quart pan half full of water and bring it to a boil over medium-high heat. Add about a third of the drained apple slices to the water. Bring the water back to a boil and cook the apple slices for 2 minutes. Using a large slotted spoon, transfer the apples to a strainer. Drain well, then pour into a bowl. Cover and keep warm.

Return the water to a boil and cook the remaining apples in 2 batches.

In an 8-quart pan, whisk together the superfine sugar, Clearjel, cinnamon and nutmeg until very well combined. Add the warm apple juice to the sugar mixture all at once. Using a spoon, stir gently to thoroughly blend the juice into the dry ingredients. Do not use a whisk, as it will cause the pie filling to contain air bubbles.

Over low heat, stirring gently, gradually heat the mixture until it is warm, the Clearjel is completely dissolved and the mixture turns translucent, 1 to 2 minutes. Do not allow the filling to boil or it will contain air bubbles. Stir in the lemon juice and butter until well blended. Gently fold in the apple slices and heat 1 minute. Remove the pan from the heat.

Spoon the pie filling into hot jars, removing as many air bubbles as possible and leaving ½-inch headspace. Using a plastic knife, remove any trapped air bubbles. Wipe the jar rims and threads with a clean, damp cloth. Cover with hot lids and apply screw rings. Process both pint and quart jars in a 200F (93C) water bath for 30 minutes.

Apricot Pie Filling

Old-fashioned goodness packed with intense flavor describes this pie filling. To easily slip the skins from the apricots, heat the whole fruit in simmering water for 30 seconds, then plunge them into ice water for 1 minute. Drain well and slip the skins from the fruit using a paring knife.

MAKES ABOUT 8 PINT JARS OR 4 QUART JARS

3 quarts cold water
3 tablespoons antioxidant crystals or
 ascorbic acid crystals
4 quarts peeled, pitted and sliced firm, ripe
 apricots

4⅔ cups superfine sugar
1⅓ cups Instant Clearjel powder
3 cups warm water
1 cup strained fresh lemon juice
2 tablespoons unsalted butter
½ teaspoon pure almond extract

In a large bowl or pan, combine the cold water and antioxidant crystals. Stir until the crystals are completely dissolved.

As you cut the apricots, place the slices into the antioxidant solution to prevent browning. Do not allow the apricots to soak in the solution for longer than 20 minutes or they may absorb too much of the solution and turn sour. Rinse the apricots thoroughly under cool running water and drain well.

Fill an 8-quart pan half full of water and bring it to a boil over medium-high heat. Add about a third of the drained apricot slices to the water. Bring the water back to a boil and cook the apricot slices for 1 minute. Using a large slotted spoon, transfer the apricots to a strainer. Drain well, then pour into a bowl. Cover and keep warm.

Return the water to a boil and cook the remaining apricots in 2 batches.

In an 8-quart pan, whisk together the superfine sugar and the Clearjel until very well combined. Add the warm water to the sugar mixture all at once. Using a spoon, stir gently to thoroughly blend the water into the dry ingredients. Do not use a whisk, as it will cause the pie filling to contain air bubbles.

Over low heat, stirring gently, gradually heat the mixture until it is warm, the Clearjel is completely dissolved and the mixture turns translucent, 1 to 2 minutes. Do not allow the filling to boil or it will contain air bubbles. Stir in the lemon juice and butter until well blended. Gently fold in the apricot slices and heat 1 minute. Remove the pan from the heat and stir in the almond extract.

Spoon the pie filling into hot jars, removing as many air bubbles as possible and leaving ½-inch headspace. Using a plastic knife, remove any trapped air bubbles. Wipe the jar rims and threads with a clean, damp cloth. Cover with hot lids and apply screw rings. Process both pint and quart jars in a 200F (93C) water bath for 30 minutes.

Blueberry Pie Filling

If you are using frozen blueberries, do not defrost them before making the pie filling.

MAKES ABOUT 6 PINT JARS OR 3 QUART JARS

10 cups fresh or frozen blueberries
2⅔ cups superfine sugar
⅔ cup Instant Clearjel powder
½ teaspoon ground cinnamon (optional)
4 cups warm water
Few drops red and blue food coloring
  (optional)
¼ cup strained fresh lemon juice
2 tablespoons unsalted butter

Remove stems from blueberries and rinse the berries in cool water. Drain well. If using frozen blueberries, do not rinse.

In an 8-quart pan, whisk together the superfine sugar, Clearjel and cinnamon until very well combined. If desired, add a few drops of food coloring to the water. Add the warm water to the sugar mixture all at once. Using a spoon, stir gently to

thoroughly blend the water into the dry ingredients. Do not use a whisk, as it will cause the pie filling to contain air bubbles.

Over low heat, stirring gently, gradually heat the mixture until it is warm, the Clearjel is completely dissolved and the mixture turns translucent, 1 to 2 minutes. Do not allow the filling to boil or it will contain air bubbles. Stir in the lemon juice and butter until well blended. Gently fold in the blueberries and heat 1 minute. Remove the pan from the heat.

Spoon the pie filling into hot jars, removing as many air bubbles as possible and leaving ½-inch headspace. Using a plastic knife, remove any trapped air bubbles. Wipe the jar rims and threads with a clean, damp cloth. Cover with hot lids and apply screw rings. Process both pint and quart jars in a 200F (93C) water bath for 30 minutes.

Cherry Pie Filling

Nothing beats a cherry pie made with fresh-picked sour cherries, and this pie filling makes it possible to have that fresh taste all year 'round.

MAKES ABOUT 6 PINT JARS OR
3 QUART JARS

2 quarts cold water

2 tablespoons antioxidant crystals or ascorbic acid crystals

12 cups pitted fresh sour cherries

2 cups water

2 tablespoons strained fresh lemon juice

3⅔ cups superfine sugar

½ cup Instant Clearjel powder

2 tablespoons unsalted butter

¾ teaspoon pure almond extract

In a large bowl or pan, combine the cold water and antioxidant crystals. Stir until the crystals are completely dissolved.

As you pit the cherries, place them into the antioxidant solution to prevent browning. Do not allow the cherries to soak in the solution for longer than 20 minutes or they may absorb too much of the solution and turn sour. Rinse the cherries thoroughly under cool running water and drain well.

In an 8-quart pan, combine the cherries, 2 cups water and the lemon juice. Over medium heat, gradually bring the mixture to a boil, stirring occasionally to prevent sticking or scorching. Boil gently for 1 minute. Remove the pan from the heat and skim off any foam. Using a large slotted spoon, transfer the cherries to a strainer placed over a heatproof bowl. Drain well, reserving the juice. Combine the drained juice with the juice in the pan and set aside. Pour the cherries into a bowl. Cover and keep warm.

In an 8-quart pan, whisk together the superfine sugar and the Clearjel until very well combined. Add the warm reserved cherry juice to the sugar mixture all at once. Using a spoon, stir gently to thoroughly blend the cherry juice into the dry ingredients. Do not use a whisk, as it will cause the pie filling to contain air bubbles.

Over low heat, stirring gently, gradually heat the mixture until it is warm, the Clearjel is completely dissolved and the mixture turns translucent, 1 to 2 minutes. Do not allow the filling to boil or it will contain air bubbles. Stir in the butter until well blended. Remove the pan from the heat. Stir in the almond extract, then fold in the cherries.

Spoon the pie filling into hot jars, removing as many air bubbles as possible and leaving ½-inch headspace. Using a plastic knife, remove any trapped air bubbles. Wipe the jar rims and threads with a clean, damp cloth. Cover with hot lids and apply screw rings. Process both pint and quart jars in a 200F (93C) water bath for 30 minutes.

Tip

When making cherry pie filling, or any other preserved food that requires a lot of cherries, save the pits. They make terrific pie weights for baking empty pie shells using the baking blind method. The pits work much better than beans, rice or store-bought weights and can be used over and over again without ever turning rancid.

After pitting cherries, rinse the pits several times in cold water, changing the water with each rinsing. Gently rub the pits between the palms of your hands to remove any remaining fruit pulp. Rinse the pits thoroughly and drain well.

Preheat oven to 300F (150C). Line a jelly-roll pan or baking pan with foil. Spread the drained pits in a single layer on the lined pan. Bake for 30 minutes, stirring the pits halfway through the baking time. Remove the pan from the oven. Allow the pits to cool completely, at least 2 hours or overnight. Store them in a covered container or heavy plastic storage bag in a dry location.

When baking unfilled pie shells, line the crust with foil and spread the cherry pits 2 layers deep. Fold the foil inward slightly so it does not overhang the crust. Bake in a preheated 400F (200C) oven for 8 to 10 minutes. Carefully remove the foil and pits together. Return the pie shell to the oven and bake for 3 to 4 minutes more. Remove the pie shell from the oven. Allow the cherry pits to cool completely before returning them to the storage container.

Peach Pie Filling

In addition to pies, this filling is great for making cobblers. Select firm, ripe, yellow-fleshed peaches for making the pie filling. White-fleshed peaches have a milder flavor and will not hold their shape well when canned. They are best when eaten fresh. Yellow-fleshed nectarines also work well in this recipe. For a more attractive filling, use a thin-bowled spoon to remove the red fibers from the center of the peaches or nectarines before slicing.

MAKES ABOUT 8 PINT JARS OR
4 QUART JARS

3 quarts cold water
3 tablespoons antioxidant crystals or
  ascorbic acid crystals
4 quarts peeled, pitted and sliced firm, ripe
  peaches
4²⁄₃ cups superfine sugar
1¹⁄₃ cups Instant Clearjel powder
3 cups warm water
1 cup strained fresh lemon juice
2 tablespoons unsalted butter

In a large bowl or pan, combine the cold water and antioxidant crystals. Stir until the crystals are completely dissolved.

As you cut the peaches, place the slices into the antioxidant solution to prevent browning. Do not allow the peaches to soak in the solution for longer than 20 minutes or they may absorb too much of the solution and turn sour. Rinse the peaches thoroughly under cool running water and drain well.

Fill an 8-quart pan half full of water and bring it to a boil over medium-high heat. Add about a third of the drained peach slices to the water. Bring the water back to a boil and cook the peach slices for 1 minute. Using a large slotted spoon, transfer the peaches to a strainer. Drain well, then pour into a bowl. Cover and keep warm.

Return the water to a boil and cook the remaining peaches in 2 batches.

In an 8-quart pan, whisk together the superfine sugar and the Clearjel until very well combined. Add the warm water to the sugar mixture all at once. Using a spoon, stir gently to thoroughly blend the water into the dry ingredients. Do not use a whisk, as it will cause the pie filling to contain air bubbles.

Over low heat, stirring gently, gradually heat the mixture until it is warm, the Clearjel is completely dissolved and the mixture turns translucent, 1 to 2 minutes. Do not allow the filling to boil or it will contain air bubbles. Stir in the lemon juice and butter until well blended. Gently fold in the peach slices and heat 1 minute. Remove the pan from the heat.

Spoon the pie filling into hot jars, removing as many air bubbles as possible and leaving ½-inch headspace. Using a plastic knife, remove any trapped air bubbles. Wipe the jar rims and threads with a clean, damp cloth. Cover with hot lids and apply screw rings. Process both pint and quart jars in a 200F (93C) water bath for 30 minutes.

Green-Tomato Mincemeat

Green tomatoes make an excellent version of mincemeat—without the meat. For all those vegetarians out there who love the smell of holiday mincemeat but must abstain, rejoice! This recipe is for you.

MAKES ABOUT 10 PINT JARS OR 5 QUART JARS

8 cups chopped green tomatoes

1 tablespoon salt

4 cups boiling water

10 cups chopped tart green apples

4 cups firmly packed light brown sugar

2 cups raisins

2 cups currants

½ cup distilled white vinegar

3 tablespoons finely chopped orange zest

1 tablespoon finely chopped lemon zest

2 teaspoons ground cinnamon

1 teaspoon ground nutmeg

½ teaspoon ground ginger

½ teaspoon ground allspice

2 tablespoons unsalted butter

Place the tomatoes in a large bowl. Sprinkle the salt over the tomatoes and let stand for 1 hour to draw excess moisture from the tomatoes. Rinse the tomatoes and drain well. Pour boiling water over the tomatoes and let stand for 5 minutes. Drain well.

In an 8- to 10-quart pan, combine the drained tomatoes and all of the remaining ingredients in the order listed, except the butter, stirring gently after each addition. Over medium heat, bring the mixture to a boil, stirring constantly. Reduce the heat and simmer until the apples are tender when pierced with a fork. Stir frequently to prevent sticking. Stir in the butter. Remove the pan from the heat.

Ladle the mincemeat into hot jars, removing as many air bubbles as possible and leaving ½-inch headspace. Using a plastic knife, remove any trapped air bubbles. Wipe the jar rims and threads with a clean, damp cloth. Cover with hot lids and apply screw rings. Process both pint and quart jars in a 200F (93C) water bath for 30 minutes.

Mixed-Fruit Mincemeat

Here is a delightful and flavorful mincemeat made from a variety of fresh and dried fruits with just a hint of spice.

MAKES ABOUT 8 PINT JARS OR 4 QUART JARS

½ pound dried apricots, chopped
½ pound dried cherries, chopped
½ pound dried dates, chopped
½ pound golden raisins
½ pound currants or dark raisins
2 cups apple cider or apple juice
¾ cup brandy
¾ cup sherry
1 pound tart apples
1 pound firm, ripe Bartlett pears
½ cup fresh orange juice
¼ cup fresh lemon juice
3 tablespoons finely chopped orange
   zest
2 tablespoons finely chopped lemon zest
3 cups firmly packed light brown sugar
1 teaspoon ground cinnamon
½ teaspoon ground allspice
½ teaspoon ground nutmeg
½ teaspoon ground ginger

In a large bowl, combine the apricots, cherries, dates, raisins, currants, apple cider, brandy and sherry. Stir until well combined. Cover loosely with plastic wrap and set aside to macerate for 24 hours, stirring occasionally.

Peel, core and chop the apples and pears.

In an 8- to 10-quart pan, combine the apples, pears, orange juice and lemon juice. Stir in the dried fruit mixture, orange zest and lemon zest. Combine the brown sugar, cinnamon, allspice, nutmeg and ginger until well blended. Stir the sugar mixture into the fruit in the pan.

Over medium heat, bring the mincemeat mixture to a boil, stirring frequently to prevent sticking. Reduce the heat and simmer until the apples are tender, about 40 minutes, stirring frequently to prevent sticking. If mixture becomes too dry, add a little more apple cider.

Ladle the mincemeat into hot jars, removing as many air bubbles as possible and leaving ½-inch headspace. Using a plastic knife, remove any trapped air bubbles. Wipe the jar rims and threads with a clean, damp cloth. Cover with hot lids and apply screw rings. Process both pint and quart jars in a 200F (93C) water bath for 30 minutes.

Vermont Tomato Mincemeat

My sister-in-law, Challis Amendt, kindly shared this wonderful recipe for this traditional Vermont mincemeat made from green tomatoes. The recipe has been in her family since the late 1800s, passed down from her grandmother, Blanche Baker Adams, to her mother, Evelyn Adams Hodge.

McIntosh apples are the preferred choice of Vermonters, but another tart, crisp apple, such as Jonathon or Granny Smith, may be substituted in a pinch. Cherries and even grated carrot were added to the mincemeat pot from time to time as a way to use up some of the garden extras. While cooking, the whole house fills with the mincemeat's spicy aroma. The cooking time will vary depending on the water content of the tomatoes and apples.

MAKES ABOUT 8 PINT JARS OR 4 QUART JARS

4 pounds green tomatoes, chopped
4 pounds McIntosh apples, peeled, cored and chopped
1 pound currants
1 pound raisins
½ cup distilled white vinegar
4 pounds (about 10 cups) sugar
2 teaspoons ground cinnamon
2 teaspoons ground cloves
2 teaspoons ground allspice
2 teaspoons ground nutmeg
½ pound (2 sticks) unsalted butter, softened

In an 8- to 10-quart pan, combine the tomatoes, apples, currants, raisins and vinegar, mixing well after each addition. Stir in about half of the sugar.

In a large bowl, combine the remaining sugar with the cinnamon, cloves, allspice and nutmeg until well blended. Stir the sugar-spice mixture into the mincemeat. Mix in the butter.

Over medium heat, bring the mixture to a boil, stirring constantly until the sugar is completely dissolved. Reduce the heat and boil gently until most of the liquid evaporates and the mincemeat reaches the desired consistency, 2 to 4 hours. Watch the pot carefully and stir frequently to prevent sticking and scorching. Remove the pan from the heat.

Ladle the mincemeat into hot jars, removing as many air bubbles as possible and leaving ½-inch headspace. Using a plastic knife, remove any trapped air bubbles. Wipe the jar rims and threads with a clean, damp cloth. Cover with hot lids and apply screw rings. Process both pint and quart jars in a 200F (93C) water bath for 30 minutes.

Blackberry Sauce

This elegantly flavored sauce is loaded with juicy blackberries. Boysenberries, loganberries and olallieberries work equally well.

MAKES ABOUT 4 HALF-PINT JARS OR 2 PINT JARS

7 cups fresh ripe blackberries
1⅓ cups sugar
½ cup water
2 tablespoons strained fresh lemon juice
1 tablespoon zested fresh lemon peel
¼ cup unsalted butter

Rinse the blackberries in cool water and drain well. Set aside.

In a 4-quart saucepan, combine 4 cups of the blackberries, the sugar, water, lemon juice and lemon zest. Over low heat, stirring constantly, heat until the sugar is completely dissolved. Increase the heat to medium and bring the mixture to a gentle boil, stirring frequently to prevent scorching. Reduce the heat and simmer, stirring frequently, until the berries fall apart and the sauce has thickened slightly, about 20 minutes. Remove the pan from the heat.

Strain the sauce through a fine sieve to remove the seeds. Rinse and dry the pan and return the strained sauce to the pan. Over medium heat, stir in the butter until melted and well blended. Add the remaining blackberries and heat the sauce, stirring gently for 1 to 2 minutes. Remove the pan from the heat.

Ladle the blackberry sauce into hot jars, leaving ½-inch headspace. Using a plastic knife, remove any trapped air bubbles. Wipe the jar rims and threads with a clean, damp cloth. Cover with hot lids and apply screw rings. Process half-pint jars in a 200F (93C) water bath for 10 minutes, pint jars for 15 minutes.

Blueberry Topping

Filled with plump, tender blueberries, spoon this topping over ice cream, cheesecake or pound cake for a quick and elegant dessert.

MAKES ABOUT 4 HALF-PINT JARS OR 2 PINT JARS

5 cups fresh blueberries
1 cup sugar
⅔ cup water

Remove stems from blueberries and rinse the berries in cool water. Drain well. Using a vegetable masher, gently crush 2 cups of the berries. Set the remaining blueberries aside.

In a 3-quart saucepan, combine the sugar and water. Over low heat, stirring constantly, heat until the sugar is completely dissolved. Stir in the crushed blueberries. Increase the heat to medium-high and bring the mixture to a boil. Reduce the heat and simmer the mixture for 5 minutes, stirring frequently to prevent sticking. Stir in the remaining blueberries and simmer, stirring con-

stantly, for 2 minutes. Remove the pan from the heat.

Ladle the blueberry topping into hot jars, leaving ½-inch headspace. Using a plastic knife, remove any trapped air bubbles. Wipe the jar rims and threads with a clean, damp cloth. Cover with hot lids and apply screw rings. Process half-pint jars in a 200F (93C) water bath for 10 minutes, pint jars for 15 minutes.

Brandy-Pecan Sauce

This rich, slightly spicy sauce is also wonderful made with walnuts or with a combination of walnuts and pecans.

MAKES ABOUT 4 HALF-PINT JARS

¼ cup unsalted butter
3 cups whole pecan halves
½ cup unsalted butter
¼ cup water
1¾ cups firmly packed dark brown sugar
¼ teaspoon ground cinnamon
¼ teaspoon ground nutmeg
⅛ teaspoon ground ginger
⅛ teaspoon salt
½ cup brandy

In a large nonstick sauté pan over low heat, melt the ¼ cup butter. Stir in the pecan halves, coating well. Cook the pecans, stirring constantly, until they have absorbed all of the butter and developed a rich, nutty aroma, about 5 to 7 minutes. Remove the pan from the heat and set aside.

In a medium saucepan, combine the remaining ½ cup butter, water and brown sugar. Over low heat, stirring constantly, heat until the sugar is completely dissolved. Increase heat to medium and cook, stirring constantly, until the mixture reduces slightly and starts to thicken, about 3 to 4 minutes. Add the cinnamon, nutmeg, ginger and salt, stirring until well blended. Stir in the brandy. Continue cooking, stirring constantly, until the mixture reduces to a medium syrup, about 5 minutes. Stir in the toasted pecans and cook 2 minutes more. Remove the pan from the heat.

Ladle the pecans and syrup into hot jars, leaving ½-inch headspace. Using a plastic knife, remove any trapped air bubbles. Wipe the jar rims and threads with a clean, damp cloth. Cover with hot lids and apply screw rings. Process half-pint jars in a 200F (93C) water bath for 10 minutes.

Butterscotch Topping

An old-fashioned topping with a warm buttery flavor, it is reminiscent of days gone by.

MAKES ABOUT 6 (4-OUNCE) JARS OR 3 HALF-PINT JARS

    1 (11-ounce) package butterscotch chips
    ¼ cup firmly packed dark brown sugar
    ⅓ cup light corn syrup
    ¾ cup water
    ⅓ cup unsalted butter
    ½ teaspoon pure vanilla extract

In a medium saucepan, combine the butterscotch chips, brown sugar, corn syrup, water and butter. Over low heat, stirring constantly, heat until the sugar is completely dissolved and the butterscotch chips and butter are thoroughly melted.

Increase heat to medium-low and continue cooking, stirring constantly, until the topping starts to thicken and becomes glossy, about 5 to 7 minutes. Do not allow the topping to boil or it may taste burned. Remove the pan from the heat and stir in the vanilla. The topping will thicken as it cools.

Ladle the butterscotch topping into hot jars, leaving ½-inch headspace. Using a plastic knife, remove any trapped air bubbles. Wipe the jar rims and threads with a clean, damp cloth. Cover with hot lids and apply screw rings. Process both 4-ounce jars and half-pint jars in a 200F (93C) water bath for 15 minutes.

For best results, use the topping within 4 months.

Cherry-Amaretto Dessert Sauce

This wonderful sauce turns dessert into a special occasion any day of the week. Serve it over vanilla ice cream or spoon it over a rich, buttery pound cake for a quick, elegant dessert.

Either sweet or sour cherries may be used to make this sauce, depending on your personal taste and what you have available that is fresh and of high quality. Avoid sweet cherries that are very ripe, as they will tend to become mushy and the sauce will end up being too sweet. If you use sour cherries, use the smaller quantity of lemon juice.

MAKES ABOUT 6 HALF-PINT JARS OR 3 PINT JARS

8 cups pitted fresh cherries

½ cup strained fresh lemon juice for sweet cherries or 2 tablespoons strained fresh lemon juice for sour cherries

2½ cups light corn syrup

1¼ cups sugar

1 (3-ounce) pouch liquid pectin

1 teaspoon pure almond extract or 2 to 3 tablespoons amaretto

❧ Rinse and stem the cherries. Using a cherry pitter, remove the pits from the cherries.

In an 8-quart pan, layer the cherries, lemon juice, corn syrup and sugar. Over medium-low heat, gradually heat the mixture until the sugar has completely dissolved, gently shaking the pan occasionally to prevent scorching.

Increase the heat to medium and bring the cherry mixture to a boil. Simmer gently for 5 minutes, stirring occasionally.

Increase the heat to medium-high. Bring the cherries to a boil, stirring constantly, but gently. Stir in the entire contents of the pectin pouch. Boil, stirring constantly, for 1 minute. Remove the pan from the heat. Skim off any foam. Stir in the almond extract or amaretto. Cool 5 minutes, occasionally stirring gently.

Ladle the cherries and sauce into hot jars, leaving ½-inch headspace. Using a plastic knife, remove any trapped air bubbles. Wipe the jar rims and threads with a clean, damp cloth. Cover with hot lids and apply screw rings. Process half-pint jars in a 200F (93C) water bath for 10 minutes, pint jars for 15 minutes.

Rich Dark Chocolate Sauce

This wonderful chocolate sauce is great served over ice cream or drizzled over angel food cakes and pound cakes.

MAKES ABOUT 6 (4-OUNCE) JARS OR 3 HALF-PINT JARS

8 ounces bittersweet chocolate, chopped

1⅓ cups superfine sugar

⅔ cup light corn syrup

1 cup water

6 tablespoons unsalted butter

2 teaspoons pure vanilla extract

❧ In a medium saucepan, combine the chocolate, superfine sugar, corn syrup, water and butter. Over low heat, stirring constantly, heat until the sugar is completely dissolved and the chocolate and butter are thoroughly melted.

Increase heat to medium-low and continue cooking, stirring constantly, until the sauce starts to thicken and becomes glossy, about 10 minutes. Do not allow the sauce to boil or it may taste burned. Remove the pan from the heat and stir in the vanilla. The sauce will thicken as it cools.

Ladle the chocolate sauce into hot jars, leaving ½-inch headspace. Using a plastic knife, remove any trapped air bubbles. Wipe the jar rims and threads with a clean, damp cloth. Cover with hot lids and apply screw rings. Process both 4-ounce jars and half-pint jars in a 200F (93C) water bath for 15 minutes.

For best results, use the sauce within 4 months.

Island Topping

The fresh taste of the tropical islands makes for a very special fruit topping. The judges praised the excellent blend of flavors.

MAKES ABOUT 4 HALF-PINT JARS

1 (20-ounce) can crushed pineapple packed
   in heavy syrup
¾ cup unsweetened pineapple juice
1¼ cups sugar
⅔ cup shredded or flaked coconut
2 tablespoons bottled lemon juice
½ cup chopped roasted macadamia nuts

🦋 Drain the pineapple, reserving the syrup. Set pineapple aside.

In a medium saucepan, combine the reserved pineapple syrup, pineapple juice and sugar. Over medium heat, heat and stir the mixture until the sugar is completely dissolved. Bring the mixture to a boil, reduce the heat and boil gently for 3 minutes. Stir in the reserved pineapple, coconut and lemon juice. Heat for 2 minutes. Remove the pan from the heat and stir in the macadamia nuts.

Ladle the topping into hot jars, leaving ½-inch headspace. Using a plastic knife, remove any trapped air bubbles. Wipe the jar rims and threads with a clean, damp cloth. Cover with hot lids and apply screw rings. Process half-pint jars in a 200F (93C) water bath for 10 minutes.

Maple Walnut Sauce

Grade B maple syrup has a stronger, more intense maple flavor than Grade A syrup, the kind most commonly used on pancakes. If you cannot find Grade B maple syrup, you may use Grade A, but the sauce will have a milder maple flavor.

MAKES ABOUT 4 HALF-PINT JARS

¼ cup unsalted butter
3 cups coarsely chopped walnuts
1½ cups Grade B maple syrup
½ cup light corn syrup
⅓ cup water
¼ cup sugar

🦋 In a large nonstick sauté pan over low heat, melt the butter. Stir in the chopped walnuts, coating the pieces well. Cook the walnuts, stirring constantly, until they have absorbed all of the butter and developed a rich, nutty aroma, about 5 to 7 minutes. Remove the pan from the heat and set aside.

In a medium saucepan, combine the maple syrup, corn syrup, water and sugar. Over low heat, stirring constantly, heat until the sugar is completely dissolved. Increase the heat to medium and bring the mixture to a boil. Reduce the heat and simmer 15 minutes, stirring frequently to prevent sticking. Stir in the toasted walnuts and cook 2 minutes more. Remove the pan from the heat.

Ladle the walnuts and syrup into hot jars, leaving ½-inch headspace. Using a plastic knife, remove any trapped air bubbles. Wipe the jar rims and threads with a clean, damp cloth. Cover with hot lids and apply screw rings. Process half-pint jars in a 200F (93C) water bath for 10 minutes.

Pecan Praline Sauce

A traditional southern taste, it's just as good in a dessert sauce.

MAKES ABOUT 4 HALF-PINT JARS

¼ cup unsalted butter
3 cups coarsely chopped pecans
1⅓ cups dark corn syrup
⅓ cup Grade A maple syrup
⅓ cup water
⅓ cup firmly packed dark brown sugar
1 teaspoon pure vanilla extract

In a large nonstick sauté pan over low heat, melt the butter. Stir in the chopped pecans, coating the pieces well. Cook the pecans, stirring constantly, until they have absorbed all of the butter and developed a rich, nutty aroma, about 5 to 7 minutes. Remove the pan from the heat and set aside.

In a medium saucepan, combine the corn syrup, maple syrup, water and brown sugar. Over low heat, stirring constantly, heat until the sugar is completely dissolved. Increase the heat to medium and bring the mixture to a boil. Reduce the heat and simmer 10 minutes, stirring frequently to prevent sticking. Stir in the toasted pecans and cook 3 minutes more. Remove the pan from the heat and stir in the vanilla extract.

Ladle the pecans and syrup into hot jars, leaving ½-inch headspace. Using a plastic knife, remove any trapped air bubbles. Wipe the jar rims and threads with a clean, damp cloth. Cover with hot lids and apply screw rings. Process half-pint jars in a 200F (93C) water bath for 10 minutes.

Pineapple Upside-Down Topping

Brown sugar and pineapple make a heavenly combination.

MAKES ABOUT 5 HALF-PINT JARS

2 (20-ounce) cans crushed pineapple packed in heavy syrup
1 cup firmly packed dark brown sugar
3 tablespoons light rum (optional)

Drain the pineapple well, reserving the syrup.

In a 3-quart saucepan, combine the reserved pineapple syrup and the brown sugar. Heat over low heat, stirring constantly, until sugar is completely dissolved. Increase heat to medium-high and bring the syrup to a boil. Reduce the heat and simmer the syrup for 5 minutes.

Add the drained pineapple to the syrup. Return mixture to a boil. Reduce the heat and simmer for 2 minutes. Remove the pan from the heat. Stir in the rum if using.

Ladle the pineapple topping into hot jars, leaving ½-inch headspace. Using a plastic knife, remove any trapped air bubbles. Wipe the jar rims and threads with a clean, damp cloth. Cover with hot lids and apply screw rings. Process half-pint jars in a 200F (93C) water bath for 10 minutes.

Raspberry Hot Fudge Sauce

A decadent blending of two luscious flavors, use the sauce for ice-cream sundaes and with other rich desserts.

MAKES ABOUT 6 (4-OUNCE) JARS OR
3 HALF-PINT JARS

6 ounces bittersweet chocolate, chopped
5 tablespoons unsalted butter
1¼ cups superfine sugar
½ cup light corn syrup
½ cup water
⅓ cup raspberry liqueur

In the top of a double boiler, combine the chocolate and butter. Place the pan over a saucepan of gently simmering water, making sure that the water does not touch the bottom of the top pan. Heat, stirring frequently, until the chocolate and butter are melted and combined. Remove the double boiler from the heat and keep the chocolate mixture warm over the hot water until ready to use.

In a large saucepan, combine the superfine sugar, corn syrup and water. Over low heat, stirring constantly, heat until the sugar is completely dissolved. Increase the heat to medium-high and bring the mixture to a boil, stirring constantly to prevent sticking. Reduce the heat to medium-low and simmer until the syrup is clear, about 3 minutes. Remove the pan from the heat.

Whisk the melted chocolate mixture into the hot syrup. Return the pan to the heat and cook the hot fudge, stirring constantly, until the sauce starts to thicken and becomes glossy, about 10 minutes. Do not allow the sauce to boil or it may taste burned. Remove the pan from the heat and gently stir for 2 to 3 minutes to cool the sauce and release any trapped air bubbles. Stir in the raspberry liqueur until well blended.

Ladle the raspberry fudge sauce into hot jars, leaving ½-inch headspace. Using a plastic knife, remove any trapped air bubbles. Wipe the jar rims and threads with a clean, damp cloth. Cover with hot lids and apply screw rings. Process both 4-ounce jars and half-pint jars in a 200F (93C) water bath for 15 minutes.

For best results, use the fudge sauce within 4 months.

Note

Raspberry Hot Fudge Sauce may also be stored in the refrigerator, without processing, for up to 2 days. Spread a piece of plastic wrap over the surface of the sauce, pressing out any air bubbles. Cover the container tightly. Allow the sauce to come to room temperature before heating.

Silky Hot Fudge Sauce

Pure heaven for chocolate lovers, this version of an old favorite is rich, dark and decadent, perfect for banana splits and hot fudge sundaes. Warm the fudge sauce in a small saucepan over low heat or in a glass dish in the microwave before serving. Be careful not to overheat or allow the sauce to boil.

MAKES ABOUT 6 (4-OUNCE) JARS OR 3 HALF-PINT JARS

8 ounces bittersweet chocolate, chopped
½ cup unsalted butter
1½ cups superfine sugar

⅔ cup light corn syrup

⅔ cup water

3 teaspoons pure vanilla extract

In the top of a double boiler, combine the chocolate and butter. Place the pan over a saucepan of gently simmering water, making sure that the water does not touch the bottom of the top pan. Heat, stirring frequently, until the chocolate and butter are melted and combined. Remove the double boiler from the heat and keep the chocolate mixture warm over the hot water until ready to use.

In a large saucepan, combine the superfine sugar, corn syrup and water. Over low heat, stirring constantly, heat until the sugar is completely dissolved. Increase the heat to medium-high and bring the mixture to a boil, stirring constantly to prevent sticking. Reduce the heat to medium-low and simmer until the syrup is clear, about 3 minutes. Remove the pan from the heat.

Whisk the melted chocolate mixture into the hot syrup. Return the pan to the heat and cook the hot fudge, stirring constantly, until the sauce starts to thicken and becomes glossy, about 10 minutes. Do not allow the sauce to boil or it may taste burned. Remove the pan from the heat and gently stir for 2 to 3 minutes to cool the sauce and release any trapped air bubbles. Stir in the vanilla extract until well blended.

Ladle the hot fudge sauce into hot jars, leaving ½-inch headspace. Using a plastic knife, remove any trapped air bubbles. Wipe the jar rims and threads with a clean, damp cloth. Cover with hot lids and apply screw rings. Process both 4-ounce jars and half-pint jars in a 200F (93C) water bath for 15 minutes.

For best results, use the fudge sauce within 4 months.

Note

Silky Hot Fudge Sauce may also be stored in the refrigerator, without processing, for up to 2 days. Spread a piece of plastic wrap over the surface of the sauce, pressing out any air bubbles. Cover the container tightly. Allow the sauce to come to room temperature before heating.

Strawberry Topping

Add a bit of springtime flavor to desserts all year long.

MAKES ABOUT 4 HALF-PINT JARS OR 2 PINT JARS

5 cups hulled and sliced fresh strawberries

1½ cups sugar

¾ cup water

2 tablespoons strained fresh lemon juice

Using a vegetable masher, gently crush 2 cups of the strawberries. Set the remaining berries aside.

In a 3-quart saucepan, combine the sugar and water. Over low heat, stirring constantly, heat until the sugar is completely dissolved. Stir in the crushed strawberries. Increase the heat to medium-high and bring the mixture to a boil. Reduce the heat and simmer the mixture for 5 minutes, stirring frequently to prevent sticking. Stir in the remaining strawberries and the lemon juice. Simmer, stirring constantly, for 1 minute. Remove the pan from the heat.

Ladle the strawberry topping into hot jars, leaving ½-inch headspace. Using a plastic knife, remove any trapped air bubbles. Wipe the jar rims and threads with a clean, damp cloth. Cover with hot lids and apply screw rings. Process half-pint jars in a 200F (93C) water bath for 10 minutes, pint jars for 15 minutes.

Almond Liqueur

This liqueur is abundant with the fragrant aroma and flavor of almonds. Hazelnuts may be substituted for the almonds to make Hazelnut Liqueur.

MAKES ABOUT 3 CUPS

    1¾ pounds almonds, coarsely chopped
    3 cups vodka
    1⅓ cups sugar
    1 vanilla bean, coarsely chopped

Place the almonds in a 1½- to 2-quart glass jar.

In a medium saucepan, over low heat, heat the vodka just until warm. Add the sugar and stir until the sugar is completely dissolved. Remove the pan from the heat, add the vanilla bean and set aside to cool.

Pour the cooled vodka mixture into the jar with the almonds. Cover the jar opening with 2 layers of plastic wrap, then screw on the jar lid or a screw ring. Swirl the jar gently to mix the ingredients. Place the jar in a paper bag and set it in a cool, dry, dark location for 3 to 4 weeks.

Wash decorative liqueur bottles in hot, soapy water and rinse well. Turn the bottles upside down to dry.

Place a fine-meshed sieve over a bowl or pan and strain the liqueur. Discard the nuts and

vanilla bean. Rinse the sieve and line it with 3 layers of clean, damp cheesecloth. Strain the liqueur through the cheesecloth. Line the sieve with a paper coffee filter and strain the liqueur one more time. Using a funnel, pour the liqueur into the clean glass bottles and close with clean screw caps or clamp closures.

Apricot Brandy

A classic pairing of flavors with a refreshing taste, use within 3 to 4 months for the best flavor.

MAKES ABOUT 5 CUPS

    1½ pounds dried apricots, chopped
    3 cups Johannisberg Riesling
    1 cup brandy
    2 cups sugar

Place the apricots in a 1½- to 2-quart glass jar.

In a medium saucepan, over low heat, heat the wine and brandy just until warm. Add the sugar and stir until the sugar is completely dissolved. Remove the pan from the heat and cool.

Pour the cooled wine mixture into the jar with the apricots. Cover the jar opening with 2 layers of plastic wrap, then screw on the jar lid or a screw ring. Swirl the jar gently to mix the ingredients. Place the jar in a paper bag and set it in a cool, dry, dark location for 6 weeks.

Wash decorative liqueur bottles in hot, soapy water and rinse well. Turn the bottles upside down to dry.

Place a fine-meshed sieve over a bowl or pan and strain the cordial. Discard the pulp. Rinse the sieve and line it with 3 layers of clean, damp cheesecloth. Strain the cordial through the cheesecloth. Line the sieve with a paper coffee filter and strain the cordial one more time. Using a funnel, pour the cordial into the clean glass bottles and close with clean screw caps or clamp closures.

Blackberry Cordial

This fruity liqueur may also be made with boysenberries or red raspberries.

MAKES ABOUT 4½ CUPS

1½ quarts ripe fresh or frozen
    blackberries
3 cups framboise (raspberry brandy) or
    kirsch (cherry brandy)
1 cup sugar

 Rinse the blackberries in cool water and drain well. If using frozen berries, defrost, reserving the juice, but do not rinse.

In a medium saucepan, over low heat, heat the framboise just until warm. Add the sugar and stir until the sugar is completely dissolved. Remove the pan from the heat and cool.

In a flat-bottomed bowl or pan, using a vegetable masher, slightly crush the berries in small batches. Transfer the berries and juice to a 2-quart glass jar. Pour the cooled framboise into the jar with the berries. Cover the jar opening with 2 layers of plastic wrap, then screw on the jar lid or a screw ring. Swirl the jar gently to mix the ingredi-

ents. Place the jar in a paper bag and set it in a cool, dry, dark location for 6 weeks.

Wash decorative liqueur bottles in hot, soapy water and rinse well. Turn the bottles upside down to dry.

Place a fine-meshed sieve over a bowl or pan and strain the cordial. Discard the seeds and pulp. Rinse the sieve and line it with 3 layers of clean, damp cheesecloth. Strain the cordial through the cheesecloth. Line the sieve with a paper coffee filter and strain the cordial one more time. Using a funnel, pour the cordial into the clean glass bottles and close with clean screw caps or clamp closures.

Cherry Brandy

A light layer of foam may develop on top of the cherry cordial during steeping. This is a normal occurrence with cherries. The foam may be skimmed from the surface of the cordial before straining.

MAKES 3½ TO 4 CUPS

1½ pounds dried pitted cherries, chopped
2 cups Johannisberg Riesling
1 cup kirsch (cherry brandy)
1½ cups sugar

 Place the cherries in a 1½- to 2-quart glass jar.

In a medium saucepan, over low heat, heat the wine and the kirsch just until warm. Add the sugar and stir until the sugar is completely dissolved. Remove the pan from the heat and cool.

Pour the cooled wine mixture into the jar with the cherries. Cover the jar opening with 2 layers of plastic wrap, then screw on the jar lid or a screw ring. Swirl the jar gently to mix the ingredients. Place the jar in a paper bag and set it in a cool, dry, dark location for 6 weeks.

Wash decorative liqueur bottles in hot, soapy water and rinse well. Turn the bottles upside down to dry.

Place a fine-meshed sieve over a bowl or pan and strain the cordial. Discard the pulp. Rinse the sieve and line it with 3 layers of clean, damp cheesecloth. Strain the cordial through the cheesecloth. Line the sieve with a paper coffee filter and strain the cordial one more time. Using a funnel, pour the cordial into the clean glass bottles and close with clean screw caps or clamp closures.

Coffee Liqueur

This liqueur has a rich coffee flavor and is excellent on its own or mixed with a little fresh cream just before serving. Or try it over vanilla ice cream for an adult dessert. If you do not have a coffee grinder, use a fresh can of ground coffee.

MAKES ABOUT 6 TO 6½ CUPS

2 cups fresh ground coffee beans, preferably
    French roast
3 cups boiling water
2½ cups granulated sugar
1 cup firmly packed light brown sugar
1 vanilla bean, coarsely chopped
2¼ cups vodka
¾ cup brandy

In a heatproof glass bowl or stainless steel saucepan, combine the ground coffee and the boiling water. Stir for 1 to 2 minutes.

Line a sieve with a coffee filter and place the sieve over a medium saucepan. Strain the coffee through the filter. Discard the coffee grounds. Add the granulated sugar and brown sugar to the coffee. Place the pan over low heat and heat, stirring constantly, just until the sugars are completely dissolved. Remove the pan from the heat, add the vanilla bean and set aside to cool.

In a 1½- to 2-quart glass jar, combine the cooled coffee mixture, the vodka and the brandy. Cover the jar opening with 2 layers of plastic wrap, then screw on the jar lid or a screw ring. Swirl the jar gently to mix the ingredients. Place the jar in a paper bag and set it in a cool, dry, dark location for 3 to 4 weeks.

Wash decorative liqueur bottles in hot, soapy water and rinse well. Turn the bottles upside down to dry.

Line a fine-meshed sieve with a coffee filter and place it over a bowl or pan. Strain the liqueur through the filter, discarding the vanilla bean. Using a funnel, pour the liqueur into the clean glass bottles and close with clean screw caps or clamp closures.

Raspberry Sherry

This refreshing cordial is also wonderful served over fresh fruit or ice cream.

MAKES ABOUT 5 CUPS

2 quarts fresh or frozen raspberries
2 cups golden sherry
2½ cups sugar

☙ Rinse the raspberries in cool water and drain well. If using frozen berries, defrost, reserving the juice, but do not rinse.

In a medium saucepan, over low heat, heat the sherry just until warm. Add the sugar and stir until the sugar is completely dissolved. Remove the pan from the heat and cool.

In a flat-bottomed bowl or pan, using a vegetable masher, slightly crush the raspberries in small batches. Transfer the berries and juice to a 1½- to 2-quart glass jar. Pour the cooled sherry into the jar with the berries. Cover the jar opening with 2 layers of plastic wrap, then screw on the jar lid or a screw ring. Swirl the jar gently to mix the ingredients. Place the jar in a paper bag and set it in a cool, dry, dark location for 6 weeks.

Wash decorative liqueur bottles in hot, soapy water and rinse well. Turn the bottles upside down to dry.

Place a fine-meshed sieve over a bowl or pan and strain the cordial. Discard the seeds and pulp. Rinse the sieve and line it with 3 layers of clean, damp cheesecloth. Strain the cordial through the cheesecloth. Line the sieve with a paper coffee filter and strain the cordial one more time. Using a funnel, pour the cordial into the clean glass bottles and close with clean screw caps or clamp closures.

Strawberry Sherry

A delicately flavored cordial, it has a tantalizing aroma of fresh fruit.

MAKES ABOUT 5 CUPS

2 quarts strawberries
2 cups golden sherry
2½ cups sugar

☙ Rinse the strawberries in cool water and drain well. Remove the hulls. In a flat-bottomed bowl or pan, using a vegetable masher, slightly crush the strawberries in small batches. Transfer the berries to a 1½- to 2-quart glass jar.

In a medium saucepan, over low heat, heat the sherry just until warm. Add the sugar and stir until the sugar is completely dissolved. Remove the pan from the heat.

Pour the warm sherry into the jar with the crushed berries. Swirl the jar gently to mix the ingredients, then set aside to cool. When the mixture is cool, cover the jar opening with 2 layers of plastic wrap, then screw on the jar lid or a screw ring. Place the jar in a paper bag and set it in a cool, dry, dark location for 6 weeks.

Wash decorative liqueur bottles in hot, soapy water and rinse well. Turn the bottles upside down to dry.

Place a fine-meshed sieve over a bowl or pan and strain the cordial. Discard the seeds and pulp. Rinse the sieve and line it with 3 layers of clean, damp cheesecloth. Strain the cordial through the cheesecloth. Line the sieve with a paper coffee filter and strain the cordial one more time. Using a funnel, pour the cordial into the clean glass bottles and close with clean screw caps or clamp closures.

Troubleshooting Guide

This guide lists the major problems that can occur following the home canning of preserved foods. Many of these problems may appear during storage and are directly related to the conditions under which the food was stored. Others are a result of poor handling and improper techniques. Always use the correct and safe methods of preparation and processing when home canning preserved foods. Inspect the seals of all jars after canning and before storing. Within 24 hours of canning, reprocess or refrigerate any jars that fail to seal.

Any food in a jar that is unsealed or has a bulging lid should not be eaten. If the food inside the jar shows any sign of spoilage, such as mold, mildew, fermentation, rising air bubbles, cloudy liquid, spurting liquid, sediment in the liquid, foaming, soft or mushy food, slimy food or has an unpleasant odor, the food should not be tasted. Dispose of any contaminated food in a safe manner so that no human or animal can come in contact with it.

All Preserved Foods

PROBLEM	CAUSE	SOLUTION
Jars fail to seal or do not retain a vacuum (Do not taste or use.)	Jars were not processed properly.	Always process jars in a water bath or pressure canner.
	Jars were not covered by water during water bath processing.	Make sure jars are covered by at least 1 to 2 inches of water.
	Jars were inverted after processing.	Do not invert the jars.
	Product on rim of the jar.	Wipe jar rims with a clean, damp towel before applying lids.

PROBLEM	CAUSE	SOLUTION
Jars fail to seal or do not retain a vacuum (Do not taste or use.)	Too much headspace in jar to form a vacuum.	Use the correct amount of headspace.
	Nicked, chipped or cracked jar or jar rim.	Inspect all jars before use.
Liquid or food boils out of jars during processing	Jars were filled too full.	Always leave the correct amount of headspace.
	Packing fruits and vegetables into jars too solidly or tightly.	Pack jars snugly but not too tightly.
	Processing jars at too high of a temperature.	Monitor the temperature of water bath canners during processing.
	Processing jars at too high of a pressure.	Monitor the pressure gauge during pressure canner processing.
Mold or spoilage (Do not taste or use.)	Use of overripe or damaged produce.	Use only top-quality produce for canning.
	Jars stored in a location that was too warm.	Store jars in a cool location.
	Jars were not properly processed after filling.	Always process jars of preserved foods in a water bath or pressure canner.
	Seal broken by inverting jars after processing.	Never invert jars after processing.
Fermentation (Do not taste or use.)	Jars stored in a location that was too warm.	Store jars in a cool location.
	Unsealed jars.	Process all jars in a water bath or pressure canner.
Mildew (Do not taste or use.)	Jars stored in a damp location.	Store jars in a dry location.
	Jars not properly sealed.	Process all jars in a water bath or pressure canner.
	Food poured into cold, wet jars.	Always add food to hot jars.

PROBLEM	CAUSE	SOLUTION
Moving or rising bubbles (Do not taste or use.)	Denotes spoilage or fermentation.	Process all jars according to the instructions in the recipe for the type of food.
Contents of jars darken during storage	Weak seals on jars.	Process all jars in a water bath or pressure canner.
	Jars stored in a location that was too light.	Store jars in a dark location.
	Jars stored in a location that was too warm.	Store jars in a cool location.

Soft Spreads

PROBLEM	CAUSE	SOLUTION
Spread does not set, is too soft or is syrupy	Incorrect amount of sugar— too little or too much.	Do not reduce or increase the quantity of sugar in the recipe. Measure the sugar carefully.
	Not enough acid.	Increase acid level by adding lemon juice.
	Overripe fruit.	Use fruit that is fully ripe but not overripe.
	Not enough pectin.	Be sure to use the entire contents of the pectin pouch.
	Old, outdated pectin.	Check date on pectin box. Use pectin before the expiration date.
	Cooking too much fruit at one time. Insufficient surface area in pan to allow for evaporation.	Do not double batches. Cook each batch separately.
	Spread was cooked too long after adding the pectin, causing the pectin to break down.	Cook only for the amount of time indicated in the recipe.
	Fruit or juice was not brought to a full rolling boil before adding pectin.	Bring to a full rolling boil before and after adding pectin.
	Mixture not boiled long enough after adding pectin.	Boil for the full amount of time indicated in the recipe to distribute the pectin.

Soft Spreads (*cont.*)

PROBLEM	CAUSE	SOLUTION
Spread is too stiff	Overcooking, resulting in evaporation of too much liquid or juice.	Cook the spread for the amount of time indicated in the recipe.
	Underripe fruit.	Use fully ripe fruit.
Tough or rubbery texture	Overcooking or boiling spread too long.	Boil for the amount of time indicated in the recipe.
	Cooking too slowly, at too low a temperature, for too long a period of time.	After sugar is dissolved, rapidly bring mixture to a full boil. Boil only for the amount of time indicated in the recipe.
	Not enough sugar.	Do not reduce the amount of sugar. Measure the sugar c arefully.
	Too much acid.	Measure the lemon juice or other acid carefully.
	Too much pectin in proportion to the fruit.	Measure the fruit carefully. Use fully ripe fruit.
	Underripe fruit.	Use fully ripe fruit.
Air bubbles in spread	Spread ladled into jars too slowly. Jars filled too slowly.	Pour spread from ladle quickly into the jars. Fill the jars quickly.
	Spread ladled into jars from too great a height.	Keep ladle close to the funnel when filling jars.
	Spread too cool when ladled into jars.	Cool spread only for the amount of time indicated in the recipe.
Crystals in spread	Too much sugar was used.	Measure sugar carefully.
	Spread brought to a boil before sugar was completely dissolved.	Make sure sugar is completely dissolved before bringing the mixture to a boil.
	Sugar was not completely dissolved before adding pectin.	Make sure sugar is completely dissolved before adding pectin.
	Not enough acid.	Increase amount of lemon juice.

PROBLEM	CAUSE	SOLUTION
Crystals in spread	Pouring spread into jars directly from pan, picking up undissolved sugar on side of pan.	Use a ladle to fill jars.
	Tartaric acid in grape jelly.	Chill juice overnight to allow acid to settle to the bottom of container. Pour or ladle juice into another container without disturbing sediment.
Cloudy jelly	Starch from underripe fruit.	Use fully ripe fruit.
	Homemade apple pectin used to make jelly.	Use commercial pectin.
	Poor method of preparing fruit for extracting juice.	Do not puree fruit. Remove skins.
	Fruit cooked too long before straining juice.	Cook fruit for the amount of time indicated in recipe.
	Squeezing cheesecloth or jelly bag during juice extraction.	Do not squeeze cheesecloth or bag. Allow the juice to drip.
	Did not filter juice after extraction.	Filter juice through paper coffee filters.
	Did not skim foam from surface before filling jars.	Quickly skim foam from surface of jelly.
	Jelly was too cool when ladled into jars.	Immediately ladle jelly into jars.
	Jelly was ladled into jars too slowly.	Ladle jelly into jars quickly.
Weeping jelly	Too much acid.	Use less lemon juice or other acid.
	Jars stored in a location that was too warm.	Store jars in a cool location.
Separation of fruit and juice in jars	Underripe fruit.	Use fully ripe fruit.
	Not enough sugar or acid.	Measure sugar and lemon juice carefully.
	Pectin was not fully distributed throughout the spread.	After adding pectin, boil for the full amount of time indicated in recipe.

PROBLEM	CAUSE	SOLUTION
Separation of fruit and juice in jars	Did not cool and stir the spread before filling the jars.	Cool and stir the spread for the amount of time indicated in recipe.
Spread darkens during storage	Fruit was cooked too long.	Cook fruit as instructed and for the amount of time indicated in recipe. Use a pectin recipe to avoid overcooking fruit.
	Jars stored in a location that was too light.	Store jars in a dark location.
	Jars stored in a location that was too warm.	Store jars in a cool location.
	Weak seals on jars.	Process all jars in a water bath for amount of time indicated in recipe.
Spread has poor flavor	Use of underripe, overripe or damaged fruit.	Use fully ripe, undamaged fruit.
	Use of inferior-quality ingredients.	Use top-quality ingredients.
	Poor preparation techniques.	Prepare the fruit according to the recipe.
Mold or spoilage (Do not taste or use.)	Not enough acid.	Increase lemon juice or other acid. Measure acid carefully.
	Not enough sugar.	Do not reduce the amount of sugar called for in the recipe. Measure sugar carefully.
	Unsealed jars.	Jars may have been inverted after canning or processing. Do not invert jars. Process all jars in a water bath.
	Use of the outdated Open-Kettle Method of canning. Jars were not processed in a water bath.	Do not use the Open-Kettle Method. Process all jars in a water bath for the amount of time indicated in the recipe.
	Jars stored in a location that was too warm.	Store jars in a cool location.

Reprocessing Soft Spreads

If a soft spread does not set properly and is either too thick or too thin, you have a couple of options—you can either find a use for the spread the way it is or reprocess it. A thin spread can be used as a pancake syrup or ice-cream topping, while a thick spread can be heated with a little water and used as a glaze or sauce for meats and other foods.

Finding a use for the spread is usually a better option than reprocessing it. When you reprocess a spread, there is an increased chance of air bubbles becoming trapped in the spread. The flavor and texture can also be affected, causing the spread to lose some of its fresh taste and silky smoothness.

If you do decide to reprocess a soft spread to thin its texture, you will need to reheat the spread and add either some juice or water. To thicken the texture of a thin spread, you will need to cook the spread again with some additional sugar, lemon juice and pectin.

Be sure to use clean, hot jars and new, heated lids when reprocessing any preserved food.

Reprocessing jellies, especially firm jellies, is not recommended because of the increased probability of a cloudy appearance and tiny air bubbles or pectin wisps becoming trapped in the jelly. If you reprocess a jelly, use filtered fresh lemon juice or the jelly will be cloudy.

To reprocess a soft spread that has set too firm (jellies not recommended):

Empty the jars of soft spread into the same size pan as used in the recipe. Add 2 to 3 tablespoons of water or juice, depending on the thickness of the spread, for each half-pint jar of spread being reprocessed.

Over low heat, stirring gently and constantly, heat until the spread melts and the mixture is smooth and well combined. Increase the heat to medium-high and bring the mixture to a boil. Remove the pan from the heat. Skim off any foam. (If reprocessing jelly, immediately ladle the spread into the hot jars.)

Cool and stir the spread for 5 minutes. Ladle the spread into clean, hot jars, leaving ¼-inch headspace. Wipe the rims with a clean, damp cloth. Cover with new, hot lids and apply screw rings. Process half-pint jars in a 200F (93C) water bath for 10 minutes, pint jars for 15 minutes or for the length of time indicated in the recipe.

To reprocess a soft spread that is too thin and did not set (jellies not recommended):

Empty the jars of soft spread into the same size pan as used in the recipe.

Over low heat, stirring gently and constantly, heat until the spread melts and is smooth. Add 3 tablespoons sugar and 1½ teaspoons strained fresh lemon juice for each half-pint jar of spread being reprocessed. Heat the mixture, stirring constantly, until the sugar is completely dissolved.

Increase the heat to medium-high and bring the mixture to a full rolling boil. Stir in 1½ teaspoons of liquid pectin for each half-pint jar of spread being reprocessed. Return the mixture to a full rolling boil, stirring constantly. Boil and stir for 1 minute. Remove the pan from the heat. Skim off any foam. (If reprocessing jelly, immediately ladle the jelly into the hot jars.)

Cool and stir the spread for 5 minutes. Ladle the spread into clean, hot jars, leaving 1/4-inch headspace. Wipe the rims with a clean, damp cloth. Cover with new, hot lids and apply screw rings. Process half-pint jars in a 200F (93C) water bath for 10 minutes, pint jars for 15 minutes or for the length of time indicated in the recipe.

To reprocess 4 half-pint jars of a thin soft spread, you will need:

3/4 cup sugar

2 tablespoons strained fresh lemon juice

2 tablespoons liquid pectin

To reprocess 6 half-pint jars of a thin soft spread, you will need:

1 cup plus 2 tablespoons sugar

3 tablespoons strained fresh lemon juice

3 tablespoons liquid pectin

Fruits

PROBLEM	CAUSE	SOLUTION
Fruit in top of jar darkens	Syrup did not cover the fruit.	Cover fruit completely with syrup before applying lids.
	Trapped air bubbles were not removed.	Remove air bubbles and replace with more syrup before applying lids.
	Headspace too large.	Measure the headspace carefully.
	Vacuum was not produced in jar.	Process all jars in water bath for the time and at the temperature indicated in the recipe.
	Jars were not processed long enough to deactivate enzymes.	Process jars for the length of time indicated in the recipe.
Fruit floats in the jar	Fruit canned using the raw pack method contains air trapped in the cells.	Can fruit using the hot pack method, where applicable.
	Syrup is heavier than the fruit.	Can fruit in a light or medium syrup.
	Underripe fruit.	Use firm, ripe fruit.

PROBLEM	CAUSE	SOLUTION
Cloudy liquid	Overripe fruit or overcooked fruit falls apart during processing or storage.	Use firm, ripe fruit. Do not heat fruit in syrup too long before packing into jars.
	Spoilage resulting from underprocessing. Do not taste or use.	Process jars for the length of time indicated in the recipe.

Vegetables

PROBLEM	CAUSE	SOLUTION
Vegetables in top of jar darken	Liquid did not cover the vegetables.	Cover vegetables completely with liquid before applying lids.
	Trapped air bubbles were not removed.	Remove air bubbles and replace with more liquid before applying lids.
	Headspace too large.	Measure headspace carefully.
	Vacuum was not produced in jar. Do not taste or use.	Process all jars in a pressure canner for the time and at the pressure indicated in the recipe.
Vegetables float in jars	Vegetables canned using the raw pack method contain air bubbles trapped in the cells.	Can vegetables using the hot pack method.
Light-colored vegetables turn brown during processing	Vegetables were blanched or cooked at too high of a temperature before filling jars.	Blanch or cook vegetables at a simmer or a gentle boil rather than a full boil.
	Iron or other minerals in water used for canning.	Use soft water or distilled water for canning.
	Vegetables processed at too high of a temperature or pressure.	Process vegetables in a pressure canner at the pressure indicated in the recipe. Watch the pressure gauge closely.
Color of green vegetables fades	Natural reaction to heat processing.	None. A little baking soda or lemon juice added to cooking liquid may help reduce color loss.

PROBLEM	CAUSE	SOLUTION
Beets fade in color or turn white	Beets used were too old or mature.	Select fresh, young, tender beets for canning.
	Beets were stored too long before canning.	Can beets as soon after harvest as possible.
	Beets were cooked without the stems.	Leave 2 inches of stem on beets during cooking.
Corn turns brown in jars	Corn was too old or mature.	Select fresh, young, tender ears of corn.
	Corn was stored too long before canning.	Can corn as soon after harvest as possible.
	Variety of corn was not suitable for canning.	Use a yellow variety of corn that is good for canning.
Liquid in jars turns cloudy	Vegetables used were too old or overripe.	Select, fresh young, tender vegetables for canning.
	Vegetables were overcooked.	Cook vegetables at a simmer or a gentle boil only for the amount of time indicated in the recipe.
	Iron or other minerals in water used for canning.	Use soft water or distilled water for canning.
	Fillers in table salt.	Use canning, pickling or kosher salt.
	Starch in vegetables such as corn.	Can vegetables as soon after harvest as possible.
	Too high of a processing pressure caused vegetables to burst.	Process vegetables in a pressure canner at the pressure indicated in the recipe. Watch the pressure gauge closely.
	Spoilage from underprocessing. Do not taste or use.	Process vegetables in a pressure canner for the length of time indicated in the recipe.

Pickles

PROBLEM	CAUSE	SOLUTION
Hollow cucumber pickles	Cucumbers were too mature when harvested.	Harvest cucumbers before they reach full maturity.
	Cucumbers were too old or stored too long before canning.	Use cucumbers within 24 hours of harvest.
	Wrong type of cucumber used for making pickles.	Use only pickling cucumbers. Do not use salad-type cucumbers for making pickles.
	Imperfect development of cucumber.	None.
Soft pickles	High mineral level in water.	Use soft water or distilled water for pickling liquid.
	Not enough salt in brine.	Use full amount of salt called for in the recipe.
	Not enough vinegar in pickling liquid.	Use full amount of vinegar called for in the recipe.
	Pickles were heated too long before filling the jars.	Heat pickles for the length of time indicated in the recipe.
	Vinegar with less than 5 percent acidity strength.	Use a vinegar with a known acidity level of at least 5 percent.
	Overprocessing in water bath.	Process pickles in water bath for the time and at the temperature indicated in the recipe.
Shriveled pickles	Too much time between harvest and pickling.	Can pickles as soon after harvest as possible. Use cucumbers within 24 hours of harvest.
	Salt brine too strong.	Use less salt in brine. Measure salt carefully.
	Too much sugar in syrup, or too much sugar added to syrup at one time.	Use the amount of sugar indicated in the recipe. Measure sugar carefully. Follow recipe closely for making sweet pickles.

PROBLEM	CAUSE	SOLUTION
Shriveled pickles	Too much vinegar in pickling liquid.	Measure vinegar carefully.
Pickles darken in jars during storage	Iron, lime or other minerals in water used for canning.	Use soft water or distilled water for canning.
	Iodized salt.	Use canning, pickling or kosher salt.
	Cider vinegar or red wine vinegar used in pickling liquid for light-colored vegetables.	Use white vinegar or white wine vinegar for light-colored vegetables.
	Pans, bowls, utensils or other equipment made of aluminum, copper, iron, brass or zinc.	Only use stainless steel pans and utensils and stainless steel or glass bowls for making pickles.
Pickling liquid in jars turns cloudy	Vegetables used were too old or overripe.	Select fresh, young, tender vegetables for pickling.
	Iron or other minerals in water used for canning.	Use soft water or distilled water for canning.
	Fillers in table salt.	Use canning, pickling or kosher salt.
	Ground spices.	Use whole spices for pickling.
	Spoilage from underprocessing. Do not taste or use.	Process pickles for the length of time indicated in the recipe.
Scum on pickles in jars (Do not taste or use.)	Presence of bacteria.	Scrub vegetables well before making pickles.
	Exposure to air. Jars not sealed properly.	Process all jars in a water bath for the time and at the temperature indicated in the recipe.
Slippery or slimy pickles (Do not taste or use.)	Spoilage from underprocessing and unsealed jars.	Process all jars in a water bath for the time and at the temperature indicated in the recipe.

Mail-Order Sources

The following companies offer canning equipment and other supplies by mail. Merchandise catalogs are available upon request by calling or writing to the companies. These catalogs can be very useful resources for the home canner.

Alltrista Corporation
P.O. Box 2005
Muncie, IN 47307-0005
(800) 240-3340
Ball and Kerr canning supplies, jars, equipment, utensils, Norpro cheesecloth, Instant Clearjel and the *Ball Blue Book Canning Guide*

The Baker's Catalog
P.O. Box 876
Norwich, VT 05055-0876
(800) 827-6836
KingArthurFlour.com
Instant Clearjel, chocolate, dried fruit, dried spices and seasonings and utensils

Chef's Catalog
P.O. Box 620048
Dallas, TX 75262-0048
(800) 338-3232
www.chefscatalog.com

Cooking equipment, utensils, knives and specialty gadgets

Colorful Images
2910 Colorful Avenue
Longmont, CO 80504-6214
(800) 458-7999
Personalized labels for canning jars

A Cook's Wares
211 37th Street
Beaver Falls, PA 15010-2103
(800) 915-9788
www.cookswares.com
Cooking equipment, utensils, specialty tools, thermometers, scales, knives, dried fruits and dried herbs and spices

Cumberland General Store
#1 Highway 68
Crossville, TN 38555
(800) 334-4640
Canning equipment, utensils and tools

The Food Crafter's Supply Catalog
Kitchen Krafts, Inc.
P.O. Box 442
Waukon, IA 52172-0442

(800) 776-0575
www.kitchenkrafts.com
Home-canning equipment, canning jars, utensils, tools, cooking supplies, Instant Clearjel and vinegar bottles

Penzeys Spices
P.O. Box 933
Muskego, WI 53150-0933
(800) 741-7787
www.penzeys.com
Dried spices and seasonings

Walnut Acres Organic Farms
Penns Creek, PA 17862-0800
(800) 344-9025 (Customer Service)
(800) 433-3998

www.walnutacres.com
Organic dried fruits and nuts and dried herbs and spices

William Glen
Mail-Order Department
2651 El Paseo Lane
Sacramento, CA 95821
(800) 842-3322
Fine cooking equipment, tools and utensils

Williams-Sonoma
Mail-Order Department
P.O. Box 7456
San Francisco, CA 94120
(800) 541-2233
Fine cooking equipment, tools and utensils

Fair Addresses

Most of the following state, county and regional fairs responded to my request for a copy of their exhibitor handbook. I appreciate their generous assistance in providing this information to me. Many other counties throughout the country also hold annual fairs that include a preserved foods competition. Check with your local fair for specific information about their entry rules and exhibit requirements.

The information listed here was accurate at the time this list was compiled. I have indicated the fairs that welcome entries from exhibitors who live outside the state or region where the fair is held.

ALABAMA
Alabama National Fair
P.O. Box 3304
Montgomery AL, 36109-0304
(334) 272-6831
www.alnationalfair.org

ALASKA
Alaska State Fair, Inc.
2075 Glenn Highway
Palmer, AK 99645-6799
(907) 745-4827
www.akstatefair.org
Request: Exhibitor Guide
Competitive exhibits are open to all.

ARIZONA
Arizona State Fair
1826 W. McDowell Road
Phoenix, AZ 85005
(602) 252-6771
www.azstatefair.com
Request: Premium Book

ARKANSAS
Arkansas State Fair
P.O. Box 166660
Little Rock, AR 72216
(501) 372-8341
www.arkfairgrounds.com

Clothesline Fair
Prairie Grove Battlefield State Park
P.O. Box 306

Prairie Grove, AR 72753
(501) 846-2990

CALIFORNIA
California State Fair
P.O. Box 15649
Sacramento, CA 95852
(916) 263-3146 (May 1 to September 30)
(916) 263-3010 (October 1 to April 30)
www.bigfun.org
Request: California Living Competition
Handbook

Kern County Fair
1142 South P Street
Bakersfield, CA 93307
(805) 833-4914 (Entry Department)
Request: Exhibit Catalog

Los Angeles County Fair
P.O. Box 2250
Pomona, CA 91769
(909) 623-3111
www.fairplex.com
Request: Creative Living Exhibits Competition
Premium Book
Competitive exhibits are open to the world.

Orange County Fair
88 Fair Drive
Costa Mesa, CA 92626
(714) 708-1553 (Entry Department)
www.ocfair.com
Request: Competition Handbook

Sonoma-Marin Fair
175 Fairgounds Drive
Petaluma, CA 94952-7321
(707) 763-0931 (Entry Office)
www.sonoma-marinfair.org
Request: Exhibitor Handbook

COLORADO
Colorado State Fair & Exposition
State Fairgrounds
Pueblo, CO 81004
(719) 561-8484 or (800) 876-4567
www.coloradosfair.com
Request: Contestant Handbook
Competitive exhibits are open to nonresidents.

CONNECTICUT
Brooklyn Fair
P.O. Box 410
Brooklyn, CT 06234
(860) 779-0012
www.ctfairs.org

Durham Fair
Durham Agricultural Fair Association, Inc.
Box 225
Durham, CT 06442-0225
(860) 349-9495
www.durhamfair.com
Request: Exhibitor Guide

North Haven Fair
Greater North Haven Convention & Visitors
Bureau
One Long Wharf Drive
New Haven, CT 06511
(203) 777-8550
www.northhaven-fair.com
Request: Premium List

Woodstock Fair
P.O. Box 1
South Woodstock, CT 06267
(860) 928-3246

DELAWARE
Delaware State Fair
P.O. Box 28

Harrington, DE 19952-0028
(302) 398-3269
www.delawarestatefair.com
Request: Exhibitor Handbook

FLORIDA
Florida State Fair
P.O. Box 11766
Tampa, FL 33680
(813) 621-7821
www.dos.state.fl.us/statefair
Request: Rules and Prize List

GEORGIA
Georgia National Fair
P.O. Box 1367
Perry, GA 31069
(912) 987-3247
www.gnfa.com

Georgia State Fair
P.O. Box 4105
Macon, GA 31208-4105
(912) 746-7184
www.georgiastatefair.org

HAWAII
Hawaii State Fair
Hawaii Visitors and Convention Bureau
2270 Kalakaua Avenue, Suite 801
Honolulu, HI 96815
Does not have a preserved foods
competition.

IDAHO
Eastern Idaho State Fair
P.O. Box 250
Blackfoot, ID 83221
(208) 785-2480
Request: Exhibitor Handbook

Western Idaho Fair
5610 Glenwood
Boise, ID 83714
(208) 376-3247

ILLINOIS
Illinois State Fair
P.O. Box 19427
Springfield, IL 62794-9427
(217) 782-6661
www.state.il.us/fair
Request: General Premium Book

INDIANA
Indiana State Fair
Entry Department
1202 E. 38th Street
Indianapolis, IN 46205-2869
(317) 927-7515 (Entry Department)
www.indianastatefair.com
Request: Open Class Premium Book

IOWA
Iowa State Fair, Statehouse
400 E. 14th Street
Des Moines, IA 50319-0198
(515) 262-3111
www.iowastatefair.com
Request: Iowa Family Living Premium
Book

KANSAS
Kansas State Fair
2000 N. Poplar
Hutchinson, KS 67502-5598
(316) 669-3600
Request: Exhibitor Handbook Premium List

KENTUCKY
Kentucky State Fair
Kentucky Fair & Exposition Center

P.O. Box 37130
Louisville, KY 40233
(502) 367-5190 (Entry Department)
www.kyfair.org
Request: Premium List & General Rules
Competitive exhibits are open to
nonresidents.

LOUISIANA

State Fair of Louisiana
P.O. Box 38327
Shreveport, LA 71133
(318) 635-1361

MAINE

Acton Fair
RR1, Box 3140
Shapleigh, ME 04076
(207) 636-2026
Request: Premium List

Blue Hill Fair
P.O. Box 390
Blue Hill, ME 04614
(207) 374-3701

Common Ground Country Fair
Maine Organic Farmers and Gardeners
Association
P.O. Box 2176
Augusta, ME 04338-2176
(207) 623-5115
Request: Exhibition Hall Rules

Fryeburg Fair
P.O. Box 78
Fryeburg, ME 04037
(207) 935-3268
Request: Exhibitor Handbook

Skowhegan State Fair
Skowhegan State Fair Association
P.O. Box 39

Skowhegan, ME 04976
(207) 474-2947
www.skowheganstatefair.com

MARYLAND

Maryland State Fair
State Fairgrounds
P.O. Box 188
Timonium, MD 21094
(410) 252-0200

Montgomery County Agricultural Fair
16 Chestnut Street
Gaithersburg, MD 20877
(301) 926-3100
www.mcafair.com

MASSACHUSETTS

The Big E
Eastern States Exposition
1305 Memorial Avenue
West Springfield, MA 01089
www.thebige.com
Does not have a preserved foods competition.

Franklin County Fair
P.O. Box 564
Greenfield, MA 01302
(413) 774-4282

New England Grange Fair
Eastern States Exposition
45 Oakland Street
West Springfield, MA 01089-2854
Request: Entry Handbook

MICHIGAN

Michigan State Fair
Community Arts Department
1120 W. State Fair
Detroit, MI 48203
(313) 369-8260

www.michiganstatefair.net
Request: Community Arts & Crafts Premium
List and Rules

West Michigan Fair
Ludington Area Convention and Visitors
Bureau
5827 W. U.S. 10
Ludington, MI 49431
(800) 542-4600

MINNESOTA
Minnesota State Fair
1265 Snelling Avenue North
St. Paul, MN 55108-3099
(612) 642-2217
www.mnstatefair.org
Request: Creative Activities Rules & Premiums
Competitive exhibits are open to nonresidents,
but preserved foods jars must be hand-delivered
to the fairgrounds. No preserved foods exhibits
will be accepted by mail.

MISSISSIPPI
Neshoba County Fair
Philadelphia-Neshoba County Chamber of
Commerce
P.O. Box 51
Philadelphia, MS 39350
(601) 656-1742

Mississippi State Fair
P.O. Box 892
Jackson, MS 39205
(601) 961-4000
Request: Premium Book

MISSOURI
Missouri State Fair
2503 W. 16th Street
Sedalia, MO 65301

(816) 530-5605
Request: Premium Book

Ozark Empire Fair
P.O. Box 630
Springfield, MO 65801
(417) 833-2660
Request: Exhibitor Handbook

Southeast Missouri District Fair
SEMO District Fair Association
P.O. Box 234
Cape Girardeau, MO 63702-0234
(573) 334-9250 or (800) 455-3247

MONTANA
MontanaFair
MetraPark
P.O. Box 2514
Billings, MT 59103
(406) 256-2400
www.metrapark.com
Request: Exhibitor Handbook
Competitive exhibits are open to nonresidents.

Montana State Fair
Box 1888
Great Falls, MT 59403-1888
(406) 727-8900
Request: Exhibitor Handbook
Competitive exhibits are open to nonresidents.

NEBRASKA
Fairfest
947 South Baltimore
Hastings, NE 68901
(402) 462-3247
www.adamscountyfairgrounds.com

Garfield County Fair
Garfield County Frontier Fair Association
Box 747
Burwell, NE 68823

The fair prints information about the competitive exhibit open classes in local newspapers prior to the opening of the fair.

Nebraska State Fair
P.O. Box 81223
Lincoln, NE 68501
(402) 474-5371
www.statefair.org
Request: Foods Entry/Award Book

Scotts Bluff County Fair
Box 157
Mitchell, NE 69357
(308) 623-1828
Request: Exhibitor Handbook

NEVADA
Nevada State Fair
1350-A N. Wells Avenue
Reno, NV 89512
(775) 688-5767
www.nevadastatefair.org
Request: Creative Living Competition Guide

NEW HAMPSHIRE
Rochester Fair
72 Lafayette Street
Rochester, NH 03867-2624
(603) 332-6585
Request: Exhibitor Handbook

Sandwich Fair
P.O. Box 161
Center Sandwich, NH 03227
(603) 284-7062

NEW JERSEY
Flemington Agricultural Fair
P.O. Box 293, Rt. 31
Flemington, NJ 08822
(908) 782-2413

NEW MEXICO
New Mexico State Fair
P.O. Box 8546
Albuquerque, NM 87198
(505) 265-1791
www.nmstatefair.com
Request: Competition Handbook

Southern New Mexico State Fair
P.O. Box 1145
Las Cruces, NM 88004
(505) 524-8602
www.snmstatefair.org

NEW YORK
Dutchess County Fair
P.O. Box 389
Rhinebeck, NY 12572
(914) 876-4001

New York State Fair
581 State Fair Boulevard
Syracuse, NY 13209
(315) 487-7711
www.nysfair.com
Request: Art & Home Center Competition Handbook

NORTH CAROLINA
North Carolina State Fair
1025 Blue Ridge Boulevard
Raleigh, NC 27607
(919) 821-7400
www.ncstatefair.org

NORTH DAKOTA
North Dakota State Fair
Box 1796
Minot, ND 58702
(701) 857-7620
Request: Exhibitor Handbook

OHIO

Canfield Fair
P.O. Box 250
Canfield, OH 44406
(216) 533-4107
www.canfieldfair.com

Ohio State Fair
717 E. 17th Avenue
Columbus, OH 43211-2698
(614) 644-4052 (Entry Department)
www.ohiostatefair.com
Request: Family Arts & Crafts Exhibitor
Handbook

OKLAHOMA

State Fair of Oklahoma
P.O. Box 74943
Oklahoma City, OK 73147
(405) 948-6700
www.oklafair.org
Request: Premium Book

Tulsa State Fair
P.O. Box 4735
Tulsa, OK 74159
(918) 744-1113
www.tulsastatefair.com
Request: Creative Arts Premium Book

OREGON

Hood River County Fair
Hood River Chamber of Commerce
Box 385
Odell, OR 97044-0385
(514) 354-2865
Exhibitor Handbooks may be obtained at the
Fair Office or the Hood River Chamber of
Commerce.

Marion County Fair
P.O. Box 703

Salem, OR 97308
(503) 585-9998
Request: Open Class Exhibitor Handbook

Oregon State Fair
2330 17th Street SE
Salem, OR 97303
(503) 378-3247
www.fair.state.or.us
Request: Premium List and Rules

PENNSYLVANIA

Big Knob Grange Fair
Beaver County Tourist Promotion Agency
215 B Ninth Street
Monaca, PA 15061-2028
(724) 728-0212

Hookstown Fair
Beaver County Tourist Promotion Agency
215 B Ninth Street
Monaca, PA 15061-2028
(724) 728-0212

South Mountain Fair
Gettysburg Convention and Visitors Bureau
35 Carlisle Street
Gettysburg, PA 17325-1899
(717) 334-6274
www.gettysburg.com

RHODE ISLAND

Washington County Fair
Box 78
Richmond Townhouse Road
Carolina, RI 02812
(401) 782-8139

SOUTH CAROLINA

South Carolina State Fair
P.O. Box 393

Columbia, SC 29202
(803) 799-3387

SOUTH DAKOTA
Sioux Empire Fair
W. H. Lyons Fairgrounds
4000 West 12th Street
Sioux Falls, SD 57107
(605) 367-7178
Request: Premium List and Regulations

South Dakota State Fair
P.O. Box 1275
Huron, SD 57350-1275
(605) 353-7340 or (800) 529-0900

TENNESSEE
Mid-South Fair
940 Early Maxwell Boulevard
Memphis, TN 38104
(901) 274-8800
www.midsouthfair.com
Request: Creative Arts Exhibitor
Handbook

Tennessee State Fair
Tennessee Fair Office
P.O. Box 40208
Melrose Station
Nashville, TN 37204
(615) 862-8980
Request: Premium List

TEXAS
State Fair of Texas
P.O. Box 150009
Dallas, TX 75315
(214) 421-8744
www.bigtex.com
Request: Creative Arts Premium List
Competitive exhibits are open to the world.

Texas/Oklahoma Fair
Wichita Falls Convention & Visitors Bureau
1000 5th Street
Wichita Falls, TX 76301
(940) 716-5500

UTAH
Utah State Fair
155 N. 1000 W
Salt Lake City, UT 84116
(801) 538-3246
www.utah-state-fair.com
Request: Living Arts Handbook

VERMONT
Champlain Valley Fair
P.O. Box 209
Essex Junction, VT 05453
(802) 878-5545
www.cvfair.com
Welcomes all exhibitors.

Vermont State Fair
175 S. Main Street
Rutland, VT 05701
(802) 775-5200

VIRGINIA
Five County Fair
P.O. Box 877
Farmville, VA 23901
(804) 392-7002
www.fivecountyfair.org

The Rockbridge Regional Fair
Lexington Visitors Bureau
106 E. Washington Street
Lexington, VA 24450
(540) 463-6263
Request: Exhibitor Handbook

Salem Fair
P.O. Box 886
Salem, VA 24153-0886
(540) 375-3004
Request: Premium Book
Competitive exhibits are open to the world.

State Fair of Virginia
Atlantic Rural Exposition, Inc.
P.O. Box 26805
Richmond, VA 23261
(804) 228-3200
www.statefair.com

WASHINGTON
Central Washington State Fair
General Manager
P.O. Box 1381
Yakima, WA 98907
(509) 248-7160
www.fairfun.com
Request: Exhibitor Guidebook
Competitive exhibits are open to nonresidents.

Evergreen State Fair
P.O. Box 129
Monroe, WA 98272
(360) 805-6700
www.homestead.com/ESFfoodpreservation

Western Washington Fair
P.O. Box 430

Puyallup, WA 98371-0162
(253) 841-5017
www.thefair.com
Request: Home Arts Premium List
Competitive exhibits are open to nonresidents,
but all entries must be hand-delivered to the
fairgrounds. No entries will be accepted by mail.

WEST VIRGINIA
State Fair of West Virginia
P.O. Drawer 986
Lewisburg, WV 24901
(304) 645-1090
www.wvstatefair.com

WISCONSIN
Wisconsin State Fair
P.O. Box 14990
West Allis, WI 53214-0990
(414) 266-7052
www.wsfp.state.wi.us
Request: Exhibitor Handbook & Premium
List

WYOMING
Wyoming State Fair
P.O. Drawer 10
Douglas, WY 82633
(307) 358-2398
Request: Premium Book

Bibliography

Anonymous. *Making Jellies, Jams and Preserves*. University of California, Cooperative Extension, Division of Agricultural Sciences Leaflet 2803. Berkeley: April 1981.

———. *Ball Blue Book: Guide to Home Canning, Freezing and Dehydration, Volume 1*. Muncie, Indiana: Alltrista Corporation, 1999.

———. *Certo Liquid Fruit Pectin and Sure-Jell Fruit Pectin Leaflets*. White Plains, New York: Kraft General Foods, Inc., n.d.

———. *Complete Guide to Home Canning*. U.S. Department of Agriculture, Extension Service, Agriculture Information Bulletin No. 539. Washington, D.C.: Government Printing Office, May 1989.

Groppe, Christine C., and George K. York, revised by George K. York, Kathryn J. Boor and Joan E. Byers. *Safe Methods for Preparing Pickles, Relishes & Chutneys*. Oakland: University of California, Cooperative Extension, Division of Agriculture and Natural Resources Leaflet 4080, 1989.

Joslyn, Maynard A. assisted by G. L. Marsh, revised by George K. York and Paulette DeJong. *Bottling, Canning, Freezing Fruit Juices and Tomato Juices*. Berkeley: University of California Cooperative Extension, Division of Agricultural Sciences Leaflet 2423, September 1980.

York, George K., and Paulette DeJong. *Home Canning of Fruits and Vegetables*. Berkeley: University of California, Cooperative Extension, Division of Agriculture and Natural Resources Leaflet 21392, July 1984.

Metric Conversions for Canning

The use of precise measurements and temperatures is very important in creating successful preserved foods. For your convenience, I have provided the nearest metric equivalents for the standard American measurements I have used throughout this book. The following measurements are approximate and have been rounded up or down slightly to the nearest whole number for easier measuring. This minor variation should not affect the quality of your preserved foods.

Volume Equivalents

AMERICAN	METRIC
¼ teaspoon	1.25 ml spoon
½ teaspoon	2.5 ml spoon
1 teaspoon	5 ml spoon
½ tablespoon	7.5 ml spoon
1 tablespoon	15 ml spoon
¼ cup	59 ml
⅓ cup	79 ml
½ cup	118 ml
⅔ cup	158 ml
¾ cup	177 ml
1 cup	237 ml
1¼ cups	296 ml
1½ cups	355 ml

Volume Equivalents (*cont.*)

AMERICAN	METRIC
1 pint	473 ml
1 quart	946 ml
1 gallon	3.79 liters

Weight Equivalents

AMERICAN	METRIC
¼ ounce	7 grams
½ ounce	14 grams
1 ounce	28 grams
2 ounces	57 grams
3 ounces	85 grams
4 ounces (¼ pound)	113 grams
5 ounces	142 grams
6 ounces	170 grams
7 ounces	198 grams
8 ounces (½ pound)	227 grams
9 ounces	255 grams
10 ounces	284 grams
11 ounces	312 grams
12 ounces (¾ pound)	340 grams
13 ounces	369 grams
14 ounces	397 grams
15 ounces	425 grams
1 pound	454 grams
1½ pounds	680 grams
2 pounds	907 grams
2¼ pounds	1.02 kilograms
2½ pounds	1.13 kilograms
3 pounds	1.36 kilograms
3½ pounds	1.59 kilograms
4 pounds	1.81 kilograms
4½ pounds	2.04 kilograms
5 pounds	2.27 kilograms

Temperatures

FAHRENHEIT	CELSIUS
5 degrees	-15 degrees
40 degrees	4 degrees
60 degrees	16 degrees
65 degrees	18 degrees
70 degrees	21 degrees
75 degrees	24 degrees
80 degrees	27 degrees
100 degrees	38 degrees
120 degrees	49 degrees
140 degrees	60 degrees
150 degrees	66 degrees
160 degrees	71 degrees
170 degrees	77 degrees
180 degrees	82 degrees
190 degrees	88 degrees
200 degrees	93 degrees
210 degrees	99 degrees
212 degrees	100 degrees
220 degrees	104 degrees
230 degrees	110 degrees
240 degrees	116 degrees
250 degrees	121 degrees

Standard American Measurements

1 tablespoon	3 teaspoons	½ fluid ounce
¼ cup	4 tablespoons	2 fluid ounces
⅓ cup	5⅓ tablespoons	2½ fluid ounces
½ cup	8 tablespoons	4 fluid ounces
⅔ cup	10⅔ tablespoons	5 fluid ounces
¾ cup	12 tablespoons	6 fluid ounces
1 cup	16 tablespoons	8 fluid ounces
1 pint	2 cups	16 fluid ounces
1 quart	2 pints	32 fluid ounces
1 gallon	4 quarts	128 fluid ounces

Depending on the type of ingredient, weight measurements for the standard volume measurements can vary significantly. The following charts provide the weights of many common home canning ingredients and will assist you in measuring the correct quantities of ingredients for use in home canning. The correct quantities are essential to the success of the preserved food and to attain the best flavor and texture.

Sugar

GRANULATED	PRESERVING OR CASTER	
1 teaspoon	4 grams	0.15 ounce
1 tablespoon	12 grams	0.44 ounce
1/4 cup	50 grams	1.75 ounces
1/3 cup	66 grams	2.33 ounces
1/2 cup	99 grams	3.5 ounces
2/3 cup	132 grams	4.66 ounces
3/4 cup	149 grams	5.25 ounces
1 cup	198 grams	7 ounces

Brown Sugar

(FIRMLY PACKED)

1 teaspoon	4 grams	0.16 ounce
1 tablespoon	13 grams	0.47 ounce
1/4 cup	53 grams	1.88 ounces
1/3 cup	71 grams	2.5 ounces
1/2 cup	107 grams	3.76 ounces
2/3 cup	142 grams	5 ounces
3/4 cup	160 grams	5.64 ounces
1 cup	213 grams	7.5 ounces

Corn Syrup

1 teaspoon	7 grams	0.23 ounce
1 tablespoon	20 grams	0.7 ounce
1/4 cup	79 grams	2.8 ounces
1/3 cup	106 grams	3.73 ounces
1/2 cup	159 grams	5.6 ounces
2/3 cup	212 grams	7.46 ounces
3/4 cup	238 grams	8.4 ounces
1 cup	318 grams	11.2 ounces

Honey

1 teaspoon	7 grams	0.25 ounce
1 tablespoon	21 grams	0.75 ounce
1/4 cup	85 grams	3 ounces
1/3 cup	113 grams	4 ounces
1/2 cup	170 grams	6 ounces
2/3 cup	220 grams	7.75 ounces
3/4 cup	255 grams	9 ounces
1 cup	340 grams	12 ounces

Cornstarch or Clearjel Powder

1 tablespoon	7.6 grams	0.27 ounce
1/4 cup	31 grams	1.08 ounces
1/3 cup	41 grams	1.44 ounces
1/2 cup	61 grams	2.16 ounces
2/3 cup	82 grams	2.88 ounces
3/4 cup	92 grams	3.24 ounces
1 cup	122 grams	4.3 ounces

Salt

AMERICAN	METRIC
1/8 teaspoon	0.63 gram
1/4 teaspoon	1.25 grams
1/2 teaspoon	2.5 grams
1 teaspoon	5 grams
1 tablespoon	15 grams
1/4 cup	60 grams
1/2 cup	120 grams
1 cup	240 grams

Ground Spices

AMERICAN	METRIC
1/8 teaspoon	0.25 gram
1/4 teaspoon	0.50 gram
1/2 teaspoon	1 gram

Ground Spices (*cont.*)

AMERICAN	METRIC
1 teaspoon	2 grams
1 tablespoon	6 grams
1½ tablespoons	9 grams

Unsalted Butter

1 tablespoon	0.5 ounce	14 grams
¼ cup (4 tablespoons or ½ stick)	2 ounces	57 grams
½ cup (8 tablespoons or 1 stick)	4 ounces	113 grams
1 cup (2 sticks)	8 ounces	227 grams

Eggs

1 large egg, out of shell	50 grams	1.75 ounces
1 large egg yolk	18 grams	0.65 ounce

Index

About the Author

Creating delicious and intensely flavorful homemade preserved foods has become a rewarding adventure for **Linda J. Amendt.** She never anticipated that her first batch of jam would lead to a world of tantalizing tastes and aromas, the whirl and excitement of competition, or the satisfaction, rewards and recognition in achieving excellence.

Impressing the judges with her jams, jellies and other preserves, Linda earned 618 awards in just 11 years of fair competitions, including 315 first place ribbons, 111 second place ribbons and 69 special awards for excellence in preserved foods. In special recognition of her outstanding achievements and excellence in the field of jam and jelly making, she was inducted as a Lifetime Member into the 1997 Inaugural Class of the *Sure-Jell Hall of Fame.* Successfully exhibiting her preserved foods in state, county and regional fair competitions across the nation, Linda became the top competitor in the United States. Still in her thirties, she officially retired from competition in the fall of 2000. She now serves as a judge at state and county fairs.

Linda Amendt's remarkable accomplishments in home canning and competitive preserved foods exhibits at fairs include:

- *Sure-Jell Hall of Fame*, Lifetime Member, Inaugural Class of 1997

- Top Preserved Foods Competitor in the United States (1999 and 2000)

- California's Top Preserved Foods Competitor (1996, 1997, 1998, 1999 and 2000)

- 5 Los Angeles County Fair *Preserved Foods Blue Ribbon Sweepstakes Awards* (1996, 1997, 1998, 1999 and 2000)

- 2 Special *Sweepstakes Awards*

- 3 *Best of Show Awards*

- 15 *Alltrista Premium Food Preservation Awards*

- 2 *Sure-Jell Outstanding Jam Competition First Place Awards*

- 2 *Alltrista Home Canning Best of Category: Soft Spreads Awards*

- 16 *Best of Division Awards*

- 23 Special Awards of Merit in Preserved Foods

A self-taught home canner, Linda enjoys passing along her knowledge to home canners of all skill levels, helping others to discover the joys and rewards of creating their own home-made preserves. Sharing her expertise with both beginning and experienced home canners, she takes the mystery and intimidation out of preserving foods so they can approach making their own jams, jellies and other preserves with confidence. Besides being an expert in home canning, Linda is also an accomplished baker, winning numerous awards for her delicious cakes, pies, cookies and breads.

SELMA AND DALLAS COUNTY LIBRARY

3 6054 00160 9028

PUBLIC LIBRARY OF
SELMA & DALLAS CTY
1103 SELMA AVENUE
SELMA, AL 36701